Other Books and Series by Jeff Bowen

Applications for Enrollment of Chickasaw Newborn Act of 1905
Volumes I thru VII

Cherokee Intermarried White 1906 Volume I thru X

Applications for Enrollment of Creek Newborn Act of 1905
Volumes I, II, III, IV, V, VI, VII, VIII, IX, X, XI, XII & XIII

Visit our website at **www.nativestudy.com** to learn more about these and other books and series by Jeff Bowen

APPLICATIONS FOR ENROLLMENT OF CREEK NEWBORN ACT OF 1905
VOLUME XIV

TRANSCRIBED BY
JEFF BOWEN
NATIVE STUDY
Gallipolis, Ohio
USA

Other Books and Series by Jeff Bowen

1901-1907 Native American Census Seneca, Eastern Shawnee, Miami, Modoc, Ottawa, Peoria, Quapaw, and Wyandotte Indians (Under Seneca School, Indian Territory)

1932 Census of The Standing Rock Sioux Reservation with Births And Deaths 1924-1932

Census of The Blackfeet, Montana, 1897- 1901 Expanded Edition

Eastern Cherokee by Blood, 1906-1910, Volumes I thru XIII

Choctaw of Mississippi Indian Census 1929-1932 with Births and Deaths 1924-1931   Volume I
Choctaw of Mississippi Indian Census 1933, 1934 & 1937, Supplemental Rolls to 1934 & 1935 with Births and Deaths 1932-1938, and Marriages 1936-1938 Volume II

Eastern Cherokee Census Cherokee, North Carolina 1930-1939 Census 1930-1931 with Births And Deaths 1924-1931 Taken By Agent L. W. Page Volume I
Eastern Cherokee Census Cherokee, North Carolina 1930-1939 Census 1932-1933 with Births And Deaths 1930-1932 Taken By Agent R. L. Spalsbury   Volume II
Eastern Cherokee Census Cherokee, North Carolina 1930-1939 Census 1934-1937 with Births and Deaths 1925-1938 and Marriages 1936 & 1938 Taken by Agents R. L. Spalsbury And Harold W. Foght Volume III

Seminole of Florida Indian Census, 1930-1940 with Birth and Death Records, 1930-1938

Texas Cherokees 1820-1839 A Document For Litigation 1921

Choctaw By Blood Enrollment Cards 1898-1914 Volumes I thru XVII

Starr Roll 1894 (Cherokee Payment Rolls) Districts: Canadian, Cooweescoowee, and Delaware Volume One
Starr Roll 1894 (Cherokee Payment Rolls) Districts: Flint, Going Snake, and Illinois   Volume Two
Starr Roll 1894 (Cherokee Payment Rolls) Districts: Saline, Sequoyah, and Tahlequah; Including Orphan Roll   Volume Three

Cherokee Intruder Cases Dockets of Hearings 1901-1909 Volumes I & II

Indian Wills, 1911-1921 Records of the Bureau of Indian Affairs Books One thru Seven;
Native American Wills & Probate Records 1911-1921

Other Books and Series by Jeff Bowen

Turtle Mountain Reservation Chippewa Indians 1932 Census with Births & Deaths, 1924-1932

Chickasaw By Blood Enrollment Cards 1898-1914 Volume I thru V

Cherokee Descendants East An Index to the Guion Miller Applications Volume I
Cherokee Descendants West An Index to the Guion Miller Applications Volume II (A-M)
Cherokee Descendants West An Index to the Guion Miller Applications Volume III (N-Z)

Applications for Enrollment of Seminole Newborn Freedmen, Act of 1905

Eastern Cherokee Census, Cherokee, North Carolina, 1915-1922, Taken by Agent James E. Henderson   Volume I (1915-1916)
Volume II (1917-1918)
Volume III (1919-1920)
Volume IV (1921-1922)

Complete Delaware Roll of 1898

Eastern Cherokee Census, Cherokee, North Carolina, 1923-1929, Taken by Agent James E. Henderson   Volume I (1923-1924)
Volume II (1925-1926)
Volume III (1927-1929)

Applications for Enrollment of Seminole Newborn Act of 1905 Volumes I & II

North Carolina Eastern Cherokee Indian Census 1898-1899, 1904, 1906, 1909-1912, 1914 Revised and Expanded Edition

1932 Hopi and Navajo Native American Census with Birth & Death Rolls (1925-1931) Volume 1 - Hopi
1932 Hopi and Navajo Native American Census with Birth & Death Rolls (1930-1932) Volume 2 - Navajo

Western Navajo Reservation Navajo, Hopi and Paiute 1933 Census with Birth & Death Rolls 1925-1933

Cherokee Citizenship Commission Dockets 1880-1884 and 1887-1889 Volumes I thru V

Copyright © 2012
by Jeff Bowen

ALL RIGHTS RESERVED
No part of this publication may be reproduced
or used in any form or manner whatsoever
without previous written permission from the
copyright holder or publisher.

Originally published:
Baltimore, Maryland
2012

Reprinted by:

Native Study LLC
Gallipolis, OH
www.nativestudy.com
2020

Library of Congress Control Number: 2020917992

ISBN: 978-1-64968-093-8

Made in the United States of America.

This series is dedicated to the descendants of the Creek newborn listed in these applications.

DEPARTMENT OF THE INTERIOR.

Commissioner to the Five Civilized Tribes.

NOTICE.

Opening of Land Office at Wewoka,
IN THE SEMINOLE NATION, INDIAN TERRITORY.

Notice is hereby given that on Monday, September 4, 1905, the Commissioner to the Five Civilized Tribes will establish a land office at Wewoka, in the Seminole Nation, Indian Territory, for the purpose of allowing citizens and freedmen of the Seminole Nation to select allotments of land for their minor children enrolled under the Act of Congress approved March 3, 1905 (33 Stat. L 1060), and for the further purpose of allowing citizens and freedmen of the Seminole Nation, whose allotments are incomplete, to select additional land in order to bring the value of their allotments up to the standard of $309.09, as nearly as may be practicable.

Each child whose enrollment in accordance with the Act of March 3, 1905, has been duly approved by the Secretary of the Interior, is entitled to receive an alllotment of forty acres without regard to the character or value of the land selected.

Selection of allotments for minor children must be made by their citizen or freedmen parents or by a duly appointed guardian, or curator, or by a duly appointed administrator.

TAMS BIXBY,
Commissioner.

Muskogee, Indian Territory,
July 29, 1905.

This particular notice makes mention of the Act of 1905. The Creek and Seminole were closely related tribes. Both tribes' notices were similar in nature.

DEPARTMENT OF THE INTERIOR,
Commission to the Five Civilized Tribes.

Closing of Citizenship Rolls
OF THE MUSKOGEE OR CREEK NATION.

WHEREAS, on June 13, 1904, the Secretary of the Interior, under the authority in him vested by the provisions of the act of Congress approved March 3, 1901, (31 Stat., 1058) ordered that September 1, 1904, be and the same is hereby fixed as the time when the rolls of the Muskogee or Creek Nation shall be closed:

Notice is hereby given that the Commission to the Five Civilized Tribes will, at its office in Muskogee, Indian Territory, up to and inclusive of September 1, 1904, receive applications for the enrollment of citizens and freedmen of the Muskogee or Creek Nation, and that after that date the application of no person whomsoever for enrollment as a citizen or freedman of said nation will be received by the Commission.

Commission to the Five Civilized Tribes,
TAMS BIXBY, Chairman,
T. B. NEEDLES,
C. R. BRECKINRIDGE,
Commissioners.

Muskogee, Indian Territory,
June 25, 1904.

A notice like this was printed in newspapers and posted throughout Indian Territory.

INTRODUCTION

This series concerns Applications for Enrollment of Creek Newborn, National Archive film M-1301 (Act of 1905), as described in the National Archives publication *American Indians*. It falls under the heading Applications for Enrollment of the Commission to the Five Civilized Tribes, 1898-1914, M-1301 and is transcribed from microfilm rolls 414-419. This shows the application forms filled out by individuals applying for enrollment in the Five Civilized Tribes under the Dawes Commission. These applications contain additional information that wasn't abstracted to the census cards that you find in series M-1186. This particular roll (Creek by Birth) contains its own series of numbers separate from M-1186. To find each party's roll number you would have to reference M-1186. On July 25, 1898, there was an Indian Territory Division created in the Office of the Department of Interior. This division was created because of the increased work caused by what was called the Curtis Act, named after Senator Charles Curtis. Basically, this law stated that the tribal rolls needed to be descriptive and pointed out that each tribal roll was without description and had to be redone. At this point there was such a struggle among the Creeks to accept that the Government was going to change their way of life, again, that their leaders were refusing to cooperate in handing over their census information. The Commission had found that enrolling the Creeks was a difficult task not only because the Creek feared what was coming but also because their tribal structure was consistent with being a confederacy with forty-four different bands whose tribesmen lived in different towns of which each had a king that was supposed to keep track of their citizenry. The Commission reported that there was very little evidence of any census that existed and what there was had been kept carelessly. There were attempts and tribal conflicts along the way, but the Curtis Act would make it so they had to do it again no matter what effort from the past. In 1899, Agent Wesley Smith educated Washington to the fact that it was difficult to verify Creek eligibility. The acts passed by the Creeks themselves concerning enrollment since 1893 had been strewn amongst the archives of the Creek Council in Muskogee, I.T., and there was no provision ever approved for the printing of the those enrollments. There was confusion and difficulty let alone the fact that surnames were practically unknown among the Creek. But there was no confusion on March 9, 1905, when the Commission stated they would come to seven towns in the Creek Nation and accept applications that had to be made on a standardized blank form and contain a notarized affidavit from the mother and the attending doctor or midwife. A few by mail, but most of them were offered to a field party led by Commissioner Needles. The Commission took in applications for 2,410 children by the deadline of midnight, May 2, 1905.

This series contains applications and correspondence from 1,171 of those claimants. Realizing there were over 2,400 applicants originally, it is understood that not all were accepted. Also included are names of doctors, lawyers, mid-wives, and others who attended to the Creek Nation before and during this time in history.

Jeff Bowen
Gallipolis, Ohio
NativeStudy.com

Applications for Enrollment of Creek Newborn
Act of 1905   Volume XIV

2467 B

DEPARTMENT OF THE INTERIOR,
COMMISSION TO THE FIVE CIVILIZED TRIBES.
Eufaula, I. T., April 14, 1905.

In the matter of the application for the enrollment of Amy Kelly as a citizen by blood of the Creek Nation.

JOHNSON LEWIS, being duly sworn, testified as follows:

Through Alex Posey Official Interpreter:

BY COMMISSION;
Q What is your name? A Johnson Lewis.
Q How old are you? A Forty-five.
Q What is your post office address? A Eufaula.
Q Are you a citizen of the Creek Nation? A Yes, sir.
Q To what town do you belong? A Eufaula Canadian.
Q Are you acquainted with Susie Johnson? A Yes, sir.
Q To what town does she belong? A Hickory Ground.
Q Do you know a child of hers named Amy Kelly? A Yes, sir.
Q Who is the father of that child? A Jim Kelly.
Q Is he a citizen of the Creek Nation? A Yes, sir.
Q To what town does he belong? A Eufaula Canadian.
Q Is he the lawful husband of Susie Johnson? A No, sir. The child is illegitimate.
Q Do you know whether or not he recognizes the child as his? A Yes, sir, he does.
Q Do you know whether or not he contributes towards the support of the child? A I do not know as to that but I do know that he goes to visit the child quite often.
Q How old is the child? A The father told me the other day that the child was nearly two years old.
Q The child is living is it? A Yes, sir.

------:o:------

I, D. C. Skaggs, on oath state that the above and foregoing is a full and true transcript of my stenographic notes as taken in said cause on said date.

D. C. Skaggs

Subscribed and sworn to before me this 12th day of May, 1905.

Henry G Hains
Notary Public.

Applications for Enrollment of Creek Newborn
Act of 1905   Volume XIV

No. 2467.
DEPARTMENT OF THE INTERIOR,
COMMISSION TO THE FIVE CIVILIZED TRIBES.
Eufaula, I. T., May 18, 1905.

In the matter of the application for the enrollment of Amy Kelly as a citizen by blood of the Creek Nation.

ADELINE WHITE, being duly sworn, testified as follows:

BY COMMISSION:
Q What is your name? A Adeline White.
Q How o/ld[sic] are you? A I do not know my age.

Witness appears to be about fifty years old.

Q What is your post office address? A Eufaula.
Q Are you a citizen of the Creek Nation? A Yes, sir.
Q To what town do you belong? A Tuskegee.
Q Are you acquainted with Jim Kelly and Susie Johnson? A Yes, sir.
Q Is Jim Kelly the lawfull[sic] husband of Susue[sic] Johnson? A No, sir.
Q They were never married? A No, sir.
Q Did you attend on Susie Johnson at the time the child was born? A Yes, sir.
Q Do you know when the child was born? A I don't know the date but it is a little over two years old.
Q Do you know in what time of the year it was born? A No, sir.
Q The child is living is it? A Yes, sir.
Q Is it old enough to talk? A Yes, sir, it is talking.
Q Are you positive that the child is about two years old? A Yes, sir.
Q Are you positive that the child is not three years old? A No, sir, it is not three. It is about two and a half.

---oooOOOooo---

I, D. C. Skaggs, on oath state that the above and foregoing is a full and true transcript of my stenographic notes as taken in said cause on said date.
D. C. Skaggs
Subscribed and sworn to before me this 18" day of July 1905.
Edw C Griesel
Notary Public.

Applications for Enrollment of Creek Newborn
Act of 1905   Volume XIV

No. 2467.

DEPARTMENT OF THE INTERIOR,
COMMISSION TO THE FIVE CIVILIZED TRIBES.
Eufaula, I. T., May 18, 1905.

In the matter of the application for the enrollment of Amy Kelly as a citizen by blood of the Creek Nation.

JEANETTA BROOK, being duly sworn, testified as follows:

BY COMMISSION:
Q What is your name? A Jeanetta Brook.
Q How old are you? A Thirty-two.
Q What is your post office address? A Eufaula.
Q Are you a citizen of the Creek Nation? A Yes, sir.
Q To what town do you belong? A Hickory Ground.
Q Are you acquainted with Susie Johnson and Jim Kelly? A Yes, sir.
Q Are they any relation to you? A Susie is a distant relative.
Q Is Jim Kelly the lawful husband of Susie Johnson? A No, sir.
Q Have they a child named Amy? A I don't know what the child's name is. They have one there but I don't know its name.
Q Do you know when the child was born? A No, I don't.
Q About how old is the child? A I guess it is about two years old. It may be a little over two years old.
Q The child is living is it? A Yes, sir.

---oooOOOooo---

I, D. C. Skaggs, on oath state that the above and foregoing is a full and true transcript of my stenographic notes as taken in said cause on said date.

D. C. Skaggs

Subscribed and sworn to before me this 18" day of July 1905.

Edw C Griesel

Notary Public.

N.C. 1080.

DEPARTMENT OF THE INTERIOR,
COMMISSIONER TO THE FIVE CIVILIZED TRIBES.
Eufaula, I. T., September 30, 1905.

In the matter of the application for the enrollment of Amy Kelly as a citizen by blood of the Creek Nation.

JIM KELLY, being duly sworn, testified as follows:

Through Alex Posey Official Interpreter:

Applications for Enrollment of Creek Newborn
Act of 1905   Volume XIV

BY THE COMMISSIONER:
Q What is your name? A Jim Kelly.
Q How old are you? A Twenty-four.
Q What is your post office address? A Eufaula.
Q Are you a citizen of the Creek Nation? A Yes, sir.
Q To what town do you belong? A Eufaula Canadian.
Q Have you a child named Amy Kelly? A Yes, sir, she is also called Bettie.
Q What is the name of her mother? A Susie Johnson.
Q Is Susie Johnson your wife? A No, sir.
Q You were never married to her? A No sir.
Q Do you recognize the child as your own? A Yes, sir.
Q Do you know when the child was born? A I do not know on what day she was born. She was born in the month of May, 1903.
Q Are you positive as to the date? A Yes, sir.
Q To what town does the mother belong? A Hickory Ground.
Q The child is living is it? A Yes, sir.
Q Was the child born during the first or last of May? A Sometimes in the middle of the month.

---oooOOOooo---

I, D. C. Skaggs, on oath state that the above and foregoing is a full and true transcript of my stenographic notes as taken in said cause on said date.

D. C. Skaggs

Subscribed and sworn to before me this 16 day of October 1906.

Edw C Griesel
Notary Public.

N.C. 1080.   F.H.W.

DEPARTMENT OF THE INTERIOR,
COMMISSIONER TO THE FIVE CIVILIZED TRIBES.

In the matter of the application for the enrollment of Amy Kelly as a citizen by blood of the Creek Nation.

DECISION.

The record in this case shows that on April 14, 1905, Johnson Lewis appeared before the Creek Enrollment Field Party, at Eufaula, Indian Territory, and made application for the enrollment of Amy Kelly as a citizen by blood of the Creek Nation, under the provisions of the Act of Congress approved March 3, 1905 (33 Stats., 1048). Affidavits as to the birth of said child filed May 20, 1905, and October 17, 1905, are

Applications for Enrollment of Creek Newborn
Act of 1905   Volume XIV

attached to and made part of the record herein. Further proceedings were had on May 18, 1905, and September 30, 1905.

The evidence shows that Amy Kelly is the illegitimate child of Jim Kelly and Susie Johnson, duly enrolled citizens of the Creek Nation whose names appear upon the approved roll of citizens by blood of the said nation, opposite Nos. 9152 and 8648 respectively.

The evidence further shows that said Amy Kelly was born in May, 1903, and was living on the date of the last proceedings herein.

The Act of Congress approved March 3, 1905, (33 Stats., 1048), provides in part as follows:

"That the Commission to the Five Civilized Tribes is authorized for sixty days after the date of the approval of this act to receive and consider applications for enrollment, of children, born subsequent to May twenty-fifth, nineteen hundred and one, and prior to March fourth, nineteen hundred and five, and living on said latter date, to citizens of the Creek tribe of Indians whose enrollment has been approved by the Secretary of the Interior prior to the approval of this act; and to enroll and make allotments to such children."

It is, therefore, ordered and adjudged that the said Amy Kelly is entitled to be enrolled as a citizen by blood of the Creek Nation, in accordance with the provisions of law above quoted, and the application for her enrollment as such is accordingly granted.

Muskogee, Indian Territory,   Tams Bixby   COMMISSIONER.
JAN 7_ 1907

BIRTH AFFIDAVIT.

DEPARTMENT OF THE INTERIOR.
COMMISSION TO THE FIVE CIVILIZED TRIBES.

IN RE APPLICATION FOR ENROLLMENT, as a citizen of the Creek Nation, of Amy Kelly, ~~born on the   day of~~ in May   , 1903

Name of Father: James Kelly   a citizen of the   Creek   Nation.
Eufaula Canadian
Name of Mother: Susie Johnson   a citizen of the   Creek   Nation.
Hickory Ground
                                Postoffice   Eufaula, I.T.

Applications for Enrollment of Creek Newborn
Act of 1905   Volume XIV

AFFIDAVIT OF MOTHER.

UNITED STATES OF AMERICA, Indian Territory, ⎫
    Western   DISTRICT. ⎬

    I, James Kelly , on oath state that I am 24 years of age and a citizen by blood, of the Creek Nation; that I am not the lawful ~~wife~~ husband of Susie Johnson , who is a citizen, by *(blank)* of the *(blank)* Nation; that a female child was born to me ~~on~~ in ~~day of~~ May , 1903 , that said child has been named Amy Kelly , and was living March 4, 1905.

                                                    James Kelley

Witnesses To Mark:
{

    Subscribed and sworn to before me this 30 day of September , 1905.

                                                Drennan C Skaggs
                                                      Notary Public.

AFFIDAVIT OF ATTENDING PHYSICIAN OR MID-WIFE.

UNITED STATES OF AMERICA, Indian Territory, ⎫
    (blank)   DISTRICT. ⎬

                                                      are personally acquainted with
    We, the undersigned , ~~a~~ , on oath state that ~~I~~ we ~~attended on~~ Mrs. Susie Johnson , ~~wife of   on the   day of   , 1~~ ; that there was born to her sometime in May, 1903, ~~on said date~~ a female child; that said child was living March 4, 1905, and is said to have been named Amy Kelly

                                                Johnson Lewis

Witnesses To Mark: Daniel Lewis
{

    Subscribed and sworn to before me this 30 day of Sept , 1905.

                                                Drennan C Skaggs
                                                    Notary Public.

Applications for Enrollment of Creek Newborn
Act of 1905   Volume XIV

BIRTH AFFIDAVIT.

DEPARTMENT OF THE INTERIOR.
COMMISSION TO THE FIVE CIVILIZED TRIBES.

IN RE APPLICATION FOR ENROLLMENT, as a citizen of the Creek Nation, of Amy Kelly, born on the *(blank)* day of *(blank)*, 1*(blank)*.

Name of Father: Jim Kelly   a citizen of the   Creek   Nation.
Eufaula Canadian Town
Name of Mother: Susie Johnson   a citizen of the   Creek   Nation.
Hickory Ground Town

Postoffice   Eufaula, I.T.

AFFIDAVIT OF ATTENDING PHYSICIAN OR MID-WIFE.

UNITED STATES OF AMERICA, Indian Territory,
   Western   DISTRICT.

I, Adeline White, a mid-wife, on oath state that I attended on Miss. Susie Johnson, ~~wife of   on the   day of   , 1~~ a little over two (2) years ago; that there was born to her on said date a female child; that said child is now living and is said to have been named Amy Kelly

                                            her
Witnesses To Mark: Adeline x White
   { DC Skaggs   mark
   { Alex Posey

Subscribed and sworn to before me this 18 day of   May   , 1905.

                             Drennan C Skaggs
                             Notary Public.

C 1080

Dustin, Indian Territory, June 3, 1905.

Commission to the Five Civilized Tribes,
    Muskogee, Indian Territory.

Gentlemen:

I return herewith copies of testimony taken in the following cases. as I find it impossible to secure further evidence:

Applications for Enrollment of Creek Newborn
Act of 1905   Volume XIV

Sarty, Enrollment No. 520.
Chepe and Folle Homahta, Creek Indian Card Field No. 2871.
Katy and Nicey Gano, No. 2465 B.
William Tiger, No. ___ B.
> Amy Kelly, No. 2467 B.
Heliswa and Kaska Beaver, No. 2466 B.
Lena Bear, No. ___ B.
Setepake Scott, No. 2447 B.
Susanna and Onate Johnson, No. 2468 B.
Mahlahsee Mitchell, No. 2447 B.

        Respectfully,

            (Signed) Alex Posey,
           Clerk in Charge Creek Field Party.

NC 1080.

       Muskogee, Indian Territory, November 30, 1906.

Jesse McDermott,
  Creek Enrollment Field Party,
    Dustin, Indian Territory.
Dear Sir:

  On May 20, 1905, application was made in affidavit form for the enrollment of Amy Kelly, born in the year 1903, to James Kelly and Susie Johnson, as a citizen of the Creek Nation.

  A copy of the record in the case is herewith enclosed and you are advised that you should secure evidence in the matter of the application for the enrollment of identification of the mother of said child as a citizen of the Creek Nation.

        Respectfully,

LM-566.   Commissioner.

N.C. 1080.

       Muskogee, Indian Territory, March 1, 1907.

Susie Johnson,
  Eufaula, Indian Territory.

Dear Madam:

  You are hereby advised that on February 15, 1907, the Secretary of the Interior approved the enrollment of your minor child, Amy Kelly, as a citizen by blood of the Creek Nation, and that the name of said child appears upon the roll of new born citizens

Applications for Enrollment of Creek Newborn
Act of 1905   Volume XIV

by blood of the Creek Nation, enrolled under the Act of Congress approved March 3, 1905, as number 1210.

This child is now entitled to allotment and application therefor should be made without delay at the Creek Land Office, Muskogee, Indian Territory.

Respectfully,

Commissioner.

BIRTH AFFIDAVIT.

DEPARTMENT OF THE INTERIOR.
COMMISSION TO THE FIVE CIVILIZED TRIBES.

IN RE APPLICATION FOR ENROLLMENT, as a citizen of the Creek Nation, of Oscar Lovick Letts, born on the 26th day of September, 1902

Name of Father: Frank B. Letts	a citizen of the U.S.	Nation.
Name of Mother: Susan L. Letts	a citizen of the Creek	Nation.

Postoffice   Wagoner, I.T.

AFFIDAVIT OF MOTHER.

UNITED STATES OF AMERICA, Indian Territory, ⎫
    Western   DISTRICT. ⎬
                                  (nee Susan L. Garner)

I, Susan L. Letts , on oath state that I am 32 years of age and a citizen by blood, of the Creek Nation; that I am the lawful wife of Frank B. Letts , who is a citizen, by *(blank)* of the U.S. ~~Nation~~; that a male child was born to me on 26th day of September , 1902 , that said child has been named Oscar Lovick Letts , and is now living.

                                    Susan L. Letts

Witnesses To Mark:

Applications for Enrollment of Creek Newborn
Act of 1905 Volume XIV

Subscribed and sworn to before me this 8th day of April , 1905.

(Name Illegible)

My Com. expires May 7, 1908.   Notary Public.

AFFIDAVIT OF ATTENDING PHYSICIAN OR MID-WIFE.

UNITED STATES OF AMERICA, Indian Territory, }
     Western   DISTRICT.

I, Sarah E. Bearden , a mid-wife , on oath state that I attended on Mrs. Susan L Letts , wife of Frank B. Letts on the 26th day of September , 1902 ; that there was born to her on said date a male child; that said child is now living and is said to have been named Oscar Lovick Letts

                                  Sarah E Bearden

Witnesses To Mark:

{

Subscribed and sworn to before me this 8th day of April , 1905.

(Name Illegible)

My Com. expires May 7, 1908.   Notary Public.

DEPARTMENT OF THE INTERIOR,
COMMISSION TO THE FIVE CIVILIZED TRIBES.
MUSKOGEE, I.T. AUGUST 25, 1904.

In the matter of the application for the enrollment of Major Barbee Pitts as a citizen by blood of the Creek Nation.

APPEARANCE: M. L. Mott, attorney for Creek Nation.

Emma Pitts being duly sworn testified as follows:

Examination by the Commission:

Q What is your name? A Emma Pitts.
Q How old are you? A 29.

Applications for Enrollment of Creek Newborn
Act of 1905   Volume XIV

Q What is your post office address? A Wagoner.
Q Do you make application for the enrollment of your child, Major Barbee Pitts, as a citizen by blood of the Creek Nation? A Yes sir.
Q What is the name of his father? A Frank Pitts.
Q Is he a citizen of the Creek Nation? A Yes sir, claims to be but he didn't get on the roll.
Q You are the mother of the child, are you? A Yes sir.

The records of the Commission show that Emma Pitts is listed for enrollment on Creek Indian card Field No. 697 and that her name is contained in the partial list of Creeks by blood approved by the Secretary of the Interior March `13, 1902, No. 2278.

Q When was your child, Major Barbee born? A In July, 1900.
Q What day of the month? A The 15th.
Q The child is living is he? A Yes sir; here he is.
Q Do you know Charles W. Hatfield, a Notary Public? A Yes sir, I have seen him.
Q Did you go before him and execute an affidavit about the birth of this child? A Yes sir.
Q How long had that child been born when you went before him? A It had been born a little over a year.
Q What date did you give him at that time? A I give him 1900, the 15th of July.
Q Did you learn that a different date was inserted in that affidavit? A I learnt that there was a mistake; that it was put down there 1901 instead of 1900.
Q Do you know Louisa Jones? A Yes sir.
Q Was she with you when the child was born? A Yes sir.
Q Does she know the date of this child's birth? A I guess she does.
Q How many children have you younger than Major Barbee? A Yes sir. One.
Q Just one? A Yes sir.
Q Have you ever had any other except that one? A No sir.
Q How old ism[sic] this child you have in our arms? A She was a year old last March.
Q How old was Major Barbee when this child you have in your arms was born? About? As near as you can come at it? A I can't tell unless I count it up now; a person don't think about these things; I never kept count of it.
Q Could Major Barbee walk when this child was born? A Yes sir.
Q Could he talk? A Talked a little; not much yet.
Q Was this child that you have in your arms born when you went before that Notary Public and executed the affidavit about Major Barbee? A No sir.
Q About how old do you say that Major Barbee was when you made that affidavit? A I had not said yet.
Q I understood you to say; about how old was he when you made that affidavit? A He must have been a year or so old now; I don't remember when that paper was fixed now.

Frank F. Pitts being duly sworn testified as follows:

Examination by the Commission:

Q What is your name? A Frank F. Pitts.

Applications for Enrollment of Creek Newborn
Act of 1905   Volume XIV

Q How old are you? A 64.
Q What is your post office address? A Wagoner.
Q Are you the father of Major Barbee Pitts? A So says my wife.
Q Were you with her when she executed an affidavit before a Notary Public named Hatfield? About the date of the birth of the child? A Yes sir I went in with them; I had some other business to transact and I stepped out and come back.
Q You was there? A Yes sir.
Q About how old was Major Barbee at that time? A I'll be doggoned if I can tell you exactly. We sent it down here and they said it would do no good, and never jogged my memory with it any more until the notice came down that there was a chance to file the child.
Q Did you take the child there with you when you went to make this affidavit? A Yes sir, running around the house.
Q Can't you form some idea about how old that child was at that time? A It seems to me that he was along about 3 years old.
Q How old is he now- the child Major Barbee? A He is about 4 years old; got it all on the Bible at home.

The witness is advised that it will be necessary for him to produce the bible in which he states there is a record of the birth of Major Barbee Pitts.

Q You have a record of the birth of the balance of your family on there? A Yes sir.
Q Your wife too? A Yes sir.
Q Written with a pen or pencil? A All with a pencil I think, I don't think we have put any down with a pen for we haven't had a pen in the house since I was married.
Q Who did the writing in there-, your wife? A I think she did; all of them.
Q Is the date of your birth in there and your wife's and all your children? A Yes sir.
Q Where is Mr. Hatfield now? A I think he is dead. I think I saw in the paper this morning that he is dead. *(Three lines are illegible.)*
A Dr. Hamilton is in town; he is the man that issued the medicine.
Q Did he attend on your wife after her sickness or soon after the child was born? A After he was born.
Q Did you, pay him at the time or afterwards? A Sometimes I would owe him a month or two.

The applicant is advised that the testimony of Dr/[sic] Hamilton is desired, and that he produce his book here in which he made an entry of the charge for waiting on the mother at the time of the child's birth.

Emma Pitts recalled:

Examination by Mr. Mott:

Q Did that child have on pants when you took it to the Notary Public? A No sir; he was wearing dresses.
Q Could it talk then? A No he couldn't talk very much yet; its[sic] only been the last year or so he can talk a little.

Applications for Enrollment of Creek Newborn
Act of 1905   Volume XIV

Q How old is your oldest child?   A Living?
Q How many have you got dead?   A Three.
Q Is your oldest child dead?   A Yes sir.
Q How long has your youngest child that died- how long has it been dead-- what's its name?   A William Robinson Pitts.
Q How long has he been dead?   A I guess it will be 6 years this coming April.
Q He is filed is he?   A Yes sir; 6 or 7 I won't be positive.
Q What is his name?   A William Robinson.
Q He has been dead 6 or 7 years this coming April?   A Yes sir.
Q Well, you have one older dead?   A Two older ones dead.
Q But the youngest one that's dead is William Robinson?   A Yes sir.
Q And it has been dead 6 or 7 years this coming April?   A Yes sir; I think so; I won't be positive now.
Q You mean 6 years this last April or 7 this coming April?   A I won't say but I, think its[sic] 6 years this coming April.

Frank F. Pitts recalled:

By Mr. Mott:

Q What do you say about that?   A I think its[sic] 7 this coming April; I wont[sic] be positive; it may be 6; I am not right certain.
Q What day in April did it die?   A I believe the 6th of April; the whole outfit has the measles.

Emma recalled:

By the Commission:

[sic] Mrs. Pitts, how long had William Robinson been dead when Major Barbee was born, do you remember that?   A You have asked me one too much; I can't tell you.

(To Frank: Q What do you say about that Mr. Pitts?   A Well, now, Frank here was in bed with her a little baby when William died with the measles that baby was in bed with her with the measles.
Q Well, how long had William been dead when Major Barbee was born; can't you remember as to that?   A I can't answer that.

An affidavit heretofore filed relative to the birth of Major Barbee Pitts is made part of the record herein.

By Mr. Mott:

Q When did this Notary Public die Mr. Pitts?   A I can't tell when; we was sitting down in the office this morning and somebody said Hatfield was dead.
Q You live at Wagoner, Indian Territory don't you?   A Out a mile from Wagoner.

Applications for Enrollment of Creek Newborn
Act of 1905 Volume XIV

Q Well, don't you know about his burial? A Had not heard anything about it except what was in the paper.
Q When did they say this morning he was dead? A I don't know; nobody said; I didn't look at it with my specs. Somebody was telling about him.
Q Was your wife sitting there then? A No sir; she had not come from home then; I think this morning is the first time I remember hearing anything about it.
Q What time did you get here? A Yes sir, this train this evening.
Q What time did you get in? A Left Wagoner 2:15; we got here just 19 minutes of 4.
Q How far is it from here to Wagoner? A 15 miles.

- - - - -

Henry G. Hains being sworn on his oath states that as stenographer to the Commission to the Five Civilized Tribes he reported the above case and that this is a full, true and correct transcript of his stenographic notes in same.

Henry G. Hains

Subscribed and sworn to before me this 29 day of September, 1904.

W^mMartinJr.
Notary Public.

En. 709.

DEPARTMENT OF THE INTERIOR,
COMMISSION TO THE FIVE CIVILIZED TRIBES.
MUSKOGEE, INDIAN TERRITORY, APRIL 5, 1905.

-ooOoo-

In the matter of the application for the enrollment of Major Barbee Pitts, as a citizen by blood of the Creek Nation.

EMMA PITTS, being duly sworn, testified as follows:

EXAMINATION BY COMMISSION:
Q What is your name? A Emma Pitts.
Q Have you heretofore made application for the enrollment of your child, Major Barbee Pitts? A Yes.
Q When was that child born? A He was born the 15th of July, 1901.
Q Are you sure that he was born in 1901? A Yes.
Q How old will he be this coming July? A Four years old.
Q Have you the record with you that you spoke of in your former testimony? A Yes.

There is exhibited a Testament and on the back of the fly-leaf entitled "The New Testament" is written the dates of the birth and death of different children, among said entries is found the following: "Major Barbee Pitts was borne[sic] July 15 1901."

Applications for Enrollment of Creek Newborn
Act of 1905 Volume XIV

Q Is that child living? A Yes, here he is.
(Child is present and appears to be about as old as indicated).

Zera Ellen Parrish, being sworn on her oath states that as stenographer to the Commission to the Five Civilized Tribes she reported the above case and that this is a full, true and correct transcript of her stenographic notes in same.

                                          Zera Ellen Parrish

Subscribed and sworn
to before me this   7
day of April, 1905.

                                          Edw C Griesel
                                                  Notary Public.

(The below note typed as given.)

Towe the commission of the five civilized tribe we made a mistake in the date of the year when we made statment of Barbee Pitts was Born in 1900 in the place of 1901 for it was sick and botheard at the time the papers was made out and ~~was~~ now tell me what to do about it and he will be 3 years old in 15 of July 1903

                                    Emma Pitts and
                                    Frank F. Pitts

BIRTH AFFIDAVIT.

DEPARTMENT OF THE INTERIOR,
COMMISSION TO THE FIVE CIVILIZED TRIBES.

In Re Application for Enrollment, as a citizen of the Creek Nation, of Major Barbee Pitts , born on the 15th day of July, 1901

                                                                           by adoption
Name of Father: Frank Field Pitts   a citizen of the Creek Nation Nation.
Name of Mother: Emma Pitts   a citizen of the Creek Nation Nation.

                             Post-office   Wagoner, I.T.

Applications for Enrollment of Creek Newborn
Act of 1905   Volume XIV

AFFIDAVIT OF MOTHER.

UNITED STATES OF AMERICA,
   INDIAN TERRITORY,
      Western   District.

I, Emma Pitts , on oath state that I am 27 years of age and a citizen by blood , of the Creek Nation; that I am the lawful wife of Frank Field Pitts , who is a citizen, by adoption of the Creek Nation; that a male child was born to me on 15th day of July , 1901, that said child has been named Major Barbee Pitts , and is now living.

                                    Emma Pitts

WITNESSES TO MARK:

Subscribed and sworn to before me this 28th day of August , 1902.

                                    Charles W. Hatfield
My Com Expires July 2^d 1906   NOTARY PUBLIC.

AFFIDAVIT OF ATTENDING PHYSICIAN OR MID-WIFE.

UNITED STATES OF AMERICA,
   INDIAN TERRITORY,
      Western   District.

I, Louisa Jones , a neighbor , on oath state that I attended on Mrs. Emma Pitts , wife of Frank Field Pitts on the 15th day of July , 1901 ; that there was born to her on said date a male child; that said child is now living and is said to have been named Major Barbee Pitts

                                    her
                            Louisa x Jones
WITNESSES TO MARK: mark
   Ed Mullins
   W J *(Illegible)*

Subscribed and sworn to before me this 28th day of August , 1902.

                                    Charles W. Hatfield
My Com Expires July 2^d 1906   NOTARY PUBLIC.

Applications for Enrollment of Creek Newborn
Act of 1905 Volume XIV

BIRTH AFFIDAVIT.

DEPARTMENT OF THE INTERIOR.
COMMISSION TO THE FIVE CIVILIZED TRIBES.

IN RE APPLICATION FOR ENROLLMENT, as a citizen of the Creek Nation, of Major Barbee Pitts, born on the 15th day of July, 1901

Name of Father: Frank Fields Pitts   a citizen of the   Creek   Nation.
Name of Mother: Emma Pitts   a citizen of the   Creek   Nation.

Postoffice   Wagoner IT

AFFIDAVIT OF MOTHER.

UNITED STATES OF AMERICA, Indian Territory, }
Western   DISTRICT.

I, Emma Pitts, on oath state that I am 30 years of age and a citizen by blood, of the Creek Nation; that I am the lawful wife of Frank Fields Pitts, who is a citizen, by adoption of the Creek Nation; that a male child was born to me on 15th day of July, 1901, that said child has been named Major Barbee Pitts, and was living March 4, 1905.

Emma Pitts

Witnesses To Mark:
{

Subscribed and sworn to before me this 4th day of November, 1905.

My Com Ex July 15th 1906   H.R. Bonnet
                                   Notary Public.

AFFIDAVIT OF ATTENDING PHYSICIAN OR MID-WIFE.

UNITED STATES OF AMERICA, Indian Territory, }
Western   DISTRICT.

I, J.N. Fain, a Physician, on oath state that I attended on Mrs. Emma Pitts, wife of Frank Fields Pitts on the 15 day of July, 1901; that there was born to her on said date a male child; that said child was living March 4, 1905, and is said to have been named Major Barbee Pitts

J. N. Fain M.D.

Witnesses To Mark:
{

Applications for Enrollment of Creek Newborn
Act of 1905   Volume XIV

Subscribed and sworn to before me 7 day of   Nov. , 1905.
My Com exprs
    May 12-1908   Anna Farrow
                                                Notary Public.

NC-1082.

Muskogee, Indian Territory, October 23, 1905.

Emma Pitts,
    Wagoner, Indian Territory.

Dear Madam:

    In the matter of the application for the enrollment of your minor child, Major Barbee, born July 15, 1901, as a citizen by blood of the Creek Nation, you are advised that it will be necessary for you to furnish this office with the affidavits of yourself and the physician or midwife, who attended at the birth of said child, relative to his birth and a blank for that purpose, which has been properly filled out, is inclosed herewith.

    In having the same executed be careful to see that the notary public, before whom the affidavits are sworn to, affixes his name and seal to each affidavit. In case any signature is by mark the same must be attested by two disinterested witnesses. When the affidavits have been properly executed return them to this office in the inclosed envelope.

                               Respectfully,

CTD-16   Commissioner.
Env.

DEPARTMENT OF THE INTERIOR,
COMMISSION TO THE FIVE CIVILIZED TRIBES.

Muskogee, Indian Territory, April 15, 1905

    In the matter of the application for the enrollment of certain new-born children as citizens of the Creek Nation.

    Alex Posey, being duly sworn, testified as follows:

Applications for Enrollment of Creek Newborn
Act of 1905 Volume XIV

EXAMINATION BY THE COMMISSION:
Q State your name, age and postoffice address. A Alex Posey; 31; Muskogee.
Q Are you a citizen of the Creek Nation? A Yes sir.
Q Got your land, have you? A Yes sir.
Q Have you been engaged recently in the "field work" of the Dawes Commission in securing evidence about Creek citizens or new-borns? A Yes sir.
Q Have you a list of children for whom application could not be made and about whom you have succeeded in obtaining some information? A Yes sir.
Q You may state the conditions and the names of those children that you desire to make application for. A Yes sir.
Q Name them. A Annie Deere. Born July 10, 1902, a child of _____ Deere and Louina Deere. The father belongs to Okfuskee Canadian, and the mother is a citizen of the Seminole Nation.

Noda Pologee I understand has some children, but I have not been able to learn their names, or the name of their father. The mother lives near Eufaula.

Maxey Lewis, of Eufaula Canadian Town, I learn has one child, but I have not been able to learn its name or the name of its mother.

Q This information you received from relatives right around there on April 15, 1905? A Yes sir.
Q Were you informed that the parents of these children were unwilling to make application for their enrollment? A Yes sir.

Q This was the only way the rights of these children could be save by? A Yes, sir. I made every effort to obtain direct information from the parents, but in every instance they refused to give testimony.

INDIAN TERRITORY, Western District.
I, J. Y. Miller, a stenographer to the Commission to the Five Civilized Tribes, do hereby certify that the above and foregoing is a true and complete translation of my notes as same appear in my stenographic report of this case.

JY Miller

Subscribed and sworn to before me
this the 15th day of April,
1905.

Drennan C Skaggs
Notary Public.

Applications for Enrollment of Creek Newborn
Act of 1905   Volume XIV

DEPARTMENT OF THE INTERIOR,
COMMISSION TO THE FIVE CIVILIZED TRIBES.
Eufaula, I.T., May 16, 1905.

In the matter of the application for the enrollment of Lena Bear as a citizen by blood of the Creek Nation.

LYDIA BEAR, being duly sworn, testified as follows:

Through Alex Posey Official Interpreter:

BY COMMISSION:
Q What is your name? A Lydia Bear.
Q How old are you? A About twenty-five/[sic]
Q What is your post office address? A Eufaula.
Q Are you a citizen of the Creek Nation? A Yes, sir.
Q To what town do you belong? A Okfuske Canadian.
Q Do you now make application for the enrollment of your minor child, Lena Bear, as a citizen by blood of the Creek Nation? A Yes, sir.
Q Who is her father? A Thomas Bear.
Q Is Thomas Bear your lawfull[sic] husband? A Yes, sir.
Q Is he living? A No, sir, he is dead.
Q Was he a citizen of the Creek Nation? A Yes, sir.
Q To what town did he belong? A Okfuske Canadian.
Q When was your child Lena, born? A The last of December, after Christmas. It will be four years old next December.
Q The child is living is it? A Yes, sir.

---ooo OOoooo---[sic]

I, D. C. Skaggs, on oath state that the above and foregoing is a full and true transcript of my stenographic notes as taken in said cause on said date.

Subscribed and sworn to before me this ___ day of _____ 1905.

Notary Public.

DEPARTMENT OF THE INTERIOR,
COMMISSIONER TO THE FIVE CIVILIZED TRIBES.
Eufaula, I. T., September 11, 1905.

In the matter of the application for the enrollment of certain new born children as citizens of the Creek Nation.

JAMES SULPHUR, being duly sworn, testified as follows:

Applications for Enrollment of Creek Newborn
Act of 1905 Volume XIV

Through Alex Posey Official Interpreter:

BY THE COMMISSIONER:
Q What is your name? A James Sulphur.
Q How old are you? A About twenty-nine.
Q What is your post office address? A Eufaula.
Q Are you a citizen of the Creek Nation? A Yes, sir.
Q To what town do you belong? A Hickory Ground.
Q Do you know Neda Pologee? A I do.
Q Is she known by any other name? A She is known both as Lydia Pologee and Lydia Bear. Her last husband's name was Thomas Bear.
Q To what town does she belong? A Okfuske Canadian.
Q Has she any new born children? A Yes, sir.
Q How many? A She has three.
Q Do you know their names? A I do not know the name of any one of them.
Q How old is the oldest one? A The oldest child is about six years old.
Q How old is the next? A About five years old.
Q How old is the next child? A About three years old.
Q Is Thomas Bear the father of all three children? A No, sir. The father of the oldest child was Loney Charte, who is now dead.
Q Was he a citizen of the Creek NATION[sic]? A Yes, sir.
Q To what town did he belong? A I do not know but I think he belonged to Eufaula Canadian. He died about six years ago, when the child was an infant.
Q Who is the father of the other two children? A Thomas Bear.
Q To what town does he belong? A Okfuske Canadian. He is also dead
Q How long has he been dead? A He has been dead three years.
Q Was the youngest child born before his death A The child was born shortly after his death.
Q How old was his other child at the time of his death? A Something like two years old.
Q Was Loney Charte known by any other name? A No, sir. Loney Charte was an orphan who was raised by William McCombs.
Q Was Thomas Bear known by any other name? A He was sometimes known as Cusamacher.

---oooooooooo---

I, D. C. Skaggs, on oath state that the above and foregoing is a full and true transcript of my stenographic notes as taken in said cause on said date.

D. C. Skaggs

Subscribed and sworn to before me this 16 day of October 1905.

Edw C Griesel
Notary Public.

Applications for Enrollment of Creek Newborn
Act of 1905   Volume XIV

DEPARTMENT OF THE INTERIOR,
COMMISSIONER TO THE FIVE CIVILIZED TRIBES.
Eufaula, I. T., September 12, 1905.

In the matter of the application for the enrollment of certain new born children as citizens of the Creek Nation.

WICEY ASBURY, being duly sworn, testified as follows:

Through Alex Posey Official Interpreter Posey:

BY THE COMMISSIONER:
Q What is your name? A Wicey Asbury.
Q How old are you? A About thirty.
Q What is your post office address? A Eufaula.
Q Are you a citizen of the Creek Nation? A Yes, sir.
Q To what town do you belong? A Tulladega.
Q Do you know Neda Pologee? A Yes, sir. Her correct name is Lydia Pologee.
Q Is she sometimes known as Lydia Bear? A Yes, sir.
Q To what town does she belong? A Okfuske Canadian.
Q Has she any children? A Yes, sir.
Q How many? A She has three living and one dead.
Q What is he name of the oldest living child? A Cristie Charte, her father was Loney Charte.
Q How old is she? A I think she is about eight years old.
Q Is Loney Charte living or dead? A He is dead.
Q What is the name of the next oldest child? A Its name is Rhoda. I do not know who her father is.
Q How old is Rhoda? A I think she is about four years old. She may be five.
Q What is the name of the next child? A I do not know.
Q Do you know who is the father of it? A Thomas Bear.
Q How old is that child? A About three years old.
Q What is the name of the child that is dead? A I don't know.
Q When did it die? A The child died shortly after the father died and he has been dead about two years.
Q How old was the child at the time of its death? A About a year old.

JIMSY ASBURY, being duly sworn, testified as follows:

Through Alex Posey Official Interpreter:

BY THE COMMISSIONER:
Q What is your name? A Jimsy Asbury.
Q How old are you? A I do not know my age, but white people guess my age at about forth-eight.
Q What is your post office address? A Eufaula.
Q Are you a citizen of the Creek Nation? A Yes, sir.

Applications for Enrollment of Creek Newborn
Act of 1905   Volume XIV

Q To what town do you belong? A Tuskegee.
Q Do you know Lydia Pologee or Bear? A Yes, sir.
Q Has she any children? A Yes, sir.
q How many? A She has three. Three girls.
q Do you know the name of her oldest child? A I do not know the names of her children.
q How old is the oldest child? A I think she is at least ten years old.
Q Do you know whether or not land has been selected for her? A I do not know. If she was allotted she was arbitrarilly[sic] filed by the Commission. All of her people were arbitrarilly[sic] filed.
Q What is the name of her father? A Loney Charte.
Q To what town did he belong? A I think he belonged to Eufaula Canadian Town, but I am not positive. Bill McCombs would know because he raised him as an orphan.
Q How old is the next oldest child? A She is between four and five years old.
Q Who is that child's father? A The father is unknown, but it is generally supposed that Ben Kiddo, who is also known as Ben Corser, is the father. He belongs to Cussehta Town.
Q How old is the youngest child? A About three years old.
Q Who is the father of that child? A Thomas Bear.
Q To what town does Thomas Bear belong? A Okfuske Canadian.

---oooOOOooo---

I, D. C. Skaggs, on oath state that the above and foregoing is a full and true transcript of my stenographic notes as taken in said cause on said date.

D. C. Skaggs

Subscribed and sworn to before me this 16 day of October 1905.

Edw C Griesel
Notary Public.

N.C. 1064.

Department of the Interior,
Commissioner to the Five Civilized Tribes.
Eufaula, I. T., August 18, 1906.

In the matter of the application for the enrollment of Lena Bear as a citizen by blood of the Creek Nation.

SUPPLEMENTAL TESTIMONY.

LYDIA BEAR being duly sworn testified as follows:

Applications for Enrollment of Creek Newborn
Act of 1905   Volume XIV

Through Alex Posey Official Interpreter:

BY THE COMMISSIONER:

Q What is your name? A Lydia Bear.
Q What is your age? A About 25.
Q What is your postoffice address? A Eufaula.
Q You testified in this case yesterday, did you not? A Yes sir.
Q Have you the marriage license you were advised to furnish in the matter of the application for the enrollment of your child, Lena Bear? A Yes sir. (The witness presents license and certificate of marriage issued April 3, 1902, to Thos. Bear and Miss Lydia Johnson).
Q Your name is given in this marriage license as Miss Lydia Johnson. Is that your correct name? A No sir, it is a mistake; we have a number of relatives named Johnson and Thomas Bear, through mistake, gave my surname as Johnson when he applied for our marriage license.

James B. Myers, being first duly sworn, states, that as stenographer to the Commissioner to the Five Civilized Tribes, he recorded the testimony in the foregoing proceedings, and that the above is a true, and correct transcript of his stenographic notes thereof.

James B Myers

Subscribed and sworn to before me this the 20 day of August, 1906.

JBM

Alex Posey
Notary Public.

BIRTH AFFIDAVIT.

DEPARTMENT OF THE INTERIOR.
COMMISSION TO THE FIVE CIVILIZED TRIBES.

IN RE APPLICATION FOR ENROLLMENT, as a citizen of the Creek Nation, of Lena Bear, born on the *(blank)* day of December, 1901

Name of Father: Thomas Bear   a citizen of the   Creek   Nation.
Okfuske Canadian Town
Name of Mother: Lydia Bear   a citizen of the   Creek   Nation.
Okfuske Canadian Town

Postoffice   Eufaula, I.T.

Applications for Enrollment of Creek Newborn
Act of 1905   Volume XIV

AFFIDAVIT OF MOTHER.

Child present

UNITED STATES OF AMERICA, Indian Territory, ⎫
   Western   DISTRICT.   ⎭

I, Lydia Bear , on oath state that I am about 25 years of age and a citizen by blood , of the Creek Nation; that I am the lawful wife of Thomas Bear, deceased , who is a citizen, by blood of the Creek Nation; that a female child was born to me on *(blank)* day of December , 1901 , that said child has been named Lena Bear , and ~~is now~~ was living. March 4, 1905

                                            her
Witnesses To Mark: Lydia x Bear
   { DC Skaggs   mark
   { Alex Posey

Subscribed and sworn to before me this   16 day of   May   , 1905.

                                            Drennan C Skaggs
                                            Notary Public.

AFFIDAVIT OF ATTENDING PHYSICIAN OR MID-WIFE.

UNITED STATES OF AMERICA, Indian Territory, ⎫
   Western   DISTRICT.   ⎭

I, Susie Deere , a mid-wife , on oath state that I attended on Mrs. Lydia Bear, wife of Thomas Bear on the *(blank)* day of December , 1901 ; that there was born to her on said date a female child; that said child ~~is now~~ was living on March 4, 1905 and is said to have been named Lena Bear

                                            her
                                        Susie x Deere
Witnesses To Mark: mark
   { DC Skaggs
   { Alex Posey

Subscribed and sworn to before me this   16 day of   May   , 1905.

                                            Drennan C Skaggs
                                            Notary Public.

Applications for Enrollment of Creek Newborn
Act of 1905   Volume XIV

C 1083

Dustin, Indian Territory, June 3, 1905.

Commission to the Five Civilized Tribes,
   Muskogee, Indian Territory.

Gentlemen:

   I return herewith copies of testimony taken in the following cases, as I find it impossible to secure further evidence:

   Sarty, Enrollment No. 520.
   Chepe and Folle Homahta, Creek Indian Card Field No. 2871.
   Katy and Nicey Gano, No. 2465 B.
   William Tiger, No. ____ B.
   Amy Kelly, No. 2467 B.
   Heliswa and Kaska Beaver, No. 2466 B.
   ✓Lena Bear, No. ____ B.
   Setepake Scott, No. 2447 B.
   Mahlahsee Mitchell, No. 2447 B.
   Susanna and Onate Johnson, No. 2468 B.

                     Respectfully,
                     (Signed) Alex Posey,
                     Clerk in Charge Creek Field Party.

CERTIFICATE OF RECORD.

United States of America,
INDIAN TERRITORY,   } ss.
Northern District.

   I, **CHARLES A. DAVIDSON**, Clerk of the United States Court in the Northern District, Indian Territory, do hereby certify that the instrument hereto attached was filed for record in my office the   31"   day of   May   1902 at   8 A- M., and duly recorded in Book   M   , Marriage Record, Page   457

   WITNESS my hand and seal of said Court at Muscogee, in said Territory,
            this   31"   day of   May   A. D. 1902

                     Chas A Davidson   Clerk.
            By...Deputy.

Applications for Enrollment of Creek Newborn
Act of 1905   Volume XIV

MARRIAGE LICENSE

United States of America, ⎫
   INDIAN TERRITORY,   ⎬ ss.
   Northern District. ⎭

To Any Person Authorized by Law to Solemnize Marriage---Greeting:

You are Hereby Commanded to Solemnize the Rite and publish the Banns of Matrimony between Mr.   Thos Bear   of   Eufaula , in the Indian Territory, aged   34   years and Miss Lydia Johnson   of   Eufaula   in the Indian Territory aged   30   years according to law, and do you officially sign and return this License to the parties therein named.

     WITNESS my hand and official seal at Muscogee Indian Territory this   3rd day of   April   A.D. 190 2

                               Chas. A. Davidson
                               Clerk of the U.S. Court

By .... Deputy

CERTIFICATE OF MARRIAGE.

United States of America, ⎫
   INDIAN TERRITORY,   ⎬ ss.
   Northern District. ⎭

    I,   Johnson J. Phillips   , a Minister of the Gospel, DO HEREBY CERTIFY that on the   17   day of   ~~April~~   May   A. D. 1902, I did duly and according to law as commanded in the foregoing License, solemnize the Rite and publish the Banns of Matrimony between the parties therein named.

    WITNESS my hand this   17   day of   May   A. D. 1902

    My credentials are recorded in the office of the Clerk of the United States Court, Indian Territory, Northern District, Book   B   , Page   29   .

                               Johnson J Phillips
                               A Minister of the Gospel

Applications for Enrollment of Creek Newborn
Act of 1905 Volume XIV

Note—This License and Certificate of Marriage must be returned to the Office of the Clerk of the United States Court in the Northern District, Indian Territory, from whence it was issued, within sixty days from the date thereof, or the party to whom the license was issued will be liable in the amount of the One Hundred Dollars ($100.00)

N.C. 1064
BIRTH AFFIDAVIT.

DEPARTMENT OF THE INTERIOR,
COMMISSIONER TO THE FIVE CIVILIZED TRIBES.

ENROLLMENT OF MINORS. ACT OF CONGRESS, APPROVED APRIL 26, 1906.

IN RE APPLICATION FOR ENROLLMENT, as a citizen of the Creek Nation, of Lena Bear, born on or about the 15 day of October, 1901

deceased
Name of Father: Thomas Bear (or Cussamacha) a citizen of the Creek Nation.
Name of Mother: Lydia Bear (nee Poloke) C.F. 3602 a citizen of the Creek Nation.

Tribal enrollment of father Okfuske Canadian Tribal enrollment of mother Okfuske Canadian

Postoffice Eufaula, Indian Territory

AFFIDAVIT OF MOTHER.

UNITED STATES OF AMERICA, Indian Territory,
Western District.

I, Lydia Bear (nee Poloke), on oath state that I am about 25 years of age and a citizen by blood, of the Creek Nation; that I am the lawful wife of Thomas Bear (or Cussamacha) deceased, who is was a citizen, by blood of the Creek Nation; that a female child was born to me on or about 15 day of October, 1901, that said child has been named Lena Bear, and was living March 4, 1906.

her
Lydia x Bear
mark

WITNESSES TO MARK:
{ Alex Posey
{ Dan Polk

Subscribed and sworn to before me this 16 day of August, 1906.

Alex Posey
Notary Public.

Applications for Enrollment of Creek Newborn
Act of 1905   Volume XIV

AFFIDAVIT OF ATTENDING PHYSICIAN OR MID-WIFE.

UNITED STATES OF AMERICA, Indian Territory, }
   Western   District.

    I, Susie Poloke , a midwife , on oath state that I attended on Lydia Bear , wife of Thomas Bear deceased on or about the 15 day October , 1901 ; that there was born to her on said date a   female   child; that said child was living March 4, 1906, and is said to have been named Lena Bear

                                                       her
                                                 Susie x Poloke
WITNESSES TO MARK: mark
  { Alex Posey
    Dan Polk

Subscribed and sworn to before me this   16   day of   August   , 1906.

                                                 Alex Posey
                                                         Notary Public.

BIRTH AFFIDAVIT.

DEPARTMENT OF THE INTERIOR.
COMMISSION TO THE FIVE CIVILIZED TRIBES.

    IN RE APPLICATION FOR ENROLLMENT, as a citizen of the Creek Nation, of Elmer Gillis , born on the 25" day of May , 1904

Name of Father: E.L. Gillis   a non ~~a~~ citizen of the   Creek   Nation.
Name of Mother: Anna Perryman   a citizen of the   Creek   Nation.

                              Postoffice   Broken Arrow, I.T.

AFFIDAVIT OF MOTHER.

UNITED STATES OF AMERICA, Indian Territory, }
   Western   DISTRICT.

    I,   Anna Perryman , on oath state that I am 19 years of age and a citizen by blood , of the Creek   Nation; that I am ~~the~~ not the lawful wife of E.L. Gillis , who is a

Applications for Enrollment of Creek Newborn
Act of 1905   Volume XIV

non citizen, by ———of the Creek Nation; that a male child was born by him to me on 25" day of May, 1904, that said child has been named Elmer Gillis, and is now living.

Anna Perryman

Witnesses To Mark:
{

    Subscribed and sworn to before me this 18" day of   April   , 1905.

Z.I.J. Holt

my commission expires May 9" 1907   Notary Public.

AFFIDAVIT OF ATTENDING PHYSICIAN OR MID-WIFE.

UNITED STATES OF AMERICA, Indian Territory, ⎤
    Western   DISTRICT. ⎦

    I, A. J. Pollard, a Physician, on oath state that I attended on ~~Mrs.~~ Miss Anna Perryman, wife of ══ on the 25" day of May, 1904; that there was born to her on said date a male child; that said child is now living and is said to have been named Elmer Gillis

AJ Pollard MD

Witnesses To Mark:
{

    Subscribed and sworn to before me this 18" day of   April   , 1905.

Z.I.J. Holt

my commission expires May 9" 1907   Notary Public.

Applications for Enrollment of Creek Newborn
Act of 1905 Volume XIV

BIRTH AFFIDAVIT.

DEPARTMENT OF THE INTERIOR.
COMMISSION TO THE FIVE CIVILIZED TRIBES.

IN RE APPLICATION FOR ENROLLMENT, as a citizen of the Creek Nation, of Roy Collins, born on the 6 day of Sept, 1903

Name of Father: Jacob M Collins   a citizen of the   Creek   Nation.
Name of Mother: Nancy D. Collins   a citizen of the   U. S.   Nation.

Postoffice   Paden

AFFIDAVIT OF MOTHER.

UNITED STATES OF AMERICA, Indian Territory,
     Western   DISTRICT.

I, Nancy D Collins, on oath state that I am 20 years of age and a citizen by U.S. , ~~of the Nation~~; that I am the lawful wife of Jacob M Collins , who is a citizen, by blood of the Creek Nation; that a male child was born to me on 6 day of September , 1903 , that said child has been named Roy Collins , and was living March 4, 1905.

                                                     her
                                     Nancy D   x   Collins
Witnesses To Mark: mark
    { D J Mansker
      John I. Brown

Subscribed and sworn to before me this 25th day of Nov , 1905.

                             (Name Illegible)
My commission expires Feby 19" 1909   Notary Public.

BIRTH AFFIDAVIT.

DEPARTMENT OF THE INTERIOR.
COMMISSION TO THE FIVE CIVILIZED TRIBES.

IN RE APPLICATION FOR ENROLLMENT, as a citizen of the Creek Nation, of Roy Collins, born on the 6" day of Sept, 1903

Name of Father: Jacob M Collins   a citizen of the   Creek   Nation.
Name of Mother: Nancy D. Collins   a citizen of the   U. S.   Nation.

                  Postoffice   Paden, I.T.
                  Address until Sept 1, Briartown, I.T.

Applications for Enrollment of Creek Newborn
Act of 1905   Volume XIV

(Child present)

AFFIDAVIT OF MOTHER.

UNITED STATES OF AMERICA, Indian Territory, }
Western   DISTRICT.

I, Nancy D. Collins , on oath state that I am 20 years of age and a citizen by ---, of the U.S. Nation; that I am the lawful wife of Jacob M Collins , who is a citizen, by blood of the Creek Nation; that a *(blank)* child was born to me on 6" day of Sept , 1903 , that said child has been named Roy Collins , and is now living.

(Name Illegible)

Witnesses To Mark:
{

Subscribed and sworn to before me this 15" day of   April   , 1905.

My Com expires Apr 16, 1909.   Zera E Parrish
                                                       Notary Public.

AFFIDAVIT OF ATTENDING PHYSICIAN OR MID-WIFE.

UNITED STATES OF AMERICA, Indian Territory, }
Western   DISTRICT.

I, S.E. Laudermilk, a midwife , on oath state that I attended on Mrs. Nancy D Collins , wife of Jacob M Collins on the 6" day of Sept , 1903 ; that there was born to her on said date a male child; that said child is now living and is said to have been named Roy Collins

S E Laudermilk

Witnesses To Mark:
{

Subscribed and sworn to before me this 15" day of   April   , 1905.

My Com expires Apr 16, 1909.   Zera E Parrish
                                                       Notary Public.

Applications for Enrollment of Creek Newborn
Act of 1905   Volume XIV

BIRTH AFFIDAVIT.

DEPARTMENT OF THE INTERIOR.
COMMISSION TO THE FIVE CIVILIZED TRIBES.

IN RE APPLICATION FOR ENROLLMENT, as a citizen of the Creek Nation, of Roy Collins, born on the 6" day of Sept, 1903

Name of Father: Jacob M Collins   a citizen of the   Creek   Nation.
Name of Mother: Nancy D. Collins   a citizen of the   U. S.   Nation.

Postoffice   Paden, I.T.
Address until Sept 1, Briartown, I.T.

(Father presents *(illegible)*)

AFFIDAVIT OF MOTHER.

UNITED STATES OF AMERICA, Indian Territory,
 Western   DISTRICT.

I, Jacob M Collins, on oath state that I am 28 years of age and a citizen by blood, of the Creek Nation; that I am the lawful ~~wife~~ husband of Nancy D Collins, who is a citizen, by ~~blood~~ of the ~~Creek~~ U.S. Nation; that a male child was born to me on 6" day of Sept, 1903, that said child has been named Roy Collins, and is now living.

Jacob M Collins

Witnesses To Mark:
{

Subscribed and sworn to before me this 15" day of April, 1905.

My Com expires Apr 16, 1909.   Zera E Parrish
                                          Notary Public.

NC-1087.

Muskogee, Indian Territory, November 9, 1905.

Nancy D. Collins,
    c/o Jacob M. Collins,
        Paden, Indian Territory.

Dear Madam:

In the matter of the application for the enrollment of your minor child Roy Collins, born September 6, 1903, as a citizen by blood of the Creek Nation, the signature to the affidavit executed by you April 15, 1905, relative to the birth of said child, is illegible. Your name is given in the body of the affidavit as Nancy D. Collins.

Applications for Enrollment of Creek Newborn
Act of 1905   Volume XIV

There is herewith inclosed form of birth affidavit which has been properly filled out. You are requested to execute same signing your name as the same appears in the body of the affidavit. In the event that you are unable to write legibly and the signature is by mark same must be attested by two disinterested witnesses.

                       Respectfully,
                                           Commissioner.

CTD-24.
Env.

(Affidavit below handwritten)

Affidavit of Midwife

United States of America
    Indian Territory
Western Judicial District

I Mary Barnett Midwife on oath state that I attended Mrs. Sukey Barnett wife of Tom Barnett on the 29th day of June 1903 that there was born to her on said date a male child that said child is now living and is said to have been named John Barnett

                                          her

Witness   Mary x Barnett
x Rosie Fisher   mark
x Seaborn Fisher   Subscribed and sworn to ~~me~~ before me a Notary Public this 11th day of April 1905   E E Schock Notary Public
                                            My Commission Expires
                                                 Jan 18th 1908

(Affidavit below handwritten)

Birth Affidavit

Department of Interior
Commission to the Five Civilized Tribes

In re aplication[sic] for enrollment as a citizen of the Creek Nation of John Barnett born on the 29th day of June 1903 Name of Father Tom Barnett a citizen of the Creek Nation Name of Mother Sukey Barnett a citizen of the Creek Nation
Post office Bryant I.T

Applications for Enrollment of Creek Newborn
Act of 1905   Volume XIV

United States of America   Affidavit of Mother
    Indian Territory
Western Judicial District

I Sukey Barnett on oath state that I am 24 years old and a citizen by blood of the Creek Nation that I am the lawful wife of Tom Barnett who is a citizen by blood of the Creek Nation that a male child was born to me on 29th day of June 1903. That said child has been named John Barnett and is now living

                                              Sukey Barnett

Subscribed and sworn to before me this 11th day of April 1905 The child being present

                                        E E Schock Notary Public
                                        My commission Expires
                                             Jan 18th 1908

(Affidavit below handwritten)

                              Affidavit of Midwife

United States of America
    Indian Territory
Western Judicial District

I Mary Barnett Midwife on oath state that I attended Mrs. Sukey Barnett wife of Tom Barnett on the 24th day of September 1904 that there was born to her on that date a male child that said child is now living and is said to have been named Charlie Barnett

                                                  her
Witness   Mary x Barnett
Rosie Fisher   mark
Seaborn Fisher

Subscribed and sworn to before me this 11th day of April 1905

                                        E E Schock Notary Public
                                        My Commission Expires
                                         Jan 18th 1908

(Affidavit below handwritten)

Birth Affidavit

                              Department of Interior
                       Commission to the Five Civilized Tribes

In re aplication[sic] for enrollment as a citizen of the Creek Nation Charley Barnett born on the 24th day of September 1904 Name of Father Tom Barnett a citizen of the Creek Nation Name of Mother Sukey Barnett a citizen of the Creek Nation

                                         Post office Bryant I.T

Applications for Enrollment of Creek Newborn
Act of 1905 Volume XIV

Affidavit of Mother

United States of America
Indian Territory
Western Judicial District

    I Sukey Barnett on oath state that I am 24 years old and a citizen by blood of the Creek Nation that I am the lawful wife of Tom Barnett who is a citizen by blood of the Creek Nation that a male child was born to me on 24th day of September 1904 That said child has been named Charlie Barnett and is now living

                                            Sukey Barnett

Subscribed and sworn to before me this 11th day of April 1905 The child being present

                                    E E Schock Notary Public
                                    My commission Expires
                                        Jan 18th 1908

Child was present when papers
were made out
                E E Schock N.P.

BIRTH AFFIDAVIT.

DEPARTMENT OF THE INTERIOR.
COMMISSION TO THE FIVE CIVILIZED TRIBES.

    IN RE APPLICATION FOR ENROLLMENT, as a citizen of the Creek Nation, of Alice Barnett, born on the 31st day of Jan, 1902

Name of Father: Tom Barnett   a citizen of the   Creek   Nation.
    Hutchechubbe
Name of Mother: Sukey Barnett (nee Lowe)   a citizen of the   Creek   Nation.
    Tulsa Canadian
                            Postoffice   Bryant I.T.

AFFIDAVIT OF MOTHER.

UNITED STATES OF AMERICA, Indian Territory,
    Western Judicial   **DISTRICT.**

    I, Sukey Barnett, on oath state that I am 24 years of age and a citizen by blood, of the Creek Nation; that I am the lawful wife of Tom Barnett, who is a citizen, by blood of the Creek Nation; that a Female child was born to me on 31st day of January, 1902, that said child has been named Alice Barnett, and is now living.

Applications for Enrollment of Creek Newborn
Act of 1905   Volume XIV

Sukey Barnett

Witnesses To Mark:
{

Subscribed and sworn to before me this 11th day of   Jan   , 1905.

E. E. Schock
Notary Public.
My Commission Expires
Jan 18th 1908

AFFIDAVIT OF ATTENDING PHYSICIAN OR MID-WIFE.

UNITED STATES OF AMERICA, Indian Territory, }
Western Judicial   DISTRICT.

I, Mary Barnett , a midwife , on oath state that I attended on Mrs. Sukey Barnett , wife of Tom Barnett on the 31st day of January , 1902 ; that there was born to her on said date a Female child; that said child is now living and is said to have been named Alice Barnett

                          her
               Mary x Barnett

Witnesses To Mark: mark
{ Seaborn Fisher
{ Rosie Fisher

Subscribed and sworn to before me this 11th day of   Jan   , 1905.

E. E. Schock
Notary Public.
My Commission Expires
Jan 18th 1908

Applications for Enrollment of Creek Newborn
Act of 1905   Volume XIV

NC-1089.

Muskogee, Indian Territory, October 23, 1905.

Nancy Barnett,
    c/o Dave Barnett,
        Bryant, Indian Territory.

Dear Madam:
    In the matter of the application for the enrollment of your minor child, Mary Barnett, born December 24, 1901, as a citizen by blood of the Creek Nation, you are advised that this office is unable to identify Dave Barnett, the father of said child, upon the final roll of citizens by blood of the Creek Nation.

    You are, therefore, requested to state the name under which he was finally enrolled, the names of his parents and other members of his family, his age, the Creek Indian town to which he belongs and his final roll number as the same appears upon his allotment certificate and deeds.

                Respectfully,

                          Commissioner.

(Handwritten)
Tom Barnett appeared 11/21/05 & identified father at Roll 18, 4851   J.D.

(Affidavit below handwritten)

                Affidavit of Midwife

United States of America }
    Indian Territory }
Western Judicial District }

I Mary Barnett a midwife on oath state that I attended Mrs. Nancy Barnett wife of Dave Barnett on the 24th day of December 1901. that there was born to her on that date a female child that said child is now living and is said to have been named Mary Barnett

                                      her
Witness   Mary x Barnett
x Seaborn Fisher   mark
x Rosie Fisher

Subscribed and sworn to before me this 11th day of April 1905

                        E E Schock Notary Public
My Commission Expires Jan 18th 1908

Applications for Enrollment of Creek Newborn
Act of 1905   Volume XIV

(Affidavit below handwritten)

Birth Affidavit

Department of Interior
Commission to the Five Civilized Tribes

In re aplication[sic] for enrollment as a citizen of the Creek Nation of Mary Barnett born on the 24th day of December 1901 Name of Father Dave Barnett Name of Mother Nancy Barnett both citizens of the Creek Nation

Post office Bryant I.T

Affidavit of Mother

United States of America ⎫
   Indian Territory   ⎬
Western Judicial Dist   ⎭

    I Nancy Barnett on oath state that I am 35 years of age and a citizen by blood of the Creek Nation that I am the lawful wife of Dave Barnett who is a citizen by blood of the Creek Nation that a female child was born to me on 24th day of December 1901 that said child has been named Mary Barnett and is now living

Witness to mark	her
x Rosie Fisher	Nancy x Barnett
x Seaborn Fisher	mark

Subscribed and sworn to before me this 11th day of April 1905 The child being present
E E Schock Notary Public
My commission Expires
Jan 18th 1908

Applications for Enrollment of Creek Newborn
Act of 1905 Volume XIV

NC-1090.

Muskogee, Indian Territory, October 23, 1905.

Lizzie Harjo,
    c/o Sulphur Harjo,
        Bald Hill, Indian Territory.

Dear Madam:

    In the matter of the application for the enrollment of your minor child, Ethel Harjo, born August 15, 1904, as a citizen by blood of the Creek Nation, this office desires the affidavit of the physician or midwife who attended at the birth of said child and a blank for that purpose is inclosed herewith.

    If there was no physician or midwife in attendance at the birth of said Ethel Harjo it will be necessary for you to furnish this office with the affidavits of two disinterested persons relative to the birth of said child. Sad affidavits to set forth said child's name, the date of her birth, the names of her parents and whether or not she was living on March 4, 1905.

                      Respectfully,

                              Commissioner.

AFFIDAVIT OF DISINTERESTED WITNESSES.

United States of America,
    Indian Territory,
        Western District.

    We, the undersigned, on oath state that we are personally acquainted with Eliza Harjo wife of Sulphur Harjo, and that there was born to her on or about the 15th day of August, 1904, a female child; that said child was living March 4, 1905, N is said to have been named Ethel Harjo

We further state that we have no interest in this case.

                          Martin L. Checote
                                  her
                          Celina Bighead x
(2) Witnesses to mark: mark
Hugh E *(Illegible)*
Geo. McLagan

Subscribed and sworn to before me this 11th day of November 1905.

                          Walter A Saunders
                              Notary Public.

Applications for Enrollment of Creek Newborn
Act of 1905 Volume XIV

BIRTH AFFIDAVIT.

DEPARTMENT OF THE INTERIOR.
COMMISSION TO THE FIVE CIVILIZED TRIBES.

    IN RE APPLICATION FOR ENROLLMENT, as a citizen of the Creek Nation, of Ethel Harjo, born on the 15 day of Aug , 1904

Name of Father: Sulphur Harjo   a citizen of the   Creek   Nation.
Artussee Town
Name of Mother: Liza   "   a citizen of the   Creek   Nation.
Artussee Town

           Postoffice   Edna, I.T.

(Child present)

AFFIDAVIT OF MOTHER.

UNITED STATES OF AMERICA, Indian Territory,
    Western   DISTRICT.

    I, Liza Harjo , on oath state that I am 33 years of age and a citizen by blood , of the Creek Nation; that I am the lawful wife of Sulphur Harjo , who is a citizen, by blood of the Creek Nation; that a female child was born to me on 15 day of Aug , 1904 , that said child has been named Ethel Harjo , and was living March 4, 1905.

                   Liza Harjo

Witnesses To Mark:
{

    Subscribed and sworn to before me this 12" day of April , 1905.

(Seal)   J McDermott
                         Notary Public.

                 Father
AFFIDAVIT OF ~~ATTENDING PHYSICIAN OR MID-WIFE~~.

UNITED STATES OF AMERICA, Indian Territory,
    Western   DISTRICT.

    I, Sulphur Harjo , a husband , on oath state that I attended on ~~Mrs.~~ my , wife ~~of~~ when on the 15 day of Aug , 1904 ; that there was born to her on said date a *(blank)* child; that said child was living March 4, 1905, and is said to have been named Ethel Harjo
                           his
                 Sulphur x Harjo
                       mark

Applications for Enrollment of Creek Newborn
Act of 1905   Volume XIV

Witnesses To Mark:
{ EC Griesel
{ Jesse McDermott

    Subscribed and sworn to before me this 12" day of   April   , 1905.

(Seal)　　　　　　　　　　　　　　J McDermott
　　　　　　　　　　　　　　　　　　　　Notary Public.

BIRTH AFFIDAVIT.

DEPARTMENT OF THE INTERIOR.
COMMISSION TO THE FIVE CIVILIZED TRIBES.

    IN RE APPLICATION FOR ENROLLMENT, as a citizen of the Creek Nation, of Edward Harjo (D), born on the 15 day of May, 1902

Name of Father: Sulphur Harjo　　　a citizen of the   Creek   Nation.
Artussee Town
Name of Mother: Liza　　"　　　　a citizen of the   Creek   Nation.
Artussee Town
　　　　　　　　　　Postoffice　　Edna, I.T.

AFFIDAVIT OF MOTHER.

UNITED STATES OF AMERICA, Indian Territory, }
    Western　　　　　　　DISTRICT.　　}

    I, Liza Harjo , on oath state that I am 33   years of age and a citizen by blood , of the Creek   Nation; that I am the lawful wife of Sulphur Harjo , who is a citizen, by blood of the Creek   Nation; that a male   child was born to me on 15" day of May, 1902 , that said child has been named Edward Harjo , and ~~was living March 4, 1905~~. died Sept 12-1903
　　　　　　　　　　　　　　　　Liza Harjo

Witnesses To Mark:
{

    Subscribed and sworn to before me this 12" day of   April   , 1905.

(Seal)　　　　　　　　　　　　　　J McDermott
　　　　　　　　　　　　　　　　　　　　Notary Public.

Applications for Enrollment of Creek Newborn
Act of 1905   Volume XIV

NC 1090   JLD

DEPARTMENT OF THE INTERIOR,
COMMISSIONER TO THE FIVE CIVILIZED TRIBES.

In the matter of the application for the enrollment of Edward Harjo, deceased, as a citizen by blood of the Creek Nation.

....

STATEMENT AND ORDER.

The record in this case shows that on April 17, 1905, application was made, in affidavit form, for the enrollment of Edward Harjo, deceased, as a citizen by blood of the Creek Nation, under the provisions of the act of Congress approved March 3, 1905.

It appears from the affidavit filed in this matter that said Edward Harjo, deceased, was born May 15, 1902, and died September 12, 1903.

The Act of Congress approved March 3, 1905, (33 Stats., 1048), provides:

"That the Commission to the Five Civilized Tribes is authorized for sixty days after the date of the approval of this act to receive and consider applications for enrollment, of children, <u>born subsequent to May twenty-fifth, nineteen hundred and one, and prior to March fourth, nineteen hundred and five, and living on said latter date,</u> to citizens of the Creek tribe of Indians whose enrollment has been approved by the Secretary of the Interior prior to the approval of this act; and to enroll and make allotments to such children."

It is, therefore, ordered that the application for the enrollment of said Edward Harjo, deceased, as a citizen by blood of the Creek Nation, be, and the same is hereby dismissed.

                                                                Tams Bixby   Commissioner.

Muskogee, Indian Territory.
JAN 4 – 1907

Applications for Enrollment of Creek Newborn
Act of 1905   Volume XIV

DEPARTMENT OF THE INTERIOR,
COMMISSION TO THE FIVE CIVILIZED TRIBES.
MUSKOGEE, I.T. AUGUST 30. 1904.
Muskogee[sic]

In the matter of the application for the enrollment of Minnie Richard as a citizen by blood of the Creek Nation.

S. J. Logan being duly sworn testified as follows:

Examination by the Commission:

Q State your name, age and post office address? A S.J. Logan; Brush Hill; about 49.
Q You are town king of Arbeka Deep Fork town, are you? A Yes sir.
Q You want to make application for the enrollment of Minnie Richard? A Yes sir.
Q How old is that child? A Its[sic] over three years old.
Q When was it born? A Born in September, 1900.
Q What is the name of the father of the child? A Eastman Richard.
Q What is the name of the mother? A Yarner Richard.
Q[sic]
The records of the Commission show that Eastman and Yarner Richard are listed for enrollment on Creek Indian card Field No. 2605, and that their names are contained in the partial list of Creek Indians by blood approved by the Secretary of the Interior March 28, 1902, Nos. 7664 and 7665, respectively.

Q The father of these children[sic] belongs to the Snake Faction, does he? A Yes sir.
Q You have no interest in this case except to see that the member of your town that are[sic] entitled are enrolled. A That's all.

Henry G. Hains being sworn on his oath states that as stenographer to the Commission to the Five Civilized Tribes he reported the above case and that this is a full, true and correct transcript of his stenographic[sic] of his stenographic notes in same.

Henry G. Hains

Subscribed and sworn to before me this 22 day of October, 1904.

Charles H. *(Illegible)*
Notary Public.

Applications for Enrollment of Creek Newborn
Act of 1905   Volume XIV

DEPARTMENT OF THE INTERIOR,
COMMISSION TO THE FIVE CIVILIZED TRIBES.
MUSKOGEE, I.T. DEC. 9, 1904.

761

In the matter of the application for the enrollment of Minnie Richard as a citizen by blood of the Creek Nation.

Eastman Richard being duly sworn, testified as follows:

BY THE COMMISSSION[sic]:

Q What is your name? A Eastman Richard.
Q How old are you? A About 31.
Q What is your post office address? A Brush Hill.
Q Have you a child named Minnie? A Yes sir, I have got a child named Minnie.
Q What is the name of the child's mother? A Yarna Richard.
Q Is Minnie living? A Yes sir.
Q How old is she? A Five years old.
Q Do you know what year she was born? A I have it on the paper; but I can't remember exactly what it is. its[sic] on the book.
Q You have a boy named Samuel, have you? A Yes sir, Samuel and Jennetta and--
Q Is Minnie the next child to Samuel? A Yes sir.
Q How old was Samuel when Minnie was born? A Samuel is about 10 years old; Sam is about three years ahead of Minnie.
Q What month was Minnie born? A It was in the last of September.
Q Sam Logan says that the child was four years old last September. A Well, Sam didn't know; my wife and Sam is cousins; he didn't know and come and asked the mother, and Yarna didn't tell Sam how old they was; Sam said he thought it was 4 years old when it was 5.
Q You know it is over 4 do you? A Yes sir.
Q You say you have a record of it at home? A Yes sir.
Q Got it set down on paper? A Yes sir.

- - - - -

Henry G. Hains being sworn on his oath states that as stenographer to the Commission to the Five Civilized Tribes he reported the above case and that this is a full, true and correct transcript of his notes in same.

Henry G. Hains

Subscribed and sworn to before me this 10th day of December, 1904

Edw C Griesel
Notary Public.

Applications for Enrollment of Creek Newborn
Act of 1905   Volume XIV

En. 761.

DEPARTMENT OF THE INTERIOR,
COMMISSIONER TO THE FIVE CIVILIZED TRIBES.
Brush Hill, I. T., September 14, 1905.

In the matter of the application for the enrollment of Minnie Richard as a citizen by blood of the Creek Nation.

EASTMAN RICHARD, being duly sworn, testified as follows

Through Alex Posey Official Interpreter:

BY THE COMMISSIONER:
Q What is your name? A Eastman Richard.
Q How old are you? A Thirty-three.
Q What is your post office address? A Brush Hill, I. T.
Q Are you a citizen of the Creek Nation? A Yes, sir.
Q To what town do you belong? A Arbeka Deep Fork.
Q Have you a child named Minnie? A Yes, sir, that is the child. (indicating a little girl)
Q When was Minnie born? A September 30, 1902.

Witness presents a Family Bible, on the record page of which appears the following entry:
"Name
Name Richard. Place of birth Brush Hill, I. T., date of birth Septe 30, 1902."

Q Did you make this record? A Yes, sir.
Q When did you make it? A Shortly after the child was born.
Q What is the name of Minnie's mother? A Yana.
Q Does Mane refer to Minnie? A Yes, sir.
Q To what town does the mother belong? A Arbeka Deep Fork.

---oooOOOooo---

I, D. C. Skaggs, on oath state that the above and foregoing is a full and true transcript of my stenographic notes as taken in said cause on said date.

D. C. Skaggs

Subscribed and sworn to before me this 25 day of Sept 1905.

JC *(Illegible)*
Notary Public.

Applications for Enrollment of Creek Newborn
Act of 1905 Volume XIV

N.C. 1091.	F.H.W.

DEPARTMENT OF THE INTERIOR,
COMMISSIONER TO THE FIVE CIVILIZED TRIBES.

In the matter of the application for the enrollment of Minnie Richard as a citizen by blood of the Creek Nation.

DECISION.

The record in this case shows that on August 30, 1904, S. J. Logan appeared before the Commission to the Five Civilized Tribes and made application for the enrollment of Minnie Richard as a citizen by blood of the Creek Nation. Further proceedings were had December 9, 1904, and September 14, 1905. Supplemental affidavits filed April 18, 1905, and September 14, 1905, are attached to and made part of the record herein.

It appears from the evidence that the said Minnie Richard is the child of Eastman and Yarna Richard, whose names appear upon a schedule of citizens by blood of the Creek Nation approved by the Secretary of the Interior March 28, 1902, opposite Nos. 7664 and 7665 respectively.

The evidence further shows that the said Minnie Richard was born either January 29, 1902 or September 30, 1901. It is conclusively shown that she was living on March 4, 1905.

The Act of Congress approved March 3, 1905, (33 Stats. 1048) provides in part as follows:

> "That the Commission to the Five Civilized Tribes is authorized for sixty days after the date of the approval of this act to receive and consider applications for enrollment, of children, born subsequent to May twenty-fifth, nineteen hundred and one, and prior to March fourth, nineteen hundred and five, and living on said latter date, to citizens of the Creek tribe of Indians whose enrollment has been approved by the Secretary of the Interior prior to the approval of this act; and to enroll and make allotments to such children."

It is therefore, ordered and adjudged that the said Minnie Richard is entitled to enrollment as a citizen by blood of the Creek Nation, in accordance with the provisions of the law above quoted, and the application for her enrollment as such is accordingly granted.

Tams Bixby Commissioner.

Muskogee, Indian Territory.
JAN 7_ 1907

Applications for Enrollment of Creek Newborn
Act of 1905 Volume XIV

BIRTH AFFIDAVIT.

DEPARTMENT OF THE INTERIOR.
COMMISSION TO THE FIVE CIVILIZED TRIBES.

IN RE APPLICATION FOR ENROLLMENT, as a citizen of the Creek Nation, of Minnie Richard, born on or about the 29 day of January, 1902

Name of Father: Eastman Richard   a citizen of the Creek Nation.
Arbeka North Fork Town
Name of Mother: Yanah Richard   a citizen of the Creek Nation.
Arbeka North Fork Town
                           Postoffice   Brush Hill, Ind. Ter.

Relation
AFFIDAVIT OF ~~MOTHER~~.

UNITED STATES OF AMERICA, Indian Territory,
    Western   DISTRICT.   Child not present.

I, John Timothy, on oath state that I am about 41 years of age and a citizen by blood, of the Creek Nation; that I am the ~~lawful wife~~ brother of Yanah Richard, who is a citizen, by blood of the Creek Nation; that a female child was born to ~~me~~ her on or about 29 day of January, 1902, that said child has been named Minnie Richard, and was living March 4, 1905.

                                        John Timothy
Witnesses To Mark:
{

Subscribed and sworn to before me this 14 day of April, 1905.

                           Drennan C Skaggs
                           Notary Public.

BIRTH AFFIDAVIT.

DEPARTMENT OF THE INTERIOR.
COMMISSION TO THE FIVE CIVILIZED TRIBES.

IN RE APPLICATION FOR ENROLLMENT, as a citizen of the Creek Nation, of Minnie Richard, born on or about the 30" day of Sept, 1902

Name of Father: Eastman Richard   a citizen of the Creek Nation.
Arbeka North Fork
Name of Mother: Yana Richard   a citizen of the Creek Nation.
Arbeka North Fork
                           Postoffice   Brush Hill, Ind. Ter.

Applications for Enrollment of Creek Newborn
Act of 1905   Volume XIV

AFFIDAVIT OF MOTHER.

UNITED STATES OF AMERICA, Indian Territory, }
Western   DISTRICT.

I, Yana Richard, on oath state that I am 29 years of age and a citizen by blood, of the Creek Nation; that I am the lawful wife of Eastman Richard, who is a citizen, by blood of the Creek Nation; that a female child was born to me on 30" day of September, 1902, that said child has been named Minnie Richard, and was living March 4, 1905.

                                                her
                                      Yana x Richard

Witnesses To Mark: mark
{ DC Skaggs
  Alex Posey

Subscribed and sworn to before me this 14" day of September, 1905.

                                      Drennan C Skaggs
                                      Notary Public.

AFFIDAVIT OF ATTENDING PHYSICIAN OR MID-WIFE.

UNITED STATES OF AMERICA, Indian Territory, }
Western   DISTRICT.

                                                my wife
I, Eastman Richard, a ~~(blank)~~, on oath state that I attended on ^ Mrs. Yana Richard, ~~wife of~~ *(blank)* on the 30 day of Sept, 1902; that there was born to her on said date a female child; that said child was living March 4, 1905, and is said to have been named Minnie Richard
                                        hix
                                   Eastman x Richard

Witnesses To Mark: mark
{ DC Skaggs
  Alex Posey

Subscribed and sworn to before me this 14 day of September, 1905.

                                      Drennan C Skaggs
                                      Notary Public.

Applications for Enrollment of Creek Newborn
Act of 1905   Volume XIV

COMMISSIONERS:
TAMS BIXBY,
THOMAS B. NEEDLES,
C.R. BRECKINBRIDGE.

DEPARTMENT OF THE INTERIOR,
COMMISSIONER TO THE FIVE CIVILIZED TRIBES.

WM. O. BEALL
Secretary

HGH

En. 761..

ADDRESS ONLY THE
COMMISSION TO THE FIVE CIVILIZED TRIBES.

Muskogee, Indian Territory, May 22, 1906.

Eastman Richard,
    Brushhill, Indian Territory.

Dear Sir:

    The Commission desires further evidence in the matter of the application for the enrollment of your minor child, Minnie Richard, as a citizen by blood of the Creek Nation. The Commission requires the affidavits of the mother and midwife or physician in attendance at the birth of said child.

    There is herewith enclosed blank form of birth affidavit, and in executing same care should be exercised to see that all blanks are properly filled, all names written in full and in the event that either of the persons signing the affidavit is unable to write, signatures by mark must be attested by two witnesses. Each affidavit must be executed before a Notary Public and the notarial seal and signature of the officer must be attached to each separate affidavit.

                    Respectfully,
                    Tams Bixby
Register.   Chairman.
BC

En. 761.

Muskogee, Indian Territory, July 10, 1905.

Sam J. Logan,
    Brushhill, Indian Territory.

Dear Sir:

    This office desires further evidence in the matter of the application for the enrollment of Minnie Richard, a citizen by blood of the Creek Nation. This office requires the affidavits of the mother and midwife or physician in attendance at the birth of said child.

    There is herewith enclosed a blank form of birth affidavit, and in executing same care should be exercised to see that all blanks are properly filled, all names written

Applications for Enrollment of Creek Newborn
Act of 1905 Volume XIV

in full and in the event that the persons signing the affidavits are unable to write, signatures by mark must be attested by two witnesses. Each affidavit must be executed before a Notary Public and the notarial seal and signature of the officer must be attached to each separate affidavit.

Respectfully,

Register.   Commissioner.
1 BA.

N.C. 1091.

Muskogee, Indian Territory, March 1, 1907.

Yanah Richard,
    Care Eastman Richard,
        Brush Hill, Indian Territory.

Dear Madam:

You are hereby advised that on February 15, 1907, the Secretary of the Interior approved the enrollment of your minor child, Minnie Richard, as a citizen by blood of the Creek Nation and that the name of said child appears upon the roll of new born citizens by blood of the said nation, enrolled under the Act of Congress approved March 3, 1905, as No. 1211.

This child is now entitled to allotment and application therefor should be made without delay at the Creek Land Office, Muskogee, Indian Territory.

Respectfully,

Commissioner.

Applications for Enrollment of Creek Newborn
Act of 1905   Volume XIV

2009
2010

DEPARTMENT OF THE INTERIOR,
COMMISSION TO THE FIVE CIVILIZED TRIBES.
April ~~May~~ 14, 1905, Okmulgee, Indian Territory.

In the matter of the application for the enrollment of Edna and Annie Monday as citizens by blood of the Creek Nation.

Lizzie Monday being duly sworn by E.C. Griesel, notary public, testified as follows:

By the Commission:
Q What is your name? A Lizzie Monday.
Q What is your age? A 22.
Q What is your post office? A Schulton[sic], I.T.
Q You have two children born since May 25, 1901, have you not? A Yes sir.
Q What are their names and when were they born? A Edna born September 2, 1902, and Annie born December 13, 1903.
Q Both of these children are living now are they? A Yes, sir, they are both present.
Q Who is the father of these children? A March Monday.
Q Is he a citizen of the Creek Nation? A Yes sir.
Q What town does he belong to? A Cusseta.
Q Are you a citizen of the Creek Nation? A No sir, I am a Seminole.
Q Have you an allotment in the Seminole Nation? A Yes, sir.
Q If it should be found that your children Edna and Annie Monday are entitled to enrollment in both the Creek and Seminole Nations, in which Nation do you elect to have them enrolled and receive their allotments of land? A In the Creek Nation.
Q Is you husband, March living with you now? A No sir.
Q How long have you been separated? A He left me last August.
Q Your husband has no objection to taking the allotments in the Creek Nation? A No sir.

E.C. Griesel, being duly sworn, state that the above and foregoing is a true and correct transcript of his stenographic notes as taken in said cause on said date.

Edw C Griesel

Subscribed and sworn to before me this 5 day of May, 1905.

Zera E Parrish
Notary Public.

Applications for Enrollment of Creek Newborn
Act of 1905 Volume XIV

NC-1093

DEPARTMENT OF THE INTERIOR,
COMMISSIONER TO THE FIVE CIVILIZED TRIBES.

Muskogee, Indian Territory, November 14, 1905.

In the matter of the application for the enrollment of Edna and Annie Monday as citizens of the Creek Nation.

Lizzie Monday, being duly sworn, testified as follows (through Jesse McDermott, Official Interpreter):

EXAMINATION BY THE COMMISSIONER:
Q What is your name? A Lizzie Monday.
Q How old are you? A I don't know.
Q What is your postoffice address? A Schulter.
Q Are you a citizen of any tribe in Indian Territory? A Seminole.
Q Have you some new-born children? if so, name them. A Yes. I have one. This one here and one named Edna.
Q What is the name of this one here? A Annie.
Q Have you ever called this one by any other name? A No.
Q What was your name before it was Monday? A Lizzie Randall.
Q Was it ever known as "London?" A Yes, that's my Indian name.
Q Sam Hayney applied for this child, Annie, and called it Elizabeth. Do you know anything about it? A Yes, he told me about it.
Q The child he called Elizabeth he meant the one you named Annie? A Yes, sir. He told me that he did not know her name, and just gave her the mother's name.
Q When was your child, Annie, who was incorrectly called Elizabeth by Hayney, born? A Annie was born December 13, 1904--I am mistaken; it was 1903.
Q How old will it be this December? A 2 years old.
Q Are you sure of that? A Yes sir.
Q Who was the midwife when it was born? A My mother, Mina Randall.
Q And that is the child there? A Yes sir.
Q You made application for this child--you made out an affidavit for the enrollment of this child and so did your mother, Mina Randall; you said that the child was born the 13th of December, 1904. Was it then a mistake, as you now say in your testimony? A Yes sir.
Q This first affidavit you made in April before Mr. McDermott, in the field; that was correct was it? A Yes sir.
Q Have you another child just older than this one? A Yes sir.
Q What is its name? A Edna.
Q When was Edna born? A September 2.
Q What year? A 1903.
Q It couldn't have been born in 1903, and then this one in December of the same year, only about three months apart. A It was 1902.
Q How old it is now? A Past three.

53

Applications for Enrollment of Creek Newborn
Act of 1905   Volume XIV

Q The first affidavit you made about Edna, Indian Territory and Mina made one also, giving the date 1902 is correct, and this last one, giving the year 1903 is a mistake, is it?
A Yes sir. The last affidavits are written down 1903, and they are errors.
Q Now, Lizzie, if it should be found that Edna and Annie, your two children, are entitled to rights in either the Creek or Seminole Nation, in which Nation do you elect to have them enrolled and take their allotments of land? A In the Creek Nation.
Q You elect to have them enrolled in the Creek Nation, do you? A Yes sir.
Q Is Edna living? A Yes sir.

March Monday, being duly sworn, testified as follows (through Jesse McDermott, Official interpreter).

EXAMINATION BY THE COMMISSIONER:
Q What is your name? A March Monday.
Q What is the name of your father? A Monday.
Q What is the name of your mother? A Millie Annie.
Q How old are you? A I am not sure, but think I am about 32.
Q What is the name of your Creek Indian Town? A Cussehta.
Q What is your postoffice address? A Schulter.
Q Have you two newborn children by the names of Edna and Annie Monday? A Yes sir.
Q You have one named Elizabeth, have you? A No sir, never did.
Q You never did have a child named Elizabeth? A No sir.
Q If Haney made application for Elizabeth, he meant to refer to Annie, do you think? A Yes sir.
Q How old is Edna? A Three years old, past.
Q How old is this little one, here? A She's going to be two years old.
Q In what month, do you remember? A December.
Q Next month? A Yes sir.
Q Is Edna living? A Yes sir.
Q If it should be found that Edna and Annie, these two children, are entitled to rights in either the Creek or Seminole Nation, in which Nation do you elect to have them enrolled and take their allotments of land? A Creek Nation.
Q You elect for them to be enrolled in the Creek Nation, do you? A Yes sir.
Q Are you married to Lizzie, the mother of these children? A Yes sir.
Q Have you ever had any children by her before these two? A No sir. Sam Checotah has my license and I did not bring it with me.
Q How about Jennette? Is she dead, or are you divorced from her? A We were married according to the Indian custom and separated likewise.
Q You had a child by her, didn't you? A Yes sir.
Q What is its name? A Martin.
Q These two children are your children? A Yes sir.
Q By this woman, Lizzie? A Yes sir.

Applications for Enrollment of Creek Newborn
Act of 1905   Volume XIV

INDIAN TERRITORY, Western District

I, J. Y. Miller, a stenographer to the Commissioner to the Five Civilized Tribes, do hereby certify that the above and foregoing is a true and complete translation of my notes as same appear in my stenographic report of this case.

JY Miller

Sworn to and subscribed before me this the 15th day of November, 1905.

J McDermott
Notary Public.

BIRTH AFFIDAVIT.

DEPARTMENT OF THE INTERIOR.
COMMISSION TO THE FIVE CIVILIZED TRIBES.

IN RE APPLICATION FOR ENROLLMENT, as a citizen of the Creek Nation, of Edna Monday, born on the 2 day of Sept , 1902

Name of Father: March Monday	a citizen of the Creek Nation.
Name of Mother: Lizzie "	a citizen of the Seminole Nation.

Postoffice   Schulter, I.T.

AFFIDAVIT OF MOTHER.

UNITED STATES OF AMERICA, Indian Territory,
Western   DISTRICT.

I, March Monday , on oath state that I am 32 years of age and a citizen by blood , of the Creek Nation; that I am the lawful ~~wife~~ husband of Lizzie Monday , who is a citizen, by blood of the Seminole Nation; that a female child was born to ~~me~~ her on 2^d day of September , 1902 , that said child has been named Edna Monday , and was living March 4, 1905.

March Monday

Witnesses To Mark:

{

Subscribed and sworn to before me this 14" day of Nov , 1905.

My Commission
Expires July 25" 1907

J McDermott
Notary Public.

Applications for Enrollment of Creek Newborn
Act of 1905   Volume XIV

Indian Territory, I
          I ss
Western District. I

    We, the undersigned, do hereby elect to have our child, Edna Monday, born on the 2 day of Sept., 1902, enrolled as a citizen of the Creek Nation, and to have said child receive her allotment of land and distribution of moneys in said nation.

                                          March Monday
Witnesses to mark:

_____
_____   Lizzie Monday
_____

    Subscribed and sworn to before me this 26 day of Sept 1906.

                                          H.G. Hains
                                          Notary Public.

Indian Territory, I
          I ss
Western District. I

    We, the undersigned, do hereby elect to have our child, Annie Monday, born on the 13 day of Dec., 1903, enrolled as a citizen of the Creek Nation, and to have said child receive her allotment of land and distribution of moneys in said nation.

                                          March Monday
Witnesses to mark:

_____
_____   Lizzie Monday
_____

    Subscribed and sworn to before me this 26 day of Sept 1906.

                                          H.G. Hains
                                          Notary Public.

Applications for Enrollment of Creek Newborn
Act of 1905   Volume XIV

BIRTH AFFIDAVIT.   Copy

DEPARTMENT OF THE INTERIOR.
COMMISSION TO THE FIVE CIVILIZED TRIBES.

IN RE APPLICATION FOR ENROLLMENT, as a citizen of the Creek Nation, of Annie Monday, born on the 13th day of December, 1904

Name of Father: March Monday   a citizen of the Creek Nation.
Name of Mother: Lizzie Monday   a citizen of the Seminole Nation.

Postoffice   Schulter, Ind. Ter.

AFFIDAVIT OF MOTHER.

UNITED STATES OF AMERICA, Indian Territory, }
   Western   DISTRICT.

I, Lizzie Monday, on oath state that I am 22 years of age and a citizen by blood, of the Seminole Nation; that I am the lawful wife of March Monday, who is a citizen, by blood of the Creek Nation; that a female child was born to me on 13th day of December, 1904, that said child has been named Annie Monday, and was living March 4, 1905.

                                        Lizzie Monday

Witnesses To Mark:
{

Subscribed and sworn to before me this 24 day of July, 1905.

My Commission expires July 12, 1906   (Signed) C.E. Regmer
                                                Notary Public.

AFFIDAVIT OF ATTENDING PHYSICIAN OR MID-WIFE.

UNITED STATES OF AMERICA, Indian Territory, }
   Western   DISTRICT.

I, Minor Randall, a mid-wife, on oath state that I attended on Mrs. Lizzie Monday, wife of March Monday on the 13th day of Dec., 1904; that there was born to her on said date a female child; that said child was living March 4, 1905, and is said to have been named Annie Monday
                                                her
                                        Minor x Randall

Witnesses To Mark: mark
{ W.H. Russell
  Samuel J Checote

Applications for Enrollment of Creek Newborn
Act of 1905 Volume XIV

Subscribed and sworn to before me 30th day of July , 1905.

        (Signed) Samuel J. Checote
             Notary Public.
Com Exp Nov. 6-1906

BIRTH AFFIDAVIT.

DEPARTMENT OF THE INTERIOR.
COMMISSION TO THE FIVE CIVILIZED TRIBES.

IN RE APPLICATION FOR ENROLLMENT, as a citizen of the Creek Nation, of Annie Monday, born on the 13 day of Dec , 1903

Name of Father: March Monday	a citizen of the Creek Nation.
Name of Mother: Lizzie Monday	a citizen of the Seminole Nation.

      Postoffice Schulter, I.T.

AFFIDAVIT OF MOTHER.

UNITED STATES OF AMERICA, Indian Territory, ⎫
  Western   DISTRICT. ⎭

  I, March Monday , on oath state that I am 32 years of age and a citizen by blood , of the Creek Nation; that I am the lawful ~~wife~~ husband of Lizzie Monday , who is a citizen, by blood of the Seminole Nation; that a female child was born to ~~me~~ her on 13th day of December , 1903 , that said child has been named Annie Monday , and was living March 4, 1905.

            March Monday

Witnesses To Mark:
{

  Subscribed and sworn to before me this 14" day of Nov , 1905.

My Commission   J McDermott
Expires July 25" 1907   Notary Public.

Applications for Enrollment of Creek Newborn
Act of 1905   Volume XIV

BIRTH AFFIDAVIT.

DEPARTMENT OF THE INTERIOR.
COMMISSION TO THE FIVE CIVILIZED TRIBES.

IN RE APPLICATION FOR ENROLLMENT, as a citizen of the Creek Nation, of Annie Monday, born on the 13 day of Dec, 1902

Name of Father: March Monday   a citizen of the   Creek   Nation.
Name of Mother: Lizzie   "   a citizen of the   Seminole   Nation.

Postoffice   Schulter, I.T.

AFFIDAVIT OF MOTHER.

Child Present

UNITED STATES OF AMERICA, Indian Territory, }
       Western   DISTRICT.

I, Lizzie Monday, on oath state that I am 22 years of age and a citizen by blood, of the Seminole Nation; that I am the lawful wife of March Monday, who is a citizen, by blood of the Creek Nation; that a female child was born to me on 13 day of December, 1903, that said child has been named Annie Monday, and is now living.

Lizzie Monday

Witnesses To Mark:
{ Jesse McDermott

Subscribed and sworn to before me this 14" day of April, 1905.

J McDermott
Notary Public.

AFFIDAVIT OF ATTENDING PHYSICIAN OR MID-WIFE.

UNITED STATES OF AMERICA, Indian Territory, }
       Western   DISTRICT.

I, Minah Randel, a midwife, on oath state that I attended on Mrs. Lizzie Monday, wife of March Monday on the 13" day of Dec, 1903; that there was born to her on said date a *(blank)* child; that said child is now living and is said to have been named Annie Monday

Minah x Randel
her   mark

Witnesses To Mark:
{ EC Griesel
  Jesse McDermott

Applications for Enrollment of Creek Newborn
Act of 1905 Volume XIV

Subscribed and sworn to before me this 14" day of April , 1905.

J McDermott
Notary Public.

BIRTH AFFIDAVIT.

DEPARTMENT OF THE INTERIOR.
COMMISSION TO THE FIVE CIVILIZED TRIBES.

IN RE APPLICATION FOR ENROLLMENT, as a citizen of the Creek Nation, of Edna Monday, born on the 2 day of Sept , 1902

Name of Father: March Monday   a citizen of the   Creek   Nation.
Cussehta
Name of Mother: Lizzie Monday   a citizen of the Seminole   Nation.
Seminole

Postoffice   Schulter, I.T.

AFFIDAVIT OF MOTHER.

Child Present

UNITED STATES OF AMERICA, Indian Territory, ⎫
      Western   DISTRICT. ⎬

I, Lizzie Monday , on oath state that I am 22 years of age and a citizen by blood, of the ~~Creek~~ Seminole Nation; that I am the lawful wife of March Monday , who is a citizen, by blood of the Creek Nation; that a female child was born to me on 2 day of Sept , 1902 , that said child has been named Edna Monday , and is now living.

Lizzie Monday

Witnesses To Mark:

Jesse McDermott

Subscribed and sworn to before me this 14" day of April , 1905.

J McDermott
Notary Public.

Applications for Enrollment of Creek Newborn
Act of 1905   Volume XIV

AFFIDAVIT OF ATTENDING PHYSICIAN OR MID-WIFE.

UNITED STATES OF AMERICA, Indian Territory,
Western   DISTRICT.

    I, Minah Randel, a midwife, on oath state that I attended on Mrs. Lizzie Monday, wife of March Monday on the 2 day of Sept, 1902; that there was born to her on said date a *(blank)* child; that said child is now living and is said to have been named Edna Monday

                                                her
                                  Minah x Randel
Witnesses To Mark: mark
- EC Griesel
- Jesse McDermott

    Subscribed and sworn to before me this 14" day of April, 1905.

                                  J McDermott
                                      Notary Public.

Sem. NB-171.
NBC-1093.

                            Muskogee, Indian Territory, January 2, 1905.

Chief Clerk of Seminole Enrollment Division,
        Muskogee, Indian Territory.

Dear Sir:

    Receipt is acknowledged of your letter of December 29, 1905, in which you ask to be informed as to the status of the application for the enrollment of Annie and Edna Monday as citizens of the Creek Nation, together with their Roll numbers if their enrollment has been approved by the Department.

    In reply you are advised that the matter of the application for the enrollment of said children, as citizens of the Creek Nation, is pending, and when final action is had in the same you will be duly notified.

                          Respectfully,
                                        Commissioner.

Applications for Enrollment of Creek Newborn
Act of 1905   Volume XIV

NC-1093.

Muskogee, Indian Territory, July 15, 1905.

Chief Clerk,
    Seminole Enrollment Division,
        Muskogee, Indian Territory.

Dear Sir:

    April 18, 1905, application was made to the Commission to the Five Civilized Tribes for the enrollment of Edna Monday, born September 2, 1902 and Annie Monday, born December 13, 1903, as citizens by blood of the Creek Nation. It is stated in said application that the father of said children is March Monday, a citizen of the Creek Nation, and that the mother is Lizzie Monday, a citizen of the Seminole Nation.

    You are requested to inform the Creek Enrollment Division as to whether application has been made for the enrollment of said children as citizens of the Seminole Nation, and if so, what disposition has been made of the same.

                      Respectfully,

                                      Commissioner.

W.F.

DEPARTMENT OF THE INTERIOR.
COMMISSION TO THE FIVE CIVILIZED TRIBES.

Muskogee, Indian Territory, July 18, 1905.

Chief Clerk,
    Creek Enrollment Division.

Dear Sir:

    Receipt is acknowledged of your letter of June 15, 1905 (N C-1093) stating that an application was made to the Commission to the Five Civilized Tribes for the enrollment of Edna Monday, born September 2, 1902, and Annie Monday, born December 13, 1903, children of March Monday, a citizen of the Creek Nation, and Lizzie Monday, a citizen of the Seminole Nation, as citizens by blood of the Creek Nation and requesting to be advised as to whether application has been made for the enrollment of said children as citizens of the Seminole Nation.

    In reply to your letter you are advised that on May 31, 1905 Sam Haney appeared before the Commission and made application for the enrollment of his nieces, Edna Monday and Elizabeth Monday, as citizens by blood of the Seminole Nation. He stated in his testimony given at that time that the father of said children was a Creek

Applications for Enrollment of Creek Newborn
Act of 1905 Volume XIV

citizen, that their mother was Lizzie Monday, and that said Elizabeth was born in August, 1904. The name of the father of said children and the date of the birth of Edna Monday are not given. The post office address of said Lizzie Monday is given as Shulter, Indian Territory.

It does not appear from the records of this office that any application has been made for the enrollment of Annie Monday as a citizen of the Seminole Nation.

Respectfully,
Tams Bixby   Commissioner.

N.C. 1093

Muskogee, Indian Territory, September 15, 1905.

March Monday,
Schulter, Indian Territory.

Dear Sir:

Receipt is acknowledged of your letter of September 9, 1905, in which you ask if *(illegible)* two blank applications for allotment for your children Edna and Annie be sent you.

You are requested to write this office at once giving the names of the parents and date of birth of your children born since May 25, 1901.

You are also requested to furnish this office with the joint affidavit of yourself and the mother of said new-born children electing in which nation you desire to have them enrolled.

You are advised that this office has no blank applications for allotment and that when the matter of the application for enrollment of new-born children has been finally approved, the citizen parent is notified to appear in person at the land office and file.

Respectfully,
Acting Commissioner.

Applications for Enrollment of Creek Newborn
Act of 1905   Volume XIV

NC-1093.

Muskogee, Indian Territory, October 23, 1905.

Lizzie Monday,
    c/o March Monday,
        Schulter, Indian Territory.

Dear Madam:

    In the matter of the application for the enrollment of children, Edna Monday, born February 2, 1902, and Annie Monday, born December 13, 1903, as citizens by blood of the Creek Nation, this office requires evidence of your marriage to March Monday, the father of said children.

    Such evidence may consist of either the original or a certified copy of your marriage license and certificate.

                           Respectfully,

                                          Commissioner.

N C 1093

REFER IN REPLY TO THE FOLLOWING:

DEPARTMENT OF THE INTERIOR,
COMMISSIONER TO THE FIVE CIVILIZED TRIBES.

Muskogee, Indian Territory, November 16, 1905.

Chief Clerk,
    Creek Enrollment Division.

Dear Sir:

    Receipt is hereby acknowledged of a copy of the testimony taken in the matter of the application for the enrollment of Edna and Annie Monday, wherein their mother, Lizzie Monday, elects that they be enrolled as citizens by blood of the Creek Nation under the provisions of the Act of Congress approved March 3, 1905.

                           Respectfully,

                                    Tams Bixby Commissioner.

Applications for Enrollment of Creek Newborn
Act of 1905 Volume XIV

N.C. 1093.

Muskogee, Indian Territory, December 19, 1905.

Chief Clerk,
  Seminole Enrollment Division.

Dear Sir:

  You are requested to furnish the Creek Enrollment Division with a copy of the affidavit of Lizzie Monday, filed in the matter of the application for the enrollment of her minor child, Annie (Elizabeth) Monday, as a citizen by blood of the Seminole Nation (Sem.N.B. 171).

  Kindly give this matter your early attention.

        Respectfully,
            Commissioner.

REFER IN REPLY TO THE FOLLOWING:
_____

DEPARTMENT OF THE INTERIOR,
COMMISSIONER TO THE FIVE CIVILIZED TRIBES.

Muskogee, Indian Territory, December 20, 1905.

Chief Clerk,
  Creek Enrollment Division,
    General Office.

Dear Sir:

  In compliance with letter of the Commissioner to the Five Civilized Tribes, dated December 19, 1905, you are furnished with a copy of the affidavit of Lizzie Monday, filed in the matter of the application for the enrollment of her minor child, Annie (Elizabeth) Monday, as a citizen by blood of the Seminole Nation. (Sem. N. B. 171.)

        Respectfully,
        HC *(Name Illegible)*
        Clerk in charge Seminole Div.

Applications for Enrollment of Creek Newborn
Act of 1905 Volume XIV

W^mOB

REFER IN REPLY TO THE FOLLOWING:

Sem. N B 171

DEPARTMENT OF THE INTERIOR,
COMMISSIONER TO THE FIVE CIVILIZED TRIBES.

Muskogee, Indian Territory, December 29, 1905.

Chief Clerk,
    Creek Enrollment Division.

Dear Sir:

    On May 31, 1905, application was made to the Commission to the Five Civilized Tribes, under the provisions of the act of Congress approved March 3, 1905, for the enrollment as citizens of the Seminole Nation of Annie and Edna Monday, children of March Monday a citizen of the Creek Nation, and Lizzie Monday, a citizen of the Seminole Nation.

    It appears from the record in this case that application has also been made for the enrollment of these children as new born citizens of the Creek Nation, and You are requested to inform the Seminole Enrollment Division the status of the application for the enrollment of these two children as citizens of the Creek Nation, and if they have been enrolled, that you advise their roll numbers and the date of the approval of their enrollment by the Department.

                  Respectfully,
                  Tams Bixby Commissioner.

N.C. 1093

Muskogee, Indian Territory, March 1, 1907.

March Monday,
    Schulter, Indian Territory.

Dear Sir:

    You are hereby advised that on February 15, 1907, the Secretary of the Interior approved the enrollment of your minor children, Edna and Annie Monday, as citizens by blood of the Creek Nation, and that the names of said children appear upon the roll of new born citizens by blood of said nation, enrolled under the Act of Congress approved March 3, 1905, as numbers 1212 and 1213 respectively.

    These children are now entitled to allotments and application therefor should be made without delay at the Creek Land Office, Muskogee, Indian Territory.

                    Respectfully,
                            Commissioner.

Applications for Enrollment of Creek Newborn
Act of 1905   Volume XIV

AB

REFER IN REPLY TO THE FOLLOWING:
Sem. N.B. 171

DEPARTMENT OF THE INTERIOR,
COMMISSIONER TO THE FIVE CIVILIZED TRIBES.

Muskogee, Indian Territory, March 7, 1907.

Chief Clerk,
    Creek Enrollment Division.

Dear Sir:-

    You are hereby notified that the Commissioner to the Five Civilized Tribes on February 20, 1907, rendered his decision dismissing the application for the enrollment of Edna Monday and Annie Monday as citizens of the Seminole Nation.

                    Respectfully,
                    Tams Bixby   Commissioner.

COMMISSIONERS:
TAMS BIXBY,
THOMAS B. NEEDLES,
C.R. BRECKINBRIDGE.

DEPARTMENT OF THE INTERIOR,
COMMISSIONER TO THE FIVE CIVILIZED TRIBES.

REFER IN REPLY TO THE FOLLOWING:
REFER IN REPLY TO THE FOLLOWING:

WM. O. BEALL
   Secretary

ADDRESS ONLY THE
COMMISSION TO THE FIVE CIVILIZED TRIBES.

Sapulpa I.T.
April 26, 1905

Commission to Five Tribes
    Muskogee I.T.

Gentlemen:

    On April 24, 1905 there was transmitted to your he application for the enrollment of Henry Marshall, Creek infant, father Charley Marshall, mother Martha Marshall. You

Applications for Enrollment of Creek Newborn
Act of 1905   Volume XIV

are advised that Martha Marshall the mother appears upon the app^r rolls as Martha Snow and that her roll N° is 6109. She appeared yesterday and exhibited her patent.

Yrs. truly
David Shelby

BIRTH AFFIDAVIT.

DEPARTMENT OF THE INTERIOR.
COMMISSION TO THE FIVE CIVILIZED TRIBES.

IN RE APPLICATION FOR ENROLLMENT, as a citizen of the Creek Nation, of Henry Marshall, born on the 2 day of Feb, 1903

Name of Father: Charlie Marshall (Euchee)	a citizen of the	Creek Nation.
Name of Mother: Martha " nee Tiger (Euchee)	a citizen of the	" Nation.

Postoffice   Sapulpa

AFFIDAVIT OF MOTHER.   Child Present

UNITED STATES OF AMERICA, Indian Territory,
Western   DISTRICT.

I, Martha Marshall, on oath state that I am 26 years of age and a citizen by blood, of the Creek Nation; that I am the lawful wife of Charlie Marshall, who is a citizen, by blood of the Creek Nation; that a male child was born to me on 2 day of Feb, 1903, that said child has been named Henry Marshall, and was living March 4, 1905.

Martha Marshall

Witnesses To Mark:
{ David Shelby

Subscribed and sworn to before me this 24 day of April, 1905.

(Seal)
Edw C Griesel
Notary Public.

Applications for Enrollment of Creek Newborn
Act of 1905   Volume XIV

AFFIDAVIT OF ATTENDING PHYSICIAN OR MID-WIFE.

UNITED STATES OF AMERICA, Indian Territory,
    Western   DISTRICT. }

    I, He-ka-wa-thla-ny , a Midwife , on oath state that I attended on Mrs. Martha Marshall , wife of Charlie Marshall on the 2 day of Feb , 1903 ; that there was born to her on said date a male child; that said child was living March 4, 1905, and is said to have been named Henry Marshall

                                                     her
Witnesses To Mark: He-ka-wa-thla-ny x
   { David Shelby   mark
    Jesse McDermott

    Subscribed and sworn to before me this 24 day of April , 1905.

(Seal)   Edw C Griesel
                                               Notary Public.

BIRTH AFFIDAVIT.

DEPARTMENT OF THE INTERIOR.
COMMISSION TO THE FIVE CIVILIZED TRIBES.

    IN RE APPLICATION FOR ENROLLMENT, as a citizen of the Creek Nation, of Henry Marshall , born on the 2nd day of February , 1903

Name of Father: Charlie Marshall   a citizen of the   Creek   Nation.
Name of Mother: Martha Marshall   a citizen of the   Creek   Nation.

                          Postoffice   Sapulpa Ind Ter

AFFIDAVIT OF MOTHER.

UNITED STATES OF AMERICA, Indian Territory,
    Western   DISTRICT. }

    I, Martha Marshall , on oath state that I am 22 years of age and a citizen by blood , of the Creek Nation; that I am the lawful wife of Charlie Marshall , who is a citizen, by blood of the Creek Nation; that a male child was born to me on 2nd day of February , 1903 , that said child has been named Henry Marshall , and is now living.

                                             Martha Marshall

Witnesses To Mark:
   { W.B. Mathis
    E.B. Day

Applications for Enrollment of Creek Newborn
Act of 1905 Volume XIV

Subscribed and sworn to before me this 14th day of April, 1905.

My term expires   GC Hughes
July 25 1906   Notary Public.

AFFIDAVIT OF ATTENDING PHYSICIAN OR MID-WIFE.

UNITED STATES OF AMERICA, Indian Territory,
    Western   **DISTRICT.**

I, Har-ka-wa-thlany, a *(blank)*, on oath state that I attended on Mrs. Martha Marshall, wife of Charlie Marshall on the 2nd day of February, 1903; that there was born to her on said date a male child; that said child is now living, and is said to have been named Henry Marshall

                                  her
                        He-ka- x wa-thla-ny
Witnesses To Mark: mark
   { W.B. Mathis
     E.B. Day

Subscribed and sworn to before me this 14th day of April, 1905.

My term expires   GC Hughes
July 25 1906   Notary Public.

N.C. 1095
DEPARTMENT OF THE INTERIOR,
COMMISSIONER TO THE FIVE CIVILIZED TRIBES.
Muskogee, Indian Territory, July 26, 1905.

In the matter of the application for the enrollment of Charlie McIntosh as a citizen by blood of the Creek Nation.

Ben McIntosh being duly sworn, testified as follows:

Q What is your name? A Ben McIntosh
Q What is your age? A 44
Q Are you a citizen of the Creek Nation? A I am.
Q What is your post office? A Okmulgee.

Applications for Enrollment of Creek Newborn
Act of 1905   Volume XIV

Q Have you a brother named Charlie McIntosh? A Yes, sir
Q Do you know his wife, Bertha? A Yes, sir
Q Do you know a child of theirs named Charlie McIntosh? A Yes, sir.
Q When was this child born do you know? A I don't know of my own knowledge just exactly.
Q What is the correct name of that child? A Charles Curtis McIntosh.
Q The mother of the child made an affidavit and it was called that and she made another affidavit calling it Charlie, which is correct? A Charles Curtis McIntosh
Q They some times call him Charlie? A Yes, sir
Q But his real name is Charles Curtis McIntosh, you know that to be a fact? A Yes, sir
Q You go to see them? A Yes, sir
Q When was the last time you saw that child? A Ten days ago.
Q Its[sic] alive now? A Yes, sir

Anna Garrigues on oath states that the above and foregoing is a true and correct transcript of her stenographic notes taken in said cause on said date.

Anna Garrigues

Subscribed and sworn to before me
this 29th day of July 1905.   Notary Public C Griesel
                                                         Notary Public Public.

BIRTH AFFIDAVIT.

DEPARTMENT OF THE INTERIOR.
COMMISSION TO THE FIVE CIVILIZED TRIBES.

     IN RE APPLICATION FOR ENROLLMENT, as a citizen of the Creek Nation, of Charlie McIntosh , born on the 2 day of June, 1902

Name of Father: Charlie E. McIntosh   a citizen of the   Creek   Nation.
  Coweta Town
Name of Mother: Bertha A. McIntosh   a citizen of the United States Nation.

Postoffice   Stroud, Oklahoma.

AFFIDAVIT OF MOTHER.

UNITED STATES OF AMERICA, Indian Territory, ⎫
    Western   **DISTRICT.**   ⎭

    I, Bertha A. McIntosh , on oath state that I am 23 years of age and a citizen by ——— , of the United States ~~Nation~~; that I am the lawful wife of Charlie E. McIntosh , who is a citizen, by blood of the Creek Nation; that a male child was

Applications for Enrollment of Creek Newborn
Act of 1905   Volume XIV

born to me on 2 day of June, 1902, that said child has been named Charlie McIntosh, and was living March 4, 1905.

Bertha A. McIntosh

Witnesses To Mark:
{

    Subscribed and sworn to before me this 5 day of   April , 1905.

Drennan C Skaggs
Notary Public.

AFFIDAVIT OF ATTENDING PHYSICIAN OR MID-WIFE.

UNITED STATES OF AMERICA, Indian Territory, }   State of Kansas   County- Ford } SS
Western   DISTRICT.

I, Alice Orcutt, a mid-wife, on oath state that I attended on Mrs. Bertha A McIntosh, wife of Charlie E. McIntosh on the 2 day of June, 1902; that there was born to her on said date a male child; that said child was living March 4, 1905, and is said to have been named Charlie McIntosh

Alice Orcutt

Witnesses To Mark:
{

    Subscribed and sworn to before me 13 day of   April , 1905.

W. J. Spencer
Notary Public.

My Commission expires May 24-1907

BIRTH AFFIDAVIT.

Department of the Interior,
COMMISSION TO THE FIVE CIVILIZED TRIBES.

IN RE APPLICATION FOR ENROLLMENT, as a citizen of the Creek Nation, of Charles Curtis McIntosh, born on the 2 day of June, 1902

Name of Father: Charles E. McIntosh   a citizen of the   Creek   Nation.
Name of Mother: Bertha A. McIntosh   a citizen of the   U. S.   Nation.

Post-Office: Fort Dodge Kansas
Ford Co

Applications for Enrollment of Creek Newborn
Act of 1905   Volume XIV

AFFIDAVIT OF MOTHER.

UNITED STATES OF AMERICA,
   INDIAN TERRITORY,
   (blank)   District.

State of Kansas
County of Ford } SS

I, Bertha A. McIntosh , on oath state that I am 21   years of age and a citizen by Marriage , of the Creek   Nation; that I am the lawful wife of   Charles E. McIntosh , who is a citizen, by Blood   of the Creek   Nation; that a male   child was born to me on 2 day of June , 1902 , that said child has been named Charles Curtis McIntosh , and is now living.

Mrs. Bertha A. McIntosh

WITNESSES TO MARK:
{

Subscribed and sworn to before me this 29 day of   Sept   , 1902.

W. J. Spencer
Notary Public.
My Commission Expires May 24-1903

AFFIDAVIT OF ATTENDING PHYSICIAN OR MID-WIFE.

UNITED STATES OF AMERICA,
   INDIAN TERRITORY,
   (blank)   District.

State of Kansas
County of Ford } SS

I, Alice Orcutt , a   Nurse , on oath state that I attended on Mrs. Bertha A. McIntosh , wife of   Charles E. McIntosh   on the 2 day of June , 1902 ; that there was born to her on said date a Male child; that said child is now living and is said to have been named Charles Curtis McIntosh

x   Mrs Alice Orcutt

WITNESSES TO MARK:
{

Subscribed and sworn to before me this 29 day of   Sept   , 1902.

My Commission Expires May 24-1903   W. J. Spencer
Notary Public.

Applications for Enrollment of Creek Newborn
Act of 1905   Volume XIV

N.C. 1095
Muskogee, Indian Territory, July 19, 1905.

Bertha McIntosh,
    Stroud, Oklahoma.

Dear Madam:

    Receipt is acknowledged of your letter of July 18, 1905, in which you ask if this office has received an affidavit in the matter of the birth of Charles Curtis McIntosh.

    You asked if you could have his allotment set aside for him.

    You are advised that there are on file in this office, affidavits relative to the birth of Charlie McIntosh, new born child of Bertha A. McIntosh non-citizen and Charlie E. McIntosh an alleged citizen of the Creek Nation.

    Without further information, it is impossible to identify said Charlie E. McIntosh, the father of the child, as a citizen of the Creek Nation and you are requested to furnish this office with the names of his parents, the Creek Indian town to which he belongs and, if possible, the number on his deeds to lands in the Creek Nation.

    You are further advised that at this time no reservation of land in the Creek Nation can be made for new born children.

                    Respectfully,

                                    Commissioner.

NC-1095

Muskogee, Indian Territory, July 20, 1905.

Bertha A. McIntosh,
    Stroud, Oklahoma Territory.

Dear Madam:

    In the matter of the application for the enrollment of your minor child, Charlie E. (or Charles Curtis) McIntosh, as a citizen of the Creek Nation, you are advised that this office requests further proof of your marriage to Charles E. McIntosh, the father of said child.

    You are requested to furnish a certified copy of the marriage license and certificate, or other satisfactory proof of your marriage to said Charles E. McIntosh.

    You are further advised that in order to identify said Charles E. McIntosh as a citizen of the Creek Nation, it will be necessary that you advise this office as to his age,

Applications for Enrollment of Creek Newborn
Act of 1905 Volume XIV

the names of his parents, the Creek Indian town to which he clams to belong, and, if possible, the roll number as same appears on his deeds to lands in the Creek Nation.

       Respectfully,
           Commissioner.

BIRTH AFFIDAVIT.

DEPARTMENT OF THE INTERIOR.
COMMISSION TO THE FIVE CIVILIZED TRIBES.

IN RE APPLICATION FOR ENROLLMENT, as a citizen of the Creek Nation, of Charlie Deere, born on the 15 day of April, 1903

Name of Father: Noah Deere   a citizen of the   Creek   Nation.
 Okfuske Canadian Town
Name of Mother: Maley Deere   a citizen of the   Creek   Nation.
 Hutchechuppa Town

      Postoffice   Eufaula, I.T.

AFFIDAVIT OF MOTHER.

UNITED STATES OF AMERICA, Indian Territory, }
  Western   DISTRICT.

  I, Noah Deere, on oath state that I am about 35 years of age and a citizen by blood, of the Creek Nation; that I am the lawful ~~wife~~ husband of Maley Deere, who is a citizen, by blood of the Creek Nation; that a male child was born to ~~me~~ her on 15 day of April, 1903, that said child has been named Charlie Deere, and was living March 4, 1905.
               his
            Noah x Deere
Witnesses To Mark: mark
 { DC Skaggs
   Alex Posey

   Subscribed and sworn to before me this 14 day of April, 1905.

            Drennan C Skaggs
              Notary Public.

Applications for Enrollment of Creek Newborn
Act of 1905 Volume XIV

NC 1096

OCH
JCL

DEPARTMENT OF THE INTERIOR,
COMMISSIONER TO THE FIVE CIVILIZED TRIBES.

In the matter of the application for the enrollment of Lumsey Deere and Charlie Deere, as citizens by blood of the Creek Nation.

DECISION.

The record in this case shows that on April 18, 1905, application was made in affidavit form, for the enrollment of Lumsey Deere and Charlie Deere as citizens by blood of the Creek Nation, under the provisions of the Act of Congress approved March 3, 1905, (33 Stats. L. 1048).

The evidence and the records of this office show that said Lumsey Deere and Charlie Deere are the children of Maley Deere and Noah Deere, whose names appear as Mary Deere and Noah Deere upon a schedule of citizens by blood of the Creek Nation approved by the Secretary of the Interior March 28, 1902 opposite numbers 8554 and 8554, respectively.

The evidence further shows that said Lumsey Deere was born in the month of June 1901; that said Charlie Deere was born April 15, 1903; and that both of said children were living March 4, 1905.

The evidence in this case is not as full and complete as has heretofore been required by this office to establish a right to be enrolled as a citizen of the Creek Nation, but in view of the provisions of the Act of Congress approved April 26, 1906, (34 Stats. L. 137) fixing March 4, 1907 as the date after which the Secretary of the Interior shall have no jurisdiction to approve the enrollment of any person as a citizen of said Nation, it is believed that the evidence herein should be considered sufficient to establish the facts necessary to support the rights of the applicants herein to enrollment.

It is therefore, ordered and adjudged that said Lumsey Deere and Charlie Deere are entitled to be enrolled as citizens by blood of the Creek Nation, under the provisions of the Act of Congress approved March 3, 1905 (33 Stat. L., 1048), and the application for their enrollment as such is accordingly granted.

Tams Bixby Commissioner.

Muskogee, Indian Territory.
FEB 19 1907

Applications for Enrollment of Creek Newborn
Act of 1905 Volume XIV

BIRTH AFFIDAVIT.

DEPARTMENT OF THE INTERIOR.
COMMISSION TO THE FIVE CIVILIZED TRIBES.

                                                                                                              Lumsey

       IN RE APPLICATION FOR ENROLLMENT, as a citizen of the Creek Nation, of ~~Charlie~~ Deere, born on the *(blank)* day of June, 1901

Name of Father: Noah Deere	a citizen of the	Creek Nation.
Okfuske Canadian Town		
Name of Mother: Maley Deere	a citizen of the	Creek Nation.
Hutchechuppa Town		

                            Postoffice   Eufaula, I.T.

                                                                  Child present

                        AFFIDAVIT OF MOTHER.

UNITED STATES OF AMERICA, Indian Territory,
    Western   DISTRICT.

      I, Noah Deere, on oath state that I am about 35 years of age and a citizen by blood, of the Creek Nation; that I am the lawful ~~wife~~ husband of Maley Deere, who is a citizen, by blood of the Creek Nation; that a male child was born to ~~me~~ her ~~on~~ sometime in day of June, 1901, that said child has been named ~~Charlie~~ Deere, and was living March 4, 1905.

                                                      his   Lumsey
                                           Noah x Deere
Witnesses To Mark: mark
   { DC Skaggs
     Alex Posey

      Subscribed and sworn to before me this 14 day of April, 1905.

                                              Drennan C Skaggs
                                              Notary Public.

NC-1096.

                          Muskogee, Indian Territory, October 23, 1905.

Noah Deere,
     Eufaula, Indian Territory.

Dear Sir:

      In the matter of the application for the enrollment of your minor children, Lumsey Deere, born in the month of June 1901, and Charlie Deere, born April 15, 1903, as citizens by blood of the Creek Nation this office requires the affidavits of the mother of

Applications for Enrollment of Creek Newborn
Act of 1905   Volume XIV

said children and the physician or midwife who attended at their birth and blanks for that purpose are inclosed herewith.

In having the same executed be careful to see that all blank spaces are properly filled, all names written in full and that the notary public, before whom the affidavits are sworn to, attaches his name and seal to each affidavit. In case any signature is by mark it must be attested by two disinterested witnesses.

If there was no physician or midwife in attendance when said children were born it will be necessary for you to furnish this office with the affidavits of two disinterested persons relative to their birth. Said affidavits to set forth the names of said children, the dates of their birth, the names of their parents and whether or not they were living on March 4, 1905.

This office is unable to identify the mother of said children upon the final roll of citizens by blood of the Creek Nation. You are requested to state the name under which she is finally enrolled, the names of her parents and other members of her family, the Creek Indian town to which she belongs, her age and her final roll number as the same appears upon her allotment certificate and deeds.

Respectfully,

Commissioner.

2 BC
Env.

N.C. 1096.

Muskogee, Indian Territory, January 11, 1907.

Jesse McDermott,
    Clerk in charge Creek Field Party,
        Okemah, Indian Territory.

Dear Sir:

In the matter of the application for the enrollment of Lumsey and Charlie Deere, as citizens by blood of the Creek Nation, you are advised that this office requires, for each applicant, the affidavit of the attending physician or midwife or the affidavit of two disinterested witnesses. Said affidavits should set forth the names of the children, the names of their parents, the date of their birth and whether or not said children were living March 4, 1905.

Copies of the records in this case are herewith enclosed.

Respectfully,

N.C. 1096.   Commissioner.

Applications for Enrollment of Creek Newborn
Act of 1905   Volume XIV

REFER IN REPLY TO THE FOLLOWING:
NC-1096

DEPARTMENT OF THE INTERIOR,
COMMISSIONER TO THE FIVE CIVILIZED TRIBES.

Muskogee, Indian Territory, February 14, 1907.

Commissioner to the Five Civilized Tribes,
    Muskogee, Indian Territory.

Sir :--

    I have the honor to report in the matter of the application for the enrollment of Lumsey and Charlie Deere as citizens by blood of the Creek Nation that I was informed on February 9, 1907, that both of said children were living on that date.

                  Respectfully,
                            Jesse McDermott

JWH

N C 1096

                Muskogee, Indian Territory, March 9, 1907.

Maley Deere,
    c/o Noah Deere,
        Eufaula, Indian Territory.

Dear Madam :--

    You are hereby advised that on March 2, 9107, the Secretary of the Interior approved the enrollment of your minor children, Lumsey and Charlie Deere, as citizens by blood of the Creek Nation, and that the name of said child[sic] appears upon the roll of new born citizens by blood of the Creek Nation, enrolled under the Act of Congress approved March 3, 1905, as numbers 1278 and 1279, respectively.

    These children are now entitled to allotments and application therefor should be made without delay at the Creek Land Office, Muskogee, Indian Territory.

                    Respectfully,
                            Commissioner.

Applications for Enrollment of Creek Newborn
Act of 1905 Volume XIV

BIRTH AFFIDAVIT.

DEPARTMENT OF THE INTERIOR.
COMMISSION TO THE FIVE CIVILIZED TRIBES.

IN RE APPLICATION FOR ENROLLMENT, as a citizen of the Creek Nation, of Tuxey Derrisaw, born on the 4 day of June, 1902

Name of Father: Barney Derrisaw   a citizen of the Creek Nation.
Name of Mother: Toche Derrisaw   a citizen of the Creek Nation.

Postoffice   Lesma, Ind. Ter.

AFFIDAVIT OF MOTHER.

UNITED STATES OF AMERICA, Indian Territory,
Western DISTRICT.

I, Barney Derrisaw, on oath state that I am about 50 years of age and a citizen by blood, of the Creek Nation; that I am the lawful ~~wife~~ husband of Toche Derrisaw, who is a citizen, by blood of the Creek Nation; that a female child was born to ~~me~~ her on 4 day of June, 1902, that said child has been named Tuxey Derrisaw, and was living March 4, 1905. and is now living.

                                  his
                         Barney x Derrisaw
Witnesses To Mark: mark
   { J McDermott
   { Andrew Brashar

Subscribed and sworn to before me this 12" day of February, 1907.

My Commission   J McDermott
Expires July 25" 1907   Notary Public.

BIRTH AFFIDAVIT.

DEPARTMENT OF THE INTERIOR.
COMMISSION TO THE FIVE CIVILIZED TRIBES.

IN RE APPLICATION FOR ENROLLMENT, as a citizen of the Creek Nation, of Tuxey Derrsaw[sic], born on the 4 day of june[sic], 1902

Name of Father: Barney Derrsaw   a citizen of the Creek Nation.
Coweta Town
Name of Mother: Togie Derrsaw   a citizen of the Creek Nation.
Coweta Town

Postoffice   stidham, indian territory[sic]

Applications for Enrollment of Creek Newborn
Act of 1905 Volume XIV

AFFIDAVIT OF MOTHER.

UNITED STATES OF AMERICA, Indian Territory, }
    Western   DISTRICT.   Child not present

    I, Barey[sic] Derrsaw , on oath state that I am about 50 years of age and a citizen by Blood , of the Creek Nation; that I am the lawful ~~wife~~ Husband of Togie Derrsaw wife died Dec 28 1904 , who is a citizen, by blood of the Creek Nation; that a Female child was born to me on 4 day of June , 1902 , that said child has been named Tuxey Derrsaw , and was living March 4, 1905.
  I was the lawfull[sic] Husband of Togie Derrsaw

                                                         his
Witnesses To Mark: Barney Derrsaw x
  { Thomas L. Boone   mark
  { Lewis Collins

    Subscribed and sworn to before me this 8 day of April , 1905.

                                        Preston Janway
                                        Notary Public.

AFFIDAVIT OF ATTENDING PHYSICIAN OR MID-WIFE.

UNITED STATES OF AMERICA, Indian Territory, }
    Western   DISTRICT.
                             had no midwife or Doctor
    I, Barney Derrsaw , a Husband , on oath state that I attended on Mrs. my wife Togie Derrsaw , wife of *(blank)* on the 4 day of June , 1902 ; that there was born to her on said date a female child; that said child was living March 4, 1905, and is said to have been named Tuxey Derrsaw

                                                        his
                                        Barney Derrsaw x
Witnesses To Mark: mark
  { Thomas L. Boone
  { Lewis Collins

    Subscribed and sworn to before me this 8 day of April , 1905.
My commission
Expires May 19th 1908   Preston Janway
                                        Notary Public.

(The above Birth Affidavit given again.)

Applications for Enrollment of Creek Newborn
Act of 1905   Volume XIV

NC 1097

OCH
CM

DEPARTMENT OF THE INTERIOR,
COMMISSIONER TO THE FIVE CIVILIZED TRIBES.

In the matter of the application for the enrollment of Tuxey Derrisaw as a citizen by blood of the Creek Nation.

DECISION.

The record in this case shows that on April 18, 1905 application was made, in affidavit form, for the enrollment of Tuxey Derrsaw as a citizen by blood of the Creek Nation under the provisions of the Act of Congress approved March 3, 1905 (33 Stat. L. 1048). Supplemental affidavit was filed February 14. 1907.

It appears from the evidence and the records of this office that the correct name of this child is Tuxey Derrisaw and reference to the applicant herein will hereafter be made accordingly.

The evidence and the records of this office show that said Tuxey Derrisaw is the child of Barney Derrisaw and Toche Derrisaw whose names appear upon a schedule of citizens by blood of the Creek Nation approved by the Secretary of the Interior March 28, 1902, opposite Nos. 7243 and 7244 respectively.

The evidence shows that said Tuxey Derrisaw was born June 4, 1902 and was living February 12, 1907.

The evidence is not as full and complete as has heretofore been required by this office to establish the right of the person to be enrolled as a citizen of the Creek Nation, but in view of the provision of the Act of Congress approved April 26, 1906 (34 Stat. L. 137), fixing March 4, 1907 as the date after which the Secretary of the Interior shall have no jurisdiction to approve the enrollment of any person as a citizen of said nation, it is believed that the evidence herein should be considered sufficient to establish the facts necessary to enrollment.

It is therefore, ordered and adjudged that said Tuxey Derrisaw is entitled to be enrolled as a citizen by blood of the Creek Nation under the provisions of the Act of Congress approved March 3, 1905 (33 Stat. L. 1048), and the application for his enrollment as such is accordingly granted.

Tams Bixby COMMISSIONER.

Muskogee, Indian Territory.
FEB 19 1907

Applications for Enrollment of Creek Newborn
Act of 1905   Volume XIV

NC-1097.

Muskogee, Indian Territory, October 24, 1905.

Toche Derrisaw,
    c/o Barney Derrisaw,
        Stidham, Indian Territory.

Dear Madam:

    In the matter of the application for the enrollment of your minor child Tuxey Derrisaw, born June 4, 1902, as a citizen by blood of the Creek Nation, this office desires the affidavits of two disinterested witnesses relative to the birth of said child. Said affidavits must set forth said child's name, the date of her birth, the names of her parents and whether or not she was living March 4, 1905.

                Respectfully,

                            Commissioner.

COPY

N. C. 1097.

Eufaula, Indian Territory, February 13, 1907.

Commissioner to the Five Civilized Tribes,
    Muskogee, Indian Territory.

Sir:

    There are herewith enclosed copies of record in the matter of the application for the enrollment of Tuxey Derrisaw, as a citizen by blood of the Creek Nation, together with the affidavit of Barney Derrisaw, the father of said child. The mother having died and there being no midwife, the Creek Enrollment Field Party is unable to secure the affidavits of two disinterested witnesses relative to the birth of said child.

                Respectfully,
                (Signed) Jesse McDermott
                        Clerk in Charge.

Applications for Enrollment of Creek Newborn
Act of 1905   Volume XIV

N C 1097

JWH

Muskogee, Indian Territory, March 9, 1907.

Toche Derrisaw,
    % Barney Derrisaw,
        Stidham, Indian Territory.

Dear Madam :--

You are hereby advised that on March 2, 1907, the Secretary of the Interior approved the enrollment of your minor child, Tuxey Derrisaw, as a citizen by blood of the Creek Nation, and that the name of said child appears upon the roll of new born citizens by blood of the Creek Nation, enrolled under the Act of Congress approved March 3, 1905, as number 1280.

This child is now entitled to allotment and application therefor should be made without delay at the Creek Land Office, Muskogee, Indian Territory.

                Respectfully,

                            Commissioner.

BIRTH AFFIDAVIT.

DEPARTMENT OF THE INTERIOR.
COMMISSION TO THE FIVE CIVILIZED TRIBES.

IN RE APPLICATION FOR ENROLLMENT, as a citizen of the Creek Nation, of Jannetta Raiford , born on the 20 day of February, 1903

Name of Father: Arthur E. Raiford   a citizen of the   Creek   Nation.
Coweta Town
Name of Mother: Tookah Raiford (McCombs)   a citizen of the   Creek   Nation.
Tuskegee Town
                      Postoffice   Eufaula, I.T.

Applications for Enrollment of Creek Newborn
Act of 1905   Volume XIV

AFFIDAVIT OF MOTHER.

Child present.

UNITED STATES OF AMERICA, Indian Territory, ⎱
    Western   DISTRICT.   ⎰

    I, Tookah Raiford , on oath state that I am 23 years of age and a citizen by blood , of the Creek Nation; that I am the lawful wife of Arthur E. Raiford , who is a citizen, by blood of the Creek Nation; that a female child was born to me on 20 day of February , 1903 , that said child has been named Jannetta Raiford , and was living March 4, 1905.

                                              Tookah Raiford

Witnesses To Mark:
{

    Subscribed and sworn to before me this 3 day of April , 1905.

                                              Drennan C Skaggs
                                              Notary Public.

AFFIDAVIT OF ATTENDING PHYSICIAN OR MID-WIFE.

UNITED STATES OF AMERICA, Indian Territory, ⎱
    Western   DISTRICT.   ⎰

    I, Bettie Drew , a Midwife , on oath state that I attended on Mrs. Tookah Raiford , wife of Arthur E. Raiford on the 20th day of February , 1903 ; that there was born to her on said date a female child; that said child was living March 4, 1905, and is said to have been named Jannetta Raiford

                                              Bettie Drew

Witnesses To Mark:
{

    Subscribed and sworn to before me 12th day of April , 1905.

                                              R.C. Allen
                                              Notary Public.

My Commission Expires March 15, 1908.

Applications for Enrollment of Creek Newborn
Act of 1905   Volume XIV

NC-1099.

Muskogee, Indian Territory, October 24, 1905

Lava Doyle,
    c/o Arthur Doyle,
        Brush Hill, Indian Territory.

Dear Madam:

In the matter of the application for the enrollment of your minor child, Clarrance William Doyle, born April 13, 1904, as a citizen by blood of the Creek Nation, this office requires evidence of your marriage to Arthur Doyle, the father of said child.

Such evidence may consist of either the original or a certified copy of your marriage license and certificate.

                Respectfully,

                          Commissioner.

NC-1099

CHECOTAH, I. T. Nov. 21, 1905.

Hon. Commissioner.

I enclose herein our Marriage License in reply to above, and ask you to kindly return the same to me at Brush Hill, I. T.

                Respectfully,

                          LAVA DOYLE,
    authorized.   By J. B. Morrow.

NC-1099

Muskogee, Indian Territory, November 24, 1905.

Lava Doyle,
    Care of Arthur Doyle,
        Brushhill, Indian Territory.

Dear Madam:

In compliance with your request, there is herewith enclosed you[sic] marriage license. A copy thereof has been made and filed with the record in the matter of the application for the enrollment of your minor child, Clarrance William Doyle, as a citizen by blood of the Creek Nation.

                Respectfully,

JYM-24-1   Acting Commissioner.

Applications for Enrollment of Creek Newborn
Act of 1905   Volume XIV

NC-1099

MARRIAGE LICENSE

UNITED STATES OF AMERICA,
   Indian Territory,   ss.   NO. 176
   Western District.

TO ANY PERSON AUTHORIZED BY LAW TO SOLEMNIZE MARRIAGE--GREETING:

    You are hereby commanded to Solemnize the Rite and publish the Banns of Matrimony between Mr. Arthur Doyle of Fame, in the Indian Territory, aged 22 years, and Miss Laura Bashaw, of Brush Hill, in the Indian Territory, aged 19 years, according to law, and do you officially sign and return this License to the parties therein named.

    Witness my hand and official seal at Eufaula, Indian Territory, this 29th day of June, A. D. 1903.

                                            R. P. HARRISON,
By C. E. Wilcox, Deputy.   Clerk of the U.S. Court.
   (SEAL)

CERTIFICATE OF MARRIAGE.

United States of America,
     Indian Territory,   ss.
     Western District.
    I, B. F. McElwain, a Minister of the Gospel, do hereby certify that on the 3 day of July, A. D. 1903, did duly and according to law as commanded in the foregoing License, solemnize the Rite and Publish the Banns of Matrimony between the parties therein named.
    Witness my hand this 3 day of July, A. D. 1903.
    My credentials are recorded in the office of the Clerk of the United States Court, Indian Territory, Western District, Book C. Page 150.
                                  (signed) B. F. McELWAIN,
                                        a Minister of the Gospel.

CERTIFICATE OF RECORD.

United States of America,
     Indian Territory,   ss.
     Western District.
    I, Robert P. Harrison, Clerk of the United States Court in the Western District, Indian Territory, do hereby certify that the instrument hereto attached was filed for record in my office the 4th day of August, 1904, at ....M., and duly recorded in Book P. Marriage Record, Page 39.

Applications for Enrollment of Creek Newborn
Act of 1905 Volume XIV

Witness my hand and seal of said Court at Muskogee, in said Territory this 4th day of August, A. D. 1903.

R. P. HARRISON, Clerk.
By J. Harlan, Deputy.
(SEAL)

INDIAN TERRITORY, Western District.

I, J. Y. Miller, a stenographer to the Commissioner to the Five Civilized Tribes, do hereby certify that the above and foregoing is a true and complete translation of my notes as same appear in my stenographic report of this case.

JY Miller

Sworn to and subscribed before me this the 23rd day of November, 1905.

J McDermott
Notary Public.

BIRTH AFFIDAVIT.

DEPARTMENT OF THE INTERIOR.
COMMISSION TO THE FIVE CIVILIZED TRIBES.

IN RE APPLICATION FOR ENROLLMENT, as a citizen of the Creek Nation, of Clarrance William Doyle, born on the 13 day of April, 1904

Name of Father: Author Doyle   a citizen of the Creek Nation.
Broken Arrow Town
Name of Mother: Laura Doyle   a citizen of the United States Nation.
~~Broken Arrow Town~~

Postoffice   Brush Hill Ind Ter

AFFIDAVIT OF MOTHER.

UNITED STATES OF AMERICA, Indian Territory,
Western DISTRICT.

Child present

I, Laura Doyle , on oath state that I am 19 years of age and a citizen by marriage , of the Creek Nation; that I am the lawful wife of Author Doyle , who is a citizen, by blood of the Creek Nation; that a male child was born to me on 13 day of April , 1904, that said child has been named Clarrance William Doyle , and was living March 4, 1905.

Laura Doyle

Witnesses To Mark:

Applications for Enrollment of Creek Newborn
Act of 1905   Volume XIV

Subscribed and sworn to before me this 8 day of   April   , 1905.

                                   Preston Janway
                                   Notary Public.

AFFIDAVIT OF ATTENDING PHYSICIAN OR MID-WIFE.

UNITED STATES OF AMERICA, Indian Territory,
    Western   **DISTRICT.**

    I,   Sarah A. Doyle , a   midwife , on oath state that I attended on Mrs. Lara Doyle, wife of Author Doyle on the 13 day of April , 1904 ; that there was born to her on said date a   male   child; that said child was living March 4, 1905, and is said to have been named Clarrance William Doyle

                                   Sarah A Doyle

Witnesses To Mark:

Subscribed and sworn to before me this 8 day of   April   , 1905.
My commission
expires May 19 1908   Preston Janway
                                   Notary Public.

NC-1100.

                     Muskogee, Indian Territory, October 24, 1905.

Roseter E. Doyle,
    c/o Thomas E. Doyle,
        Brush Hill, Indian Territory.

Dear Madam:

    In the matter of the application for the enrollment of your minor child, Mose Doyle, born July 29, 1902, as a citizen by blood of the Creek Nation, this office requires evidence of your marriage to Thomas E. Doyle the father of said child.

Applications for Enrollment of Creek Newborn
Act of 1905   Volume XIV

Such evidence may consist of either the original or a certified copy of your marriage license and certificate.

                        Respectfully,

                                    Commissioner.

NC-1100

                        Muskogee, Indian Territory, November 18, 1905.

Thomas E. Doyle,
    Brushhill, Indian Territory.

Dear Sir:

In compliance with your request, there is herewith enclosed you[sic] marriage license. A copy thereof has been made and filed in the matter of the application for the enrollment of your minor child, Mose Doyle, as a citizen by blood of the Creek Nation.

                        Respectfully,

                                      Acting Commissioner.

JYM-18-1

NC-1100

MARRIAGE LICENSE

UNITED STATES OF AMERICA,
    Indian Territory,   ss.   No. 232
    Northern District.

TO ANY PERSON AUTHORIZED BY LAW TO SOLEMNIZE MARRIAGE--GREETING:

You are hereby commanded to Solemnize the Rite and publish the Banns of Matrimony between Mr. Thomas E. Doyle of Brush Hill, in the Indian Territory, aged 21 years, and Miss Rosetta McGill, of Brush Hill, in the Indian Territory, aged 16 years, according to law, and do you officially sign and return this License to the parties therein named.

Witness my hand and official seal at Muscogee[sic], Indian Territory, this 15 day of May, A. D. 1900.

                                      C. A. DAVIDSON,
By P. M. Ford, Deputy.   Clerk of the U.S. Court.
    (SEAL)

Applications for Enrollment of Creek Newborn
Act of 1905   Volume XIV

CERTIFICATE OF MARRIAGE.

United States of America,
 Indian Territory. ss.
 Northern District.

 I, R. C. McGee, a Minister of the Gospel, do hereby certify that on the 19 day of May, A. D. ~~1900~~, I did duly and according to law, as commanded in the foregoing License, solemnize the Rite and publish the Banns of Matrimony between the parties therein names.

 Witness my hand this 19 day of May, A. D. 1900.

 My credentials are recorded in the office of the Clerk of the United States Court, Indian Territory, Northern District, Book A Page 31.

(signed)   R. C. McGEE,
a Minister of the Gospel.

CERTIFICATE OF RECORD.

United States of America,
 Indian Territory. ss.
 Northern District.

 I, Charles A. Davidson, Clerk of the United States Court in the Northern District, Indian Territory, do hereby certify that the instrument hereto attached was filed for record in my office the 21 day of May, 1900, at ……M., and duly recorded in Book I, Marriage Record, Page 442.

 Witness my hand and seal of said Court at Muscogee[sic], in said Territory this 25 day of May, A. D. 1900.

(signed)   CHAS. A. DAVIDSON, Clerk

By ……………………..Deputy.

Northern Dist. Ind. Ter.
FILED
MAY 21, 1900
CHAS. A. DAVIDSON,
Clerk U.S. Courts.

INDIAN TERRITORY, Western District.   :   I, J. Y. Miller, a stenographer to the Commissioner to the Five Civilized Tribes, do hereby certify that the above and foregoing is a true and complete translation of my notes as same appear in my stenographic report of this case.

JY Miller

Applications for Enrollment of Creek Newborn
Act of 1905   Volume XIV

Sworn to and subscribed before me
this the 17th day of November,
1905.

J McDermott
Notary Public.

BIRTH AFFIDAVIT.

DEPARTMENT OF THE INTERIOR.
COMMISSION TO THE FIVE CIVILIZED TRIBES.

IN RE APPLICATION FOR ENROLLMENT, as a citizen of the Creek Nation, of Mose Doyle, born on the 29 day of July, 1902

Name of Father: Thomas E. Doyle   a citizen of the   Creek   Nation.
Big Spring Town
Name of Mother: Roseter E Doyle   a citizen of the United States Nation.
~~Big Spring Town~~

Postoffice   Brush Hill Ind Ter

AFFIDAVIT OF MOTHER.

UNITED STATES OF AMERICA, Indian Territory,   } Child
    Western   **DISTRICT.**   present

I, Roseter E. Doyle, on oath state that I am 20 years of age and a citizen by Mariage[sic], of the Creek Nation; that I am the lawful wife of Thomas E Doyle, who is a citizen, by blood of the Creek Nation; that a male child was born to me on 29 day of July, 1902, that said child has been named Mose Doyle, and was living March 4, 1905.

                                    her
                          Roseter x Doyle
Witnesses To Mark: mark
  { Robert Crowson
  { Charley Hagan

Subscribed and sworn to before me this 8 day of April, 1905.

Preston Janway
Notary Public.

Applications for Enrollment of Creek Newborn
Act of 1905 Volume XIV

AFFIDAVIT OF ATTENDING PHYSICIAN OR MID-WIFE.

UNITED STATES OF AMERICA, Indian Territory, }
Western DISTRICT.

I, Sarah A. Doyle , a midwife , on oath state that I attended on Mrs. Roseter E. Doyle , wife of Thomas E. Doyle on the 29 day of July , 1902 ; that there was born to her on said date a male child; that said child was living March 4, 1905, and is said to have been named Mose Doyle

Sarah A. Doyle

Witnesses To Mark:
{

Subscribed and sworn to before me this 8 day of April , 1905.

My commission Preston Janway
Expires May 19 1908 Notary Public.

BIRTH AFFIDAVIT.

DEPARTMENT OF THE INTERIOR.
COMMISSION TO THE FIVE CIVILIZED TRIBES.

IN RE APPLICATION FOR ENROLLMENT, as a citizen of the Creek Nation, of Julia Lavinia Bethel , born on the 10th day of June , 1903

Name of Father: David F. Bethel a citizen of the United States Nation.
Name of Mother: Dora Bethel, nee Holman a citizen of the Creek Nation.

Postoffice Wagoner, I.T.

AFFIDAVIT OF MOTHER.

UNITED STATES OF AMERICA, Indian Territory, }
Western DISTRICT.

I, Dora Bethel, nee Holman , on oath state that I am 37 years of age and a citizen by blood , of the Creek Nation; that I am the lawful wife of David F. Bethel , who is a citizen, by *(blank)* of the United States Nation; that a female child was born

Applications for Enrollment of Creek Newborn
Act of 1905   Volume XIV

to me on 10th day of June, 1903, that said child has been named Julia Lavinia Bethel, and was living March 4, 1905.

                                    Dora Bethel nee Holman

Witnesses To Mark:
{

    Subscribed and sworn to before me this 5th day of April, 1905.

                                    Estelle Simpson
                                    Notary Public.

AFFIDAVIT OF ATTENDING PHYSICIAN OR MID-WIFE.

UNITED STATES OF AMERICA, Indian Territory, }
    Western   DISTRICT.

    I, George W. Ruble, a physician, on oath state that I attended on Mrs. Dora Bethel, nee Holman, wife of David F. Bethel on the 10th day of June, 1903; that there was born to her on said date a female child; that said child was living March 4, 1905, and is said to have been named Julia Lavinia Bethel

                                    George W. Ruble

Witnesses To Mark:
{

    Subscribed and sworn to before me this 14th day of April, 1905.

                                    Estelle Simpson
                                    Notary Public.

NC 1102

                DEPARTMENT OF THE INTERIOR,
     COMMISSIONER TO THE FIVE CIVILIZED TRIBES.
             MUSKOGEE, INDIAN TERRITORY.
                    JULY 20, 1906.

    In the matter of the application for the enrollment of Robert and Hannah Harjo, as citizens by blood of the Creek Nation.

Applications for Enrollment of Creek Newborn
Act of 1905   Volume XIV

Susie Harjo, being duly sworn, testified as follows, through Official Interpreter, Lona Merrick.

Q What is your name? A Susie Harjo.
Q What is your age? A 25.
Q What is your post office address? A Yeager.
Q What Creek Indian town do you belong to? A Tuckabatchee.
Q What is the name of your father? A Neha Thlocco.
Q What is the name of your mother? A Sophia Harjo.
Q Do you know how old you are, you say you are 25, aren't you older than that, aren't you about 40? A I don't know how old I am.

Witness appears to be about 30.

Q Have you got a bit grown up boy? A No sir.
Q Who is Peter Harjo? A He is my brother.
Q Has the same father and mother you have? A We have the same mother and different fathers.
Q What is the name of his father? A Sundulla Harjo. He is my husband and also the father of my brother Peter.
Q Was Sundulla Harjo known by any other name? [sic] Peter Hodge is his christian[sic] name.
Q Sundulla Harjo is an old man isn't he? A Yes sir.
Q Good deal older than you? A Yes sir.
Q Is he living? A He is dead.
Q When did he die? A Died the 7th day of this month.
Q Is your half brother living? A He is dead.
Q When did he die? A Been dead about two years I think.
Q What is the name of the girl you have in your lap? A Hannah Harjo.
Q Are you her mother? A Yes sir.

Witness is identified as Susie Harjo, opposite Creek Indian Roll No. 5302.

Q What is the name of Hannah?[sic] A Sundulla.
Q When was this child Hannah born?

Midwife Phebe Beaver presents a piece of paper, which shows Hannah was born Feb. 9, 1902, at 12 o'clock.
Q Now Susie here is a piece of paper which gives the date as 1902, and you and the midwife on the 28th day of June, this year, went before a Notary Public named Clawson, and swore that Hannah was born in 1903, and you went before the same Notary Public last year and swore that the child was born 1901, you have the given three years, 1901, 1902, 1903, now which of those three is correct? A The date on the piece of paper must be correct, we didn't wrire[sic] out the affidavits, the Notary Public made the mistakes.
Q Is this one correct; this child is four years old past, and not five years or three years as those other affidavits give t, is that one right, the one which says she was born 1902, that

Applications for Enrollment of Creek Newborn
Act of 1905   Volume XIV

would make the child over four years old? A Yes, that is correct, she is little over four years old.
Q That child has never been enrolled? A I thought she was enrolled by Alex Posey.
Q Did you have a child named Robert Harjo? A Yes sir.
Q Did he have the same father that Hannah had? A Yes sir.
Q When was Robert born? A He was born two years ago.
Q What time--what month and what day, you have an affidavit here, you and Peter, which said he was born November 12, 1904, is that correct? A Yes sir.
Q Is Robert Harjo living? A No sir.
Q When did he die? A He died last October, 1905.
Q How old was he when he died? A He was nearly a year old.
Q Was he living at the time you made application for him last year? A Yes sir, he was living, he died soon after we made application for him.
Q And this child, Peter Harjo, child of Susie and a Seminole named David Harjo, is your child isn't he? A No sir.
Q Post office address of these people is given as Sarby? A Thats[sic] some other people.
Q Was Phebe Beaver, the midwife when Hannah was born? A Yes sir.
Q Is she kind of an doctor, she said in the affidavit she was the attending physician? A Yes sir, she is a doctor.
Q Didn't you have any midwife when Robert Harjo was born? A No sir.
Q Can you furnish the affidavits of two disinterested witnesses, about the birth and death of this child, don't Peter Beaver, Phebe Beaver, Lawyer Deer or any of these people in here know anything about it? [sic] Peter and Phebe know about it.
Q You and the midwife both wish to correct these dates, which says 1902 and 1903, which would make the child over four and five years old. The date which says 1902 would make Hannah over four years, and about Robert --these disinterested witness[sic] swear about his death, you also want to join them in saying he was born last October.
A Yes sir.

Lona Merrick, being duly sworn, states that the above and foregoing is a true and correct transcript of her stenographic notes as taken in said cause on said date.

Lona Merrick

Subscribed and sworn to before me this 24th day of July, 1906.

HGHains
Notary Public,

Applications for Enrollment of Creek Newborn
Act of 1905   Volume XIV

AFFIDAVIT OF DISINTERESTED WITNESS.

UNITED STATES OF AMERICA,
Western DISTRICT,   SS
INDIAN TERRITORY.

We, the undersigned, on oath state that we are personally acquainted with   Susie Harjo   wife of   Sunduller[sic] Harjo (Dc'd)   ; that there was born to her a   male child on or about the 12 day of November 1904   ; that the said child has been named Robert Harjo   , and was living March 4, 1905 & died in October, 1905.

Witnesses: H.G. Hains
              Lona Merrick

                                      his
                             Peter x Beaver
                                      mark
                                      her
                             Phebie x Beaver
                                      mark

Subscribed and sworn to before me this 20 day of July 1906.

                                                              HGHains
                                                               Notary Public.

BIRTH AFFIDAVIT.

DEPARTMENT OF THE INTERIOR.
COMMISSION TO THE FIVE CIVILIZED TRIBES.

      IN RE APPLICATION FOR ENROLLMENT, as a citizen of the Creek Nation, of Robert Harjo , born on the 12 day of November , 1904

Name of Father: Peter Harjo   a citizen of the   Creek   Nation.
Name of Mother: Susie Harjo   a citizen of the   Creek   Nation.

                                Postoffice   Yeager Ind Ter.

AFFIDAVIT OF MOTHER.

UNITED STATES OF AMERICA, Indian Territory,
      Western   DISTRICT.

     I, Susie Harjo , on oath state that I am 25 years of age and a citizen by blood , of the Creek   Nation; that I am the lawful wife of Peter Harjo , who is a citizen, by blood of the Creek   Nation; that a male   child was born to me on   twelfth   day of

Applications for Enrollment of Creek Newborn
Act of 1905 Volume XIV

November , 1904 , that said child has been named Robert Harjo , and was living March 4, 1905.

Witnesses To Mark:
{ W.R. Clawson
  James Scott

Susie x Harjo
her   mark

Subscribed and sworn to before me this 14 day of April , 1905.

WR Clawson
Notary Public.

AFFIDAVIT OF ATTENDING PHYSICIAN OR MID-WIFE.

UNITED STATES OF AMERICA, Indian Territory,
    Western   DISTRICT.

I, Peter Harjo , a *(blank)* , on oath state that I attended on Mrs. Susie Harjo , wife of Peter Harjo on the 12 day of November , 1904 ; that there was born to her on said date a male child; that said child was living March 4, 1905, and is said to have been named Robert Harjo

Witnesses To Mark:
{ WR Clawson
  James Scott

Peter x Harjo
his   mark

Subscribed and sworn to before me this 14 day of April , 1905.

WR Clawson
Notary Public.

BIRTH AFFIDAVIT.

DEPARTMENT OF THE INTERIOR.
COMMISSION TO THE FIVE CIVILIZED TRIBES.

IN RE APPLICATION FOR ENROLLMENT, as a citizen of the Creek Nation, of Peter Harjo , born on the 21 day of July , 1903

Name of Father: David Harjo   a citizen of the   Seminole   Nation.
Seminole
Name of Mother: Susie Harjo   a citizen of the   Creek   Nation.
Thlewarthy[sic] Town

Postoffice   Sarbey ITy.

Applications for Enrollment of Creek Newborn
Act of 1905   Volume XIV

AFFIDAVIT OF MOTHER.

UNITED STATES OF AMERICA, Indian Territory,　}
　　Western　　　　　　DISTRICT.

I, Susie Harjo , on oath state that I am 22 years of age and a citizen by blood , of the Creek Nation; that I am the lawful wife of David Harjo , who is a citizen, by blood of the Seminole Nation; that a male child was born to me on 21 day of July, 1903 , that said child has been named Peter Harjo , and ~~was living March 4, 1905~~. died ~~July~~ Sept 15 1903

　　　　　　　　　　　　　　　　her
　　　　　　　　　　　　　Susie x Harjo
Witnesses To Mark:　　　　mark
　{ Jesse McDermott
　　EC Griesel

Subscribed and sworn to before me this 12" day of　April , 1905.

(Seal)　　　　　　　　　　J McDermott
　　　　　　　　　　　　　Notary Public.

AFFIDAVIT OF ATTENDING PHYSICIAN OR MID-WIFE.

UNITED STATES OF AMERICA, Indian Territory,　}
　　Western　　　　　　DISTRICT.

I, Ishulker , a midiwfe , on oath state that I attended on Mrs. Susie Harjo , wife of Peter Harjo on the 21 day of July , 1903 ; that there was born to her on said date a male child; that said child ~~was living March 4, 1905~~, and is said to have been named Peter Harjo

　　　　　　　　　　　　　　　her
　　　　　　　　　　　　Ishulker x
　　　　　　　　　　　　　mark
Witnesses To Mark:
　{ Jesse McDermott
　　EC Griesel

Subscribed and sworn to before me this 12 day of　April , 1905.

(Seal)　　　　　　　　　　J McDermott
　　　　　　　　　　　　　Notary Public.

Applications for Enrollment of Creek Newborn
Act of 1905   Volume XIV

NC 1102 　　　　　　　　　　　　　　　　　　　　　　　　JLD

DEPARTMENT OF THE INTERIOR,
COMMISSIONER TO THE FIVE CIVILIZED TRIBES.

In the matter of the application for the enrollment of Peter Harjo, deceased, as a citizen by blood of the Creek Nation.

....

STATEMENT AND ORDER.

The record in this case shows that on April 18, 1905, application was made, in affidavit form, for the enrollment of Peter Harjo, deceased, as a citizen by blood of the Creek Nation, under the provisions of the Act of Congress approved March 3, 1905.

It appears from the evidence filed in this matter that said Peter Harjo, deceased, was born July 21, 1903, and died September 15, 1903.

The Act of Congress approved March 3, 1905, (33 Stats., 1048), provides:

"That the Commission to the Five Civilized Tribes is authorized for sixty days after the date of the approval of this act to receive and consider applications for enrollment, of children, <u>born subsequent to May twenty-fifth, nineteen hundred and one, and prior to March fourth, nineteen hundred</u> and five, and living on said latter date, to citizens of the Creek tribe of Indians whose enrollment has been approved by the Secretary of the Interior prior to the approval of this act; and to enroll and make allotments to such children."

It is, therefore, ordered that the application for the enrollment of said , deceased, as a citizen by blood of the Creek Nation be, and the same is, hereby dismissed.

　　　　　　　　　　　　　　　　Tams Bixby   Commissioner.

Muskogee, Indian Territory.
　　JAN 4 – 1907

BIRTH AFFIDAVIT.

DEPARTMENT OF THE INTERIOR.
COMMISSION TO THE FIVE CIVILIZED TRIBES.

IN RE APPLICATION FOR ENROLLMENT, as a citizen of the Creek Nation, of Hannah Harjo, born on the 9 day of February, 1901

Name of Father: Peter Harjo	a citizen of the	Creek	Nation.
Name of Mother: Susie Harjo	a citizen of the	Creek	Nation.

　　　　　　　　　　　Postoffice　　　Yeager IT

Applications for Enrollment of Creek Newborn
Act of 1905 Volume XIV

AFFIDAVIT OF MOTHER.

UNITED STATES OF AMERICA, Indian Territory, } Western DISTRICT.

  I, Susie Harjo , on oath state that I am Twenty five years of age and a citizen by birth , of the Creek Nation; that I am the lawful wife of Peter Harjo , who is a citizen, by birth of the Creek Nation; that a female child was born to me on ninth day of February , 1901 , that said child has been named Hannah Harjo , and was living March 4, 1905.

                her
             Susie x Harjo
Witnesses To Mark: mark
 { W.R. Clawson
  James Scott

  Subscribed and sworn to before me this 14 day of April , 1905.

            WR Clawson
              Notary Public.

AFFIDAVIT OF ATTENDING PHYSICIAN OR MID-WIFE.

UNITED STATES OF AMERICA, Indian Territory, } Western DISTRICT.

  I, Peter Harjo , a *(blank)* , on oath state that I attended on Mrs. Susie Harjo , wife of Peter Harjo on the 9 day of February , 1901 ; that there was born to her on said date a female child; that said child was living March 4, 1905, and is said to have been named Hannah Harjo

             his
           Peter x Harjo
Witnesses To Mark: mark
 { W.R. Clawson
  James Scott

  Subscribed and sworn to before me this 14 day of April , 1905.

            WR Clawson
              Notary Public.

Father was only one present

Applications for Enrollment of Creek Newborn
Act of 1905 Volume XIV

BIRTH AFFIDAVIT.

DEPARTMENT OF THE INTERIOR,
COMMISSIONER TO THE FIVE CIVILIZED TRIBES.

ENROLLMENT OF MINORS. ACT OF CONGRESS, APPROVED APRIL 26, 1906.

IN RE APPLICATION FOR ENROLLMENT, as a citizen of the Creek Nation, of Hannah Harjo, born on the 9 day of February, 1902

Name of Father: Sunduller Harjo   a citizen of the   Creek   Nation.
Name of Mother: Susie "   a citizen of the   "   Nation.

Tribal enrollment of father Roll #I. 5301   Tribal enrollment of mother I. 5302

Postoffice   Yeager, I.T.

AFFIDAVIT OF MOTHER.

UNITED STATES OF AMERICA, Indian Territory,
Western District.   Child present

I, Susie Harjo, on oath state that I am about 25 or more years of age and a citizen by blood, of the Creek Nation; that I am the lawful wife of Sunduller Harjo (Dead), who is a citizen, by blood of the Creek Nation; that a female child was born to me on 9" day of February, 1902, that said child has been named Hannah Harjo, and was living March 4, 1906.

                                 her
                           Susie x Harjo
WITNESSES TO MARK: mark
   { HG Hains
     Lona Merrick

Subscribed and sworn to before me this 20 day of July, 1906.

                             HG Hains
                                   Notary Public.

AFFIDAVIT OF ATTENDING PHYSICIAN OR MID-WIFE.

UNITED STATES OF AMERICA, Indian Territory,
Western District.

I, Phebie Beaver, a midwife or physician, on oath state that I attended on Susie Harjo, wife of Sunduller Harjo (Dc'd) on the 9 day of Feby, 1902; that there was born to her on said date a female child; that said child was living March 4, 1906, and is said to have been named Hannah

Applications for Enrollment of Creek Newborn
Act of 1905 Volume XIV

                                  her
                              Phebie x Beaver

WITNESSES TO MARK: mark
  { HG Hains
    Lona Merrick

Subscribed and sworn to before me this 20 day of July , 1906.

                                  HG Hains
                                        Notary Public.

BIRTH AFFIDAVIT.

DEPARTMENT OF THE INTERIOR,
COMMISSIONER TO THE FIVE CIVILIZED TRIBES.

ENROLLMENT OF MINORS. ACT OF CONGRESS, APPROVED APRIL 26, 1906.

    IN RE APPLICATION FOR ENROLLMENT, as a citizen of the Creek Nation, of Hannah Harjo , born on the 9th day of February , 1903

Name of Father: Peter Harjo   a citizen of the   Creek Nation.
Name of Mother: Susie Harjo   a citizen of the   Creek Nation.

Tribal enrollment of father   Creek   Tribal enrollment of mother Creek

                        Postoffice   Yeager, Ind Ter

AFFIDAVIT OF MOTHER.

UNITED STATES OF AMERICA, Indian Territory,
    Western   District.

    I, Susie Harjo , on oath state that I am Twenty-five (25) years of age and a citizen by blood , of the Creek   Nation; that I am the lawful wife of Peter Harjo , who is a citizen, by blood of the Creek   Nation; that a female   child was born to me on ninth day of February , 1903 , that said child has been named Hannah Harjo , and was living March 4, 1906.

                                  her
                            Susie x Harjo
WITNESSES TO MARK: mark
  { James Scott
    Bert Davis

Subscribed and sworn to before me this 28th day of June , 1906.

My com Ex   *(Illegible)* D Clawson
Apr 16, 1910   Notary Public.

Applications for Enrollment of Creek Newborn
Act of 1905 Volume XIV

AFFIDAVIT OF ATTENDING PHYSICIAN OR MID-WIFE.

UNITED STATES OF AMERICA, **Indian Territory,**
Western District.

    I, Phebie Beaver , a physician , on oath state that I attended on Susie Harjo , wife of Peter Harjo on the 9th day of Feb , 1903 ; that there was born to her on said date a female child; that said child was living March 4, 1906, and is said to have been named Hannah Harjo

                                       her
                              Phebie x Beaver
WITNESSES TO MARK: mark
    { James Scott
      Bert Davis

Subscribed and sworn to before me this 28th day of June , 1906.

My com Ex   *(Illegible)* D Clawson
Apr 16, 1910   Notary Public.

N.C. 1102.

                          Muskogee, Indian Territory, July 7, 1906.

Susie Harjo,
    Care Peter Harjo,
        Yeager, Indian Territory.

Dear Madam:

    In the matter of the application for the enrollment of your minor children, Hannah and Robert Harjo, as citizens of the Creek Nation, you are advised that you will be allowed fifteen days from date hereof within which to appear at this office with witnesses to testify under oath relative to the dates of birth of said children.

                              Respectfully,
                                        Commissioner.

Applications for Enrollment of Creek Newborn
Act of 1905   Volume XIV

N.C. 1102

Muskogee, Indian Territory, March 1, 1907.

Susie Harjo,
    Care David Harjo,
        Yeager, Indian Territory.

Dear Madam:

    You are hereby advised that on February 15, 1907, the Secretary of the Interior approved the enrollment of your minor children, Hannah and Robert Harjo, as citizens by blood of the Creek Nation, and that the names of said children appear upon the roll of new born citizens by blood of the Creek Nation, enrolled under the Act of Congress approved March 3, 1905, as numbers 1214 and 1215 respectively.

    These children are now entitled to allotments and application therefor should be made without delay at the Creek Land Office, Muskogee, Indian Territory.

Respectfully,
Commissioner.

NC 1103.

DEPARTMENT OF THE INTERIOR,
COMMISSIONER TO THE FIVE CIVILIZED TRIBES.

    In the matter of the application for the enrollment of Eliza Timothy as a citizen by blood of the Creek Nation.

DECISION.

    The record in this case shows that on April 18, 1905, application was made, in affidavit form, for the enrollment of Eliza Timothy, as a citizen by blood of the Creek Nation, under the provisions of the act of Congress approved March 3, 1905 (33 Stats. L. 1048). A report made to this office under date of February 8, 1907, and a signed statement under no date filed with this office February 12, 1907, are made a part of the record in this case.

    The evidence and the records of this office show that said Eliza Timothy is the child of John Timothy and Ella Timothy, whose names are included in a schedule of

Applications for Enrollment of Creek Newborn
Act of 1905   Volume XIV

citizens by blood of the Creek Nation, approved by the Secretary of the Interior March 28, 1902, opposite numbers 7685 and 7686, respectively.

The evidence shows that said Eliza Timothy was born July 27, 1903, and was living March 4, 1905.

Although the evidence herein is not as full and complete as has heretofore been required by this office to establish the right of a person to be enrolled as a citizen of the Creek Nation, in view of the provisions of the act of Congress approved April 26, 1906 (34 Stats. L., 137), fixing March 4, 1907, as the date after which the Secretary of the Interior shall have no jurisdiction to approve of enrollment of any person as a citizen of said Nation, it is believed that the evidence herein should be considered sufficient to establish the right of the applicant to enrollment.

It is, therefore, ordered and adjudged that the said Eliza Timothy is entitled to be enrolled as a citizen by blood of the Creek Nation under the provisions of the act of Congress approved March 3, 1905 (33 Stats. L., 1048), and the application for her enrollment as such is accordingly granted.

Tams Bixby   Commissioner.

Muskogee, Indian Territory,
FEB 19 1907

BIRTH AFFIDAVIT.

DEPARTMENT OF THE INTERIOR.
COMMISSION TO THE FIVE CIVILIZED TRIBES.

IN RE APPLICATION FOR ENROLLMENT, as a citizen of the Creek Nation, of Eliza Timothy, born on the 27" day of July , 1903

Name of Father: John Timothy   a citizen of the   Creek   Nation.
A. N. F.
Name of Mother: Ella Timothy   a citizen of the   Creek   Nation.
HG
                      Postoffice   Brush Hill Ind. Ter.

Father
AFFIDAVIT OF MOTHER.   Child not present

UNITED STATES OF AMERICA, Indian Territory, }
    Western   DISTRICT.

I, John Timothy , on oath state that I am about 41 years of age and a citizen by blood , of the Creek Nation; that I am the lawful ~~wife~~ husband of Ella Timothy , who is a citizen, by blood of the Creek Nation; that a female child was born to ~~me~~ her on 27 day of July , 1903 , that said child has been named Eliza Timothy , and was living March 4, 1905.

John Timothy

Applications for Enrollment of Creek Newborn
Act of 1905   Volume XIV

Witnesses To Mark:
{

(Seal)
   Subscribed and sworn to before me this   14" day of   April   , 1905.

          Drennan C Skaggs
          Notary Public.

BIRTH AFFIDAVIT.

DEPARTMENT OF THE INTERIOR.
COMMISSION TO THE FIVE CIVILIZED TRIBES.

  IN RE APPLICATION FOR ENROLLMENT, as a citizen of the Creek Nation, of Eliza Timothy, born on the 27 day of July , 1903

Name of Father: John Timothy   a citizen of the   Creek   Nation.
Arbeka North Fork Town
Name of Mother: Ella Timothy   a citizen of the   Creek   Nation.
Hickory Ground Town
      Postoffice Brush Hill Ind. Ter.

       Father
    AFFIDAVIT OF ~~MOTHER~~. Child not present

UNITED STATES OF AMERICA, Indian Territory, ⎫
  Western   DISTRICT. ⎭

  I, John Timothy , on oath state that I am about 41 years of age and a citizen by blood , of the Creek Nation; that I am the lawful ~~wife~~ husband of Ella Timothy , who is a citizen, by blood of the Creek Nation; that a female child was born to ~~me~~ her on 27 day of July , 1903 , that said child has been named Eliza Timothy , and was living March 4, 1905.

        John Timothy
Witnesses To Mark:
{

   Subscribed and sworn to before me this   14 day of   April   , 1905.

          Drennan C Skaggs
          Notary Public.

Applications for Enrollment of Creek Newborn
Act of 1905 Volume XIV

NC 1103.

Muskogee, Indian Territory, October 24, 1905.

John Timothy,
    Brush Hill, Indian Territory.

Dear Sir:

    In the matter of the application for the enrollment of your minor child, Eliza Timothy, born July 27, 1903, as a citizen by blood of the Creek Nation, you are advised that this office requires the affidavit of the mother of said child and the physician or midwife who attended at the birth of said child and a blank for that purpose is inclosed herewith.

    In the event that no physician or midwife attended at the birth of said Eliza Timothy it will be necessary for you to furnish this office with the affidavits of two disinterested witnesses relative to the birth of said child. Said affidavits to set forth said child's name, the date of her birth, the names of her parents and whether or not she was living March 4, 1905.

                               Respectfully,

CTD 17   Commissioner.
Env.

REFER IN REPLY TO THE FOLLOWING:
N.C. 1103.

**DEPARTMENT OF THE INTERIOR,
COMMISSIONER TO THE FIVE CIVILIZED TRIBES.**

Muskogee, Indian Territory, February 8, 1907.

Commissioner to the Five Civilized Tribes,
    Muskogee, Indian Territory.

Sir:

    I have the honor to report in the matter of the application for the enrollment of Eliza Timothy, as a citizen by blood of the Creek Nation, that I am unable to secure further evidence in said case. The child is living. Copies of record are enclosed.

                                 Respectfully,

                                          Jesse McDermott

Applications for Enrollment of Creek Newborn
Act of 1905   Volume XIV

(The testimony below is handwritten.)

N.C. 1103   Eliza Timothy.

    I went to see John Timothy who is father of Eliza Timothy, but I fail to find any one at the place and I went to another place near there, but no one at that place. I think this man Timothy is out in camp somewhere. Timothy is snake. But I am satisfied this child she is entitled of allotment. The Town King told me that she is alright (Sam Logan)

                                    Bunnie McIntosh

                                                              JWH

N C 1103

                         Muskogee, Indian Territory, March 9, 1907.

Ella Timothy,
    % John Timothy,
        Brush Hill, Indian Territory.

Dear Madam :--

    You are hereby advised that on March 2, 1907, the Secretary of the Interior approved the enrollment of your minor child, Eliza Timothy, as a citizen by blood of the Creek Nation, and that the name of said child appears upon the roll of new born citizens by blood of the Creek Nation, enrolled under the Act of Congress approved March 3, 1905, as number 1281.

    This child is now entitled to allotment and application therefor should be made without delay at the Creek Land Office, Muskogee, Indian Territory.

                                Respectfully,

                                              Commissioner.

Applications for Enrollment of Creek Newborn
Act of 1905   Volume XIV

DEPARTMENT OF THE INTERIOR,
COMMISSIONER TO THE FIVE CIVILIZED TRIBES.
MUSKOGEE, INDIAN TERRITORY, JUNE 15, 1906.

In the matter of the application for the enrollment of Harpley Johnson as a citizen by blood of the Creek Nation.

APPEARANCES: E. C. Griesel, of the firm of Donovan & Griesel, Attorneys at Law, Muskogee, Indian Territory, appeared on behalf of the applicant.

LEWIS GRAY, being duly sworn testified as follows:

BY THE COMMISSIONER:

Q What is your name? A Lewis Gray.
Q How old are you? A Thirty-five years old.
Q What is your postoffice address? A Grayson, Indian Territory.
Q Are you a citizen of the Creek Nation? A Yes sir.
Q Do you know a child by the name of Harpley Johnson? A Yes sir, I know him.
Q What is the name of the child's father? A Gabriel Johnson. Well, I don't know the man but that is what they said.
Q Don't you know whether he was called anything besides Gabriel? A Yes, I know Gabriel Johnson.
Q What is the name of the child's mother? A Jennette Johnson.
Q Is Jennette living? A Yes sir.
Q Is the father of this child living? A Dead.
Q When did he die? A Well I never know. I know---
Q How long has he been dead? A I don't know how long.
Q Is this child Harpley Johnson living? A Yes sir, he is living.
Q Does Harpley live with his mother? A And this man, his mother's husband.
Q What is the name of this man you refer to? A Noah Foster.
Q Do you know whether or not the father of this child was ever called Keeper Johnson? A Yes sir.

MILLIE GRAY, being duly sworn testified as follows through Mrs. Lona Merrick, official Creek Interpreter:

BY THE COMMISSIONER:

Q What is your name? A Millie Gray.
Q How old are you? A I don't know.
Q Are you about 25 or 30? A I give my age as 29.
Q What is your postoffice? A Wildcat.
Q Are you a citizen by blood of the Creek Nation? A Yes sir.
Q Are you acquainted with a child by the name of Harpley Johnson? A Yes sir.
Q Is that child living? A Yes, it is living.
Q What is the name of the father of that child? A Keeper Johnson.

Applications for Enrollment of Creek Newborn
Act of 1905 Volume XIV

Q Is Keeper living? A He is dead.
Q When did he die? A I don't know.
Q How many years ago was it? A About three years I guess.
Q Did he die after this child was born? A Yes sir.
Q How long after? A I don't know.
Q Did he die six months after? A I guess so.
Q What is the name of this child's mother? A Jennette.
Q Jennette living? A Yes, she is living.
Q Has she remarried since the death of Keeper Johnson? A Yes, this is my husband.
Q What is the name of her husband? A Noah Foster.
Q Is this child living with his mother at the present time? A Yes.

NOAH FOSTER, being duly sworn testified as follows through Mrs. Lona Merrick, official Creek Interpreter:

BY THE COMMISSIONER:

Q Hos old are you? A Twenty-five years old.
Q What is your postoffice address? A Grayson.
Q Are you acquainted with a child called Harpley Johnson? A Yes
Q Is that child living? Yes.
Q What is the name of its father? A Keeper Johnson.
Q What is the name of its mother? A Jennette.
Q Is Keeper Johnson living? A No he is dead.
Q When did he die? A I don't know when he died, been dead about three years.
Q Did he die in the summer or fall, or what season of the year? A Died in the fall.
Q Was it three years ago last fall? A Yes.
Q That would be the fall of 1902? A Wasn't it? A Somewhere about that time.
Q Who is this child living with now? A Lives with me.
Q What is the name of your wife? A Jennette.
Q She was formerly the wife of Keeper Johnson, was she? A Yes.

S. T. Wright, being duly sworn, states that as stenographer to the Commissioner to the Five Civilized Tribes, he reported the above entitled cause on June 15, 1906, and that the same is a true and correct transcript of his stenographic notes thereof.

S.T. Wright

Subscribed and sworn to before me this 16th day of June, 1906.

Edward Merrick
NOTARY PUBLIC.

Applications for Enrollment of Creek Newborn
Act of 1905 Volume XIV

BIRTH AFFIDAVIT.

DEPARTMENT OF THE INTERIOR.
COMMISSION TO THE FIVE CIVILIZED TRIBES.

IN RE APPLICATION FOR ENROLLMENT, as a citizen of the Creek Nation, of Harpley Johnson, born on the 6 day of Mar, 1902

Name of Father: Keeper Johnson (Dead)   a citizen of the Creek   Nation.
Name of Mother: Jeanetta "   a citizen of the Creek   Nation.
Artussee Town
                           Postoffice   Edna IT

AFFIDAVIT OF MOTHER.
(Child present)

UNITED STATES OF AMERICA, Indian Territory,
    Western   DISTRICT.

I, Jeannetta Johnson, on oath state that I am 40 years of age and a citizen by blood, of the Creek Nation; that I am the lawful wife of Keeper Johnson, who is a citizen, by blood of the Creek Nation; that a male child was born to me on 6" day of Mch, 1902, that said child has been named Harpley Johnson, and was living March 4, 1905.

                                             her
                                   Jeannetta x Johnson
Witnesses To Mark: mark
   { EC Griesel
     Jesse McDermott

    Subscribed and sworn to before me this 12" day of April, 1905.
(Seal)
                                J. McDermott
                                    Notary Public.

               No one present
~~AFFIDAVIT OF ATTENDING PHYSICIAN OR MID-WIFE.~~

BIRTH AFFIDAVIT.

DEPARTMENT OF THE INTERIOR.
COMMISSION TO THE FIVE CIVILIZED TRIBES.

IN RE APPLICATION FOR ENROLLMENT, as a citizen of the Creek Nation, of Harpley Johnson, born on the 6th day of March, 1902

Name of Father: Keeper Johnson   a citizen of the Creek   Nation.
Name of Mother: Jennetta Johnson   a citizen of the Creek   Nation.

Applications for Enrollment of Creek Newborn
Act of 1905   Volume XIV

Postoffice   Edna

The child is present.

AFFIDAVIT OF MOTHER.

UNITED STATES OF AMERICA, Indian Territory,
Western Dist.   DISTRICT.

I, Jennetta Johnson, on oath state that I am Fourty[sic] years of age and a citizen by ~~Birth~~ Blood, of the Creek Nation; that I am the lawful wife of Keeper Johnson, who is a citizen, by blood of the Creek Nation; that a male child was born to me on Sixth day of March, 1902, that said child has been named Harpley Johnson, and is now living.

                    her
Jennetta x Johnson
                    mark

Witnesses To Mark:
{ J O Edwards
  J West

Subscribed and sworn to before me this 7th day of February, 1907.

Benjamin F. *(Illegible)*
Notary Public.

AFFIDAVIT OF ATTENDING PHYSICIAN OR MID-WIFE.

UNITED STATES OF AMERICA, Indian Territory,
Western   DISTRICT.

I, Bettie Miller, a mid-wife, on oath state that I attended on Mrs. Jennetta Johnson, wife of Keeper Johnson on the Sixth day of March, 1902; that there was born to her on said date a male child; that said child is now living and is said to have been named Harpley Johnson

                    her
Bettie x Miller
                    mark

Witnesses To Mark:
{ J O Edwards
  J West

Subscribed and sworn to before me this 7th day of February, 1907.

Benjamin F. *(Illegible)*
Notary Public.

Applications for Enrollment of Creek Newborn
Act of 1905   Volume XIV

NC-1104.

Muskogee, Indian Territory, October 24, 1905.

Jennetta Johnson,
    Edna, Indian Territory.

Dear Madam:

    In the matter of the application for the enrollment of your minor child, Harpley Johnson, born March 6, 1902, as a citizen by blood of the Creek Nation, this office requires the affidavits of two disinterested persons relative to the birth of said child. Said affidavits to set forth said child's name, the date of his birth, the names of his parents and whether or not he was living March 4, 1905.

                        Respectfully,

                                        Commissioner.

N.C. 1104

Muskogee, Indian Territory, March 1, 1907.

Jeannetta Johnson,
    Keeper Johnson,
        Edna, Indian Territory.

Dear Madam:

    You are hereby advised that on February 15, 1907, the Secretary of the Interior approved the enrollment of your minor child, Harpley Johnson, as a citizen by blood of the Creek Nation and that the name of said child appears upon the roll of new born citizens by blood of said nation, enrolled under the Act of Congress approved March 3, 1905, as No. 1216.

    This child is now entitled to allotment and application therefor should be made without delay at the Creek Land Office, Muskogee, Indian Territory.

                        Respectfully,

                                        Commissioner.

Applications for Enrollment of Creek Newborn
Act of 1905   Volume XIV

NC-1105

Muskogee, Indian Territory, November 6, 1905.

Susan Wisener,
   Okmulgee, Indian Territory.

Dear Madam:

In the matter of the application for the enrollment of your minor child, born July 27, 1903, as a citizen by blood of the Creek Nation, it appears from the affidavit of Ben J. Wisener, the father of said child, and of Sallie Foster, the midwife in attendance at her birth, that her name is Minnie Wisener. It appears from your affidavit in said case that the name of said child is Minnie Foster. Since you state that you are the lawful wife of Ben J. Wisener and that said child was born to you and him in lawful wedlock, it necessarily follows that the name of said child is Minnie Wisener and not Minnie Foster.

There is herewith enclosed a form of birth affidavit which you are requested to execute giving the correct name of said child, and return same to this Office in the enclosed envelope.

Respectfully,

Commissioner.

1 BA

BIRTH AFFIDAVIT.

DEPARTMENT OF THE INTERIOR.
COMMISSION TO THE FIVE CIVILIZED TRIBES.

IN RE APPLICATION FOR ENROLLMENT, as a citizen of the Creek Nation, of Bessie Wisener, born on the 10 day of Feb , 1902

Name of Father: Ben J. Wisener   a citizen of the   Creek   Nation.
(Cussehta)
Name of Mother: Susan Wisener (nee Canard)   a citizen of the   "   Nation.
(Little Eufaula)
                             Postoffice   Okmulgee

AFFIDAVIT OF ~~MOTHER~~. Father

UNITED STATES OF AMERICA, Indian Territory, ⎱
      Western   DISTRICT.   ⎰

I,   Ben J. Wisener , on oath state that I am 28 years of age and a citizen by blood , of the Creek Nation; that I am the lawful ~~wife~~ Husband of Susan Wisener , who is a citizen, by blood of the Creek Nation; that a female   child was born to me

Applications for Enrollment of Creek Newborn
Act of 1905   Volume XIV

on 10 day of Feb , 1902 , that said child has been named Bessie Wisener , and was living March 4, 1905.

                                      Ben J Wisener

Witnesses To Mark:
{

    Subscribed and sworn to before me this   12 day of   April   , 1905.

                                  Edw C Griesel
                                        Notary Public.

AFFIDAVIT OF ATTENDING PHYSICIAN OR MID-WIFE.

UNITED STATES OF AMERICA, Indian Territory, }
    Western   DISTRICT.

    I,   Sallie Foster , a Mid wife , on oath state that I attended on Mrs. Susan Wisener , wife of Ben J. Wisener on the 10 day of Feb , 1902 ; that there was born to her on said date a female child; that said child was living March 4, 1905, and is said to have been named Bessie Wisener

                                  Her
                              Sallie x Foster
Witnesses To Mark: mark
  { Jesse McDermott
    EC Griesel

    Subscribed and sworn to before me this   12 day of   April   , 1905.

                                  Edw C Griesel
                                        Notary Public.

BIRTH AFFIDAVIT.

                            DEPARTMENT OF THE INTERIOR.
COMMISSION TO THE FIVE CIVILIZED TRIBES.

    IN RE APPLICATION FOR ENROLLMENT, as a citizen of the Creek Nation, of Bessie Wisener, born on the 10 day of Feb , 1902

Name of Father: B. J. Wisener   a citizen of the   Creek   Nation.
Name of Mother: Susan Wisener   a citizen of the   Creek   Nation.

                        Postoffice   Okmulgee I.T.

Applications for Enrollment of Creek Newborn
Act of 1905   Volume XIV

AFFIDAVIT OF MOTHER.

UNITED STATES OF AMERICA, Indian Territory, }
 Western   DISTRICT.

    I, Susan Wisener, on oath state that I am 28 years of age and a citizen by Blood, of the Creek Nation; that I am the lawful wife of B.J. Wisener, who is a citizen, by Blood of the Creek Nation; that a female child was born to me on 10th day of Feby, 1902, that said child has been named Bessie Wisener, and was living March 4, 1905.

                                 Susan Wisener

Witnesses To Mark:
{

    Subscribed and sworn to before me this 28 day of April, 1905.

                                 Wesley M. Dyson
                                  Notary Public.

AFFIDAVIT OF ATTENDING PHYSICIAN OR MID-WIFE.

UNITED STATES OF AMERICA, Indian Territory, }
 Western   DISTRICT.

    I, Sallie Foster, a Mid-Wife, on oath state that I attended on Mrs. Susan Wisener, wife of B.J. Wisener on the 10th day of Feby, 1902; that there was born to her on said date a female child; that said child was living March 4, 1905, and is said to have been named Bessie Wisener

                                   Her
                               Sallie Foster x
                                   mark

Witnesses To Mark:
{ J C *(Illegible)*
  S.A. Morrison

    Subscribed and sworn to before me this 28 day of April, 1905.

                                 Wesley M. Dyson
                                  Notary Public.

Applications for Enrollment of Creek Newborn
Act of 1905   Volume XIV

BIRTH AFFIDAVIT.

DEPARTMENT OF THE INTERIOR.
COMMISSION TO THE FIVE CIVILIZED TRIBES.

IN RE APPLICATION FOR ENROLLMENT, as a citizen of the Creek Nation, of Minnie Wisener, born on the 27 day of July, 1903

Name of Father: Ben J. Wisener   a citizen of the   Creek   Nation.
(Cussehta)
Name of Mother: Susan Wisener (nee Canard) a citizen of the " Nation.
(Little Eufaula)
                    Postoffice   Okmulgee

AFFIDAVIT OF ~~MOTHER~~. Father

UNITED STATES OF AMERICA, Indian Territory,
    Western   DISTRICT.

I, Ben J. Wisener, on oath state that I am 28 years of age and a citizen by blood, of the Creek Nation; that I am the lawful ~~wife~~ Hus of Susan Wisener, who is a citizen, by blood of the Creek Nation; that a female child was born to me on 27 day of July, 1903, that said child has been named Minnie Wisener, and was living March 4, 1905.

                                  Ben J Wisener

Witnesses To Mark:
{

    Subscribed and sworn to before me this 12 day of April, 1905.

                                Edw C Griesel
                                      Notary Public.

AFFIDAVIT OF ATTENDING PHYSICIAN OR MID-WIFE.

UNITED STATES OF AMERICA, Indian Territory,
    Western   DISTRICT.

I, Sallie Foster, a Mid Wife, on oath state that I attended on Mrs. Susan Wisener, wife of Ben J. Wisener on the 27 day of July, 1903; that there was born to her on said date a female child; that said child was living March 4, 1905, and is said to have been named Minnie Wisener

                                Her
                            Sallie x Foster
Witnesses To Mark: mark
   { Jesse McDermott
    EC Griesel

Applications for Enrollment of Creek Newborn
Act of 1905   Volume XIV

Subscribed and sworn to before me this   12 day of   April   , 1905.

Edw C Griesel
Notary Public.

BIRTH AFFIDAVIT.

DEPARTMENT OF THE INTERIOR.
COMMISSION TO THE FIVE CIVILIZED TRIBES.

IN RE APPLICATION FOR ENROLLMENT, as a citizen of the Creek Nation, of Minnie Wisener, born on the 27 day of July , 1903

Name of Father: B. J. Wisener   a citizen of the   Creek   Nation.
Name of Mother: Susan Wisener   a citizen of the   Creek   Nation.

Postoffice   Okmulgee I.T.

AFFIDAVIT OF MOTHER.

UNITED STATES OF AMERICA, Indian Territory,
Western   DISTRICT.

I,   Susan Wisener , on oath state that I am   28   years of age and a citizen by Blood , of the Creek Nation; that I am the lawful wife of   B.J. Wisener , who is a citizen, by Blood of the Creek Nation; that a female   child was born to me on 27 day of July , 1903 , that said child has been named Minnie Wisener , and was living March 4, 1905.

Susan Wisener

Witnesses To Mark:
{

Subscribed and sworn to before me this 28 day of   April   , 1905.

Wesley M. Dyson
Notary Public.

AFFIDAVIT OF ATTENDING PHYSICIAN OR MID-WIFE.

UNITED STATES OF AMERICA, Indian Territory,
Western   DISTRICT.

I,   Sallie Foster , a Mid-Wife , on oath state that I attended on Mrs. Susan Wisener , wife of B.J. Wisener on the   27   day of July , 1903 ; that there was born to

Applications for Enrollment of Creek Newborn
Act of 1905 Volume XIV

her on said date a female child; that said child was living March 4, 1905, and is said to have been named Minnie Wisener

                                            Her
                                Sallie Foster x
Witnesses To Mark: mark
  { J C *(Illegible)*
    S.A. Morrison

Subscribed and sworn to before me this 28 day of April , 1905.

                                    Wesley M. Dyson
                                    Notary Public.

BIRTH AFFIDAVIT.

DEPARTMENT OF THE INTERIOR.
COMMISSION TO THE FIVE CIVILIZED TRIBES.

IN RE APPLICATION FOR ENROLLMENT, as a citizen of the Creek Nation, of Minnie Wisener, born on the 27th day of July , 1903

Name of Father: Ben J. Wisener	a citizen of the Creek	Nation.
Name of Mother: Susan Wisener	a citizen of the Creek	Nation.

                            Postoffice   Okmulgee Ind. Ter.

AFFIDAVIT OF MOTHER.

UNITED STATES OF AMERICA, Indian Territory,
     Western   DISTRICT.

    I, Susan Wisener , on oath state that I am 28 years of age and a citizen by blood , of the Creek Nation; that I am the lawful wife of Ben J. Wisener , who is a citizen, by blood of the Creek Nation; that a female child was born to me on 27th day of July , 1903 , that said child has been named Minnie Wisener , and is now living.

                                    Susan Wisener
Witnesses To Mark:
  {

Subscribed and sworn to before me this 12th day of December , 1905.

                                    M.F. Graham
My Commission Ex Oct 9-1907.   Notary Public.

Applications for Enrollment of Creek Newborn
Act of 1905   Volume XIV

AFFIDAVIT OF ATTENDING PHYSICIAN OR MID-WIFE.

UNITED STATES OF AMERICA, Indian Territory,
Western   DISTRICT.

I,   Sallie Foster , a   mid wife , on oath state that I attended on Mrs. Susan Wisener , wife of Ben J. Wisener on the 27th day of   July , 1903 ; that there was born to her on said date a female child; that said child is now living and is said to have been named Minnie Wisener

                                                        Her
                                         Sallie Foster x

Witnesses To Mark: mark

   { M.F. Graham
     P.K. Morton

Subscribed and sworn to before me this 12th day of   December   , 1905.

                                         M.F. Graham
My Commission Ex Oct 9-1907.   Notary Public.

NC-1106

                                      Muskogee, Indian Territory, September 7, 1905.

Jemima Colbert,
    Care of Daniel Colbert,
        Senora, Indian Territory.

Dear Madam:

Receipt is acknowledged of the joint affidavit of Liza Harjo and Kizzie Scott, in the matter of the birth of your minor child, William Colbert.

In order to identify you and the father of said child, Daniel Colbert, as citizens of the Creek Nation, you are requested to furnish this Office the names of your respective parents, the Creek Indian Towns to which each of you belongs, and, if possible, your respective roll numbers as same appear on your deeds to land in the Creek Nation.

Applications for Enrollment of Creek Newborn
Act of 1905   Volume XIV

This matter should receive your prompt attention.

                  Respectfully,

                                  Acting Commissioner.

United States of America,
    Western District,
Indian Territory.

AFFIDAVIT OF WITNESSES.

We, Liza Harjo and Kizzie Scott, on oath state that we are citizens by blood of the Creek Nation; that we are personally acquainted with Jemima Colbert, who is a citizen of the Creek Nation and know that she is the lawful wife of Daniel Colbert, who is also a citizen of the Creek Nation; that there was born to her on the 15th day of September 1903 a male child; that said child is said to have been named William Colbert and is now living.

                    J.W. Fowler   Her mark
Witness to mark   Liza x Harjo
                    Senora Librowski   Her
Witness to Mark   *(Name Illegible)*   Kizzie x Scott
                    Daniel Colbert   mark

Subscribed and sworn to before me this
4th   day of September   1905.   J.W. Fowler
                                                               Notary Public.
My Commission Expires July 13th 1908.

BIRTH AFFIDAVIT.
DEPARTMENT OF THE INTERIOR.
COMMISSION TO THE FIVE CIVILIZED TRIBES.

IN RE APPLICATION FOR ENROLLMENT, as a citizen of the Creek Nation, of   William Colbert , born on the   15   day of   Sept   , 1903

Name of Father: Daniel Colbert   a citizen of the   Creek   Nation.
Hickory Ground
Name of Mother: Jemima Colbert (nee Taylor)   a citizen of the   Creek   Nation.
Hickory Ground
                                Postoffice   Senora I.T.

Applications for Enrollment of Creek Newborn
Act of 1905   Volume XIV

AFFIDAVIT OF MOTHER.   Child present

UNITED STATES OF AMERICA, Indian Territory,
Western   DISTRICT.

I, Jemima Colbert , on oath state that I am 25 years of age and a citizen by blood , of the Creek Nation; that I am the lawful wife of Daniel Colbert , who is a citizen, by blood of the Creek Nation; that a male child was born to me on 15" day of Sept. , 1903 , that said child has been named William Colbert , and was living March 4, 1905.

                                                        her
                                      Jemima x Colbert
Witnesses To Mark: mark
   { EC Griesel
     Jesse McDermott

Subscribed and sworn to before me this 12" day of April , 1905.

                                   J McDermott
                                   Notary Public.

(No   one   present)
~~AFFIDAVIT OF ATTENDING PHYSICIAN OR MID-WIFE~~.

NC-1107
DEPARTMENT OF THE INTERIOR,
COMMISSIONER TO THE FIVE CIVILIZED TRIBES.

Muskogee, Indian Territory, December 29, 1905.

In the matter of the application for the enrollment of Sam Bighead as a citizen of the Creek Nation.

Salina Bighead, being sworn, testified as follows (through Jesse McDermott, Official Interpreter):

Q What is your name? A Salina Bighead.
Q What is the name of your father? A His name Pulsuma; he's dead.

Applications for Enrollment of Creek Newborn
Act of 1905   Volume XIV

Q What is your mother's name? A My mother died when I was quite small, but I have been told her name was Nagee.
Q How old are you? A I don't know; I was told I was 20 about two years ago.
Q What is your postoffice address? A Beggs.

The witness is identified as Salina Bighead, opposite Creek Indian Toll No. 3372.

Q What is the name of this boy in your lap, here? A Sam.
Q How old is Sam? A He is going on three years old.
Q Will he be three next February 4th? A Yes sir.
Q We have your affidavit, here, Salina, and on that affidavit appears a note that the father and midwife are both dead. Several letters have been written, and it does not appear that they have been received telling you that we want the affidavit of disinterested persons. We herewith hand you a form, and you are instructed to have that filled out and send back. A All right.
Q The father is dead, is he? A Yes sir.
Q He is enrolled here as Sampsey? A Yes sir.
(To the Interpreter): Tell her to send it in as soon as she can, and to see that it is properly signed and signatures by mark witnessed.

INDIAN TERRITORY, Western District.
    I, J. Y. Miller, a stenographer to the Commissioner to the Five Civilized Tribes, do hereby certify that the above and foregoing is a true and complete translation of my notes as same appear in my stenographic report of this case.

                                              JY Miller

Sworn to and subscribed before me
  this the 29th day of December,
1905.
                                          J McDermott
                                          Notary Public.

                                                                       HGH

REFER IN REPLY TO THE FOLLOWING:
NC-1107.

DEPARTMENT OF THE INTERIOR,
COMMISSIONER TO THE FIVE CIVILIZED TRIBES.

                                   Muskogee, Indian Territory, October 24, 1905.

Salina Bighead,
    Okmulgee, Indian Territory.

Dear Madam:

    In the matter of the application for the enrollment of your minor child, Sam Bighead, born February 4, 1903, as a citizen by blood of the Creek Nation, this office

Applications for Enrollment of Creek Newborn
Act of 1905 Volume XIV

requires the affidavits of two disinterested persons relative to his birth. Said affidavits to set forth said child's name, the date of his birth, the names of his parents and whether or not he was living March 4, 1905.

        Respectfully,

          Tams Bixby
          Commissioner.

N.C. 1107

        Muskogee, Indian Territory, December 20, 1905.

Salina Bighead,
  Okmulgee, Indian Territory.

Dear Madam:

  In the matter of the application for the enrollment of your minor child, Sam Bighead, born February 4, 1903, as a citizen by blood of the Creek Nation, this office desires the affidavits of two disinterested witnesses relative to his birth. Said affidavits must set forth said child's name, the names of his parents, the date of his birth and whether or not he was living on March 4, 1905.

  This matter should receive your prompt attention.

        Respectfully,

          Commissioner.

Dis.

              HGH

REFER IN REPLY TO THE FOLLOWING:

DEPARTMENT OF THE INTERIOR,
COMMISSIONER TO THE FIVE CIVILIZED TRIBES.

        Muskogee, Indian Territory, October 25, 1906.

Salina Bighead,
  c/o Sampson Bighead,
    Beggs, Indian Territory.

Dear Madam:

  You are hereby advised that the name of your minor child, Sam Bighead, is contained in the partial list of citizens by blood of the Creek Nation, approved by the Secretary of the Interior October 15, 1906, and that a selection of land in the Creek Nation may now be made for said child at the Creek Land Office in Muskogee, Indian Territory.

Applications for Enrollment of Creek Newborn
Act of 1905   Volume XIV

This matter should receive your prompt attention.

                        Respectfully,
                        Tams Bixby   Commissioner.

------------- District)
Indian Territory   )   SS

We, the undersigned, on oath state that we are personally acquainted with Salina Bighead   wife of   Sampson Bighead   ; and that on or about the 4 day of Feby , 190 3 , a male   child was born to them and has been named   Sam Bighead   ; and that said child was living March 4, 1905.

We further state that we have no interest in the above case.

                        his
                    Peter x Harjo
                       mark
                       her
                  Hepsey x Mitchell

Witness to mark: mark
W^m FA Gierkes
C.C. Kimble
W^m FA Gierkes
C.C. Kimble

Subscribed and sworn to before
me this 26th day of Jany 1906.   W^m FA Gierkes
                                  NOTARY PUBLIC.
                                My Commission Expires June 29, 1908

BIRTH AFFIDAVIT.
                        DEPARTMENT OF THE INTERIOR.
              COMMISSION TO THE FIVE CIVILIZED TRIBES.

IN RE APPLICATION FOR ENROLLMENT, as a citizen of the Creek Nation, of   Sam Bighead, born on the   4" day of Feb.   , 1903

Name of Father: Sampson Bighead (D)   a citizen of the   Creek   Nation.
Tuckabatchee Town
Name of Mother: Salina   "   a citizen of the   Creek   Nation.
Artussee Town
                      Postoffice   Okmulgee IT

Applications for Enrollment of Creek Newborn
Act of 1905   Volume XIV

AFFIDAVIT OF MOTHER.   (Child present)

UNITED STATES OF AMERICA, Indian Territory,
Western   DISTRICT.

    I, Salina Bighead , on oath state that I am 26 years of age and a citizen by blood , of the Creek Nation; that I am the lawful wife of Sam Bighead (D) , who is a citizen, by blood of the Creek Nation; that a male child was born to me on 4" day of Feb. , 1903 , that said child has been named Sam Bighead , and was living March 4, 1905.

                                                   her
                                      Salina x Bighead
Witnesses To Mark: mark
   { Edw C Griesel
     Jesse McDermott

    Subscribed and sworn to before me this 13" day of   April   , 1905.

(Seal)   J McDermott
                                   Notary Public.
                Father and Midwife Dead

BIRTH AFFIDAVIT.

DEPARTMENT OF THE INTERIOR.
COMMISSION TO THE FIVE CIVILIZED TRIBES.

    IN RE APPLICATION FOR ENROLLMENT, as a citizen of the Creek Nation, of   Laura M. Myers , born on the   27   day of   Jan , 1905

                                      non
Name of Father: Wm F Myers   a^citizen of the   Creek   Nation.
Name of Mother: Betsey   "   a citizen of the   Creek   Nation.

                          Postoffice   Okmulgee IT

Applications for Enrollment of Creek Newborn
Act of 1905   Volume XIV

AFFIDAVIT OF MOTHER.   (Child present)

UNITED STATES OF AMERICA, Indian Territory,
Western   DISTRICT.

I, Betsey Myers, on oath state that I am 30 years of age and a citizen by blood, of the Creek Nation; that I am the lawful wife of Wm F. Myers, who is not a citizen, by *(blank)* of the Creek Nation; that a female child was born to me on 27" day of Jan, 1905, that said child has been named Laura M Myers, and was living March 4, 1905.

                        her
                   Betsey x Myers
Witnesses To Mark: mark
  { EC Griesel
    Jesse McDermott

Subscribed and sworn to before me this 12" day of April, 1905.

(Seal)   J McDermott
                              Notary Public.

AFFIDAVIT OF ATTENDING PHYSICIAN OR MID-WIFE.

UNITED STATES OF AMERICA, Indian Territory,
Western   DISTRICT.

I, Della Ward, a midwife, on oath state that I attended on Mrs. Betsey Myers, wife of Wm F. Myers on the 27 day of Jan, 1905; that there was born to her on said date a female child; that said child was living March 4, 1905, and is said to have been named Laura M Myers

                        her
                   Della x Ward
Witnesses To Mark: mark
  { EC Griesel
    Jesse McDermott

Subscribed and sworn to before me this 12" day of April, 1905.

(Seal)   J McDermott
                              Notary Public.

Applications for Enrollment of Creek Newborn
Act of 1905 Volume XIV

BIRTH AFFIDAVIT.

DEPARTMENT OF THE INTERIOR.
COMMISSION TO THE FIVE CIVILIZED TRIBES.

IN RE APPLICATION FOR ENROLLMENT, as a citizen of the Creek Nation, of Oscar D. Myers, born on the 23 day of June, 1903

Name of Father: Wm F Myers	non a^citizen of the	Creek	Nation.
Name of Mother: Betsey "	a citizen of the	Creek	Nation.

Concharty Town

Postoffice   Okmulgee IT

AFFIDAVIT OF MOTHER.   (Child present)

UNITED STATES OF AMERICA, Indian Territory, }
   Western   DISTRICT.

I, Betsey Myers, on oath state that I am 30 years of age and a citizen by blood, of the Creek Nation; that I am the lawful wife of Wm F. Myers, who is not a citizen, by ~~Creek~~ of the Creek Nation; that a male child was born to me on 23" day of June, 1903, that said child has been named Oscar D Myers, and was living March 4, 1905.

                                                      her
                                         Betsey x Myers
Witnesses To Mark: mark
  { EC Griesel
    Jesse McDermott

Subscribed and sworn to before me this 12" day of April, 1905.

(Seal)   J McDermott
                                                      Notary Public.

AFFIDAVIT OF ATTENDING PHYSICIAN OR MID-WIFE.

UNITED STATES OF AMERICA, Indian Territory, }
   Western   DISTRICT.

I, L Alexander, a physician, on oath state that I attended on Mrs. Betsey Myers, wife of Wm F. Myers on the 23 day of June, 1903; that there was born to her on said date a male child; that said child was living March 4, 1905, and is said to have been named Oscar D Myers

                                        L Alexander MD
Witnesses To Mark:
  {

Applications for Enrollment of Creek Newborn
Act of 1905 Volume XIV

Subscribed and sworn to before me this 12" day of   April   , 1905.

(Seal)　　　　　　　　　　　　　J McDermott
　　　　　　　　　　　　　　　　Notary Public.

N.C. 1109.
DEPARTMENT OF THE INTERIOR,
COMMISSIONER TO THE FIVE CIVILIZED TRIBES.
Muskogee, Indian Territory, March 13, 1906.

In the matter of the application for the enrollment of Billie and Winford Pakoska as citizens by blood of the Creek Nation.

Lewis Pakoska, being duly sworn, testified as follows:

Q What is your name? A Lewis Pakoska.
Q What was the name of your father? A Joe Pakoska.
Q What is the name of your mother? A Lucy Pakoska.
Q How old are you? A About twenty three I guess.
Q What is your post office address? A Schulter.

Witness is identified as Lewis Pakoska on Creek Indian card No. 1792, opposite roll No. 5702.

Q You some times sign your name <u>Bland</u>? A Yes, some times.
Q Have you a brother named Roley Blend[sic]? A Yes.
Q Full brother? A Yes Witness states that the right name is Bland and that his full brother Roley can in here before the Commission before his mother came and got himself enrolled under the name of Roley Blend and that the witness himself often signs his name Bland, forgetting that his deed has the name Pakoska on it but he does not wish to have his deed changed from Pakoska to Blend or Bland but wants his name to stand Pakoska and he wants his children enrolled that way under which name the witness and his mother are enrolled.
Q So the correct name of these children then is Pakoska? A Yes
Q What is the name of the first one? A Billie Pakoska.
Q Is Billie living? A No, he died.
Q When did he died? A The child was born dead.

Applications for Enrollment of Creek Newborn
Act of 1905   Volume XIV

Q   We have an affidavit hereof the mother and midwife which states it was born December 26, 1902 and died that day is that correct? A Yes, sir
Q What is the name of the next child? A Winford Pakoska.
Q Is he living? A Yes, sir.
Q How old is Winford? A A year old now.
Q We have proof here that he was born May 22, 1904 is that correct? A Yes, sir.
Q What is the name of his mother? A Jennie.
Q Are you married to her? A Yes, sir.
Q Were you married before the children were born? A Yes
Q What was her name before you married her? A Jennie Foster.
Q Do you know the name of her father? [sic] Sam Foster.

Said Jennie is identified on Creek Indian care No. 497 as Jennie Foster, opposite roll No. 1622.

Q Jennie's name must be Jennie Pakoska now isn't it? A Yes I received a letter from the Commission stating that neither I or Jennie could be identified on the final roll and I had her make out another affidavit giving the name as Pakoska/.[sic]

I, Anna Garrigues, on oath state that the above and foregoing is a true and correct transcript of my stenographic notes as taken in said cause on said date.

Anna Garrigues

Subscribed and sworn to before me this 13
day of March 1906.

J McDermott
Notary Public.

BIRTH AFFIDAVIT.

DEPARTMENT OF THE INTERIOR.
COMMISSION TO THE FIVE CIVILIZED TRIBES.

IN RE APPLICATION FOR ENROLLMENT, as a citizen of the Creek Nation, of Billie Bland , born on the 26   day of Dec , 1902

Name of Father: Lewis Bland	a citizen of the Creek Nation.
Name of Mother: Jennie Blank	a citizen of the Creek Nation.

Postoffice   Schulter, I.T.

131

Applications for Enrollment of Creek Newborn
Act of 1905   Volume XIV

AFFIDAVIT OF MOTHER.

UNITED STATES OF AMERICA, Indian Territory,}
Western   DISTRICT.

I, Jennie Bland , on oath state that I am 21 years of age and a citizen by blood, of the Creek Nation; that I am the lawful wife of Lewis Bland , who is a citizen, by blood of the Creek Nation; that a male child was born to me on 26" day of Dec , 1902 , that said child has been named Billie Bland , and ~~was living March 4, 1905~~. died 26" Dec 1902

            her
            Jennie x Bland
Witnesses To Mark: mark
 { EC Griesel
  Jesse McDermott

Subscribed and sworn to before me this 12" day of April , 1905.

(Seal)   J McDermott
           Notary Public.

AFFIDAVIT OF ATTENDING PHYSICIAN OR MID-WIFE.

UNITED STATES OF AMERICA, Indian Territory,}
Western   DISTRICT.

I, Lucy Bland , a midwife , on oath state that I attended on Mrs. Jennie Bland , wife of Lewis Bland on the 26 day of Dec , 1902 ; that there was born to her on said date a male child; that said child ~~was living March 4, 1905~~, and is said to have been named Billie Bland   died 26 Dec 1902

            her
            Lucy x Bland
Witnesses To Mark: mark
 { EC Griesel
  Jesse McDermott

Subscribed and sworn to before me this 12" day of April , 1905.

(Seal)   J McDermott
           Notary Public.

Applications for Enrollment of Creek Newborn
Act of 1905   Volume XIV

NC 1109   JLD

DEPARTMENT OF THE INTERIOR,
COMMISSIONER TO THE FIVE CIVILIZED TRIBES.

In the matter of the application for the enrollment of Billie Blank, or Pakoska, deceased, as a citizen by blood of the Creek Nation.

STATEMENT AND ORDER.

The record in this case shows that on April 18, 1905, application was made in affidavit form supplemented by sworn testimony, given on March 13, 1906, for the enrollment of Billie Bland, or Pakoska, deceased, as a citizen by blood of the Creek Nation, under the provisions of the act of Congress approved March 3, 1905.

It appears from the evidence filed in this matter that said Billie Bland, or Pakoska, deceased, was born dead on December 26, 1902.

The Act of Congress approved March 3, 1905, (33 Stats., 1048) provides:

"That the Commission to the Five Civilized Tribes is authorized for sixty days after the date of the approval of this act to receive and consider applications for enrollment, of children, <u>born subsequent to May twenty-fifth, nineteen hundred and one, and prior to March fourth, nineteen hundred and five, and living on said latter date</u>, to citizens of the Creek tribe of Indians whose enrollment has been approved by the Secretary of the Interior prior to the approval of this act; and to enroll and make allotments to such children."

It is, therefore, ordered that the application for the enrollment of said Billie Bland, or Pakoska, deceased, as a Creek Freedman, be and the same is hereby dismissed.

Tams Bixby   Commissioner.

Muskogee, Indian Territory.
JAN 4- 1907

NC-1109.

Muskogee, Indian Territory, October 24, 1905.

Jennie Bland,
    c/o Lewis Bland,
        Schulter, Indian Territory.

Dear Madam:

In the matter of the application for the enrollment of your minor child, Winford Bland, born May 23, 1904, as a citizen by blood of the Creek Nation, this office is unable to identify either you or Lewis Bland, the father of said child, upon the final roll of citizens by blood of the Creek Nation.

Applications for Enrollment of Creek Newborn
Act of 1905 Volume XIV

You are therefore requested to state the names under which you and your husband, Lewis Bland, were finally enrolled, your ages, the Creek Indian towns to which you belong, the names of your parents and other members of your families and your final roll numbers as the same appear upon your allotment certificates and deeds.

In the event that your correct surname is other than Bland it will be necessary for you to execute a new affidavit, relative to the birth of said child, giving your correct surname, the correct surname of your husband and the correct surname of said child.

Please give this matter your immediate attention.

Respectfully,

Commissioner.

B C
Env.

BIRTH AFFIDAVIT.

DEPARTMENT OF THE INTERIOR.
COMMISSION TO THE FIVE CIVILIZED TRIBES.

IN RE APPLICATION FOR ENROLLMENT, as a citizen of the Creek Nation, of Winford Bland, born on the 23 day of May, 1904

Name of Father: Lewis Bland   a citizen of the   Creek   Nation.
Cussetah Town
Name of Mother: Jennie Bland   a citizen of the   Creek   Nation.
Cussetah Town

Postoffice   Schulter, I.T.

AFFIDAVIT OF MOTHER.

UNITED STATES OF AMERICA, Indian Territory,
    Western   DISTRICT.

I, Jennie Bland, on oath state that I am 21 years of age and a citizen by blood, of the Creek Nation; that I am the lawful wife of Lewis Bland, who is a citizen, by blood of the Creek Nation; that a male child was born to me on 23 day of May, 1904, that said child has been named Winford Bland, and was living March 4, 1905.

          her
        Jennie x Bland
          mark

Witnesses To Mark:
 { EC Griesel
 { Jesse McDermott

Applications for Enrollment of Creek Newborn
Act of 1905   Volume XIV

Subscribed and sworn to before me this 12 day of   April , 1905.

J McDermott
Notary Public.

AFFIDAVIT OF ATTENDING PHYSICIAN OR MID-WIFE.

UNITED STATES OF AMERICA, Indian Territory, }
  Western   DISTRICT.

    I, Lucy Bland , a midwife , on oath state that I attended on Mrs. Jennie Bland, wife of Lewis Bland on the 23 day of May , 1904 ; that there was born to her on said date a *(blank)* child; that said child was living March 4, 1905, and is said to have been named Winford Bland

                                          her
                                Lucy x Bland
Witnesses To Mark: mark
  { EC Griesel
    Jesse McDermott

Subscribed and sworn to before me this 12 day of   April , 1905.

J McDermott
Notary Public.

BIRTH AFFIDAVIT.

DEPARTMENT OF THE INTERIOR.
COMMISSION TO THE FIVE CIVILIZED TRIBES.

    IN RE APPLICATION FOR ENROLLMENT, as a citizen of the Creek Nation, of   Winford Pokoska[sic] , born on the 23rd day of May , 1904

Name of Father: Lewis Pokoska   a citizen of the   Creek   Nation.
Name of Mother: Jennie Pokoska   a citizen of the   Creek   Nation.

                    Postoffice   Schulter, I.T.

AFFIDAVIT OF MOTHER.

UNITED STATES OF AMERICA, Indian Territory, }
  Western   DISTRICT.

    I, Jennie Foster-Pokoska , on oath state that I am 22 years of age and a citizen by birth , of the Creek   Nation; that I am the lawful wife of Lewis Pokoska , who is a

Applications for Enrollment of Creek Newborn
Act of 1905   Volume XIV

citizen, by birth of the Creek Nation; that a male child was born to me on the 23rd day of May, 1904, that said child has been named Winford, and is now living.

Jennie Pokoska

Witnesses To Mark:
{ Mrs. Roena Sherwood
{ Sam Foster

Subscribed and sworn to before me this 30th day of October, 1905.

L.E. Sherwood
Notary Public.

My Commission expires Feb. 2nd 1907.

AFFIDAVIT OF ATTENDING PHYSICIAN OR MID-WIFE.

UNITED STATES OF AMERICA, Indian Territory, }
   (blank)   DISTRICT. }

I, Lucy Pokoska, a *(blank)*, on oath state that I attended on Mrs. Jennie Pokoska, wife of Lewis Pososka on the 23rd day of May, 1904; that there was born to her on said date a male child; that said child is now living, and is said to have been named Winford

her
Lucy x Pokoska
mark

Witnesses To Mark:
{ Mrs. Roena Sherwood
{ Sam Foster

Subscribed and sworn to before me this 30th day of October, 1905.

L.E. Sherwood
Notary Public.

My Commission expires Feb. 2nd 1907.

Applications for Enrollment of Creek Newborn
Act of 1905   Volume XIV

BIRTH AFFIDAVIT.

DEPARTMENT OF THE INTERIOR.
COMMISSION TO THE FIVE CIVILIZED TRIBES.

IN RE APPLICATION FOR ENROLLMENT, as a citizen of the   Creek or Muskogee Nation, of Dora Patton   , born on the   9th day of   Dec   , 1904

Name of Father: J. P. Patton   a citizen of the   U.S.   Nation.
Name of Mother: Emma Patton   a citizen of the   Creek   Nation.

Postoffice   Hitchita, I.T.

AFFIDAVIT OF MOTHER.

(Child present)

UNITED STATES OF AMERICA, Indian Territory, }
     Western   DISTRICT.

I, Emma Patton , on oath state that I am 24 years of age and a citizen by blood, of the Creek Nation; that I am the lawful wife of J. P. Patton , who is not a citizen, by *(blank)* of the Creek Nation; that a female child was born to me on 9" day of Dec , 1904 , that said child has been named Dora Patton , and was living March 4, 1905.

                                Emma Patton
Witnesses To Mark:
{

Subscribed and sworn to before me this 12" day of   April   , 1905.

(Seal)   J McDermott
                                   Notary Public.

AFFIDAVIT OF ATTENDING PHYSICIAN OR MID-WIFE.

UNITED STATES OF AMERICA, Indian Territory, }
     Western   DISTRICT.

I, A. W. Harris , a Physician , on oath state that I attended on Mrs. Emma Patton , wife of J. P. Patton on the 9th day of December, 1904 ; that there was born to her on said date a Female child; that said child was living March 4, 1905, and is said to have been named Dora Patton
                                A. W. Harris M.D.
Witnesses To Mark:
{

Applications for Enrollment of Creek Newborn
Act of 1905   Volume XIV

Subscribed and sworn to before me 11 day of April , 1905.

                                 Joseph C. Morton
                                         Notary Public.

My commission expires Feb. 29-1908

BIRTH AFFIDAVIT.

DEPARTMENT OF THE INTERIOR.
COMMISSION TO THE FIVE CIVILIZED TRIBES.

    IN RE APPLICATION FOR ENROLLMENT, as a citizen of the Creek Nation, of Lora Patton , born on the 24 day of Sept , 1902

	non		
Name of Father: J. P. Patton	a^citizen of the	*(blank*	Nation.
Name of Mother: Emma Patton	a citizen of the	Creek	Nation.

                       Postoffice   Hitchita, I.Ty.

AFFIDAVIT OF MOTHER.

                                    (Child present)

UNITED STATES OF AMERICA, Indian Territory, ⎫
    Western   DISTRICT. ⎭

    I, Emma Patton , on oath state that I am 24 years of age and a citizen by blood, of the Creek   Nation; that I am the lawful wife of J. P. Patton , who is not a citizen, ~~by~~ *(blank)* of the Creek Nation; that a female child was born to me on 24th day of Sept , 1902 , that said child has been named Lora Patton , and was living March 4, 1905.

                              Emma Patton

Witnesses To Mark:
{

    Subscribed and sworn to before me this 12" day of   April   , 1905.

(Seal)   J McDermott
                                        Notary Public.

AFFIDAVIT OF ATTENDING PHYSICIAN OR MID-WIFE.

UNITED STATES OF AMERICA, Indian Territory, ⎫
    Western   DISTRICT. ⎭

    I, Sintha Middleton , a midwife , on oath state that I attended on Mrs. Emma Patton , wife of J. P. Patton on the 24" day of Sept , 1902 ; that there was born to

Applications for Enrollment of Creek Newborn
Act of 1905   Volume XIV

her on said date a *(blank)* child; that said child was living March 4, 1905, and is said to have been named   Lora Patton

                                                              her
                                           Sintha x Middleton

Witnesses To Mark: mark
   { EC Griesel
     Jesse McDermott

      Subscribed and sworn to before me this 12" day of   April   , 1905.

(Seal)   J McDermott
                                                      Notary Public.

BIRTH AFFIDAVIT.
DEPARTMENT OF THE INTERIOR.
COMMISSION TO THE FIVE CIVILIZED TRIBES.

IN RE APPLICATION FOR ENROLLMENT, as a citizen of the   Creek or Muskogee   Nation, of   Leo Ora Patton   , born on the   10   day of   July   , 1901

Name of Father: J. P. Patton   a citizen of the   U.S.   Nation.
Name of Mother: Emma Patton   a citizen of the   Creek   Nation.

                                 Postoffice   Hitchita, I.T.

                       AFFIDAVIT OF MOTHER.
                                                   (Child present)
UNITED STATES OF AMERICA, Indian Territory, }
      Western   DISTRICT.

     I, Emma Patton , on oath state that I am   24   years of age and a citizen by blood, of the   Creek   Nation; that I am the lawful wife of   J. P. Patton , who is not a citizen, by *(blank)* of the   Creek   Nation; that a   female   child was born to me on   10 day of July , 1901 , that said child has been named   Leo Ora Patton , and was living March 4, 1905.

                                             Emma Patton
Witnesses To Mark:
   {

      Subscribed and sworn to before me this 12" day of   April   , 1905.

(Seal)   J McDermott
                                                  Notary Public.

Applications for Enrollment of Creek Newborn
Act of 1905   Volume XIV

AFFIDAVIT OF ATTENDING PHYSICIAN OR MID-WIFE.

UNITED STATES OF AMERICA, Indian Territory, }
   Western   DISTRICT.

   I, Katie Kell, a Midwife, on oath state that I attended on Mrs. Emma Patton, wife of J. P. Patton on the 10th day of July, 1901 ; that there was born to her on said date a Female child; that said child was living March 4, 1905, and is said to have been named   Leo Ora Patton

                                    her
                              Katie x Kell
Witnesses To Mark: mark
 { R. E. Parker
 { J.E. Castleberry

   Subscribed and sworn to before me 11 day of April, 1905.

                           Joseph C. Morton
                                 Notary Public.
My commission expires Feb. 29-1908

NC 1112

Muskogee, Indian Territory, July 7, 1905.

Newman Kelley,
   Okmulgee, Indian Territory.

Dear Sir:

   In the matter of the application for the enrollment of your minor child, Marshall Kelley, as a citizen by blood of the Creek Nation, you are advised that there are on file at this office, affidavits, in which the date of his birth is given as August 21, 1903 and August 21, 1904.

   To correct this discrepancy, you will be allowed reasonable time to appear before this office for the purpose of being examined under oath.

Applications for Enrollment of Creek Newborn
Act of 1905   Volume XIV

You are further advised that this office is unable to identify Susan Kelley, the mother of said child, on its roll of citizens of the Creek Nation and you are requested to state her maiden name, the names of her parents, the Creek Indian town to which she belongs, and, if possible, the number of her deed to land in the Creek Nation.

Respectfully,
Commissioner.

NC-1112.

Muskogee, Indian Territory, October 24, 1905.

Susan Kelley,
    c/o Newman Kelley,
        Okmulgee, Indian Territory.

Dear Madam:

In the matter of the application for the enrollment of your minor child, Marshall Kelley, as a citizen by blood of the Creek Nation, it appears that on April 12, 1905 Newman Kelley, the father of said child, and Lucy Anderson, the midwife in attendance at his birth, stated in their affidavits that the said Marshall Kelley was born August 21, 1904. On July 3, 1905 you executed an affidavit stating that the said Marshall Kelley was born August 21, 1903 and on July 3 and July 15, 1905 Lucy Anderson, the midwife, executed affidavits to the effect that Marshall Kelley was born August 21, 1903.

For the purpose of correcting the discrepancy as to the date of birth of your said child there is inclosed herewith a blank for proof of birth and you are requested to have executed and when so executed return it to this office in the inclosed envelope.

Respectfully,
Commissioner.

BC
Env.

(The Affidavit below is handwritten.)

United States of America ⎫
Western District   ⎬
Indian Territory   ⎭

Before me the undersigned authority on this day personally appeared Lucy Anderson, to me well known, who by me being duly sworn states on oath that she raised Susan Anderson, who alloted[sic] on SE 1/4 of Sec 22-15-13, and that the said Susan Anderson is now the wife of Newman Kelley, and that the said Susan Kelley is a member of leon charty[sic] Indian Town, and further states that deed for said land was delivered to said Susan Anderson on Dec 1-1904, said that her roll number is 3108, affiant further

Applications for Enrollment of Creek Newborn
Act of 1905 Volume XIV

states that she was with said Susan Kelley at the time of the birth of her child Marshall Kelley and that said child was born on August 21-1903

Witnesses
Newman Kelley
Ruth Anderson

~~Susan~~ Lucy x Anderson
her mark

Subscribed and sworn to before me on this 15th day of July 1905

Litsey L Sessions
Notary Public

My Commission expires May 31-1909-

Commission number on deed is 17624 & 17625.

BIRTH AFFIDAVIT.

DEPARTMENT OF THE INTERIOR.
COMMISSION TO THE FIVE CIVILIZED TRIBES.

IN RE APPLICATION FOR ENROLLMENT, as a citizen of the Creek Nation, of Marshall Kelley , born on the 21 day of Aug , 1904

Name of Father: Newman Kelley   a citizen of the   Creek   Nation.
Name of Mother: Susan Kelley   a citizen of the   Creek   Nation.

Postoffice   Okmulgee I.Ty.

AFFIDAVIT OF MOTHER.

UNITED STATES OF AMERICA, Indian Territory,
     Western   **DISTRICT.**

I, Newman Kelley , on oath state that I am 32 years of age and a citizen by blood , of the Creek Nation; that I am the lawful ~~wife~~ husband of Susan Kelley , who is a citizen, by blood of the Creek Nation; that a male child was born to me on 21 day of Aug , 1904 , that said child has been named Marshall Kelley , and was living March 4, 1905.

Newman Kelley

Witnesses To Mark:

Applications for Enrollment of Creek Newborn
Act of 1905   Volume XIV

Subscribed and sworn to before me this 12 day of   Apr , 1905.

(Seal)   J McDermott
                                        Notary Public.

AFFIDAVIT OF ATTENDING PHYSICIAN OR MID-WIFE.

UNITED STATES OF AMERICA, Indian Territory, ⎫
    Western   DISTRICT.   ⎬
                                          ⎭

   I, Lucy Anderson , a midwife , on oath state that I attended on Mrs. Susan Kelley , wife of Newman Kelley on the 21 day of Aug , 1904 ; that there was born to her on said date a *(blank)* child; that said child was living March 4, 1905, and is said to have been named Marshall Kelley   her
                                        Lucy x Anderson
Witnesses To Mark: mark
   ⎧ EC Griesel
   ⎨
   ⎩ Jesse McDermott

Subscribed and sworn to before me this 12 day of   Apr , 1905.

(Seal)   J McDermott
                                        Notary Public.

BIRTH AFFIDAVIT.
DEPARTMENT OF THE INTERIOR.
COMMISSION TO THE FIVE CIVILIZED TRIBES.

   IN RE APPLICATION FOR ENROLLMENT, as a citizen of the Creek Nation, of   Marshall Kelley , born on the 21st day of   August , 1903

Name of Father: Newman Kelley   a citizen of the   Creek   Nation.
Name of Mother: Susan Kelley   a citizen of the   Creek   Nation.

                        Postoffice   Okmulgee, Indian Territory

---

AFFIDAVIT OF MOTHER.

UNITED STATES OF AMERICA, Indian Territory, ⎫
    Western   DISTRICT.   ⎬
                                          ⎭

   I,   Susan Kelley , on oath state that I am 26   years of age and a citizen by blood , of the Creek   Nation; that I am the lawful wife of Newman Kelley , who is a citizen, by blood of the Creek   Nation; that a male   child was born to me on 21st day

Applications for Enrollment of Creek Newborn
Act of 1905 Volume XIV

of August, 1903, that said child has been named Marshall Kelley, and was living March 4, 1905.

Susan Kelley

Witnesses To Mark:
{ Luther Finch
A.A. Viersen

Subscribed and sworn to before me this 3rd day of July, 1905.
My Commission
expires May 31-1909.   Litsey L. Sessions
Notary Public.

AFFIDAVIT OF ATTENDING PHYSICIAN OR MID-WIFE.

UNITED STATES OF AMERICA, Indian Territory,
Western Judicial   DISTRICT.

I, Newman Kelley husband of Susan Kelley, on oath state that I attended on Mrs. Susan Kelley, wife of Newman Kelley on the 21st day of August, 1903; that there was born to her on said date a male child; that said child was living March 4, 1905, and is said to have been named Marshall Kelley

Newman Kelley

Witnesses To Mark:
{ Luther Finch
A.A. Viersen

Subscribed and sworn to before me this 3rd day of July, 1905.

My Commission expires May 31-1909.   Litsey L. Sessions
Notary Public.

BIRTH AFFIDAVIT.

DEPARTMENT OF THE INTERIOR.
COMMISSION TO THE FIVE CIVILIZED TRIBES.

IN RE APPLICATION FOR ENROLLMENT, as a citizen of the Creek Nation, of Marshall Kelley, born on the 21st day of August, 1903

Name of Father: Newman Kelley   a citizen of the Creek Nation.
Name of Mother: Susan Kelley   a citizen of the Creek Nation.

Postoffice   Okmulgee Ind. Ter.

Applications for Enrollment of Creek Newborn
Act of 1905   Volume XIV

AFFIDAVIT OF ~~MOTHER~~. Father

UNITED STATES OF AMERICA, Indian Territory, }
Western Judicial   DISTRICT.

I, Newman Kelley , on oath state that I am over 21 years of age and a citizen by blood , of the Creek Nation; that I am the father of Marshall Kelley , who is a citizen, by blood of the Creek Nation; that a male child was born to me on 21st. day of August , 1903 , that said child has been named Marshall Kelley , and is now living, and that Susan Kelley mother of said Marshall Kelley, and a citizen of the Creek Nation is dead.

Newman Kelley

Witnesses To Mark:
{ W C McAdoo
  W^m C Newman

Subscribed and sworn to before me this 14th. day of   November , 1905.

My Commission expires Apr. 23rd. 1907   W.C. McAdoo
                                                                             Notary Public.

AFFIDAVIT OF ATTENDING PHYSICIAN OR MID-WIFE.

UNITED STATES OF AMERICA, Indian Territory, }
Western Judicial   DISTRICT.

I, Lucy Anderson , a midwife , on oath state that I attended on Mrs. Susan Kelley , wife of Newman Kelley on the 21st. day of August , 1903 ; that there was born to her on said date a male child; that said child is now living and is said to have been named Marshall Kelley   her
                                                                                      Lucy x Anderson
Witnesses To Mark: mark
{ W C McAdoo
  W^m C Newman

Subscribed and sworn to before me this 14th. day of   November , 1905.

My Com. Exp. Apr. 23ed[sic]. 1907.   W.C. McAdoo
                                                                          Notary Public.

Applications for Enrollment of Creek Newborn
Act of 1905   Volume XIV

DEPARTMENT OF THE INTERIOR,
COMMISSIONER TO THE FIVE CIVILIZED TRIBES.
NEAR SENORA, I.T. April 21, 1905.

In the matter of the application for the enrollment of certain new born children of "Snake" parents.

Louie Lowe, being duly sworn, testified as follows, through Official Interpreter, Alex Posey.

Examination by the Commission:
Q What is your name? A Louie Lowe.
Q What is your age? A 25.
Q What is your post office? A Henryetta.
Q Are you a citizen of the Creek Nation? A I am a member of the Okchiye Town and Fish Pond Town.

Statement: Lijah Toney, of Hickory Ground and Losanna Lowe, of Kialigee Town, have a child named <u>Foley Toney</u>, living, it is two years two months and twenty five days old. Their Post Office if Henryetta.

Peter Sloan a Seminole, and Lodie of Weogufky Town, have a child near three years old, and the youngest about a year old; the older named <u>Lillie</u> and the <u>other's name</u> is not know[sic], but it is a boy, both are living. Their post office is Henryetta.

I think Cakochee of Thlewarthle and Lucinda, of Eufaula Canadian, have a child that hasn't been filed for yet, it is about a year old, don't know it's[sic] name, it is a <u>boy</u> and living. Their Post Office is Senora but he nevers[sic] goes after his mail, it is usually returned.

Willie Harjo of Weogufky, and Sukie Harjo of Kialigee have one child, was born in either January or February of this year, and is now living. It's[sic] mother is dead, I don't know it's[sic] name but it is under the custody of Joe and Cinda Yahdihka, whose post office is Dustin.

Letka Chupco and Jenely, Leetka is of Fish Pond or Greenleaf and Jenely of Kialigee Town; they have three children, one set of <u>twins</u>, both boys nearly three years old, and the youngest child is a girl born last October, the twins are named <u>John and Johnson,</u> and I don't know the name of the little girl; all three are living, post office, Senora. I think you have now all the children in this neighborhood except those that will be born tonight;

(The above testimony was partly given by Lewis Harjo, of Senora, about 35 years of age, who was duly sworn, through Official Interpreter).

Applications for Enrollment of Creek Newborn
Act of 1905   Volume XIV

Henry G. Hains, being duly sworn, on his oath, states that the above and foregoing is a true and correct transcript of his stenographic notes as taken in said cause on said date.   Henry G. Hains

Subscribed and sworn to before me this 11th day of May, 1905.

Drennan C Skaggs
Notary Public.

N.C. 1113   DEPARTMENT OF THE INTERIOR,
COMMISSIONER TO THE FIVE CIVILIZED TRIBES.
Muskogee, Indian Territory, December 21, 1905.

In the matter of the application for the enrollment of Nancy Tiger as a citizen by blood of the Creek Nation.

Lietka Tiger being duly sworn testified as follows through Jesse McDermott official interpreter.

Q What is your name? A Lietka Tiger.
Q What is your age? A About thirty one.
Q What is your post office address? A Senora.
Q Can you read and write? A No, sir.
Q What is the name of your father? A Heneha Cupko
Q What is the name of your mother? A Postka.

Witness is identified as Lietka Tiger on Creek Indian card opposite No. 4725.

Q Have you a child named Nancy Tiger? A Yes, sir.
Q Is that child living? A Yes, sir.
Q You have executed an affidavit about its birth? A Yes, sir
Q Is the date of birth--October 15, 1904--given in that affidavit correct? A Yes, sir.
Q What is the name of the mother of this child? A Jinalee Tiger.
Q She is your wife is she? A Yes, sir.
Q You have other children by her, enrolled? A Yes, sir.

Said mother is identified on Creek Indian card as Jinalee Tiger opposite No. 4726.

Witness is handed an affidavit partially filled out and requested to have the mother of the child execute the same and hi is also handed an affidavit of two disinterested witnesses to be filled out, in lieu of the midwife whose affidavit he says he is unable to obtain.

I, Anna Garrigues, on oath state that the above and foregoing is a true and correct transcript of my stenographic notes as taken in said cause on said date.

Anna Garrigues

Applications for Enrollment of Creek Newborn
Act of 1905   Volume XIV

Subscribed and sworn to before
me this 21 day of December 1905.

Alex Posey
Notary Public.

Indian Territory)
) SS
Western District)

We, the undersigned, on oath state that we are personally acquainted with Jinalee Tiger   wife of   Lietka Tiger   ; and that on or about the   15   day of October 1904 , a   female   child was born to them and has been named   Nancy Tiger; and that said child was living March 4, 1905.

We further state that we have no interest in the above case.

his
Lewis x Harjo
mark
her
Christy x Harjo
mark

Witnesses to mark:
Alex Posey
DC Skaggs

Subscribed and sworn to before me this 15 day of March 1906.

Alex Posey
Notary Public.

BIRTH AFFIDAVIT.

DEPARTMENT OF THE INTERIOR.
COMMISSION TO THE FIVE CIVILIZED TRIBES.

IN RE APPLICATION FOR ENROLLMENT, as a citizen of the Creek Nation, of Nancy Tiger , born on the 15   day of   October , 1904

Name of Father: Lietka Tiger   a citizen of the   Creek   Nation.
Name of Mother: Jinalee Tiger   a citizen of the   Creek   Nation.

Postoffice   Senora Ind. Ter.

Applications for Enrollment of Creek Newborn
Act of 1905 Volume XIV

AFFIDAVIT OF MOTHER.

UNITED STATES OF AMERICA, Indian Territory, }
Western   DISTRICT.

I, Jinalee Tiger , on oath state that I am about 35 years of age and a citizen by blood , of the Creek Nation; that I am the lawful wife of Lietka Tiger , who is a citizen, by blood of the Creek Nation; that a female child was born to me on 15 day of October , 1904 , that said child has been named Nancy Tiger , and was living March 4, 1905.

                                                                                       her
                                            Jinalee x Tiger

Witnesses To Mark: mark
{ Alex Posey
  DC Skaggs

Subscribed and sworn to before me this 15 day of March , 1906.

                                                                    Alex Posey
                                                                    Notary Public.

BIRTH AFFIDAVIT.

DEPARTMENT OF THE INTERIOR.
COMMISSION TO THE FIVE CIVILIZED TRIBES.

IN RE APPLICATION FOR ENROLLMENT, as a citizen of the Creek Nation, of Nancy Tiger , born on the 15 day of Oct. , 1904

Name of Father: Litka Tiger   a citizen of the   Creek   Nation.
Hickory Ground
Name of Mother: Janily "   (nee Fixico)   a citizen of the   Creek   Nation.
Hutchubbie Town
                                    Postoffice   Senora I Ty.

                                                  Father
AFFIDAVIT OF MOTHER.

UNITED STATES OF AMERICA, Indian Territory, }
Western   DISTRICT.

I, Litka Tiger, on oath state that I am 27 years of age and a citizen by blood , of the Creek Nation; that I am the lawful wife husband of Janily Tiger , who is a citizen, by blood of the Creek Nation; that a female child was born to me on 15 day of Oct , 1904 , that said child has been named Nancy Tiger , and was living March 4, 1905.

                                                                     his
                                                Litka x Tiger
                                                  mark

Applications for Enrollment of Creek Newborn
Act of 1905   Volume XIV

Witnesses To Mark:
   { EC Griesel
    Jesse McDermott

    Subscribed and sworn to before me this   12   day of   April   , 1905.

                                     J McDermott
                                        Notary Public.

NC 1064[sic]

                     Muskogee, Indian Territory, October 23, 1905.

Jinalee Tiger,
    Care Lietka Tiger,
        Senora, Indian Territory.

Dear Madam:

    In the matter of the application for the enrollment of your minor child, name unknown, said to have been born in the month of October 1904, as a citizen by blood of the Creek Nation, this office desires affidavit of the midwife or physician in attendance at the birth of said child and a blank for that purpose is herewith enclosed.

    In the event that there was no physician or midwife in attendance when said child was born, it will be necessary for you to furnish this office with the affidavits of two disinterested witnesses relative to its birth. Said affidavits must set forth said child's name, the date of its birth, the names of its parents and whether or not it was living on March 4, 1905.

    The names of yourself and husband are spelled, in this letter, as the same appear on the final roll of citizens by blood of the Creek Nation, and it is requested that you so spell them in the affidavits which you may submit in this case.

                        Respectfully,

                                        Commissioner.

BA
Env.

Applications for Enrollment of Creek Newborn
Act of 1905 Volume XIV

NC-1113.

Muskogee, Indian Territory, October 24, 1905.

Jinalee Tiger,
    c/o Litka Tiger,
        Senora, Indian Territory.

Dear Madam:

    In the matter of the application for the enrollment of your minor child, Nancy Tiger, born October 15, 1904, as a citizen by blood of the Creek Nation, you are advised that this office requires the affidavit of the physician or midwife who attended at her birth and a blank for that purpose is inclosed herewith.

    In having the same executed be careful to see that all blank spaces are properly filled, all names written in full and that the notary public, before whom the affidavit is sworn to, attaches his name and seal to the affidavit. In case the signature is by mark it must be attested by two disinterested witnesses.

    In the event that there was no physician or midwife in attendance when said child was born, it will be necessary for you to furnish this office with the affidavits of two disinterested witnesses relative to her birth. Said affidavits to set forth said child's name, the date of her birth, the names of her parents and whether or not she was living on March 4, 1905.

                      Respectfully,

                                Commissioner.

B C
Env.

Applications for Enrollment of Creek Newborn
Act of 1905   Volume XIV

NC 1114   B.A. 2049 & 2048B
DEPARTMENT OF THE INTERIOR,
COMMISSION TO THE FIVE CIVILIZED TRIBES.
Bristow, I.T. April 12, 1905.

In the matter of the application for the enrollment of Tishie M. and Rhoda Beams, as citizens by blood of the Creek Nation.

Charlie Beams, being duly sworn, by E.C. Griesel, a notary public, testified as follows:

By Commission:

Q What is your name? A Charles Beams.
Q How old are you? A About (33 Stat., 1048)
Q What is your post office address? A Henryetta
Q Do you wish to make application for the enrollment of Tishie M. and Rhoda Beams as citizens by blood of the Creek Nation? A Yes, sir
Q Who was the mother of these children? A Annie Beams
Q You are a citizen by blood of the Choctaw Nation are you? A Yes, sir
Q Your wife Annie is a citizen by blood of the Creek Nation? A Yes, sir.
Q When was Tishie born? A May 20, 1902
Q When was Rhoda born? A April 27, 1904
Q Both of these children are now living are they? A Yes, sir
Q If it should be found that your children, Tishie M. and Rhoda Beams are entitled to enrollment in both the Creek and Choctaw Nation[sic], in which nation do you elect to have them enrolled and receive their allotments of land? A In the Creek Nation.

E.C. Griesel, being dly[sic] sworn, on his oath, states that the above and foregoing is a true and correct transcript of his stenographic notes as taken in said cause on said date.

                                                    Edw C Griesel

Subscribed and sworn to before me this 27th day of July 1905
My Com
Ex July 25" 1907   J McDermott
                                                    Notary Public.

(The above testimony given again.)

Applications for Enrollment of Creek Newborn
Act of 1905 Volume XIV

Child was present when these
papers were executed   E E Schock N.P.

BIRTH AFFIDAVIT.

DEPARTMENT OF THE INTERIOR.
COMMISSION TO THE FIVE CIVILIZED TRIBES.

IN RE APPLICATION FOR ENROLLMENT, as a citizen of the Creek Nation, of Rhoda Beams , born on the 27 day of April , 1904

Name of Father: Charles Beams   a citizen of the   Choctaw   Nation.
Name of Mother: Annie Beams   a citizen of the   Creek   Nation.
   (Hutchechubbie)
                         Postoffice   Henryetta I.T.

AFFIDAVIT OF MOTHER.

UNITED STATES OF AMERICA, Indian Territory,
    Western Judicial   DISTRICT.

I, Annie Beams , on oath state that I am 30 years of age and a citizen by blood, of the Creek Nation; that I am the lawful wife of Charles Beams , who is a citizen, by blood of the Choctaw Nation; that a Female child was born to me on 27th day of April, 1904 , that said child has been named Rhoda Beams , and is now living.

                        her
                 Annie x Beams
Witnesses To Mark: mark
   M C Hickman
   Thomas Barnett

Subscribed and sworn to before me this 11th day of   April   , 1905.

                 E. E. Schock
                    Notary Public.
                 My Commission expires
                    June 18th 1908

AFFIDAVIT OF ATTENDING PHYSICIAN OR MID-WIFE.

UNITED STATES OF AMERICA, Indian Territory,
    Western Judicial   DISTRICT.

I, Mary Barnett , a midwife , on oath state that I attended on Mrs. Annie Beams , wife of Charles Beams on the 27th day of April , 1904 ; that there was born to

Applications for Enrollment of Creek Newborn
Act of 1905   Volume XIV

her on said date a Female child; that said child is now living and is said to have been named Rhoda Beams

Witnesses To Mark:
{ Seaborn Fisher
{ Rosie Fisher

Mary x Barnett
her   mark

Subscribed and sworn to before me this 11th day of   April   , 1905.

E. E. Schock
Notary Public.
My Commission expires
June 18th 1908

Child was present when these papers were executed   E E Schock N.P.
BIRTH AFFIDAVIT.

DEPARTMENT OF THE INTERIOR.
COMMISSION TO THE FIVE CIVILIZED TRIBES.

IN RE APPLICATION FOR ENROLLMENT, as a citizen of the Creek Nation, of   Tishie M. Beams , born on the 20th day of May , 1902

Name of Father: Charles Beams   a citizen of the   Choctaw   Nation.
Name of Mother: Annie Beams   a citizen of the   Creek   Nation.
  (Hutchechubbie)
                              Postoffice   Henryetta I.T.

AFFIDAVIT OF MOTHER.

UNITED STATES OF AMERICA, Indian Territory, }
  Western Judicial   **DISTRICT.** }

I, Annie Beams , on oath state that I am 30 years of age and a citizen by blood, of the Creek Nation; that I am the lawful wife of Charles Beams , who is a citizen, by blood of the Choctaw Nation; that a Female child was born to me on 20th day of May, 1902 , that said child has been named Tishie M. Beams , and is now living.

her
Annie x Beams
mark

Witnesses To Mark:
{ M C Hickman
{ Thomas Barnett

Applications for Enrollment of Creek Newborn
Act of 1905   Volume XIV

Subscribed and sworn to before me this 11th day of   April   , 1905.

         E. E. Schock
          Notary Public.
         My Commission expires
          June 18th 1908

AFFIDAVIT OF ATTENDING PHYSICIAN OR MID-WIFE.

UNITED STATES OF AMERICA, Indian Territory,
 Western Judicial DISTRICT.

  I, Mary Barnett , a midwife , on oath state that I attended on Mrs. Annie Beams , wife of Charles Beams on the 20th day of May , 1902 ; that there was born to her on said date a Female child; that said child is now living and is said to have been named Tishie M Beams

           her
         Mary x Barnett
Witnesses To Mark: mark
 { Rosie Fisher
   Seaborn Fisher

Subscribed and sworn to before me this 11th day of   April   , 1905.

         E. E. Schock
          Notary Public.
         My Commission expires
          June 18th 1908

N.C. 1114

United States of America,)
)
Western District,   )
)
Indian Territory.   )

  I, Annie Beams, on oath state that I am thirty years of age and a citizen by blood of the Creek Nation; that I am the lawful wife of Charles Beams, who is a citizen by blood of the Choctaw Nation; that I am the mother of Tishie M. Beams, born May 20, 1902, and Rhoda Beams, born April 27, 1904, and I hereby elect to have said children finally enrolled as citizens by blood of the Creek Nation and to take their allotments of lands and distribution of moneys as citizens of said nation.

           her
         Annie x Beams
          mark

Applications for Enrollment of Creek Newborn
Act of 1905   Volume XIV

Witnesses to mark:
M C Hickman
John Guire

Subscribed and sworn to before me this 24th day of October 1905.

E. E. Schock
Notary Public.
My Commission expires in
June 18th 1908

NC-1114.

Muskogee, Indian Territory, July 18, 1905.

Chief Clerk,
    Choctaw Enrollment Division,
        Muskogee, Indian Territory.

Dear Sir:

    April 19, 1905, application was made to the Commission to the Five Civilized Tribes for the enrollment of Fishie[sic] M. Beams, born May 20, 1902, and Rhoda Beams, born April 27, 1904, as citizens by blood of the Creek Nation. It is stated in said application that the father of said children is Charles Beams, a citizen of the Choctaw Nation, and that the mother is Annie Beams, a citizen of the Creek Nation.

    You are requested to inform the Creek Enrollment Division as to whether application has been made for the enrollment of said children as citizens of the Choctaw Nation, and if so, what disposition has been made of the same.

                      Respectfully,

                                  Commissioner.

Applications for Enrollment of Creek Newborn
Act of 1905   Volume XIV

REFER IN REPLY TO THE FOLLOWING:
7-4677
NC-1114

DEPARTMENT OF THE INTERIOR,
COMMISSIONER TO THE FIVE CIVILIZED TRIBES.

Muskogee, Indian Territory, July 26, 1905.

Clerk in Charge,
    Creek Enrollment Division.

Dear Sir:

    Receipt if hereby acknowledged of your letter of July 18 1905, requesting to be advised if application has been made for the enrollment as citizens of the Choctaw Nation of Fishie[sic] M. Beams and Rhoda Beams, children of Charles Beams a citizen of the Choctaw Nation and Annie Beams a citizen of the Creek Nation.

    In reply to your letter you are advised that application was made to the Commission to the Five Civilized Tribes for the enrollment as a citizen of the Choctaw Nation of Tissie M. Beams, daughter of Charles W. and Annie Beams, but it does not appear from the records of this office that application has been made for the enrollment of the child Rhoda Beams as a citizen by blood of the Choctaw Nation. It will be necessary, however, to secure the affidavits of both father and mother electing in which nation their children Fishie M. Beams and Rhoda Beams shall be enrolled and receive allotments of land.

    Respectfully,
        Tams Bixby   Commissioner.

NC 1114   Roll 895

Muskogee, Indian Territory, February 3, 1906.

Chief Clerk,
    Choctaw-Chickasaw Enrollment Division.

Dear Sir:

    Receipt is acknowledged of your letter of January 31, 1906, relative to the application for the enrollment of Tissie M. Beams, daughter of Charles Beams, a Choctaw Indian, and Annie Beams, a Creek Indian. In case an election has been made in the Creek Nation, you ask that a copy of same be sent for your records. In the event said child has been enrolled as a citizen of the Creek Nation, you ask to be furnished with her roll number and the date of approval by the Secretary of the Interior.

    You are advised that the name of Tishie M. Beams, daughter of the parents above mentioned, is contained in the partial roll of Creek new-borns by blood, opposite roll No. 895.

Applications for Enrollment of Creek Newborn
Act of 1905 Volume XIV

Copies of testimony and election affidavits are herewith enclosed.

Respectfully,

N.C. 1114   Acting Commissioner.

NC 1114

Muskogee, Indian Territory, November 13, 1905

Chief Clerk,
  Choctaw-Chickasaw Enrollment Division,
    General Office,

Dear Sir:

You are hereby advised that the names of Tishie M. and Rhoda Beams, children of Charles Beams, an alleged citizen by blood of the Creek Nation, are contained in schedule of minor citizens by blood of the Creek Nation, approved by the Secretary of the Interior, November 27, 1905 opposite Roll numbers 895 and 896,

Respectfully,

Commissioner.

BIRTH AFFIDAVIT.

DEPARTMENT OF THE INTERIOR.
COMMISSION TO THE FIVE CIVILIZED TRIBES.

IN RE APPLICATION FOR ENROLLMENT, as a citizen of the Creek Nation, of Thomas Carruth , born on the 20 day of Dec , 1902

Name of Father: Lewis Carruth (Dec'd)   a citizen of the   Creek   Nation.
Name of Mother: Dicey Tiger (nee Carruth) a citizen of the   Creek   Nation.

Postoffice   Okmulgee I.T.

Applications for Enrollment of Creek Newborn
Act of 1905 Volume XIV

AFFIDAVIT OF MOTHER.

UNITED STATES OF AMERICA, Indian Territory, }
    Western   DISTRICT.

     I, Dicey Tiger, on oath state that I am 25 years of age and a citizen by blood, of the Creek Nation; that I am the lawful wife of Albert Tiger, who is a citizen, by blood of the Creek Nation; that a male child was born to me on 20 day of Dec, 1902, that said child has been named Thomas Carruth, and ~~was living March 4, 1905~~. died July 13-1903

                                        Dicey Tiger

Witnesses To Mark:
{

     Subscribed and sworn to before me this 12" day of April, 1905.

(Seal)   J McDermott
                                          Notary Public.

AFFIDAVIT OF ATTENDING PHYSICIAN OR MID-WIFE.

UNITED STATES OF AMERICA, Indian Territory, }
    Western   DISTRICT.

     I, Sallie Soon, a midwife, on oath state that I attended on Mrs. Dicey Tiger, wife of Albert Tiger on the 20 day of Dec, 1902; that there was born to her on said date a male child; that said child was ~~living March 4, 1905, and is said to have been named~~ Thomas Carruth   died July 13- 1903

                                              her
                                        Sallie x Soon
Witnesses To Mark: mark
  { EC Griesel
    Jesse McDermott

     Subscribed and sworn to before me this 12 day of April, 1905.

(Seal)   J McDermott
                                          Notary Public.

Applications for Enrollment of Creek Newborn
Act of 1905   Volume XIV

NC 1115   JLD

DEPARTMENT OF THE INTERIOR,
COMMISSIONER TO THE FIVE CIVILIZED TRIBES.

In the matter of the application for the enrollment of Thomas Carruth, deceased, as a citizen by blood of the Creek Nation.

....
STATEMENT AND ORDER.

The record in this case shows that on April 19, 1905, application was made, in affidavit form, for the enrollment of Thomas Carruth, deceased, as a citizen by blood of the Creek Nation, under the provisions of the act of Congress approved March 3, 1905.

It appears from the affidavit filed in this matter that said Thomas Carruth, deceased, was born December 20, 1902, and died July 13, 1903.

The Act of Congress approved March 3, 1905, (33 Stats., 1048), provides:

"That the Commission to the Five Civilized Tribes is authorized for sixty days after the date of the approval of this act to receive and consider applications for enrollment, of children, <u>born subsequent to May twenty-fifth, nineteen hundred and one, and prior to March fourth, nineteen hundred and five, and living on said latter date</u>, to citizens of the Creek tribe of Indians whose enrollment has been approved by the Secretary of the Interior prior to the approval of this act; and to enroll and make allotments to such children."

It is, therefore, ordered that the application for the enrollment of said Thomas Carruth, deceased, as a citizen by blood of the Creek Nation be, and the same is, hereby dismissed.

Tams Bixby Commissioner.

Muskogee, Indian Territory.
JAN 4 – 1907

Applications for Enrollment of Creek Newborn
Act of 1905   Volume XIV

NC 1116.

DEPARTMENT OF THE INTERIOR,
COMMISSIONER TO THE FIVE CIVILIZED TRIBES.
MUSKOGEE, INDIAN TERRITORY.
JULY 7, 1906.

In the matter of the application for the enrollment of Jimmie and Lizzie Pinky, as citizens by blood of the Creek Nation.

Eliza Pinky, being duly sworn, testified as follows:

Q What is your name? A Eliza Pinky.
Q Weren't you known as Lilia sometimes? A They never got it right
Q What was the way you were enrolled, weren't you, Lilia? A Yes.
Q How old are you? A Over thirty, about thirty-one I guess.
Q What is your post office address? A Okmulgee.
Q What was your post office before Okmulgee? A Beggs.
Q Any other? A Red Fork.
Q Did you ever live at Tuskegee? A Yes sir.
Q Have you received your allotment in the Creek Nation? A Yes sir.
Q Have you your deeds with you? A No sir, I have them at home.
Q Did you ever look at them? A I can't read, I know they are deeds though.
Q What is the name of your father? A Hosey Castile.
Q He wasn't a citizen of any Nation? A He was a Mexican.
Q What is the name of your mother? A Lizzie.
Q What Creek Indian town does she belong to? [sic] Lochapoka.
Q That is your town to[sic], isn't it? A It ought to be on my mother's side.
Q What was the name of your first husband? A Charley McIntosh.
Q Is he dead? A Yes sir.
Q Did you ever have any children by him? A Three.
Q Are they enrolled? A Yes sir.
Q What are their names? A The oldest one is Katie, next is David and the other is Lee.
Q Was their father Charley McIntosh? A Yes sir.
Q Are these three children living? A Yes sir.
Q Living with you? A Yes sir.
Q That is all you had by Charley? A Yes sir.
Q What is the name of your next child? A Sammy Taylor.
Q Is he living? A Yes sir.
Q Where? A At home.
Q At Okmulgee? A Yes sir.
Q What is the name of his father? A Abram Taylor.
Q Is he living? A No sir.
Q When did he die? A 1901.
Q Did he die before McIntosh? A After.
Q We have proof that McIntosh died in September, 1902? A McIntosh was living with me then, he was married again and I was married again, I don't know how long he has been dead.

Applications for Enrollment of Creek Newborn
Act of 1905 Volume XIV

Q But you separated from McIntosh before you married Taylor and before his death?
A Yes sir.
Q Sammy living? A Yes sir.
Q What is the name of your next child? A Jimmy Pinky. He is dead
Q How old would he be if he was living? A He was over two years old, he was born October 5, 1903.
Q If he was living next October, he would be three? A Yes sir.
Q When did he die? A He lived to be seven months old. (Died May 1904)
Q What is the name of your next child? A Lizzie.
Q That is the little girl you have here in your arms? A Yes sir.
Q We have your affidavit and the affidavit of the midwife, and a memorandum, in which it is stated this little girl here Lizzie, was born March 4, 1905, which makes her a year old this last March, is that correct? A Yes sir.
Q What is the name of the father of these two children? A Willie Pinky.
Q These are the only two children you have had by him? A Yes sir.
Q Is he living? A No sir
Q Was he a citizen of the Creek Nation? A Yes sir.
Q What town did he belong to? A Chssehta[sic].
Q When did Willie die? A 30 day of March, 1905.
Q He died after your child, Lizzie was born? A Yes sir.
Q What was the name of his father? A Ahalok Harjo.
Q Was he ever called Pinky? A Yes sir.
Q What was his mother's name? A Sissie Taylor.

Witness is identified as Lilia Taylor, opposite Creek Indian Roll No. 3709. The father of said child here present is identified opposite Creek Indian Roll No. 3724 under the name of Willie Pinky.

Q Were you married to Willie Pinky? A Yes sir.
Q Have you your marriage license with you? A No sir.
Q Witness is advised she should furnish this office with a certified copy of that marriage license. You are not married now are you? A No sir.

Lona Merrick, being duly sworn, states that the above and foregoing is a true and correct transcript of her stenographic notes as taken in said cause on said date.

Lona Merrick

Subscribed and sworn to before me this 10th day of July, 1906.

HG Hains
Notary Public.

Applications for Enrollment of Creek Newborn
Act of 1905 Volume XIV

NC 1116　　　　　　　　　　　　　　　　　　　　　　　　　JLD

DEPARTMENT OF THE INTERIOR,
COMMISSIONER TO THE FIVE CIVILIZED TRIBES.

In the matter of the application for the enrollment of Jimmie Pinky, deceased, as a citizen by blood of the Creek Nation.

STATEMENT AND ORDER.

The record in this case shows that on April 19, 1905, application was made, in affidavit form, supplemented by sworn testimony, taken on July 7, 1906, for the enrollment of Jimmie Pinky, deceased, as a citizen by blood of the Creek Nation, under the provisions of the Act of Congress approved March 3, 1905.

It appears from the evidence filed in this matter that said Jimmie Pinky, deceased, was born October 5, 1903, and died May 23, 1904.

The Act of Congress approved March 3, 1905, (33 Stats., 1048), provides:

"That the Commission to the Five Civilized Tribes is authorized for sixty days after the date of the approval of this act to receive and consider applications for enrollment, of children, <u>born subsequent to May twenty-fifth, nineteen hundred and one, and prior to March fourth, nineteen hundred and five, and living on said latter date</u>, to citizens of the Creek tribe of Indians whose enrollment has been approved by the Secretary of the Interior prior to the approval of this act; and to enroll and make allotments to such children."

It is, therefore, ordered that the application for the enrollment of Jimmie Pinky, deceased, as a citizen by blood of the Creek Nation be, and the same is, hereby dismissed.

　　　　　　　　　　　　　　　　　　　Tams Bixby Commissioner.

Muskogee, Indian Territory.
JAN 4 – 1907

BIRTH AFFIDAVIT.

DEPARTMENT OF THE INTERIOR.
COMMISSION TO THE FIVE CIVILIZED TRIBES.

IN RE APPLICATION FOR ENROLLMENT, as a citizen of the Creek Nation, of Jimmie Pinkey , born on the　5　day of　Oct　, 1903

Name of Father: Willie Pinkey　　　　　a citizen of the　Creek　Nation.
Name of Mother: Lillia[sic] Pinkey　　　a citizen of the　Creek　Nation.

　　　　　　　　　　　　Postoffice　　Okmulgee

Applications for Enrollment of Creek Newborn
Act of 1905   Volume XIV

AFFIDAVIT OF MOTHER.

UNITED STATES OF AMERICA, Indian Territory, ⎫
    Western   DISTRICT.   ⎬

    I, Lillia Pinkey , on oath state that I am 30 years of age and a citizen by blood, of the Creek   Nation; that I am the lawful wife of   Willie Pinkey , who is a citizen, by blood of the Creek   Nation; that a male   child was born to me on 5   day of Oct, 1903, that said child has been named   Jimmie Pinkey , and ~~was living March 4, 1905~~. died May 23-1904

                                                Lilia Pinkey

Witnesses To Mark:

    Subscribed and sworn to before me this 12 day of   April , 1905.

                                                Edw C Griesel
                                                  Notary Public.

N.C. 1117.

DEPARTMENT OF THE INTERIOR,
COMMISSIONER TO THE FIVE CIVILIZED TRIBES.
Muskogee, Indian Territory, February 26, 1906.

    In the matter of the application for the enrollment of Jimmie Seber as a citizen by blood of the Creek Nation.

    LIZZIE SEBER, being duly sworn, testified as follows through Alex Posey official interpreter.

Q What is your name? A Lizzie Seber.
Q Were you ever known by any other name? [sic] Lizzie Cloud was my former name.
Q Lizzie Cloud was your maiden name? A Yes, sir.
Q How old are you? A Twenty seven.
Q What is your post office address? A Bristow.
Q What was the name of your father? A Laslie Cloud. My mother, Cinda Cloud.
Q Of what town are you a member? A Tuskega.
Q What is the name of your husband? A Sampson Seber.

Applications for Enrollment of Creek Newborn
Act of 1905 Volume XIV

Q Are you and your husband living together? A He is now in the penitentiary.
Q Did you make application for the enrollment of a child, Jimmie Seber? A Yes, sir.
Q Is Jimmie Seber living? A Yes, sir.

Lizzie Seber is identified as Lizzie Cloud on Creek Indian card field No. 4052 opposite roll No. 9288.

The birth affidavit now on file in this case for the application of said Jimmie Seber is insufficient to establish the matter of the birth of this child. You are requested to have the blank affidavits now handed you prepared properly and executed before a notary public and return to this office at an early date.

I, Anna Garrigues, on oath state that the above and foregoing is a true and correct transcript of my stenographic notes as taken in said cause on said date.

Anna Garrigues

Subscribed and sworn to before me
this 28 day of February 1906.

J McDermott
Notary Public.

N.C. 1117.

DEPARTMENT OF THE INTERIOR,
COMMISSIONER TO THE FIVE CIVILIZED TRIBES.
MUSKOGEE, INDIAN TERRITORY.
AUGUST 13, 1906.

In the matter of the application for the enrollment of Jimmie Seber as a citizen by blood of the Creek Nation.

LIZZIE SEBER, being duly sworn testified as follows, through Official Interpreter, Lona Merrick.

Q What is your name? A Lizzie Seber.
Q What is your age? A I don't know.
Q Have you a child named Jimmie Seber? A Yes sir.
Q Is he living? A Yes sir.
Q What is the name of his father? A Sampson Seber.
Q To what Creek Indian town does Sampson Seber belong? A Lochopoka.
Q What is the name of Sampson's father? A Seber.
Q What is the name of his mother? A Jimhoker.
Q He is now in the penitentiary? A Yes sir.
Q In February this year, Mrs. Seber, you appeared here and you were told that the proof here was not sufficient to enroll this child, and you were handed blank affidavits to have made out by two disinterested witnesses about the birth of this child, to take the place of

Applications for Enrollment of Creek Newborn
Act of 1905   Volume XIV

the midwife, you stated there was no midwife present, you haven't furnished those, we still require them? A I got one witness to sign the affidavit but I couldn't get any other witness.
Q That is the affidavit of Sam C. Davis? A Yes sir.
Q When was Sampson sent to the penitentiary? A Two years ago.
Q Was this child born then? A Yes sir.
Q Do you understand now that you will have to furnish the affidavit of a disinterested witness to go along with the affidavit of Sam C. Davis, to take the place of the missing midwife? A Yes sir, I understand. I can get the necessary witness.

Betsey Jack, being duly sworn, testified as follows, through official Interpreter, Lona Merrick.

Q What is your name? A Betsey Jack.
Q How old are you? A I don't know my age. (Witness appears to be about 21).
Q Are you related to the witness here? A yes, she is my sister.
Q Do you know her child, Jimmie Seber? A Yes sir.
Q Is it living? A Yes sir.
Q When did you see it last? A I saw it yesterday.
Q How old is it? A I don't know.
Q About how old? A I don't know.
Q Do you know when it was born? A No sir.
Q What is the name of its father? A Sampson Seber.
Q Was your sister married to him? A They were not married; they lived together as man and wife.
Q When was Sampson sent to the Pen? A About two years ago.

Lona Merrick, being duly sworn, states that the above and foregoing is a true and correct transcript of her stenographic notes as taken in said cause on said date.

Lona Merrick

Subscribed and sworn to before me
this 13th day of August, 1906.

Alex Posey
Notary Public.

AFFIDAVIT OF DISINTERESTED WITNESS.

UNITED STATES OF AMERICA,
Western DISTRICT,   SS
INDIAN TERRITORY.

We, the undersigned, on oath state that we are personally acquainted with   Lizzie Seber (nee Cloud)   wife of   Sampson Seber   ; that there was born to her a   male

Applications for Enrollment of Creek Newborn
Act of 1905   Volume XIV

child on or about the   6th   day of   December 1903   ; that the said child has been named   Jimmie Seber   and was living March 4, 1905.

We further state that we have no interest in the above case.

Witnesses: his
J McDermott   Edmond x Harry
                                            mark
Stephen Cloud   Cornelius Hary[sic]

Subscribed and sworn to before me this 13 day, Sept, 1906.

My Com
Ex July 25" 1907   J McDermott
                                                  Notary Public.

Tulsa Ind Ter April 12" 1905

Western Judicial District
Indian Territory.

I the undersigned Sam'l C Davis of lawful age and a Citizen by blood of the Creek Nation Ind Ter, being duly sworn and on oath, says that he is personally acquainted with Sampson and Lizzie Seber, and he knows they have a male child about One Year and Five Months old and he is now living and named Jimmie Seber.

Saml. C. Davis

Subscribed and acknowledged to before me this the 12" day of April 1905

My Com Expires July 3" 1906   Robert E Lynch
                                                       Notary Public.

Applications for Enrollment of Creek Newborn
Act of 1905 Volume XIV

BIRTH AFFIDAVIT.

Copy

DEPARTMENT OF THE INTERIOR,
COMMISSION TO THE FIVE CIVILIZED TRIBES.

In Re Application for Enrollment, as a citizen of the Creek Nation, of Jimmie Seber , born on the 6" day of December , 1903

Name of Father: Sampson Seber   a citizen of the   Creek   Nation.
Name of Mother: Lizzie Seber   a citizen of the   Creek   Nation.

Post-office   Bristow IT

AFFIDAVIT OF MOTHER.

UNITED STATES OF AMERICA,
INDIAN TERRITORY,
Western Judicial District.

    I, Lizzie , on oath state that I am 27 years of age and a citizen by Blood, of the Creek Nation; that I am the lawful wife of Sampson Seber , who is a citizen, by Blood of the Creek Nation; that a male child was born to me on 6" day of December , 1903 , that said child has been named Jimmie Seber , and is now living. There was no one present but myself & husband and he is now in the penitentiary at Atlanta Georgia

                       Signed   Lizzie Seber

WITNESSES TO MARK:
{

    Subscribed and sworn to before me this 12" day of April , 1905.

Com Ex 7/3/1906   Robert E Lynch
                                                      NOTARY PUBLIC.

BIRTH AFFIDAVIT.

DEPARTMENT OF THE INTERIOR,
COMMISSIONER TO THE FIVE CIVILIZED TRIBES.

    IN RE APPLICATION FOR ENROLLMENT, as a citizen of the Creek Nation, of Jimmie Seber , born on the 6" day of December , 1903

Name of Father: Sampson Seber   a citizen of the   Creek   Nation.
Name of Mother: Lizzie Seber   a citizen of the   Creek   Nation.

                       Postoffice   Bristow I.T.

Applications for Enrollment of Creek Newborn
Act of 1905 Volume XIV

AFFIDAVIT OF MOTHER.

UNITED STATES OF AMERICA, Indian Territory, }
Western Judicial District.

I, Lizzie, on oath state that I am 27 years of age and a citizen by Blood, of the Creek Nation; that I am the lawful wife of Sampson Seber, who is a citizen, by blood of the Creek Nation; that a Male child was born to me on 6" day of December, 1903, that said child has been named Jimmie Seber, and was living March 4, 1905. There was no one present but myself and husband and he is now in the penitentiary at Atlanta Georgia

Lizzie Seber

Witness to Mark:

Subscribed and sworn to before me this 12 day of April, 1905.

Com Ex 7/3/1906

Robert E Lynch
Notary Public.

Copy

NC-1117

Muskogee, Indian Territory, October 24, 1905.

Lizzie Seber,
  Bristow, Indian Territory.

Dear Madam:

In the matter of the application for the enrollment of your minor child, Jimmie Seber, born December 6, 1903, as a citizen by blood of the Creek Nation, this office requires the affidavits of two disinterested witnesses relative to his birth. Said affidavits to set forth said child's name, the date of his birth, the names of his parents and whether or not he was living March 4, 1905.

This office is unable to identify you upon the final roll of citizens by blood of the Creek Nation. It is necessary that you be identified before the rights of said child can be finally determined. You are, therefore, requested to state the name under which you were finally enrolled, the names of your parents and other members of your family, your age, the Creek Indian town to which you belong and your final roll number as the same appears upon your allotment certificate and deeds.

Respectfully,

Commissioner.

Applications for Enrollment of Creek Newborn
Act of 1905   Volume XIV

N.C. 1117.

Muskogee, Indian Territory, March 1, 1907.

Lizzie Seber,
    Care Sampson Seber,
        Bristow, Indian Territory.

Dear Madam:

You are hereby advised that on February 15, 1907, the Secretary of the Interior approved the enrollment of your minor child, Jimmie Seber, as a citizen by blood of the Creek Nation, and that the name of said child appears upon the roll of new born citizens by blood of the said nation, enrolled under the Act of Congress approved March 3, 1905, as No. 1217.

This child is now entitled to allotment and application therefor should be made without delay at the Creek Land Office, Muskogee, Indian Territory.

                Respectfully,

                Commissioner.

DEPARTMENT OF THE INTERIOR,
COMMISSION TO THE FIVE CIVILIZED TRIBES.
Mellette, I. T., July 14, 1904.

In the matter of the application for the enrollment of Jeannetta Fox as a citizen by blood of the Creek Nation.

JIM FOX, being duly sworn, testified as follows:

Through L. G. McIntosh Official Interpreter:

By Commission:
Q What is your name? A Jim Fox.
Q What is your age? A About thirty years old.
Q What is your post office address? A Stidham.
Q Are you a citizen of the Creek Nation? A Yes, sir.

Applications for Enrollment of Creek Newborn
Act of 1905   Volume XIV

Q What town do you belong to? A Tullahassoche.
Q For whom do you make application for enrollment as a citizen of the Creek Nation? A Jeannetta Fox.
Q How old is Jeannetta Fox? A About three years and a half.
Q What is the date of her birth? A About the 18th of January 1900.
Q Have you a record of the date of the birth of Jeannetta? A None.
Q What is Jeannetta's father's name? A I am her father.
Q You are the father are you of Jeannetta? A Yes, sir.
Q What is her mother's name? A Ettie Fox.
Q Is she living? A Yes, sir.
Q Is she a citizen of the Creek Nation? A Yes, sir.
Q What town does she belong to? A Tullahassoche.
Q Is Jeannetta living? A Yes, sir.
Q Have you any other children? A Only the two.
Q What is the name of the other one? A Sandy Fox.
Q What is the date of his birth? A Monday morning in February.
Q What year? A It was in last year.
Q What is the date of the month? A About the 25.
Q Can you read and write? A Never tried in English or Creek.
Q How do you fix the date of the birth of Jeannetta when you have no record? A I remember it.
Q Who was the mid-wife at the birth of Jeannetta? A No one but me.
Q Who visited you soon after the child was born? A A man by the name of Sam Long.
Q Any others? A None visited us that we paid any attention to.
Q Have you ever had executed an affidavit in the matter of the application for the enrollment of birth of your child, Jeannetta? A No, sir.
Q Why is it that you have never done so? A I didn't do it. I can not do it myself. I can't fix it up.
Q Why is it you never made application to the Commission before this time for the enrollment of your child, Jeannetta? A I went to the Commission and the Commission says "have your child recorded in the Town Roll and then let them see to fixing your papers" and I come back but they didn't fix them.
Q Why didn't they fix them for you? A They wouldn't put themselves to any trouble.
Q Who are your townsmen? A Robert Selumber and Joe Smith.

    D. C. Skaggs, on oath, states that the above and foregoing is a true and correct transcript of his stenographic notes as taken in said cause on said date.

DC Skaggs

Subscribed and sworn to before me this August *(illegible)* 1904.

Wm T. Martin Jr.
Notary Public.

Applications for Enrollment of Creek Newborn
Act of 1905 Volume XIV

BIRTH AFFIDAVIT.

DEPARTMENT OF THE INTERIOR.
COMMISSION TO THE FIVE CIVILIZED TRIBES.

IN RE APPLICATION FOR ENROLLMENT, as a citizen of the Creek Nation, of Jennetty Fox, born on the 25 day of April , 1900

Name of Father: Jim Fox   a citizen of the Creek Nation.
Name of Mother: Ada Fox   a citizen of the Creek Nation.
Tuly Hosley Town

           Postoffice   Stidham Ind Ter

AFFIDAVIT OF MOTHER.

UNITED STATES OF AMERICA, Indian Territory, }   Child present
    Western   DISTRICT.

     I, Ada Fox , on oath state that I am 20 years of age and a citizen by Blood , of the Creek Nation; that I am the lawful wife of Jim Fox , who is a citizen, by Blood of the Creek Nation; that a female child was born to me on 25 day of April , 1900 , that said child has been named Jennetty Fox , and was living March 4, 1905.

                                   her
                               Ada x Fox
Witnesses To Mark: mark
   { EH Walker
     Wm Posey

    Subscribed and sworn to before me this 11 day of April , 1905.

                               Preston Janway
                                  Notary Public.

AFFIDAVIT OF ATTENDING PHYSICIAN OR MID-WIFE.

UNITED STATES OF AMERICA, Indian Territory, }
    Western   DISTRICT.

     I, Jim Fox , a Husband , on oath state that I attended on Mrs. Ada Fox , my wife of had no doctor or midwife on the 25 day of April , 1900 ; that there was born to her on said date a female child; that said child was living March 4, 1905, and is said to have been named Jennetty Fox   his
                               Jim x Fox
Witnesses To Mark: mark
   { EH Walker
     Wm Posey

Applications for Enrollment of Creek Newborn
Act of 1905 Volume XIV

Subscribed and sworn to before me this 11 day of April , 1905.
My commission
expires May 19th 1908   Preston Janway
                                 Notary Public.

En. 566   I.D.
DEPARTMENT OF THE INTERIOR,
COMMISSIONER TO THE FIVE CIVILIZED TRIBES.

In the matter of the application for the enrollment of Jennetty Fox as a citizen by blood of the Creek Nation.

DECISION.

The record in this case shows that on July 14, 1904, Jim Fox appeared before the Commission to the Five Civilized Tribes at Mellette, Indian Territory, and made application for the enrollment of his minor child, Jennetty Fox, as a citizen by blood of the Creek Nation.

The evidence shows that said Jennetty Fox was born prior to July 1, 1900, and that she was living March 4, 1905.

The evidence further shows that said Jennetty Fox is the minor child of Jim Fox and Ettie Fox and from an examination of the records of this office said Jim Fox is identified as Jimmie Fox, and said Ettie Fox is identified as Addie Fox on the partial list of citizens by blood of the Creek Nation approved by the Secretary of the Interior March 28, 1902, opposite Nos. 8699 and 8700, respectively.

It is therefore, ordered and adjudged that said Jennetty Fox is entitled to enrollment as a citizen by blood of the Creek Nation in accordance with the provisions of the acts of Congress approved June 28, 1898 (30 Stats., 495) and March 1, 1901 (31 Stats., 861), and the application for her enrollment as such is accordingly granted.

                                 Tams Bixby Commissioner.
Muskogee, Indian Territory.
NOV 11 1905

NC 1118.   FHW
DEPARTMENT OF THE INTERIOR,   EK
COMMISSIONER TO THE FIVE CIVILIZED TRIBES.

In the matter of the application for the enrollment of Sandy Fox, deceased, as a citizen by blood of the Creek Nation.

DECISION.

The record in this case shows that on April 19, 1905, an application was filed, in affidavit form, for the enrollment of Sandy Fox, as a citizen by blood of the Creek

Applications for Enrollment of Creek Newborn
Act of 1905   Volume XIV

Nation. A supplemental affidavit as to the birth and death of said applicant, filed November 11, 1905, is attached to and made a part of the record herein.

The evidence in this case is clear with the exception of an apparent clerical error in the execution of the supplemental affidavit. In the said affidavit, the date of the birth of the applicant is given in one place as December 16, 1903, in another place as March 16, 1903. The rights of the applicant herein are the same under the law hereinafter cited, but Sandy Fox was born March 16, 1903, and died September 22, 1905.

The evidence, and the records in the possession of this office show that the applicant, Sandy Fox, it the child of James Fox and Ada Fox, enrolled as Jimmie Fox and Addie Fox, on a partial schedule of citizens by blood of the Creek Nation, approved by the Secretary of the Interior March 28, 1902, opposite numbers 8699 and 8700, respectively.

It is therefore, ordered and adjudged that the said Sandy Fox, deceased, is entitled to enrollment as a citizen by blood of the Creek Nation, under the provisions of the Act of Congress approved March 3, 1905 (33 Stat. L., 1048), and the application for his enrollment as such is accordingly granted.

Tams Bixby Commissioner.

Muskogee, Indian Territory.
FEB 7- 1907

N.C. 1118.
DEPARTMENT OF THE INTERIOR,
COMMISSIONER TO THE FIVE CIVILIZED TRIBES.
Near Lenna, Indian Territory, February 12, 1907.

In the matter of the application for the enrollment of Sandy Fox, as a citizen by blood of the Creek Nation.

RACAEL[sic] LONEY, being duly sworn, by J. McDermott, a notary public, testified as follows through Jesse McDermott, official interpreter:

BY THE COMMISSIONER:

Q What is your name? A Rachael Loney.
Q What is your age? A About 29.
Q What is your postoffice address? A Lenna.
Q Are you a Creek citizen? A Yes.
Q Do you know Jimmie Fox? A Yes.
Q Do you or did you know his wife, Addie Fox? A Yes.
Q Did she have a child by Jimmie Fox? A Yes.
Q What is the name of the child? A Sandy Fox.
Q Do you know when he was born? A I think it was in March.
Q Are you positive of that? A Yes.

It appears from your affidavit on file at the office that you at the time stated that Sandy was born in December 1903.

Applications for Enrollment of Creek Newborn
Act of 1905   Volume XIV

Q How do you account for that? A If it is stated in my affidavit that the child was born in December, it is a mistake of the notary public as I am positive that I said March. I know that Sandy was born in March. Jim and his wife were near neighbors of mine when the child was born.
Q How old will he be next month? A Four years old.
Q Is he living? A Yes, but the mother is dead.
Q When did she die, do you know? A No, I do not.

I, Jesse McDermott, on oath state that the above and foregoing is a full and true transcript of my notes as taken in said cause on said date.

Jesse McDermott

Subscribed and sworn to before me,
this 13 day of Feb, 1907.

F.L. Moss

My Commission expires Jan. 20th. 1908.   Notary Public.

N.C. 1118.

DEPARTMENT OF THE INTERIOR,
COMMISSIONER TO THE FIVE CIVILIZED TRIBES.
Near Stidham, Indian Territory, February 12, 1907.

In the matter of the application for the enrollment of Sandy Fox, as a citizen by blood of the Creek Nation.

HEPSEY HARJO, being duly sworn, by J. McDermott, a notary public, testified as follows through Jesse McDermott, official interpreter:

BY THE COMMISSIONER:

Q What is your name? A Hepsey Harjo.
Q What is your age? A About eighteen.
Q What is your postoffice address? A Stidham.
Q Are you a citizen of the Creek Nation? A I am.
Q Do you know Jimmie Fox and his wife Addie? A I do.
Q Do you know a child of theirs by the name of Sandy Fox? A Yes.
Q Do you know when that child was born? A He was born in the "Little Spring Month" (meaning the month of March).
Q Are you sure of that? A Yes, they were living just a little distance from here when he was born.

It appears from your affidavit on file at the office of the Commissioner to the Five Civilized Tribes that you stated on November 8, 1905, that Sandy was born in December 1903. Now, you state that he was born in March.

175

Applications for Enrollment of Creek Newborn
Act of 1905   Volume XIV

Q How do you account for that mistake that you have made? A That is not my mistake. I told that whiteman at Stidham that the child was born in March. Jim Fox signed an affidavit the very same day and I heard him say that Sandy was born the 16th of March. I was not certain about the date of his birth but knew all of the time that it was in March.
Q Is Sandy living? A Yes.
Q Is the mother living? A No, she is dead but I do not know when died.

I, Jesse McDermott, on oath state that the above and foregoing is a full and true transcript of my notes as taken in said cause on said date.

Jesse McDermott

Subscribed and sworn to before me, this 13 day of Feb, 1907.

F.L. Moss
Notary Public.

My Commission expires Jan. 20th. 1908.

Copy

BIRTH AFFIDAVIT.

DEPARTMENT OF THE INTERIOR.
COMMISSION TO THE FIVE CIVILIZED TRIBES.

IN RE APPLICATION FOR ENROLLMENT, as a citizen of the   *(blank)*   Nation, of   Sandy Fox , born on the 16   day of March , 1903

Name of Father: James Fox   a citizen of the   Creek   Nation.
Tullahasse
Name of Mother: Addie Fox   a citizen of the   Creek   Nation.
   Do
                          Postoffice   Stidham

AFFIDAVIT OF MOTHER.

UNITED STATES OF AMERICA, Indian Territory, ⎫   Child not present
            Western   **DISTRICT.** ⎭

I, James Fox Husband of Addie she died on the 22 day of September 1905 , on oath state that I am 30   years of age and a citizen by Blood , of the Creek   Nation; that ~~I am the lawful wife of~~ Addie Fox was my lawful wife , who ~~is~~ was a citizen, by Blood of the Creek   Nation; that a male   child was born to ~~me~~ her on 16 day of March , 1903 , that said child has been named Sandy Fox , and was living March 4, 1905.

176

Applications for Enrollment of Creek Newborn
Act of 1905   Volume XIV

                                                  his
Witnesses To Mark: James Fox x
{ TJ Ingram   mark
{ A.W. Barnett

    Subscribed and sworn to before me this 8" day of   November   , 1905.
My Commission
Expires May 19, 1908   Preston Janaway[sic]
                                              Notary Public.

AFFIDAVIT OF ATTENDING PHYSICIAN OR MID-WIFE.

UNITED STATES OF AMERICA, Indian Territory,
      Western   **DISTRICT.**

    We, Rachel Loney and Hepsey Harjo   , a   Citizens , on oath state that ~~I~~ we ~~attended on~~ knew Mrs. Addie Fox , wife of James Fox   and we are satisfied that   on the 16" day of December , 1903 ; that there was born to her on said date a male child; that said child was living March 4, 1905, and is said to have been named Sandy Fox

                                                her
                                     Rachel Loney x
Witnesses To Mark: mark
{ T J Ingram   her
{ A.W. Barnett   Hepsey Harjo x
                                             mark
    Subscribed and sworn to before me 8" day of   November , 1905.

                                          Preston Janaway[sic]
                                              Notary Public.

                              Copy
BIRTH AFFIDAVIT.
                       DEPARTMENT OF THE INTERIOR.
        COMMISSION TO THE FIVE CIVILIZED TRIBES.

    IN RE APPLICATION FOR ENROLLMENT, as a citizen of the Creek Nation, of Sandy Fox , born on the   16 day of   March   , 1903

Name of Father: Jim Fox   a citizen of the   Creek   Nation.
Tull
Name of Mother: Ada Fox   a citizen of the   Creek   Nation.
Tull
                        Postoffice   Stidham Ind Ter

Applications for Enrollment of Creek Newborn
Act of 1905   Volume XIV

AFFIDAVIT OF MOTHER.

UNITED STATES OF AMERICA, Indian Territory, }
    Western   DISTRICT.

Child present

I, Ada Fox, on oath state that I am 20 years of age and a citizen by Blood, of the Creek Nation; that I am the lawful wife of Jim Fox, who is a citizen, by Blood of the Creek Nation; that a male child was born to me on 16 day of March, 1903, that said child has been named Sandy Fox, and was living March 4, 1905.

                                          her
                                    Ada x Fox

Witnesses To Mark: mark
{ E.H. Walker
{ Wm Posey

Subscribed and sworn to before me this 11 day of April, 1905.

                                    Preston Jannaway[sic]
                                    Notary Public.

AFFIDAVIT OF ATTENDING PHYSICIAN OR MID-WIFE.

UNITED STATES OF AMERICA, Indian Territory, }
    Western   DISTRICT.

I, Jim Fox, a Husband, on oath state that I attended on Mrs. Ada Fox my, wife of had no doctor or midwife on the 16 day of March, 1903 ; that there was born to her on said date a *(blank)* child; that said child was living March 4, 1905, and is said to have been named Sandy Fox

                                        his
                                  Jim x Fox

Witnesses To Mark: mark
{ E.H. Walker
{ Wm Posey

Subscribed and sworn to before me this 11 day of April, 1905.

                                    Preston Jannaway[sic]
                                    Notary Public.

Applications for Enrollment of Creek Newborn
Act of 1905   Volume XIV

BIRTH AFFIDAVIT.

DEPARTMENT OF THE INTERIOR.
COMMISSION TO THE FIVE CIVILIZED TRIBES.

IN RE APPLICATION FOR ENROLLMENT, as a citizen of the *(blank)* Nation, of Sandy Fox , born on the 16 day of March , 1903

Name of Father: James Fox   a citizen of the   Creek   Nation.
    Town Tullyhasey
Name of Mother: Addie Fox   a citizen of the   Creek   Nation.
    Town Tullyhasey
                      Postoffice   Stidham

AFFIDAVIT OF MOTHER.

UNITED STATES OF AMERICA, Indian Territory, }   Child not present
    Western   DISTRICT.

    I, James Fox Husband of Addie she died on the 22 day of September 1905 , on oath state that I am 30 years of age and a citizen by Blood , of the Creek   Nation; that ~~I am the lawful wife of~~   Addie Fox was my lawful wife , who ~~is~~ was a citizen, by Blood of the Creek   Nation; that a male   child was born to ~~me~~ her on 16 day of March , 1903 , that said child has been named Sandy Fox , and was living March 4, 1905.
                             his
                       James Fox x
Witnesses To Mark: mark
  { TJ Ingram
    A.W. Barnett

    Subscribed and sworn to before me this 8" day of November , 1905.
My Commission
Expires May 19, 1908   Preston Janaway[sic]
                             Notary Public.

AFFIDAVIT OF ATTENDING PHYSICIAN OR MID-WIFE.

UNITED STATES OF AMERICA, Indian Territory, }
    Western   DISTRICT.

    We, Rachel Loney and Hepsey Harjo , ~~a~~ Citizens , on oath state that ~~I~~ we ~~attended on~~ knew Mrs. Addie Fox , wife of James Fox   and we are satisfied that on the 16" day of December , 1903 ; that there was born to her on said date a male child; that said child was living March 4, 1905, and is said to have been named Sandy Fox

Applications for Enrollment of Creek Newborn
Act of 1905 Volume XIV

Witnesses To Mark:	her Rachel Loney x mark
{ T J Ingram A.W. Barnett	her Hepsey Harjo x mark

Subscribed and sworn to before me 8" day of November , 1905.

Preston Janaway[sic]
Notary Public.

BIRTH AFFIDAVIT.

DEPARTMENT OF THE INTERIOR.
COMMISSION TO THE FIVE CIVILIZED TRIBES.

IN RE APPLICATION FOR ENROLLMENT, as a citizen of the Creek Nation, of Sandy Fox , born on the 16th day of March , 1903

Name of Father: Jimmie Fox   a citizen of the   Creek   Nation.
Name of Mother: Addie Fox   a citizen of the   Creek   Nation.

Postoffice   Stidham I.T.

AFFIDAVIT OF MOTHER.

UNITED STATES OF AMERICA, Indian Territory,
     Western   DISTRICT.

     I, Jimmie Fox , on oath state that I am about 32 years of age and a citizen by blood , of the Creek Nation; that I am the lawful ~~wife~~ husband of Addie Fox , who ~~is~~ was a citizen, by blood of the Creek Nation; that a male child was born to ~~me~~ her on 16" day of March , 1903 , that said child has been named Sandy Fox , and was living March 4, 1905.

                                            his
                                   Jimmie x Fox
Witnesses To Mark: mark
   { J McDermott
     Theodore T. Pyle

Subscribed and sworn to before me this 12th day of February , 1907.

My Commission   J McDermott
Expires July 25" 1907   Notary Public.

Applications for Enrollment of Creek Newborn
Act of 1905   Volume XIV

AFFIDAVIT OF TWO DISINTERESTED WITNESSES.

UNITED STATES OF AMERICA, :
WESTERN DISTRICT,   : ss
INDIAN TERRITORY,   :

We, the undersigned, on oath state that we are personally acquainted with Addie Fox the lawful wife of Jimmie Fox ;; that there was born her a male child on or about the 16 day of March 190 3 ; that said child was living March 4, 1906.

We further state that we have no interest in the above case.

Witnesses to mark:
J McDermott
Andrew Brashar
J McDermott
Andrew Brashar

            her
Rachael x Loney
            mark
            her
Hepsey x Harjo
            mark

Subscribed and sworn to before me,
this 12 day of February 1907.

                      J McDermott
                          Notary Public.

My Commission expires
25 day of July, 1907.

NC-1118.

Muskogee, Indian Territory, October 24, 1905.

Addie Fox,
    c/o Jimmie Fox,
        Stidham, Indian Territory.

Dear Madam:

In the matter of the application for the enrollment of your minor child, Sandy Fox, born March 16, 1903, as a citizen by blood of the Creek Nation, this office requires the affidavit of the physician or midwife who attended at his birth and a blank for that purpose is inclosed herewith.

In the event that no physician or midwife attended at the birth of said Sandy Fox it will be necessary for you to furnish this office with the affidavits of two disinterested persons relative to the birth of said child. Said affidavits to set forth said child's name, the date of his birth, the names of his parents and whether or not he was living March 4, 1905.

This matter should receive your immediate attention.

Applications for Enrollment of Creek Newborn
Act of 1905   Volume XIV

B C
Env.

Respectfully,

Commissioner.

NC-1118

Muskogee, Indian Territory, December 21, 1905.

James Fox,
    Stidham, Indian Territory.

Dear Sir:

    In the matter of the application for the enrollment of your minor child, Sandy Fox, born March 16, 1903, as a citizen by blood of the Creek Nation, you and your wife, Addie Fox (now deceased), state in your affidavits that said child was born March 16,

190   Muskogee, Indian Territory, December 21, 1905.

James Fox,
    Stidham, Indian Territory.

Dear Sir:

    In the matter of the application for the enrollment of your minor child, Sandy Fox, born March 16, 1903, as a citizen by blood of the Creek Nation, you and your wife, Addie Fox (now deceased), state in your affidavits that said child was born March 16, 1903; Rachel Loney and Hepsey Harjo, two disinterested witnesses, state in their affidavit on file in this case that said Sandy Fox was born December 16, 1903.

    In order that this discrepancy may be corrected, there is herewith enclosed a lank form of affidavit for two disinterested witnesses, which you are requested to have executed by said Rachel Loney and Hepsey Harjo. You will then return same to this Office in the enclosed envelope. In the event that the correct date of the birth of said Sandy Fox is other than March 16, 1903, it will be necessary for you to execute a new affidavit, giving the correct date of the birth of said child, and a blank for that purpose is herewith enclosed.

    In having the affidavits executed, care should be taken to see that all blanks are properly filled, all names spelled in full, and in the event that a person signing an affidavit is unable to write, a signature by mark must be attested by two witnesses who are able to write. The notary public must date, sign and seal each separate affidavit.

    This matter should receive your immediate attention.

Respectfully,

1 B A
Dis

Commissioner.

Applications for Enrollment of Creek Newborn
Act of 1905   Volume XIV

Cr En 566

Muskogee, Indian Territory, November 13, 1905.

M. L. Mott,
    Attorney for the Creek Nation,
        Muskogee, Indian Territory.

Sir:

There is herewith enclosed one copy of the decision of the Commissioner to the Five Civilized Tribes in the matter of the application for the enrollment of Jennetty Fox as a citizen by blood of the Creek Nation.

You are hereby notified that the Creek Nation will be allowed fifteen days from date hereof within which to protest against said decision, and if, at the expiration of that time, no protest has been filed, said Jennetty Fox will be regularly listed for enrollment as a citizen by blood of the Creek Nation.

                Respectfully,

JYM-18-5   Commissioner.

N C 1118

Muskogee, Indian Territory, March 7, 1907.

Ada Fox,
    Care of Jim Fox,
        Stidham, Indian Territory.

Dear Madam:

You are hereby advised that on March 2, 1907 the Secretary of the Interior approved the enrollment of your deceased minor child, Sandy Fox, as a citizen by blood of the Creek Nation, and that the name of said child appears upon the roll of new born citizens by blood of the Creek Nation enrolled under the Act of Congress approved March 3, 1905, as number 1263.

This child is now entitled to an allotment and application therefor should be made by a duly appointed administrator without delay at the Creek Land Office, Muskogee, Indian Territory.

                Respectfully,

                              Commissioner.

Applications for Enrollment of Creek Newborn
Act of 1905 Volume XIV

NC. 1119

Muskogee, Indian Territory, October 24, 1905.

Millie Childers,
    Care Chissoe Childers,
        Tulsa, Indian Territory.

Dear Madam:

    In the matter of the application for the enrollment of your minor child, Effie Childers, born December 6, 1904, as a citizen by blood of the Creek Nation, the name of the child is omitted in the affidavit of the midwife in attendance at her birth.

    There is herewith enclosed birth affidavit properly filled out and you are requested to have same executed before a notary public and return it to this office in the enclosed envelope.

                Respectfully,

                              Commissioner.

AG-1119

BIRTH AFFIDAVIT.

DEPARTMENT OF THE INTERIOR,
COMMISSIONER TO THE FIVE CIVILIZED TRIBES.

    IN RE APPLICATION FOR ENROLLMENT, as a citizen of the Creek Nation, of Effie Childers , born on the 6" day of December , 1904

Name of Father: Chisso Childers   a citizen of the   Creek   Nation.
Name of Mother: Millie Childers   a citizen of the   Creek   Nation.

                Postoffice   Tulsa Ind Ter

AFFIDAVIT OF MOTHER.

UNITED STATES OF AMERICA, Indian Territory, }
    Western   District. }

    I, Millie Childers , on oath state that I am 28 years of age and a citizen by Blood, of the Creek Nation; that I am the lawful wife of Chisso Childers , who is a citizen, by Blood of the Creek Nation; that a Female child was born to me on 6" day of December, 1904 , that said child has been named Effie Childers , and was living March 4, 1905.

                              Millie Childers

Witness to Mark:

Applications for Enrollment of Creek Newborn
Act of 1905 Volume XIV

Subscribed and sworn to before me this 22" day of March , 1905.

Com Ex 7/3/1906   Robert E Lynch
                                                Notary Public.

AFFIDAVIT OF ATTENDING PHYSICIAN OR MID-WIFE.

UNITED STATES OF AMERICA, Indian Territory, ⎫
    Western   District. ⎬

I, Elizabeth Gillis , a midwife , on oath state that I attended on Mrs. Millie Childers , wife of Chisso Childers on the 6" day of Dec , 1904 ; that there was born to her on said date a Female child; that said child was living March 4, 1905, and is said to have been named *(blank)*   her

                                        Elizabeth x Gillis
Witness to Mark: mark
    Ellen Gillis   ⎫
    Elizabeth Dodge ⎬

Subscribed and sworn to before me this 22 day of March , 1905.

                                    Robert E Lynch
                                    Notary Public.

BIRTH AFFIDAVIT.

DEPARTMENT OF THE INTERIOR.
COMMISSION TO THE FIVE CIVILIZED TRIBES.

IN RE APPLICATION FOR ENROLLMENT, as a citizen of the Creek Nation, of Effie Childers , born on the 6 day of December , 1904

Name of Father: Chisso Childers   a citizen of the   Creek   Nation.
Name of Mother: Millie Childers   a citizen of the   Creek   Nation.

                                  Postoffice   Tulsa

AFFIDAVIT OF MOTHER.

UNITED STATES OF AMERICA, Indian Territory, ⎫
    Western   DISTRICT. ⎬

I, Millie Childers , on oath state that I am 29 years of age and a citizen by Blood , of the Creek Nation; that I am the lawful wife of Chisso Childers , who is a citizen, by Blood of the Creek Nation; that a Female child was born to me on 6"

Applications for Enrollment of Creek Newborn
Act of 1905   Volume XIV

day of December, 1904, that said child has been named Effie Childers, and was living March 4, 1905.

                                      Millie Childers

Witnesses To Mark:
{

    Subscribed and sworn to before me this 4" day of Nov, 1905.

Com Ex 7/3/1906   Robert E Lynch
                                    Notary Public.

AFFIDAVIT OF ATTENDING PHYSICIAN OR MID-WIFE.

UNITED STATES OF AMERICA, Indian Territory, }
    Western   DISTRICT.

    I, Elizabeth Gillis, a midwife, on oath state that I attended on Mrs. Millie Childers, wife of Chisso Childers on the 6 day of December, 1904; that there was born to her on said date a female child; that said child was living March 4, 1905, and is said to have been named Effie Childers

                                        her
                                  Elizabeth x Gillis

Witnesses To Mark: mark
{ Nathanial D Christian
  James D Meadows

    Subscribed and sworn to before me this 4" day of Nov, 1905.

My Com Ex 7/3/1906   Robert E Lynch
                                    Notary Public.

Western District)
Indian Territory) SS

    We, the undersigned, on oath state that we are personally acquainted with Grace Wilson wife of Thomas Wilson; and that on or about the 8th day of May 1904, a female child was born to them and has been named Annie Wilson; and that said child was living March 4, 1905.

Applications for Enrollment of Creek Newborn
Act of 1905   Volume XIV

We further state that we have no interest in the above case.

Rasb Alexander

Witness to mark:

_____

_____

Subscribed and sworn to before
me this 23 day of Feb 1906

J.F. Panther
Notary Public.
My com exp. July 2-1906.

BIRTH AFFIDAVIT.

DEPARTMENT OF THE INTERIOR.
COMMISSION TO THE FIVE CIVILIZED TRIBES.

IN RE APPLICATION FOR ENROLLMENT, as a citizen of the *(blank)* Nation, of Annie Wilson, born on the 8 day of May, 1904

Name of Father:	Thomas Wilson	a citizen of the Creek Nation.
Name of Mother:	Grace "	a citizen of the Creek Nation.

Postoffice   Bixby I. Ty.

AFFIDAVIT OF MOTHER.

(Child present)

UNITED STATES OF AMERICA, Indian Territory,
Western   DISTRICT.

I, Grace Wilson, on oath state that I am 27 years of age and a citizen by blood, of the Creek Nation; that I am the lawful wife of Thomas Wilson, who is a citizen, by blood of the Creek Nation; that a female child was born to me on 8" day of May, 1904, that said child has been named Annie Wilson, and was living March 4, 1905.

                                                              her
Grace x Wilson

Witnesses To Mark: mark
{ Edw C Griesel
{ Jesse McDermott

Subscribed and sworn to before me this 13" day of April, 1905.

J McDermott
Notary Public.

Applications for Enrollment of Creek Newborn
Act of 1905   Volume XIV

Father
AFFIDAVIT OF ~~ATTENDING PHYSICIAN OR MID-WIFE~~.
Midwife Dead

UNITED STATES OF AMERICA, Indian Territory,
Western   DISTRICT.

I, Thomas Wilson , a husband   , on oath state that I attended on ~~Mrs~~. my , wife ~~of~~ when on the 8" day of   May , 1904 ; that there was born to her on said date a *(blank)* child; that said child was living March 4, 1905, and is said to have been named Annie Wilson

his
Thomas x Wilson
mark

Witnesses To Mark:
  { Edw C Griesel
  { Jesse McDermott

Subscribed and sworn to before me this 13" day of   April   , 1905.

J McDermott
Notary Public.

Western District)
Indian Territory) SS

We, the undersigned, on oath state that we are personally acquainted with   Grace Wilson wife of   Thomas Wilson   ; and that on or about the 16th day of May 1902 , a male child was born to them and has been named   Enus Wilson ; and that said child was living March 4, 1905.

We further state that we have no interest in the above case.

Adaline Bruner

Witness to mark: _____

_____
_____

Subscribed and sworn to before
me this 23rd day of Feb 1906   J.F. Panther
                                           Notary Public.
                                           My com exp. July 2-1906.

Applications for Enrollment of Creek Newborn
Act of 1905   Volume XIV

BIRTH AFFIDAVIT.

DEPARTMENT OF THE INTERIOR.
COMMISSION TO THE FIVE CIVILIZED TRIBES.

IN RE APPLICATION FOR ENROLLMENT, as a citizen of the Creek Nation, of Enus Wilson, born on the 16 day of May, 1902

Name of Father: Thomas Wilson   a citizen of the   Creek   Nation.
Cussetah Town
Name of Mother: Grace   "   a citizen of the   Creek   Nation.
Concharty Town

Postoffice   Bixby I. Ty.

AFFIDAVIT OF MOTHER.

(Child present)

UNITED STATES OF AMERICA, Indian Territory, ⎫
   Western   DISTRICT.   ⎬

I, Grace Wilson, on oath state that I am 27 years of age and a citizen by blood, of the Creek Nation; that I am the lawful wife of Thomas Wilson, who is a citizen, by blood of the Creek Nation; that a male child was born to me on 16 day of May, 1902, that said child has been named Enus Wilson, and was living March 4, 1905.

                                    her
                          Grace x Wilson
Witnesses To Mark: mark
  { Edw C Griesel
   Jesse McDermott

Subscribed and sworn to before me this 13" day of April, 1905.

                         J McDermott
                         Notary Public.

Father
AFFIDAVIT OF ~~ATTENDING PHYSICIAN OR MID-WIFE~~.

UNITED STATES OF AMERICA, Indian Territory, ⎫
   Western   DISTRICT.   ⎬

I, Thomas Wilson, a husband, on oath state that I attended on ~~Mrs.~~ my, wife ~~of~~ when on the 16" day of May, 1902; that there was born to her on said date a *(blank)* child; that said child was living March 4, 1905, and is said to have been named Enus Wilson

                                  his
                        Thomas x Wilson
                          mark

Applications for Enrollment of Creek Newborn
Act of 1905   Volume XIV

Witnesses To Mark:
{ Edw C Griesel
{ Jesse McDermott

    Subscribed and sworn to before me this 13" day of   April   , 1905.

                                      J McDermott
                                          Notary Public.

                                                                              HGH

| REFER IN REPLY TO THE FOLLOWING: | **DEPARTMENT OF THE INTERIOR,** |
| NC. 1121 | **COMMISSIONER TO THE FIVE CIVILIZED TRIBES.** |

                            Muskogee, Indian Territory, October 24, 1905.

Grace Wilson,
    Care Thomas Wilson,
        Bixby, Indian Territory.

Dear Madam:

    In the matter of the application for the enrollment of your minor children, Enus Wilson, born May 16, 1902, and Annie Wilson, born May 8, 1904, as citizens by blood of the Creek Nation, this office desires affidavit of the midwife or physician in attendance at the birth of said children and blanks for that purpose is enclosed herewith.

    In the event that there was no physician or midwife in attendance when said children were born, it will be necessary for you to furnish this office with the affidavits of two disinterested witnesses relative to the birth of each child. Said affidavits must set forth the names of said children, the dates of their birth, the names of their parents and whether or not they were living on March 4, 1905.

                                  Respectfully,

2 BA   Tams Bixby Commissioner.
Env.

N.C. 1121.

                          Muskogee, Indian Territory, December 20, 1905.

Witnesses relative to the birth of each child. Said affidavits must set forth the names of said children, the names of their parents, the dates of their birth and whether or not they were living on March 4, 1905.

Applications for Enrollment of Creek Newborn
Act of 1905   Volume XIV

Grace Wilson,
    Care Thomas Wilson,
        Bixby, Indian Territory.

Dear Madam:

    In the matter of the application for the enrollment of your minor children, Enus Wilson, born May 16, 1902, and Annie Wilson, born May 8, 1904, as citizens by blood of the Creek Nation, this office desires affidavit of the midwife relative to the births of said children.
    In the event that there was no midwife in attendance when said children were born, it will be necessary for you to furnish this office with the affidavits of two disinterested witnesses relative to the birth of each child. Said affidavits must set forth the names of said children, the names of their parents, the dates of their birth and whether or not they were living March 4, 1905.

                    Respectfully,

2 Dis.   Commissioner.

N.C. 1121.

                    Muskogee, Indian Territory, March 1, 1907.

Grace Wilson,
    Care Thomas Wilson,
        Bixby, Indian Territory.

Dear Madam:

    You are hereby advised that on February 15, 1907, the Secretary of the Interior approved the enrollment of your minor children, Enus and Annie Wilson, as citizens by blood of the Creek Nation and that the names of said children appear upon the roll of new born citizens by blood of the Creek Nation, enrolled under the Act of Congress approved March 3, 1905, as numbers 1218 and 1219 respectively.

    These children are now entitled to allotments and application therefor should be made without delay at the Creek Land Office, Muskogee, Indian Territory.

                    Respectfully,
                                    Commissioner.

Applications for Enrollment of Creek Newborn
Act of 1905 Volume XIV

Western District)
Indian Territory) SS

    We, the undersigned, on oath state that we are personally acquainted with Annie Artussee wife of John Artussee ; and that on or about the 1 day of Jan , 1904 a male child was born to them and has been named Mose Artussee ; and that said child was living March 4, 1905.

    We further state that we have no interest in the above case.

                                      her
                                 Lizzie x Taylor
                                      mark
                                 Thomas Harjo

Witness to mark:
Dug Sharp
Geo S. Harvison

Subscribed and sworn to before
me this 6 day of Jan 1906   Geo S. Harvison
                                        Notary Public.

BIRTH AFFIDAVIT.
                         DEPARTMENT OF THE INTERIOR.
              COMMISSION TO THE FIVE CIVILIZED TRIBES.

    IN RE APPLICATION FOR ENROLLMENT, as a citizen of the Creek Nation, of Mose Artussee , born on the 1 day of Jan , 1904

Name of Father: John Artussee   a citizen of the Creek Nation.
Hickory Ground
Name of Mother: Annie Artussee   a citizen of the Creek Nation.
Hickory Ground
                              Postoffice   Senora I.Ty.

                                        (Child present)
                        AFFIDAVIT OF MOTHER.

UNITED STATES OF AMERICA, Indian Territory,
    Western   **DISTRICT.**

    I, Annie Artussee , on oath state that I am 35 years of age and a citizen by blood , of the Creek Nation; that I am the lawful wife of John Artussee , who is a

Applications for Enrollment of Creek Newborn
Act of 1905 Volume XIV

citizen, by blood of the Creek Nation; that a male child was born to me on 1 day of Jan, 1904, that said child has been named Mose Artussee, and was living March 4, 1905.

            her
          Annie x Artussee
Witnesses To Mark: mark
 { EC Griesel
   Jesse McDermott

Subscribed and sworn to before me this 13" day of Apr , 1905.

         J McDermott
          Notary Public.

        Father (No Midwife)
AFFIDAVIT OF ~~ATTENDING PHYSICIAN OR MID-WIFE~~.

UNITED STATES OF AMERICA, Indian Territory, ⎫
 Western DISTRICT.   ⎬
             ⎭

 I, John Artussee, a (father), on oath state that I attended on ~~Mrs~~. my, wife ~~of~~ when on the 1 day of Jan 1904; that there was born to her on said date a male child; that said child is now living and is said to have been named Mose Artussee

           his
         John x Artussee
Witnesses To Mark: mark
 { EC Griesel
   Jesse McDermott

Subscribed and sworn to before me this 13" day of Apr , 1905.

         J McDermott
          Notary Public.

BIRTH AFFIDAVIT.

DEPARTMENT OF THE INTERIOR.
COMMISSION TO THE FIVE CIVILIZED TRIBES.

 IN RE APPLICATION FOR ENROLLMENT, as a citizen of the Muskogee Nation, of Mose Artussee, born on the 1st day of January, 1904

Name of Father: John Artussee   a citizen of the Muskogee Nation.
Name of Mother: Annie Artussee   a citizen of the Muskogee Nation.

        Postoffice Senora Ind. Terr.

Applications for Enrollment of Creek Newborn
Act of 1905 Volume XIV

AFFIDAVIT OF MOTHER.

UNITED STATES OF AMERICA, Indian Territory,
Western DISTRICT.

  I, Annie Artussee , on oath state that I am 32 years of age and a citizen by Blood , of the Muskogee Nation; that I am the lawful wife of John Artussee , who is a citizen, by Blood of the Muskogee Nation; that a Male child was born to me on 1st day of January , 1904 , that said child has been named Mose Artussee , and was living March 4, 1905.

                her
             Annie x Artussee
Witnesses To Mark: mark
 { Dug Sharp
  Thomas Harjo

  Subscribed and sworn to before me this 6 day of January , 1906.

             Geo S Harvison
              Notary Public.

NC. 1122

        Muskogee, Indian Territory, October 24, 1905.

Annie Artussee,
  Care John Artussee,
    Senora, Indian Territory.

Dear Madam:

  In the matter of the application for the enrollment of your minor child, Mose Artussee, born January 1, 1904, as a citizen by blood of the Creek Nation, this office desires affidavit of the midwife or physician in attendance at the birth of said child and a blank for that purpose is inclosed herewith.

  In the event that there was no physician or midwife in attendance when said child was born, it will be necessary for you to furnish this office with the affidavits of two disinterested witnesses relative to his birth. Said affidavits must set forth said child's name, the date of his birth, the names of his parents and whether or not he was living on March 4, 1905.

        Respectfully,
BC   Commissioner.
Env.

Applications for Enrollment of Creek Newborn
Act of 1905 Volume XIV

Muskogee, Indian Territory, December 20, 1905.

Annie Artussee,
    Care John Artussee,
        Senora, Indian Territory.

Dear Madam:

In the matter of the application for the enrollment of your minor child, Mose Artussee born January 1, 1904, as a citizen by blood of the Creek Nation, this office desires the affidavit of the midwife in attendance at the birth of said child, and a blank for that purpose is enclosed herewith.

In the event that there was no midwife in attendance at the birth of said child, it will be necessary for you to furnish this office with the affidavits of two disinterested witnesses relative to his birth. Said affidavits must set forth the name of said child, the names of its parents, the date of its birth and whether or not it was living March 4, 1905. said child, the date of his birth and whether or not he was living on March 4, 1905.

This matter should receive your immediate attention.

                Respectfully,

BA   Commissioner.
Dis.

N.C. 1123.

DEPARTMENT OF THE INTERIOR,
COMMISSIONER TO THE FIVE CIVILIZED TRIBES.
Senora, I. T., March 15, 1906.

In the matter of the application for the enrollment of Wiley Toney as a citizen by blood of the Creek Nation.

        ROLEY TAYLOR, being duly sworn, testified as follows:

Through Alex Posey Official Interpreter:

Applications for Enrollment of Creek Newborn
Act of 1905   Volume XIV

BY THE COMMISSIONER:
Q What is your name? A Roley Taylor.
Q How old are you? A Forty or over.
Q What is your post office address? A Senora.
Q Are you a citizen of the Creek Nation? A Yes sir.
Q To what town do you belong? A Hickory Ground.
Q Do you know Meleah Toney?? A She is my wife.
Q Was she formerly married? A Yes, sir, to Rogers Toney.
Q Is he known by any other name? A No, sir.
Q Was he sometimes known as Lijah or Lodger Toney? A No, sir., that is a corruption of his proper name, Rogers. It is hard for the Indians to pronounce the name Rogers correctly.
Q He is dead is he? A he has been dead probably three years--I con't[sic] remember exactly when he died.
Q Had he been enrolled and allotted land at the time of his death? A I do not know.
Q Did he have a child by Meleah named Wiley? A Yes, sir, the child is present.
Q Do you know when that child was born? A No, sir. He is probably going on four years of age.

This testimony is made part of the record in N. C. 1059.

---oooOOOooo---

I, D. C. Skaggs, on oath state that the above and foregoing is a full and true transcript of my stenographic notes as taken in said cause on said date.

D. C. Skaggs

Subscribed and sworn to before me this 21 day of March, 1906.

Alex Posey
Notary Public.

Western District
Indian Territory   SS

We, the undersigned, on oath state that we are personally acquainted with Maleah Toney   wife of   Rogers Toney (decd)   ; and that on or about the   sometime in day of   June 1902 , a   male   child was born to them and has been named Wiley Toney   ; and that said child was living March 4, 1905.

We further state that we have no interest in the above case.

his
Lewis x Harjo
mark

Applications for Enrollment of Creek Newborn
Act of 1905   Volume XIV

                    her
                Christy x Harjo
                    mark

Witness to mark:
Alex Posey

_____

D C Skaggs

_____

Subscribed and sworn to before
me this 15 day of March 1906

            Alex Posey
            Notary Public.

_____

N.C. 1123.

            Muskogee, Indian Territory, March 1, 1907.

Miles Toney,
    Care Lodger Toney,
        Senora, Indian Territory.

Dear Madam:

    You are hereby advised that on February 15, 1907, the Secretary of the Interior approved the enrollment of your minor child, Wiley Toney, as a citizen by blood of the Creek Nation and that the name of said child appears upon the roll of new born citizens by blood of the Creek Nation, enrolled under the act of Congress approved March 3, 1905, A No. 1220.

    This child is now entitled to allotment and application therefor should be made without delay at the Creek Land Office, Muskogee, Indian Territory.

            Respectfully,
                        Commissioner.

Applications for Enrollment of Creek Newborn
Act of 1905   Volume XIV

BIRTH AFFIDAVIT.

DEPARTMENT OF THE INTERIOR.
COMMISSION TO THE FIVE CIVILIZED TRIBES.

IN RE APPLICATION FOR ENROLLMENT, as a citizen of the Creek Nation, of Wiley Tooney[sic], born on the — day of June, 1902

Name of Father: Lodger Tooney (D)   a citizen of the   Creek   Nation. Hickory Ground
Name of Mother: Maleah " (nee Taylor)   a citizen of the   Creek   Nation. Hutchechubbee Town

    Postoffice   Senora I.T.

(Child present)

AFFIDAVIT OF MOTHER.

UNITED STATES OF AMERICA, Indian Territory, ⎫
    Western   DISTRICT.   ⎭

I, Maleah Tooney[sic], on oath state that I am 27 years of age and a citizen by blood, of the Creek Nation; that I am the lawful wife of Lodger Tooney D, who is a citizen, by blood of the Creek Nation; that a male child was born to me on *(blank)* day of June, 1902, that said child has been named Wiley Toney, and is now living.

                                  her
Witnesses To Mark: Maleah x Tooney
  { EC Griesel   mark
   Jesse McDermott

Subscribed and sworn to before me this 13" day of   April   , 1905.

(Seal)   J McDermott
                             Notary Public.

No
~~AFFIDAVIT OF ATTENDING PHYSICIAN OR MID-WIFE~~.   nor any one else

Applications for Enrollment of Creek Newborn
Act of 1905   Volume XIV

BIRTH AFFIDAVIT.

DEPARTMENT OF THE INTERIOR.
COMMISSION TO THE FIVE CIVILIZED TRIBES.

IN RE APPLICATION FOR ENROLLMENT, as a citizen of the Creek Nation, of Frank Tilley, born on the   15   day of   Aug , 1902

Name of Father: James Tilley   a citizen of the United States Nation.
Name of Mother: Eannah Tilley   a citizen of the   Creek   Nation.

Postoffice   Morse I.T.
Arbar Kachee Town

Acquaintance
AFFIDAVIT OF ~~MOTHER~~.

UNITED STATES OF AMERICA, Indian Territory, ⎫
    Western   DISTRICT.   ⎭

I,   George Hawkins , on oath state that I am 33 years of age and a citizen by blood , of the Creek   Nation; that I am ~~the lawful wife of~~ personally acquainted with Mrs. Eannah Tilley , who is a citizen, by blood of the Creek   Nation; that a male child was born to ~~me~~ her on or about   15   day of August , 1902 , that said child has been named Frank Tilley , and is now living.

His
George x Hawkins
Witnesses To Mark: mark
  ⎰ Lelah Hinha
  ⎱ Chloe Kenneda

Subscribed and sworn to before me this 31 day of   Oct , 1905.

My Commission Expires March 5th, 1908.   C. C. Eskridge
Notary Public.

Acquaintance
~~AFFIDAVIT OF ATTENDING PHYSICIAN OR MID-WIFE.~~

UNITED STATES OF AMERICA, Indian Territory, ⎫
    Western   DISTRICT.   ⎭

am personally acquainted with
I,   Ramsey Knight , a *(blank)* , on oath state that I ~~attended on~~ Mrs. Eannah Tilley , wife of James Tilley on or about the 15 day of Aug , 1902 ; that there was born to her on said date a   male   child; that said child is now living and is said to have been named Frank Tilley

Ramsey Knight

Applications for Enrollment of Creek Newborn
Act of 1905   Volume XIV

Witnesses To Mark:

{

Subscribed and sworn to before me this 31 day of   Oct , 1905.

My Commission Expires March 5th, 1908.   C. C. Eskridge
                                              Notary Public.

BIRTH AFFIDAVIT.

DEPARTMENT OF THE INTERIOR.
COMMISSION TO THE FIVE CIVILIZED TRIBES.

IN RE APPLICATION FOR ENROLLMENT, as a citizen of the Creek Nation, of   Frank Tilley, born on the   15   day of   Aug , 1902

Name of Father: James Tilley   a citizen of the   U.S.   Nation.
Name of Mother: Eannah Tilley (nee Heneha)   a citizen of the   Creek   Nation.
Arbekochee
Cr C Field No 1277   Postoffice   Lawton, Oklahoma

AFFIDAVIT OF MOTHER.
                                              Child Present

UNITED STATES OF AMERICA, Indian Territory, ⎫
        Western   DISTRICT.   ⎬
                                             ⎭

I, Eannah Tilley , on oath state that I am 23 years of age and a citizen by blood, of the Creek Nation; that I am the lawful wife of James Tilley , who is a citizen, by ——— of the U.S. Nation; that a   male   child was born to me on   15 day of Aug , 1902 , that said child has been named   Frank Tilley , and is now living.

                                  Eannah Tilley

Witnesses To Mark:

{

Subscribed and sworn to before me this 13 day of   April   , 1905.

(Seal)   Edw C Griesel
                                    Notary Public.

Applications for Enrollment of Creek Newborn
Act of 1905   Volume XIV

AFFIDAVIT OF ~~ATTENDING PHYSICIAN OR MID-WIFE~~.

UNITED STATES OF AMERICA, Indian Territory,
Western   DISTRICT.

I,   James Tilley   , a (father) , on oath state that I attended on Mrs. Eannah Tilley my, wife ~~of~~ ——on the   15   day of   Aug , 1902 ; that there was born to her on said date a   male   child; that said child is now living and is said to have been named Frank Tilley

James Tilley

Witnesses To Mark:
{

Subscribed and sworn to before me this 13 day of   April   , 1905.

(Seal)   Edw C Griesel
                                         Notary Public.

BIRTH AFFIDAVIT.

DEPARTMENT OF THE INTERIOR.
COMMISSION TO THE FIVE CIVILIZED TRIBES.

IN RE APPLICATION FOR ENROLLMENT, as a citizen of the Creek Nation, of   Laura May Tilley, born on the   28   day of   Jan   , 1904

Name of Father: James Tilley   a citizen of the United States Nation.
Name of Mother: Eannah Tilley   a citizen of the   Creek   Nation.

                    Postoffice   Morse I.T.
                                  Arbar Kochee Town

                                    Acquaintance
AFFIDAVIT OF ~~MOTHER~~.

UNITED STATES OF AMERICA, Indian Territory,
Western   DISTRICT.

I,   George Hawkins , on oath state that I am   33   years of age and a citizen by blood , of the Creek   Nation; that I am ~~the lawful wife of~~ personally acquainted with Mrs. Eannah Tilley , who is a citizen, by blood of the Creek   Nation; that a Female child was born to ~~me~~ her on or about   28   day of Jan , 1904 , that said child has been named Laura May Tilley , and is now living.

                                         His
                                George x Hawkins
                                        mark

201

Applications for Enrollment of Creek Newborn
Act of 1905   Volume XIV

Witnesses To Mark:
{ Lelah Hinha
  Chloe Kenneda

Subscribed and sworn to before me this 31 day of   Oct , 1905.

My Commission Expires March 5th, 1908.   C. C. Eskridge
                                                              Notary Public.

                                             Acquaintance
AFFIDAVIT OF ATTENDING PHYSICIAN OR MID-WIFE.

UNITED STATES OF AMERICA, Indian Territory, }
         Western   **DISTRICT.**

                                                              am personally acquainted with
I,   Ramsey Knight , a *(blank)* , on oath state that I ~~attended on~~ Mrs. Eannah Tilley , wife of   James Tilley   on or about the 28 day of Jan , 1904 ; that there was born to her on said date a Female child; that said child is now living and is said to have been named Laura May Tilley

                                             Ramsey Knight
Witnesses To Mark:
{

Subscribed and sworn to before me this 31 day of   Oct , 1905.

My Commission Expires March 5th, 1908.   C. C. Eskridge
                                                              Notary Public.

BIRTH AFFIDAVIT.
                     DEPARTMENT OF THE INTERIOR.
                     COMMISSION TO THE FIVE CIVILIZED TRIBES.

IN RE APPLICATION FOR ENROLLMENT, as a citizen of the Creek Nation, of   Laura May Tilley, born on the   28 day of   Jan , 1904

Name of Father: James Tilley   a citizen of the   U.S.   Nation.
Name of Mother: Eannah Tilley (nee Heneha)   a citizen of the   *(blank)*   Nation.
Cr C #1277
                                  Postoffice   Lawton, Oklahoma

Applications for Enrollment of Creek Newborn
Act of 1905   Volume XIV

AFFIDAVIT OF MOTHER.

Child <u>Present</u>

UNITED STATES OF AMERICA, Indian Territory,
Western   DISTRICT.

    I, Eannah Tilley, on oath state that I am 23 years of age and a citizen by blood, of the Creek Nation; that I am the lawful wife of James Tilley, who is a citizen, by ——— of the ——— Nation; that a female child was born to me on 28 day of Jan, 1904, that said child has been named Laura May Tilley, and is now living.

                                      Eannah Tilley

Witnesses To Mark:
{

    Subscribed and sworn to before me this 13 day of   April , 1905.

(Seal)   Edw C Griesel
                                        Notary Public.

AFFIDAVIT OF ~~ATTENDING PHYSICIAN OR MID-WIFE~~.

UNITED STATES OF AMERICA, Indian Territory,
Western   DISTRICT.

    I, James Tilley, a (father), on oath state that I attended on Mrs. Eannah Tilley, wife of James Tilley on the 28 day of Jan, 1904; that there was born to her on said date a female child; that said child is now living and is said to have been named Laura May Tilley

                                        James Tilley

Witnesses To Mark:
{

    Subscribed and sworn to before me this 13 day of   April , 1905.

(Seal)   Edw C Griesel
                                        Notary Public.

AFFIDAVIT.

Territory of Oklahoma,)
  County of Comanche,) ss.   Before me, G.W. Crosby, a Notary Public in and for the county and Territory aforesaid, personally appeared Mollie Woodfin, whose post-office address is Lawton, O.T., who being duly sworn according to law states that she is 40 years of age, have been personally acquainted with James Tilley and his wife Annie Tilleyy for the past four years, having lived near neighbor to them during said time. That on the 15th of August 1902, I called at the house of the said James Tilley. That the child

Applications for Enrollment of Creek Newborn
Act of 1905 Volume XIV

named Frank who then less than 24 hours old. I sometime in February, 1904, I visited the home of the said James Tilley and the child named Laura, was then about three weeks old.

I have lived as a neighbor to the said Tilleys all the said time, four years past and know them very well. I am in no way related to either of the parents and have no interest in the above claim.

I also state under oath that both children, Frank Tilley and Laura Tilley are still living.

Mollie Woodfin

Sworn to and subscribed before me, this the 11 day of October, 1905.

GW Crosby
Notary Public.

My Commission expires Oct. 22, 1906.

AFFIDAVIT.

Territory of Oklahoma,)
County of Comanche,) ss.   Before me, G.W. Crosby, a Notary Public, in and for the county and Territory aforesaid, personally appeared Laura Ray, age 37 years, who being duly sworn according to law says, that on the 28th day of January, 1904, I was present at the home of James and Annie Tilley, this being the birth of the the[sic] child Laura Tilley.

I have lived a[sic] near neighbor to the Tilleys ever since and can state that the children Frank Tilley who was born in August 1902, and Laura Tilley, who was born January 28, 1904, are both now living.

I also state that I am in no way related to the parents of the children and am not interested in their claim either present or prospective. My post-office address is Lawton, O.T.

Laura Ray

Sworn to and subscribed before me, this the 12 day of October, 1905.

GW Crosby
Notary Public.

My Commission expires Oct. 22, 1906.

AFFIDAVIT.

Territory of Oklahoma,)
County of Comanche,) ss.   Before me, G.W. Crosby, a Notary Public, in and for the county and Territory aforesaid, personally appeared James Tilley and Annie

Applications for Enrollment of Creek Newborn
Act of 1905 Volume XIV

Tilley, his wife, who being duly sworn according to law says, that they are the parents of Frank Tilley who was born on the 15 day of August 1902 and Laura Tilley who was born on the 28th day of January, 1904. That both of said children are now living.

           James Tilley

           Annie Tilley

Sworn to and subscribed before me this the 11 day of October, 1905.

           GW Crosby
           Notary Public.

My Commission expires Oct. 22, 1906.

NC-1124

         Muskogee, Indian Territory, September 27, 1905.

James Tilley,
  Lawton, Oklahoma Territory.

Dear Sir:

  Receipt is acknowledged of your communication of September 23, 1905, in which you ask when you will be permitted to file for your minor children, Frank and Laura May Tilley.

  In reply you are advised that this Office requires the affidavits of two disinterested witnesses as to the birth of each of your said children. Said affidavits must set forth said child's name, the names of its parents, the date of its birth, and whether or not it was living March 4, 1905.

         Respectfully,

              Commissioner.

NC 1124

         Muskogee, Indian Territory, October 21, 1905.

Eannah Tilley,
  Care James Tilley,
    Lawton, Oklahoma.

Dear Madam:

  In the matter of the application for the enrollment of your minor children, Frank Tilley, born August 15, 1902, and May Laura[sic] Tilley, born January 28, 1904, as citizens by blood of the Creek Nation, this office desires affidavit of the midwife or

Applications for Enrollment of Creek Newborn
Act of 1905 Volume XIV

physician in attendance at the birth of each of said children and blanks for that purpose are enclosed herewith.

In the event that there was no physician or midwife in attendance when said children were born, it will be necessary for you to furnish this office with the affidavits of two disinterested witnesses relative to the birth of each of said children. Said affidavits must set forth the names of said children, the dates of their birth, the names of their parents and whether or not they were living on March 4, 1905.

Respectfully,

Commissioner.

2 BC
Env.

2072 B
DEPARTMENT OF THE INTERIOR,
COMMISSION TO THE FIVE CIVILIZED TRIBES.
April 13, 1905, Okmulgee, I.T.

In the matter of the application for the enrollment of John Williams as a citizen of the Creek Nation.

Eli Williams, being duly sworn, by E.C. Griesel, notary public, testified as follows:

By Commission:
Q What is your name? A Eli Williams.
Q How old are you? A 42.
Q What is your post office? A Okmulgee.
Q Do you wish to make application for the enrollment of your child, John Williams, do you? A Yes, sir.
Q When was John Williams born? A August 19, 1902.
Q Who is the mother of this child? A Mary Williams.
Q Q[sic] You are a citizen of the Creek Nation, are you? A Yes.
Q Is your wife a Creek citizen? A No sir. She is a Seminole.
Q That child is living now is it? A Yes sir.
Q If it should be found that your child John Williams is entitled to enrollment in both the Seminole and Creek Nations, in what Nation do you elect to have your child enrolled and receive his allotment of land? A In the Creek Nation.

Applications for Enrollment of Creek Newborn
Act of 1905   Volume XIV

Edward C. Griesel being duly sworn, on his oath, states that he reported the above and foregoing is a true and correct transcript of his stenographic notes as taken in said cause on said date.

Edw C Griesel

Subscribed and sworn to before me this 5 day of May, 1905.

Zera E Parrish
Notary Public.

Indian Territory, I
 ss:
Western District. I

We, the undersigned, do hereby elect to have our child, John Williams, born on the 19 day of August, 1902, enrolled as a citizen of the Creek Nation, and to have said child receive his allotment of land and distribution of moneys in said nation.

Witnesses to mark:
_____
F.B. Severs
H M Harjo

his
Eli x Williams
mark
her
Mary x Williams
mark

Subscribed and sworn to before me this 10 day of March, 1906

Alex Posey
Notary Public.

BIRTH AFFIDAVIT.

DEPARTMENT OF THE INTERIOR.
COMMISSION TO THE FIVE CIVILIZED TRIBES.

IN RE APPLICATION FOR ENROLLMENT, as a citizen of the Creek Nation, of John Williams, born on the *(blank)* day of August, 1904[sic]

Name of Father: Eli Williams   a citizen of the   Creek   Nation.
Name of Mother: Mary Williams   a citizen of the   Seminole Nation.

Postoffice   Okmulgee, Indian Territory.

207

Applications for Enrollment of Creek Newborn
Act of 1905 Volume XIV

AFFIDAVIT OF MOTHER.

UNITED STATES OF AMERICA, Indian Territory, ⎫
    Western   DISTRICT.   ⎬
                                                ⎭

    I, Mary Williams, on oath state that I am 25 to 30 years of age and a citizen by Blood, of the Seminole Nation; that I am the lawful wife of Eli Williams, who is a citizen, by blood of the Creek Nation; that a male child was born to me on *(blank)* day August, 1903, that said child has been named John Williams, and was living March 4, 1905. and is still living.

                                        her
                              Mary x Williams
Witnesses To Mark: mark
  { J H Winston
    Geo C. Beidleman

    Subscribed and sworn to before me this 3rd day of March, 190.

                                        Geo. C Beidleman
                                                Notary Public.
My Commission Expires April 27th, 1908.

AFFIDAVIT OF ATTENDING PHYSICIAN OR MID-WIFE.

UNITED STATES OF AMERICA, Indian Territory, ⎫
    Western   DISTRICT.   ⎬
                                                ⎭

    I, Eli Williams, Husband of Mary Williams, on oath state that I attended on Mrs. Mary Williams my wife, ~~wife of~~ *(blank)* on the *(blank)* day of August, 1903; that there was born to her on said date a male child; that said child was living March 4, 1905, and is said to have been named John Williams and is still living

                                        his
                              John[sic] x Williams
Witnesses To Mark: mark
  { H Winston
    Geo C. Beidleman

    Subscribed and sworn to before me this 3rd day of March, 190.

                                        Geo. C Beidleman
                                                Notary Public.
My Commission Expires April 27th, 1908.

Applications for Enrollment of Creek Newborn
Act of 1905   Volume XIV

Indian Territory)
) SS
Western District)

We, the undersigned, on oath state that we are personally acquainted with   Mary Williams   wife of   Eli Williams ; and that on or about the   19   day of   August 1902 , a   male   child was born to them and has been named   John Williams ; and that said child was living March 4, 1905.

We further state that we have no interest in the above case.

Robert Wolf

(Illegible) Wolfe

Witnesses to mark:

_____
_____
_____

Subscribed and sworn to before me this 10 day of March 1906.

Alex Posey
Notary Public.

BIRTH AFFIDAVIT.

DEPARTMENT OF THE INTERIOR.
COMMISSION TO THE FIVE CIVILIZED TRIBES.

IN RE APPLICATION FOR ENROLLMENT, as a citizen of the Creek Nation, of   John Williams , born on the   19   day of   Aug   , 1902

Name of Father: Eli Williams   a citizen of the   Creek   Nation. Tulwarthlocco Town
Name of Mother: Mary Williams   a citizen of the   Seminole   Nation. Seminole

Postoffice   Okmulgee I.Ty.

Father
AFFIDAVIT OF ~~MOTHER~~.

UNITED STATES OF AMERICA, Indian Territory,
   Western   DISTRICT.

I,   Eli Williams , on oath state that I am   42   years of age and a citizen by   blood , of the   Creek   Nation; that I am the lawful ~~wife~~ husband of   Mary Williams , who is a

Applications for Enrollment of Creek Newborn
Act of 1905   Volume XIV

citizen, by blood of the Creek[sic] Nation; that a male child was born to me on 19 day of Aug , 1902 , that said child has been named John Williams , and was living March 4, 1905.

Witnesses To Mark:
{ Edw C Griesel
{ Jesse McDermott

                           his
                          Eli x Williams
                          mark

Subscribed and sworn to before me this   13" day of   April   , 1905.

(Seal)   J McDermott
                             Notary Public.

NC. 1125.

Muskogee, Indian Territory, July 15, 1905.

Chief Clerk,
    Seminole Enrollment Division,
        Muskogee, Indian Territory.

Dear Sir:

    April 19, 1905, application was made to the Commission to the Five Civilized Tribes for the enrollment of John Williams, born August 19, 1902, as a citizen by blood of the Creek Nation. It is stated in said application that the father of said child is Eli Williams, a citizen of the Creek Nation, and that the mother is Mary Williams, a citizen of the Seminole Nation.

    You are requested to inform the Creek Enrollment Division as to whether application has been made for the enrollment of said John Williams, as a citizen of the Seminole Nation, and if so, what disposition has been made of the same.

                      Respectfully,
                                Commissioner.

Applications for Enrollment of Creek Newborn
Act of 1905   Volume XIV

W.F.

DEPARTMENT OF THE INTERIOR.
COMMISSION TO THE FIVE CIVILIZED TRIBES.

Muskogee, Indian Territory, July 19, 1905.

Chief Clerk,
    Creek Enrollment Division.

Dear Sir:

    Receipt is acknowledged of your letter of July 15, 1905, (NC-1125) stating that application was made to the Commission to the Five Civilized Tribes for the enrollment of John Williams, born August 19, 1902, child of Eli Williams, a citizen of the Creek Nation, and Mary Williams, a citizen of the Seminole Nation, as a citizen by blood of the Creek Nation, and requesting to be informed as to whether application was made for the enrollment of said child as a citizen of the Seminole Nation.

    In reply to your letter you are advised that it does not appear from an examination of the records of this office that any application was made for the enrollment of said John Williams as a citizen of the Seminole Nation.

                  Respectfully,
                  Tams Bixby   Commissioner.

HGH

REFER IN REPLY TO THE FOLLOWING:
NC. 1125

DEPARTMENT OF THE INTERIOR,
COMMISSIONER TO THE FIVE CIVILIZED TRIBES.

Muskogee, Indian Territory, October 24, 1905.

Mary Williams,
    Care Eli Williams,
        Okmulgee, Indian Territory.

Dear Madam:

    In the matter of the application for the enrollment of your minor child, John Williams, born August 19, 1902, as a citizen by blood of the Creek Nation, this office desires your affidavit and affidavit of the midwife or physician in attendance at the birth of said child and a blank for that purpose is enclosed herewith.

    In the event that there was no physician or midwife in attendance when said child was born, it will be necessary for you to furnish this office with the affidavits of two

Applications for Enrollment of Creek Newborn
Act of 1905   Volume XIV

disinterested witnesses relative to his birth. Said affidavits must set forth said child's name, the date of his birth, the names of his parents and whether or not he was living on March 4, 1905.

This office desires your affidavit electing in which nation, Creek or Seminole, you wish to have said child enrolled and receive his allotment of land.

Respectfully,

BA-Env.   Tams Bixby Commissioner.

N.C. 1125

Muskogee, Indian Territory, February 21, 1906.

Beidleman & Winstor[sic],
    Okmulgee, Indian Territory.

Gentlemen:

Receipt is acknowledged of your letter of February 17, 1906 in which you state that you have been employed by Eli Williams to ascertain if it is too late to file for his minor child, John Williams, born in August 1904, and Haddie William, born in January 1906.

You are advised that this office at the present time has no knowledge of a law under which a child born in January 1906 would be entitled to enrollment as a citizen of the Creek Nation.

You are further advised that there is on file with this office an application for the enrollment of said John Williams, a citizen by blood of the Creek Nation; that a letter has been written to Mary Williams, a Seminole, the mother of said John Williams advising her that this office requires her affidavit and affidavit of the midwife or attending physician at the birth of said child; said Mary Williams was further advised that it is necessary for her to elect in which Nation, Creek or Seminole she desires to have said child enrolled.

There is herewith enclosed blank form of birth affidavit, and you are requested to have same properly executed and return to this office.

Respectfully,

Acting Commissioner.

Applications for Enrollment of Creek Newborn
Act of 1905   Volume XIV

N.C. 1125

Muskogee, Indian Territory, March 9, 1906.

Beidleman & Winston,
    Okmulgee, Indian Territory.

Gentlemen:

    Receipt is acknowledged of your letter of March 3, 1906 inclosing affidavits in the matter of the application for the enrollment of John Williams as a citizen of the Creek nation[sic]; you ask if any thing further is required in the case.

    You are advised that there is on file in this office an affidavit of the father of said child stating that it was born August 19, 1902; and the affidavits inclosed by you state that John Williams was born in August 1903. To correct said discrepancy you are advised that the parents of said John Williams will be allowed fifteen days from date hereon within which to appear at this office with two disinterested witnesses, in lieu of the midwife, for the purpose of being examined under oath.

                Respectfully,

                            Acting Commissioner.

N.C. 1125

Muskogee, Indian Territory, March 1, 1907.

Eli Williams,
    Okmulgee, Indian Territory.

Dear Sir:

    You are hereby advised that on February 15, 1907, the Secretary of the Interior approved the enrollment of your minor child, John Williams, as a citizen by blood of the Creek Nation and that the name of said child appears upon the roll of new born citizens by blood of the Creek Nation, enrolled under the Act of Congress approved March 3, 1905, as No. 1221.

    This child is now entitled to allotment and application therefor should be made without delay at the Creek Land Office, Muskogee, Indian Territory.

                Respectfully,

                            Commissioner.

Applications for Enrollment of Creek Newborn
Act of 1905   Volume XIV

BIRTH AFFIDAVIT.

Copy

DEPARTMENT OF THE INTERIOR.
COMMISSION TO THE FIVE CIVILIZED TRIBES.

IN RE APPLICATION FOR ENROLLMENT, as a citizen of the Creek Nation, of Mary Dan, born on the 29 day of Aug, 1904

Name of Father: Somecher Dan   a citizen of the   Creek   Nation. Mujoka Town
Name of Mother: Lizzie Dan (nee Mikey)   a citizen of the   Creek   Nation. Mujoka Town

Postoffice   Morse, I.T.

Father

AFFIDAVIT OF ~~MOTHER~~.

UNITED STATES OF AMERICA, Indian Territory, }
Western   DISTRICT.

I, Somecher Dan, on oath state that I am 22 years of age and a citizen by blood, of the Creek Nation; that I am the lawful ~~wife~~ husband of Lizzie Dan (nee Mikey), who is a citizen, by blood of the Creek Nation; that a female child was born to ~~me~~ her on 29" day of Aug, 1904, that said child has been named Mary Dan, and is now living.

(Signed) Somecher x Dan
                     his mark

Witnesses To Mark:
{ EC Griesel
{ Jesse McDermott

Subscribed and sworn to before me this 13 day of Apr, 1905.
(Seal)

J McDermott
Notary Public.

Applications for Enrollment of Creek Newborn
Act of 1905 Volume XIV

Copy
DEPARTMENT OF THE INTERIOR.
COMMISSION TO THE FIVE CIVILIZED TRIBES.

In the matter of the death of Mary Den a citizen of the Creek Nation, who formerly resided at or near Morse , Ind. Ter., and died on the 19 day of February , 1904

AFFIDAVIT OF RELATIVE.

UNITED STATES OF AMERICA, Indian Territory, }
Western Judicial DISTRICT.

    I, Somihehar Den , on oath state that I am 22 years of age and a citizen by blood , of the Creek Nation; that my postoffice address is Morse , Ind. Ter.; that I am Father of Mary Den who was a citizen, by blood , of the Creek Nation and that said Mary Den died on the 19 day of February , 1904

                                              his
                                    Somihehar x Den
Witnesses To Mark: mark
    { WH Dill Okemah IT
    { Tupper Dunn
(Seal)
    Subscribed and sworn to before me this 22 day of April, 1905.

My Com exp Aug 1908/   Signed Tupper Dunn
                                                        Notary Public.

AFFIDAVIT OF ACQUAINTANCE.

UNITED STATES OF AMERICA, Indian Territory, }
Western Judicial DISTRICT.

    I, Silwar , on oath state that I am 51 years of age, and a citizen by blood of the Creek Nation; that my postoffice address is Morse , Ind. Ter.; that I was personally acquainted with Mary Den who was a citizen, by blood , of the Creek Nation; and that said Mary Den died on the 19 day of February , 1904

                                              her
                                    Silwar x
Witnesses To Mark: mark
    { WH Dill Okemah IT
    { Tupper Dunn
Seal
    Subscribed and sworn to before me this 22 day of April, 1905.

Applications for Enrollment of Creek Newborn
Act of 1905 Volume XIV

My Com exp Aug 1908　　　　　　　　　Tupper Dunn
　　　　　　　　　　　　　　　　　　　　Notary Public.

BIRTH AFFIDAVIT.

Copy

DEPARTMENT OF THE INTERIOR.
COMMISSION TO THE FIVE CIVILIZED TRIBES.

IN RE APPLICATION FOR ENROLLMENT, as a citizen of the Creek Nation, of Mary Den, born on the 29" day of August, 1904.

Name of Father:　　Somihchar Den　　　a citizen of the　Creek　Nation.
Name of Mother:　　Lizzie Den　　　　　a citizen of the　Creek　Nation.

　　　　　　　　　　Postoffice　　Morse, I.T.

AFFIDAVIT OF MOTHER.

UNITED STATES OF AMERICA, Indian Territory, ⎫
　　Western Judicial　　DISTRICT. ⎭

　　I, Lizzie Den, on oath state that I am 20 years of age and a citizen by blood, of the Creek Nation; that I am the lawful wife of Somihchar Den, who is a citizen, by blood of the Creek Nation; that a female child was born to me on 29" day of August, 1904, that said child has been named Mary Den, and ~~is now living~~. died 19 day of February 1905. (This was made in former afft 2/19/04 error)

　　　　　　　　　　　　　　　　　　　her
　　　　　　　　　　　　　　　　Lizzie x Den
Witnesses To Mark:　　　　　　　　mark
　　⎰ C A Huddleston
　　⎱ Tupper Dunn Okemah I.T.
(Seal)
　　Subscribed and sworn to before me this 23 day of Aug, 1905.

　　　　　　　　　　　(Signed) Tupper Dunn
My Com exp Aug 19-1908　　　　　　　Notary Public.

Applications for Enrollment of Creek Newborn
Act of 1905   Volume XIV

AFFIDAVIT OF ATTENDING PHYSICIAN OR MID-WIFE.

UNITED STATES OF AMERICA, Indian Territory,
Western Judicial   DISTRICT.

I, Silwa , a Midwife , on oath state that I attended on Mrs. Lizzie Den , wife of Somihchar Den on the 29" day of August , 1904 ; that there was born to her on said date a female child; that said child ~~is now living~~ and is said to have been named Mary Den   died on 19 day of Feb 1905

                                            her
                                   Silwa   x
Witnesses To Mark: mark

{ ....
  .... }

Subscribed and sworn to before me this .... day of ...., 190......

                                  Notary Public.

BIRTH AFFIDAVIT.
DEPARTMENT OF THE INTERIOR.
COMMISSION TO THE FIVE CIVILIZED TRIBES.

IN RE APPLICATION FOR ENROLLMENT, as a citizen of the Creek Nation, of Ella Ruth Harjo , born on the 29" day of   May , 1903

Name of Father: H. M. Harjo   a citizen of the   Creek   Nation.
Eufaula Canadian
Name of Mother: Kate M "   a citizen of the   Creek   Nation.

                 Postoffice   Okmulgee, I.T.

Applications for Enrollment of Creek Newborn
Act of 1905   Volume XIV

AFFIDAVIT OF MOTHER.   (Child present)

UNITED STATES OF AMERICA, Indian Territory, }
Western   DISTRICT.

I, Kate M Harjo , on oath state that I am 29 years of age and a citizen by blood , of the Creek Nation; that I am the lawful wife of H. M. Harjo , who is a citizen, by blood of the Creek Nation; that a female child was born to me on 29 day of May , 1903 , that said child has been named Ella Ruth Harjo , and is now living.

                                    Kate M. Harjo

Witnesses To Mark:
{

Subscribed and sworn to before me this 13" day of April , 1905.

                                    J McDermott
                                        Notary Public.

AFFIDAVIT OF ATTENDING PHYSICIAN OR MID-WIFE.

UNITED STATES OF AMERICA, Indian Territory, }
Western   DISTRICT.

I, W. C. Mitchener , a physician , on oath state that I attended on Mrs. Kate M Harjo , wife of H. M. Harjo on the 29" day of May , 1903 ; that there was born to her on said date a female child; that said child is now living and is said to have been named Ella Ruth Harjo

                                    W. C. Mitchener M.D.

Witnesses To Mark:
{

Subscribed and sworn to before me this 13" day of April , 1905.

                                    J McDermott
                                        Notary Public.

Applications for Enrollment of Creek Newborn
Act of 1905   Volume XIV

NC 1128

                        Muskogee, Indian Territory, October 24, 1905.

Wisey Harjo,
    Care Lewis Harjo,
        Senora, Indian Territory.

Dear Madam:

    In the matter of the application for the enrollment of your minor child, Bennie Harjo, born during the month of March 1902, as a citizen by blood of the Creek Nation, this office desires the affidavits of two disinterested witnesses relative to his birth. Said affidavits must set forth said child's name, the date of his birth, the names of his parents and whether or not he was living on March 4, 1905.

    This office is unable to identify you on its final roll of citizens by blood of the Creek Nation; you are requested to state if you were ever known by the name of Nancy Tyler or Wisey Yettekahajo, also state your maiden name, the names of your parents, the Creek Indian town to which you belong and your roll number as the same appears on your deeds and allotment certificate.

                    Respectfully,

                                Commissioner.

BA
Env.

Indian Territory)
) SS
Western District)

    We, the undersigned, on oath state that we are personally acquainted with Wisey Harjo   wife of   Lewis Harjo   ; and that ~~on or about the~~ sometime in ~~day of~~ March 1902, a   male child was born to them and has been named   Bennie Harjo ; and that said child was living March 4, 1905.

    We further state that we have no interest in the above case.

                                      her
                             Jennie x Scott
                                  mark
                                    her
                             Fanny x *(Illegible)*
Witnesses to mark: mark
    Alex Posey

    DC Skaggs

Applications for Enrollment of Creek Newborn
Act of 1905 Volume XIV

Subscribed and sworn to before me this 19 day of March 1906.

                                                    Alex Posey
                                                    Notary Public.

BIRTH AFFIDAVIT.

DEPARTMENT OF THE INTERIOR.
COMMISSION TO THE FIVE CIVILIZED TRIBES.

IN RE APPLICATION FOR ENROLLMENT, as a citizen of the Creek Nation, of Bennie Harjo, born on the — day of Mar , 1902

Name of Father: Lewis Harjo   a citizen of the   Creek   Nation.
Hickory Ground
Name of Mother: Wisey " (Taylor)   a citizen of the   Creek   Nation.
Quassartte Town
                             Postoffice   Senora I.T.

                                            (Child present)
AFFIDAVIT OF MOTHER.

UNITED STATES OF AMERICA, Indian Territory,
     Western   DISTRICT.

I, Wisey Harjo , on oath state that I am 28 years of age and a citizen by blood , of the Creek Nation; that I am the lawful wife of Lewis Harjo , who is a citizen, by blood of the Creek Nation; that a male child was born to me on —day of Mar , 1902 , that said child has been named Bennie Harjo , and is now living.

                                             her
                                     Wisey x Harjo
Witnesses To Mark: mark
   { EC Griesel
      Jesse McDermott

Subscribed and sworn to before me this 13" day of April , 1905.

                                                J McDermott
                                                Notary Public.

                              No Midwife (No one present)
                  AFFIDAVIT OF ATTENDING PHYSICIAN OR MID-WIFE.

Applications for Enrollment of Creek Newborn
Act of 1905   Volume XIV

NC 1129

Muskogee, Indian Territory, October 24, 1905.

Leila Drew,
    Care Legus C. Drew,
        Broken Arrow, Indian Territory.

Dear Madam:

    In the matter of the application for the enrollment of your minor child, Madella E. Drew, born February 7, 1905, as a citizen by blood of the Creek Nation, this office is unable to identify you on its final roll of citizens by blood of the Creek Nation; you are requested to state you maiden name, the names of your parents, the Creek Indian town to which you belong and your roll number as the same appears on your deeds and allotment certificate.

                Respectfully,

                        Commissioner.

C-1129   (Copy)

                        Broken Arrow, I. T.
                        Oct. 27, 1905

Department of the Interior,
    Commissioner to the Five Civilized Tribes.
        Muskogee, Ind. Terr.

Dear Sir:

    I reply in reference to N C 1129 in regard to the enrollment of my minor child, Madella E. Drew, born February 7, 1905, as a citizen by blood of the Creek Nation;

    My maiden name was Lela S. Wright, my father's name was E. A. Wright, my ~~my~~ mother's name was Mary Ellen Wright, nee Rogers, and the Creek Indian town to which I belong is Big Springs.

    My roll number as it appears on my deeds and allotment certificate is One Thousand Five Hundred and Fifty-one (1551)

                        Respectfully,
                        (signed)   LEILA DREW
                        (Lela S. Drew, nee Wright).

Applications for Enrollment of Creek Newborn
Act of 1905   Volume XIV

BIRTH AFFIDAVIT.

DEPARTMENT OF THE INTERIOR.
COMMISSION TO THE FIVE CIVILIZED TRIBES.

IN RE APPLICATION FOR ENROLLMENT, as a citizen of the Creek Nation, of   Madella E. Drew , born on the   7th   day of   February , 1905

Name of Father: Legus C. Drew   a citizen of the   Creek   Nation.
Name of Mother: Leila Drew   a citizen of the   Creek   Nation.

Postoffice   Broken Arrow, Indian Territory.

AFFIDAVIT OF MOTHER.

UNITED STATES OF AMERICA, Indian Territory, }
        Western   DISTRICT.

I, Leila Drew , on oath state that I am 23 years of age and a citizen by blood , of the Creek   Nation; that I am the lawful wife of Legus C. Drew , who is a citizen, by blood of the Creek   Nation; that a   female   child was born to me on 7th   day of February , 1905 , that said child has been named   Madella E. Drew , and is now living.

Leila Drew

Witnesses To Mark:
{

Subscribed and sworn to before me this   13 day of   April   , 1905.

RC Allen
My Com Ex. Mch 14, 1908.   Notary Public.

AFFIDAVIT OF ATTENDING PHYSICIAN OR MID-WIFE.

UNITED STATES OF AMERICA, Indian Territory, }
        Western   DISTRICT.

I, R.S. Plumlee , a physician , on oath state that I attended on Mrs. Leila Drew, wife of Legus C. Drew on the 7th   day of February , 1905 ; that there was born to her on said date a female   child; that said child is now living and is said to have been named Madella E. Drew.

R. S. Plumlee, M.D.

Witnesses To Mark:
{

Applications for Enrollment of Creek Newborn
Act of 1905   Volume XIV

Subscribed and sworn to before me this 15 day of   April   , 1905.

(Illegible) Farmer
Notary Public.

Com Ex Jan 19, 1909

En.746.

DEPARTMENT OF THE INTERIOR,
COMMISSIONER TO THE FIVE CIVILIZED TRIBES.
Senora, I. T., October 10, 1905.

In the matter of the application for the enrollment of Selina Arbuckle as a citizen by blood of the Creek Nation.

SHAWNEE JACOBS, being duly sworn, testified as follows:

Through Alex Posey Official Interpreter:

BY THE COMMISSIONER:
Q   What is your name?   A   Shawnee Jacobs, but I am enrolled by the Commission as John Jacobs.
Q   How old are you?   A   Thirty-six.
Q   What is your post office address?   A   Senora.
Q   Are you a citizen of the Creek Nation?   A   Yes, sir.
Q   To what town do you belong?   A   Osoche.
Q   Have you a daughter named Selina Arbuckle?   A   Yes, sir. The child was named after its grandfather, Ahpale (or Arbuckle) Harjo.
Q   What was the name of the mother of this child?   A   Epsey, a daughter of Semihoye. He is now dead.
Q   Is Selina living?   A   Yes, sir.
Q   How old is she?   A   About nine years old.
Q   She has never been enrolled has she?   A   No, sir.

---oooOOOooo---

I, D. C. Skaggs, on oath state that the above and foregoing is a full and true transcript of my stenographic notes as taken in said cause on said date.

Applications for Enrollment of Creek Newborn
Act of 1905   Volume XIV

D. C. Skaggs

Subscribed and sworn to before me this 30 day of Dec, 1905.

Edw C Griesel

N.C. 1130.

DEPARTMENT OF THE INTERIOR,
COMMISSIONER TO THE FIVE CIVILIZED TRIBES.
Senora, I. T., March 15, 1906.

In the matter of the application for the enrollment of John Jacob[sic] as a citizen by blood of the Creek Nation.

JEANETTA JACOB, being duly sworn, testified as follows;

Through Alex Posey Official Interpreter:

BY THE COMMISSIONER:
Q What is your name? A Jeanetta Jacob.
Q How old are you? A About twenty-seven.
Q What is your post office address? A Senora.
Q Are you a citizen of the Creek Nation? A Yes, sir.
Q To what town do you belong? A Hickory Ground.
Q What was your maiden name and under what name are you enrolled? A Simply as Jeanetta.
Q Who are your parents? A My mother is Semihoye, is Hickory Ground Town and my father was Ahpahle (or Arbuckle) Harjo, who is also known as Willie Walker.
Q To what town did he belong? A Tuckabatchee. My mother is living but my father is dead.
Q Have you a child named John Jacob? A Yes, sir.
Q When was he born? A December 1, 1903.

---oooOOOooo---

I, D. C. Skaggs, on oath state that the above and foregoing is a full and true transcript of my stenographic notes as taken in said cause on said date.

D. C. Skaggs

Subscribed and sworn to before me this 21st day of March, 1906.

Alex Posey
Notary Public.

Applications for Enrollment of Creek Newborn
Act of 1905   Volume XIV

N.C. 1130.

DEPARTMENT OF THE INTERIOR,
COMMISSIONER TO THE FIVE CIVILIZED TRIBES.
Okmulgee, I. T., March 6, 1906.

In the matter of the application for the enrollment of John Jacobs as a citizen by blood of the Creek Nation.

Sam (or Shawnee) Jacobs, being duly sworn, testified as follows:

Through Alex Posey official interpreter:

BY THE COMMISSIONER:
Q What is your name? A Sam Jacobs.
Q How old are you? A About thirty-six.
Q What is your post office address? A Senora.
Q Are you a citizen of the Creek Nation? A Yes, sir.
Q To what town do you belong? A Osoche.
Q Under what name are you enrolled? A Sam Jacobs.

Witness presents allotment deeds Commission Nos. 8216 and 8217, Creek Indian Roll No. 8149, issued to Sam Jacob. Delivered by the Principal Chief of the Creek Nation June 4, 1904.

Q Are you know by any other name? A I am known as Sam Jacobs, Sampson Jacobs and Shawnee Jacobs. My proper name is Sam Jacobs, the name under which I am enrolled. There is but one Sam or Shawnee Jacobs in my town and I am that person.
Q Have you a child named John Jacobs? A Yes, sir.
Q When was John born? December 1, 1903.
Q Is he now living? A Yes, sir.
Q What is the name of his mother? A Jeanetta Jacobs.
Q To what town does she belong? A She is enrolled in Hickory Ground Town and is the niece of Yardeka Harjo. Her mother is Semihoye and her father was Willie Walker, who was also known as Ahpale or Arbuckle Harjo. He belonged, originally, to Tuckabatche town[sic] but was enrolled as a member of Cussehta town[sic].
Q Under what name is your wife, Jeanetta, enrolled? A I think she is enrolled simply as Jeanetta, in the family of Semihoye. We were married a long time before the Tribal Courts of the Creek Nation were abolished.
Q Is Willie Walker living? A No, sir, he is dead.
Q Do you know whether he was allotted land in the Creek Nation before his death? A I do not know. I think the certificates to his allotment were sent to him at Senora but were returned to the Commission. He belonged to the Snake Faction.
Q Did he die before or since the opening of the Creek Land Office? A He has been dead between four and five years.
Q Did he have any other children besides your wife, Jeanetta? A Yes, sir, he had three children.
Q What are their names? A Annie Walker, Sleche Walker and my wife.

Applications for Enrollment of Creek Newborn
Act of 1905   Volume XIV

Q Are Sleche and Annie living? A Yes, sir, I think they are both enrolled as Cheparnoche Walker and Annie Walker.
Q Are your parents living? A No, sir, they have been dead a long time.
Q What were their names? A My father's name was Jacobs and my mother was Loskey. My father belonged to Tuckabatche and my mother belonged to Osoche Town.
Q Did you participate in the $14.00 Payment in 1895? A Yes, sir.
Q Under what name did you draw that money? A Sam Jacob. I also participated in the 1890 Payment. I also made application for the enrollment of two other minor children of mine who are living, named John and Nicey Jacobs, when the Commission was at Okmulgee receiving applications for the enrollment of new born children. I have never heard what disposition was made of said application.

This testimony is made part of the record in Cr. En. 746.

---oooOOOooo---

I, D. C. Skaggs, on oath state that the above and foregoing is a full and true transcript of my stenographic notes as taken in said cause on said date.

D. C. Skaggs

Subscribed and sworn to before me this 12th day of March, 1906.

Alex Posey
Notary Public.

Indian Territory)
) SS
Western District)

We, the undersigned, on oath state that we are personally acquainted with Jeanetta Jacob   wife of   Sam Jacob   ; and that on or about the 1 day of Dec , 1903 , a   male   child was born to them and has been named   John Jacob ; and that said child was living March 4, 1905.

We further state that we have no interest in the above case.

Rosa McIntosh
her
Wisey x Harjo
mark

Witnesses to mark:
Alex Posey
DC Skaggs

Applications for Enrollment of Creek Newborn
Act of 1905   Volume XIV

Subscribed and sworn to before me this 15 day of March 1906.

            Alex Posey
            Notary Public.

BIRTH AFFIDAVIT.

DEPARTMENT OF THE INTERIOR.
COMMISSION TO THE FIVE CIVILIZED TRIBES.

IN RE APPLICATION FOR ENROLLMENT, as a citizen of the Creek Nation, of John Jacob, born on the 1 day of December, 1903

Name of Father: Sam Jacob   a citizen of the Creek Nation.
Name of Mother: Jeanetta Jacob a citizen of the Creek Nation.

        Postoffice Senora Ind Ter

AFFIDAVIT OF MOTHER.

UNITED STATES OF AMERICA, Indian Territory, ⎱
  Western   DISTRICT. ⎰

  I, Jeanetta Jacob, on oath state that I am about 27 years of age and a citizen by blood, of the Creek Nation; that I am the lawful wife of Sam Jacob, who is a citizen, by blood of the Creek Nation; that a male child was born to me on 1 day of December, 1903, that said child has been named John Jacob, and was living March 4, 1905.

             her
          Jeanetta x Jacob
Witnesses To Mark: mark
 ⎰ Alex Posey
 ⎱ DC Skaggs

Subscribed and sworn to before me this 15 day of March, 1906.

            Alex Posey
            Notary Public.

Applications for Enrollment of Creek Newborn
Act of 1905 Volume XIV

BIRTH AFFIDAVIT.

DEPARTMENT OF THE INTERIOR.
COMMISSION TO THE FIVE CIVILIZED TRIBES.

IN RE APPLICATION FOR ENROLLMENT, as a citizen of the Creek Nation, of John Jacobs, born on the 1 day of Dec, 1903

Name of Father: Shawnee Jacobs a citizen of the Creek Nation.
Osochee Town
Name of Mother: Jeannetta Jacobs a citizen of the Creek Nation.
Hickory Ground
Postoffice Senora IT

AFFIDAVIT OF MOTHER. (Child present)

UNITED STATES OF AMERICA, Indian Territory, }
    Western DISTRICT.

I, Jeannetta Jacobs, on oath state that I am about 27 years of age and a citizen by blood, of the Creek Nation; that I am the lawful wife of Shawnee Jacobs, who is a citizen, by blood of the Creek Nation; that a male child was born to me on 1 day of Dec, 1903, that said child has been named John Jacobs, and was living March 4, 1905.

                                    her
                        Jeannetta x Jacobs
Witnesses To Mark: mark
 { EC Griesel
   Jesse McDermott

Subscribed and sworn to before me this 13" day of April, 1905.

(Seal)   J McDermott
                                Notary Public.

No one present
~~AFFIDAVIT OF ATTENDING PHYSICIAN OR MID-WIFE.~~

AFFIDAVIT OF DISINTERESTED WITNESSES.

UNITED STATES OF AMERICA,)
INDIAN TERRITORY,   ) ss.
Western DISTRICT.   )

We, the undersigned, on oath state that we are personally acquainted with Jeanetta Jacob wife of Sam (or Shawnee) Jacob; that there was born to her a

Applications for Enrollment of Creek Newborn
Act of 1905   Volume XIV

female   child on or about the   22   of   February 1900   ; that the said child has been named   Nicey Jacob   , and was living March 4, 1906. and is now living.

her
Wisey x Davis
mark
his
Dan x Sampson
mark

WITNESSES:
Alex Posey
JB Myers
Alex Posey
JB Myers

Subscribed and sworn to before me this 22 day of Jan, 1907.

Alex Posey
Notary Public.

BIRTH AFFIDAVIT.   (See enrollment)
DEPARTMENT OF THE INTERIOR.
COMMISSION TO THE FIVE CIVILIZED TRIBES.

IN RE APPLICATION FOR ENROLLMENT, as a citizen of the Creek   Nation, of Nicey Jacobs, born on the   22   day of   Feb , 1900

Name of Father: Shawnee Jacobs   a citizen of the   Creek   Nation.
Osochee Town
Name of Mother: Jeannetta   "   a citizen of the   Creek   Nation.
Hickory Ground

Postoffice   Senora IT

AFFIDAVIT OF MOTHER.   (Child present)

UNITED STATES OF AMERICA, Indian Territory, ⎫
    Western   DISTRICT.   ⎬
                                          ⎭

    I, Jeannetta Jacobs   , on oath state that I am about 27 years of age and a citizen by blood , of the Creek Nation; that I am the lawful wife of Shawnee Jacobs , who is a citizen, by blood of the Creek   Nation; that a female   child was born to me on 22" day of Feb, 1900 , that said child has been named   Nicey Jacobs , and was living March 4, 1905.

her
Jeannetta x Jacobs
mark

Witnesses To Mark:
  ⎰ EC Griesel
  ⎱ Jesse McDermott

Applications for Enrollment of Creek Newborn
Act of 1905   Volume XIV

Subscribed and sworn to before me this 13" day of   April   , 1905.

(Seal)   J McDermott
                                             Notary Public.

No one present

~~AFFIDAVIT OF ATTENDING PHYSICIAN OR MID-WIFE~~.

(The above Birth Affidavit given again.)

NC. 1130

Muskogee, Indian Territory, October 24, 1905.

Jeanetta Jacobs,
    Care Shawnee Jacobs,
        Senora, Indian Territory.

Dear Madam:

    In the matter of the application for the enrollment of your minor child, John Jacobs, born December 1, 1903, as a citizen by blood of the Creek Nation, this office is unable to identify you and your said husband, Shawnee Jacobs, on its roll of citizens by blood of the Creek Nation; you are requested to state your maiden name, the names of the parents of yourself and of your said husband, the Creek Indian towns to which you belong and the number which appear on your deeds and allotment certificates.

Respectfully,

Commissioner.

N.C. 1130

Muskogee, Indian Territory, December 20, 1905.

Jeanetta Jacobs,
    Care Shawnee Jacobs,
        Senora, Indian Territory.

Dear Madam:

    In the matter of the application for the enrollment of your minor child, John Jacobs born December 1, 1903, as a citizen by blood of the Creek Nation, this office is unable to identify you or your said husband, Shawnee Jacobs, on its final roll of citizens by blood of the Creek Nation. You are requested to state your maiden name, the names of your parents and those of your husband, the Creek Indian town to which you each

Applications for Enrollment of Creek Newborn
Act of 1905   Volume XIV

belong and your roll numbers as the same appear on your deeds and allotment certificates.

>Respectfully,
>Commissioner.

HGH

REFER IN REPLY TO THE FOLLOWING:
N.C. 1130.

DEPARTMENT OF THE INTERIOR,
COMMISSIONER TO THE FIVE CIVILIZED TRIBES.

Muskogee, Indian Territory, January 14, 1907.

Alex Posey,
>Clerk in Charge Creek Field Party,
>>Henryetta, Indian Territory.

Dear Sir:

You are directed to procure the affidavit of two disinterested witnesses in the matter of the application for the enrollment of Nicey Jacob as a citizen of the Creek Nation.

A copy of the affidavit of the mother, the only proof now on file in said case, is herewith enclosed.

>Respectfully,
>Tams Bixby   Commissioner.

2 dis.
14-4

N.C. 1130.

Muskogee, Indian Territory, January 14, 1907.

Jeannetta Jacob,
>Care Shawnee Jacob,
>>Senora, Indian Territory.

Dear Madam:

In the matter of the application for the enrollment of your minor child, Nicey Jacob, as a citizen by blood of the Creek Nation, you are advised that this office requires the affidavit of two disinterested witnesses relative to her birth and a blank form for that purpose is herewith enclosed, which you should have properly executed and returned to this office in ten days.

>Respectfully,
Dis.
>Commissioner.

Applications for Enrollment of Creek Newborn
Act of 1905   Volume XIV

N C 1130

Muskogee, Indian Territory, March 7, 1907.

Jeannetta Jacob,
    Care of Shawnee Jacob,
        Senora, Indian Territory.

Dear Madam:

You are hereby advised that on March 2, 1907 the Secretary of the Interior approved the enrollment of your minor child, Nicey Jacob, as a citizen by blood of the Creek Nation, and that the name of said child appears upon the roll of new born citizens by blood of the Creek Nation enrolled under the Act of Congress approved March 3rd, 1905, as number 1264.

This child is now entitled to allotment and application therefor should be made without delay at the Creek Land Office, Muskogee, Indian Territory.

Respectfully,

Commissioner.

DEPARTMENT OF THE INTERIOR,
COMMISSION TO THE FIVE CIVILIZED TRIBES.

In Re: Application for enrollment, as a citizen of the Creek Nation, of Charley Dee L. Thatcher, born on the 27" day of February 1903.

Name of Father: S. B. Thatcher, non-citizen of the Creek Nation,
Name of Mother: Nancy Thatcher a citizen of the Creek Nation.

Post Office, Broken Arrow, Ind. Ter.

Applications for Enrollment of Creek Newborn
Act of 1905 Volume XIV

AFFIDAVIT OF MOTHER,

United States of America,)
Indian Territory)
Western District)

I, Nancy Thatcher, on oath state that I am 25 years of age and a citizen of the Creek Nation: that I am the lawful wife of S. B. Thatcher, who is a non-citizen of the Creek Nation; that a male child was born to me on the 27" day of February, 1903; that said child is now living and has been named Charley Dee L. Thatcher.

Nancy Thatcher

Subscribed and sworn to before me on the 15" day of April, 1905.

Z.I.J. Holt

My commission expires May 9" 1907.

AFFIDAVIT OF ATTENDING MIDWIFE,

United States of America,)
Indian Territory)
Western District)

I, Etta Castillo, a mid-wife on oath state that I attended on Mrs. Nancy Thatcher, wife of S. B. Thatcher on the 27" day of February 1903, that there was born to her on said date a Male child; that said child is now living and said to have been named Charley Dee L. Thatcher.

Etta Castillo

Witness to Mark,

Subscribed and sworn to before me on the 15" day of April 1905.

Z.I.J. Holt

My commission expires May 9", 1907.

Applications for Enrollment of Creek Newborn
Act of 1905 Volume XIV

BIRTH AFFIDAVIT.

DEPARTMENT OF THE INTERIOR.
COMMISSION TO THE FIVE CIVILIZED TRIBES.

IN RE APPLICATION FOR ENROLLMENT, as a citizen of the Creek Nation, of Julia Postoak, born on the 5th day of July, 1902

Name of Father:	Charley Postoak	a citizen of the	Creek	Nation.
Name of Mother:	Rachel Postoak	a citizen of the	Creek	Nation.

Postoffice Beggs Ind Ter

AFFIDAVIT OF MOTHER.

UNITED STATES OF AMERICA, Indian Territory,
Western DISTRICT.

I, Rachel Postoak, on oath state that I am 39 years of age and a citizen by blood, of the Creek Nation; that I am the lawful wife of Charley Postoak, who is a citizen, by adoption of the Creek Nation; that a female child was born to me on the 5th day of July, 1902, that said child has been named Julia Postoak, and was living March 4, 1905.

                                                          her
                                        Rachel x Postoak

Witnesses To Mark: mark
  M A Greene
  C.M. Keyes

Subscribed and sworn to before me this 11th day of April, 1905.

                                        Richard J. Hill
                                        Notary Public.

My commission expires Mch 25th 1909

AFFIDAVIT OF ATTENDING PHYSICIAN OR MID-WIFE.

UNITED STATES OF AMERICA, Indian Territory,
Western DISTRICT.

I, Polly McIntosh, a mid wife, on oath state that I attended on Mrs. Rachel Postoak, wife of Charley Postoak on the 5th day of July, 1902; that there was born to her on said date a female child; that said child was living March 4, 1905, and is said to have been named Julia Postoak

                                          her
                                    Polly x McIntosh
                                        mark

Applications for Enrollment of Creek Newborn
Act of 1905 Volume XIV

Witnesses To Mark:
- Annie Grayson
- Martha Harry

Subscribed and sworn to before me 15th day of April , 1905.

Richard J. Hill
Notary Public.

My commission expires March 25th 1909

BIRTH AFFIDAVIT.

DEPARTMENT OF THE INTERIOR.
COMMISSION TO THE FIVE CIVILIZED TRIBES.

IN RE APPLICATION FOR ENROLLMENT, as a citizen of the Creek Nation, of Jennie Postoak , born on the 3^d day of March , 1905

Name of Father:	Charley Postoak	a citizen of the Creek	Nation.
Name of Mother:	Rachel Postoak	a citizen of the Creek	Nation.

Postoffice   Beggs Indian Territory

AFFIDAVIT OF MOTHER.

UNITED STATES OF AMERICA, Indian Territory,
Western   DISTRICT.

I, Rachel Postoak , on oath state that I am 39 years of age and a citizen by blood , of the Creek Nation; that I am the lawful wife of Charley Postoak , who is a citizen, by Adoption of the Creek Nation; that a female child was born to me on 3^d day of March , 1905 , that said child has been named Jennie Postoak, and is now living.

            her
           Rachel x Postoak
Witnesses To Mark: mark
- M A Greene
- C.M. Keyes

Subscribed and sworn to before me this 15th day of April , 1905.

Richard J. Hill
Notary Public.

My commission expires March 25th 1909

Applications for Enrollment of Creek Newborn
Act of 1905   Volume XIV

AFFIDAVIT OF ATTENDING PHYSICIAN OR MID-WIFE.

UNITED STATES OF AMERICA, Indian Territory,
Western DISTRICT.

I, A DuBose, a Physician, on oath state that I attended on Mrs. Rachel Postoak, wife of Charley Postoak on the 3^d day of March, 1905 ; that there was born to her on said date a female child; that said child is now living and is said to have been named Jennie Postoak

A. DuBose M.D.

Witnesses To Mark:

Subscribed and sworn to before me this 15th day of April, 1905.

Richard J. Hill
Notary Public.

My commission expires March 25th 1909

BIRTH AFFIDAVIT.

DEPARTMENT OF THE INTERIOR.
COMMISSION TO THE FIVE CIVILIZED TRIBES.

IN RE APPLICATION FOR ENROLLMENT, as a citizen of the Creek Nation, of Bettie McNae, born on the 16th day of March, 1903

Freedman
Name of Father: Robison McNae   a citizen of the   Creek   Nation.
Name of Mother: Emma McNae (nee Weaver)   a citizen of the   Creek   Nation.

Postoffice   Boynton Ind. Ter.

Applications for Enrollment of Creek Newborn
Act of 1905   Volume XIV

AFFIDAVIT OF MOTHER.

UNITED STATES OF AMERICA, Indian Territory,
Western   DISTRICT.

    I, Emma McNae (nee Weaver), on oath state that I am 26 years of age and a citizen by Blood, of the Creek Nation; that I am the lawful wife of Robison McNae, who is a citizen, by Freedman of the Creek Nation; that a Female child was born to me on 16th day of March, 1903, that said child has been named Bettie McNae, and was living March 4, 1905.

                                    her
Witnesses To Mark: Emma x McNae (nee Weaver)
                                    mark
{ J.B. Morrow Checotah I.T.
{ A A Smith

    Subscribed and sworn to before me this 20th day of March, 1905.

                              J.B. Morrow
My Commission Expires July 1, 1906.   Notary Public.

AFFIDAVIT OF ATTENDING PHYSICIAN OR MID-WIFE.

UNITED STATES OF AMERICA, Indian Territory,
Western   DISTRICT.

    I, Mary Hardin (nee Weaver), a Midwife, on oath state that I attended on Mrs. Emma McNae, wife of Robison McNae on the 16th day of March, 1903; that there was born to her on said date a Female child; that said child was living March 4, 1905, and is said to have been named Bettie McNae

                                    her
Witnesses To Mark: Mary x Hardin (nee Weaver)
                                    mark
{ J B Lucus
{ Charles Buford

    Subscribed and sworn to before me this 15th day of March, 1905.

                              J.B. Morrow
My Commission Expires July 1, 1906.   Notary Public.

Applications for Enrollment of Creek Newborn
Act of 1905   Volume XIV

N.C. 1134

DEPARTMENT OF THE INTERIOR,
COMMISSIONER TO THE FIVE CIVILIZED TRIBES.,
Tulsa, Indian Territory, September 4, 1906.

In the matter of the application for the enrollment of Raymond B. Burgess as a citizen by blood of the Creek Nation.

BEN BURGESS, being duly sworn, testified as follows;

BY COMMISSIONER:

Q What is your name? A Ben Burgess.
Q What is your age? A I am thirty one.
Q What is your postoffice address? A Tulsa now.
Q Are you a Creek citizen? A Yes sir.
Q Have you selected your allotment? A Yes sir
Q Have you your deeds? A Yes sir.

The witness presents deeds issued to Ben Burgess Creek Roll No. 1220.

Q Have you a child named Raymond B. Burgess? A I have.
Q When was he born? A January 8th 1904.
Q Is he living? A Yes sir.
Q Who is the mother of Raymond? A Lydia C. Burgess. Her name was Lydia Little prior to our marriage.
Q Is the mother a Creek citizen? A No sir.
Q Were you lawfully married to her when this child was born? A Yes sir.
Q Can you produce the marriage license and certificate between you and Lydia? A Yes sir.

The witness presents his marriage license and requests that a copy of same be made and filed in the case and the original returned to him.

Q Were you ever married to anybody by the name of May Burgess? A No sir, she is the wife of another Benjiman[sic] Burgess who lives at Sapulpa.

I, Jesse McDermott, on oath state that the above and foregoing is a full and true transcript of my notes as taken in said cause on said date.

Jesse McDermott

Subscribed and sworn to before me this 5th day of November, 1905.

My com expires Dec 12-1906   MB Flesher
                                    Notary Public.

Applications for Enrollment of Creek Newborn
Act of 1905   Volume XIV

BIRTH AFFIDAVIT.

DEPARTMENT OF THE INTERIOR,
COMMISSIONER TO THE FIVE CIVILIZED TRIBES.

IN RE APPLICATION FOR ENROLLMENT, as a citizen of the Creek Nation, of Raymond B. Burgess , born on the 8th day of January , 1904

Name of Father: Benjamin E Burgess   a citizen of the   Creek   Nation.
Name of Mother: Lyddia C Burgess   a citizen of the   Creek   Nation.

Postoffice   Broken Arrow

AFFIDAVIT OF MOTHER.

UNITED STATES OF AMERICA, Indian Territory, }
Western   District. }

I, Lyddia C Burgess , on oath state that I am 38 years of age and a citizen by Marriage , of the Creek Nation; that I am the lawful wife of Benjamin E Burgess , who is a citizen, by Blood of the Creek Nation; that a Male child was born to me on 8th day of January , 1904 , that said child has been named Raymond B. Burgess , and was living March 4, 1905.

Lyddia C Burgess

Witness to Mark:
  Geo. W. Mowbray   }
  Green Yeargain   }

Subscribed and sworn to before me this 8th day of April , 1905.

My Com Exp 7/12 1906

Geo W. Mowbray
Notary Public.

AFFIDAVIT OF ATTENDING PHYSICIAN OR MID-WIFE.

UNITED STATES OF AMERICA, Indian Territory, }
Western   District. }

I, *(blank)* , a Mid wife , on oath state that I attended on Mrs. Lyddia E Burgess, wife of Benjamin E. Burgess on the 8 day of January , 1904 ; that there was born to her on said date a male child; that said child was living March 4, 1905, and is said to have been named Raymond B Burgess

D Mollie Adams

Witness to Mark:
  Geo. W. Mowbray   }
  Green Yeargain   }

Applications for Enrollment of Creek Newborn
Act of 1905   Volume XIV

Subscribed and sworn to before me this 8 day of April , 1905.

Geo W Mowbray
Notary Public.

My Com Exp 7/12 1906

BIRTH AFFIDAVIT.

DEPARTMENT OF THE INTERIOR.
COMMISSION TO THE FIVE CIVILIZED TRIBES.

IN RE APPLICATION FOR ENROLLMENT, as a citizen of the Creek Nation, of Raymond B. Burgess , born on the 8 day of January , 1904

Name of Father: Ben Burgess   a citizen of the   Creek   Nation.
Roll #1220
Name of Mother: Lydia C. "   a citizen of the   U.S.   ~~Nation~~.

Postoffice   Tulsa I.T.

AFFIDAVIT OF MOTHER.

UNITED STATES OF AMERICA, Indian Territory,
     Western   DISTRICT.

I, Ben Burgess , on oath state that I am 31 years of age and a citizen by blood , of the Creek Nation; that I am the lawful ~~wife~~ husband of Lydia C. Burgess , who is a non citizen, by *(blank)* of the Creek Nation; that a male child was born to ~~me~~ her on 8" day of January , 1904 , that said child has been named Raymond B Burgess , and was living March 4, 1905.

Ben Burgess

Witnesses To Mark:

Subscribed and sworn to before me this 4th day of Sept   , 1906.

My Com   J. McDermott
Expires July 20" 1907   Notary Public.

Applications for Enrollment of Creek Newborn
Act of 1905   Volume XIV

NC-1134

MARRIAGE LICENSE.

UNITED STATES OF AMERICA,
    Indian Territory,   ss.   NC. 179
    Northern District.

To Any Person Authorized by Law to Solemnize Marriage--Greeting:

You are hereby commanded to solemnize the Rite and publish the Banns of Matrimony between Mr. Benjamin E. Burgess of Fry, in the Indian Territory, aged 27 years, and Miss Liddie C. Little, of Fry, in the Indian Territory, aged 34 years, according to law, and do you officially sign and return this License to the parties therein named.

Witness my hand and official seal at Vinita, Indian Territory, this 21" day of September, A. D. 1901.

                        CHAS. A. DAVIDSON,
                        Clerk of the U.S. Court.
By R. H. Lybrand, Deputy.
  (SEAL)

CERTIFICATE OF MARRIAGE.

United States of America,
    Indian Territory,   ss.
    Northern District.

I, Geo. W. Mowbray, a Minister of the Gospel, do hereby certify that on the 25 day of Sept. A.D. 1901, I did duly and according to law as commanded in the foregoing License, solemnize the Rite and publish the Banns of Matrimony between the parties therein named.

Witness my hand this 25 day of September, A.D. 1901.

My credentials are recorded in the office of the clerk of the United States Court, Indian Territory, Northern District, Book Q Page 40 & 41.

                  (signed)   REV. GEO. W. MOWBRAY.
                        a Minister of the Gospel.

CERTIFICATE OF RECORD.

United States of America,
    Indian Territory,   ss.
    Northern District.

I, Charles A. Davidson, Clerk of the United States Court in the Northern District, Indian Territory, do hereby certify that the instrument hereto attached was filed for record

Applications for Enrollment of Creek Newborn
Act of 1905   Volume XIV

in my office the 1 day of October, 1901, at -------M., and duly recorded in Book L, Marriage Record, Page 213.

    Witness my hand and seal of said Court at Vinita, in said Territory this 4 day of October, A. D. 1901.

(signed) CHAS. A. DAVIDSON, Clerk.

Northern Dist. Ind. Ter.   By . . . . Deputy.
    FILED
    OCT 1, 1901
CHAS. A. DAVIDSON, Clerk U.S. Courts

INDIAN TERRITORY, Western District.   :   I, J. Y. Miller a stenographer to the Commissioner to the Five Civilized Tribes, do hereby certify that the above and foregoing is a true and complete copy of its original.

JY Miller

Sworn to and subscribed before me
    this the 4th day of November
    1905.

Edw C Griesel
        Notary Public.

BIRTH AFFIDAVIT.

DEPARTMENT OF THE INTERIOR.
COMMISSION TO THE FIVE CIVILIZED TRIBES.

IN RE APPLICATION FOR ENROLLMENT, as a citizen of the Creek Nation, of Raymond B Burgess, born on the 8" day of January, 1904

Name of Father: Benjamin E. Burgess	a citizen of the	Creek	Nation.
Name of Mother: Lydia C Burgess	a citizen of the	U.S.	Nation.

Postoffice   Broken Arrow

AFFIDAVIT OF MOTHER.

UNITED STATES OF AMERICA, Indian Territory,
    Western   DISTRICT.

    I, Lyddia C Burgess, on oath state that I am 38 years of age and a citizen by marriage, of the Creek Nation; that I am the lawful wife of Benjamin E Burgess, who is a citizen, by Blood of the Creek Nation; that a male child was born to me on

Applications for Enrollment of Creek Newborn
Act of 1905   Volume XIV

8th day of January , 1904 , that said child has been named Raymond B Burgess , and was living March 4, 1905.

             Lyddia C Burgess

Witnesses To Mark:
 { Geo W Mowbray
 { Green Yeargain

   Subscribed and sworn to before me this 8th day of   April   , 1905.

My Com   Geo W Mowbray
Exp 7/12/1906   Notary Public.

AFFIDAVIT OF ATTENDING PHYSICIAN OR MID-WIFE.

UNITED STATES OF AMERICA, Indian Territory, }
  Western   DISTRICT.

  I, *(blank)* , a Midwife , on oath state that I attended on Mrs. Lyddia E Burgess , wife of Benjamin E Burgess on the 8 day of January , 1905 ; that there was born to her on said date a male child; that said child was living March 4, 1905, and is said to have been named   Raymond B Burgess

             Mollie Adams

Witnesses To Mark:
 { GWM
 { GY

Subscribed and sworn to before me this 8 day of   April   , 1905.

My Com Exp 7/12/06   Geo W Mowbray
             Notary Public.

NC-1134.

         Muskogee, Indian Territory, October 24, 1905.

Lyddia C. Burgess,
  c/o Benjamin E. Burgess,
    Broken Arrow, Indian Territory.

Dear Madam:

  In the matter of the application for the enrollment of your minor child, Raymond Burgess, born January 8, 1904, as a citizen by blood of the Creek Nation, this office requires evidence of your marriage to Benjamin E. Burgess, the father of said child.

Applications for Enrollment of Creek Newborn
Act of 1905   Volume XIV

Such evidence may consist of either the original or a certified copy of your marriage license and certificate.

Respectfully,

Commissioner.

C 1134 (Copy)

Tulsa Ind. Ter.
Oct. 31st 1905.

Commissioner to the Five Civilized Tribes
Muskogee Ind. Ter.

Dears[sic] Sir :-

Enclosed you will please find orignal[sic] Certificate of our marriage, which you will please return when you are through with it and oblige yours truly

Lyddia C. Burges[sic]

HGH

REFER IN REPLY TO THE FOLLOWING:
NC-1134

DEPARTMENT OF THE INTERIOR,
COMMISSIONER TO THE FIVE CIVILIZED TRIBES.

Muskogee, Indian Territory, November 3, 1905.

Lyddia C. Burgess,
   Care of Benjamin E. Burgess,
      Broken Arrow Tulsa, Indian Territory.

Dear Madam:

In accordance with your request of October 31, 1905, there is herewith enclosed your marriage license and certificate, a copy of which has been made and filed with the record in the matter of the application for the enrollment of your minor child, Raymond B. Burgess, as a citizen by blood of the Creek Nation.

Respectfully,

Tams Bixby Commissioner.

JYM-3-6

Applications for Enrollment of Creek Newborn
Act of 1905   Volume XIV

N.C. 1134

Muskogee, Indian Territory, December 20, 1905.

Lydia C. Burgess,
    Tulsa, Indian Territory.

Dear Madam:

In the matter of the application for the enrollment of your minor child, Raymond B. Burgess, born January 8, 1904, as a citizen by blood of the Creek Nation, this office is unable to positively identify Benjamin E. Burgess, the father of said child, on its final roll of citizens by blood of the Creek Nation.

The name Benjamin E. Burgess does appear on the final roll of citizens by blood of the Creek Nation but it also appears from the records of this office that said Benjamin E. Burgess is the lawful husband of one May Burgess, a citizen of the Creek Nation and that said May Burgess is living and so far as the records show is still his lawful wife. It will therefore be necessary for you to advise this office as to the names of his parents, the Creek Indian town to which he belongs and his roll number as same appears on his deeds and allotment certificate.

You are further requested to advise this office whether your husband, Benjamin E. Burgess, was ever the husband of May Burgess and if so whether said May Burgess is dead or divorced from him. If said May Burgess is dead or is divorced from said Benjamin E. Burgess, you are requested to advise this office as to the date of her death or divorce.

                Respectfully,

                                      Commissioner.

NC-1134

Muskogee, Indian Territory, December 22, 1905.

Lyddia C. Burgess,
    Care of Benjamin E. Burgess,
        Broken Arrow, Indian Territory.

Dear Madam:

In compliance with your request of October 31, 1905, there is herewith enclosed your marriage license and certificate, a copy of which has been made and filed with the record in the matter of the application for the enrollment of your minor child, Raymond B. Burgess, as a citizen by blood of the Creek Nation.

                Respectfully

                                      Commissioner.

JYM-3-6

Applications for Enrollment of Creek Newborn
Act of 1905   Volume XIV

N.C. 1134

Muskogee, Indian Territory, March 1, 1907.

Ben Burgess,
    Tulsa, Indian Territory.

Dear Sir:

You are hereby advised that on February 15, 1907, the Secretary of the Interior approved the enrollment of your minor child, Raymond B. Burgess, as a citizen by blood of the Creek Nation and that the name of said child appears upon the roll of new born citizens of said nation, enrolled under the Act of March 3, 1905, as No. 1222.

This child is now entitled to allotment and application therefor should be made without delay at the Creek Land Office, Muskogee, Indian Territory.

                    Respectfully,
                              Commissioner.

Full Sister on Creek Card 1870: roll #5917

NC-1135.

Muskogee, Indian Territory, October 24, 1905.

Martha F. Boling,
    c/o W. F. Boling,
        Mounds, Indian Territory.

Dear Madam:

In the matter of the application for the enrollment of your minor child, Dixie Self Boling, born October 30, 1904, as a citizen by blood of the Creek Nation, the year is omitted in the affidavit of the midwife. It is necessary that she make a new affidavit and a blank for that purpose, partially filled out, is herewith inclosed.

Applications for Enrollment of Creek Newborn
Act of 1905   Volume XIV

You are requested to have the same executed before a notary public and when so executed to return it to this office in the inclosed envelope.

Respectfully,

Commissioner.

CTD-18
Env.

BIRTH AFFIDAVIT.

DEPARTMENT OF THE INTERIOR.
COMMISSION TO THE FIVE CIVILIZED TRIBES.

IN RE APPLICATION FOR ENROLLMENT, as a citizen of the Creek Nation, of   Dixie Self Boling , born on the   30   day of   October   , 1904

U.S.
Name of Father: W. F. Boling   a citizen of the   ~~Creek~~   ~~Nation~~.
Name of Mother: Martha F. Boling   a citizen of the   Creek   Nation.

Postoffice   Mounds, I.T.

AFFIDAVIT OF ATTENDING PHYSICIAN OR MID-WIFE.

of Texas
~~UNITED STATES OF AMERICA, Indian Territory,~~
County of Cooke   ~~DISTRICT.~~

I, Mary A. Greenhaw , a midwife , on oath state that I attended on Mrs. Martha F. Boling , wife of W. F. Boling on the 30 day of October , 1904 ; that there was born to her on said date a female child; that said child was living March 4, 1905, and is said to have been named Dixie Self Boling

Mary A Greenhaw

Witnesses To Mark:
   { Bessie Greenhaw
    Mattie Greenhaw

Subscribed and sworn to before me 16th day of Nov. , 1905.

W.L. *(Illegible)*
Notary Public.

Applications for Enrollment of Creek Newborn
Act of 1905   Volume XIV

BIRTH AFFIDAVIT.

DEPARTMENT OF THE INTERIOR.
COMMISSION TO THE FIVE CIVILIZED TRIBES.

IN RE APPLICATION FOR ENROLLMENT, as a citizen of the Creek Nation, of Dixie Self Boling , born on the 30 day of October , 1904

U.S.

Name of Father: W. F. Boling   a citizen of the   ~~Creek~~   ~~Nation~~.
Name of Mother: Martha F. Boling   a citizen of the   Creek   Nation.

Postoffice   Mounds, I.T.

AFFIDAVIT OF MOTHER.
State of Texas
UNITED STATES OF AMERICA, ~~Indian Territory~~,
County of Cooke   ~~DISTRICT~~.

I, Martha F. Boling , on oath state that I am 32 years of age and a citizen by Blood , of the Creek Nation; that I am the lawful wife of W. F. Boling , who is a citizen, by ~~United States~~ of the United States of America ~~Nation~~; that a Female child was born to me on 30th day of October , 1904 , that said child has been named Dixie Self Boling , and was living March 4, 1905.

Martha F. Boling

Witnesses To Mark:
 Clayton Brady
 Geo Y Bird Jr.

Subscribed and sworn to before me this 31st day of March , 1905.

W. L. *(Illegible)*
Notary Public.
Cooke Co Texas

AFFIDAVIT OF ATTENDING PHYSICIAN OR MID-WIFE.
State of Texas
UNITED STATES OF AMERICA, ~~Indian Territory~~,
County of Cooke   ~~DISTRICT~~.

I, Mary A. Greenhaw , a Mid-wife , on oath state that I attended on Mrs. Martha F. Boling , wife of W. F. Boling on the 30th day of October , 1...... ; that there was born to her on said date a Female child; that said child was living March 4, 1905, and is said to have been named Dixie Self Boling

Mary A Greenhaw

Applications for Enrollment of Creek Newborn
Act of 1905   Volume XIV

Witnesses To Mark:
  { Clayton Brady
    W. L. *(Illegible)*

Subscribed and sworn to before me 31$^{\underline{st}}$ day of   March   , 1905.

                                  W.L. *(Illegible)*
                                    Notary Public.
                                    Cooke Co Texas

BIRTH AFFIDAVIT.

DEPARTMENT OF THE INTERIOR.
COMMISSION TO THE FIVE CIVILIZED TRIBES.

IN RE APPLICATION FOR ENROLLMENT, as a citizen of the Creek Nation, of   Walter Gilmore Boling , born on the   2nd day of   June   , 1903

Name of Father: W. F. Boling   a citizen of the   U.S.   ~~Nation~~.
Name of Mother: Martha F. Boling   a citizen of the   Creek   Nation.

                         Postoffice   Mounds, Ind Ter

AFFIDAVIT OF MOTHER.
                       State of Texas
UNITED STATES OF AMERICA, ~~Indian Territory~~,
     County of Cooke   ~~DISTRICT.~~

    I,   Martha F. Boling , on oath state that I am   32   years of age and a citizen by Blood , of the   Creek   Nation; that I am the lawful wife of   W. F. Boling , who is a citizen, by *(blank)* of the United States of America   ~~Nation~~; that a   Male   child was born to me on   2nd day of   June , 1903 , that said child has been named   Walter Gilmore Boling , and was living March 4, 1905.

                                 Martha F. Boling

Witnesses To Mark:
  { Clayton Brady
    Geo Y Bird Jr.

Subscribed and sworn to before me this 31$^{\underline{st}}$ day of   March   , 1905.

                                  W. L. *(Illegible)*
                                  Notary Public.
                                  Cooke Co Texas

Applications for Enrollment of Creek Newborn
Act of 1905   Volume XIV

AFFIDAVIT OF ATTENDING PHYSICIAN OR MID-WIFE.

UNITED STATES OF AMERICA, Indian Territory, }
    Western   DISTRICT.

    I, M.D. Taylor , a Physician , on oath state that I attended on Mrs. Martha F. Boling , wife of W. F. Boling on the 2nd day of June , 1903 ; that there was born to her on said date a Male child; that said child was living March 4, 1905, and is said to have been named Walter Gilmore Boling

                                M.D. Taylor, M.D.

Witnesses To Mark:
{

    Subscribed and sworn to before me 17th day of April , 1905.

                                  Josiah G. Davis
                                        Notary Public.

My Com Ex 9/1/1906

BIRTH AFFIDAVIT.

DEPARTMENT OF THE INTERIOR.
COMMISSION TO THE FIVE CIVILIZED TRIBES.

    IN RE APPLICATION FOR ENROLLMENT, as a citizen of the Creek Nation, of Pearl Bruner, born on the 1 day of January , 1902

Name of Father: Nathan Bruner   a citizen of the   Creek   Nation.
Name of Mother: Lou Bruner   a citizen of the   U.S.   Nation.

                          Postoffice   Okmulgee

Applications for Enrollment of Creek Newborn
Act of 1905 Volume XIV

father
AFFIDAVIT OF ~~MOTHER~~.

UNITED STATES OF AMERICA, Indian Territory, }
Western   DISTRICT.

I, Nathan Bruner , on oath state that I am 29 years of age and a citizen by blood , of the Creek Nation; that I am the lawful ~~wife~~ husband of Lou Bruner , who is a citizen, by —— of the U.S. Nation; that a female child was born to me on 1 day of January , 1902 , that said child has been named Pearl Bruner , and was living March 4, 1905.

Nathan Bruner

Witnesses To Mark:
{

Subscribed and sworn to before me this 22" day of September , 1905.

Henry G. Hains
Notary Public.

BIRTH AFFIDAVIT.

DEPARTMENT OF THE INTERIOR.
COMMISSION TO THE FIVE CIVILIZED TRIBES.

IN RE APPLICATION FOR ENROLLMENT, as a citizen of the Creek Nation, of Pearl Bruner, born on the 1 day of January , 1902

Name of Father:	Nathan Bruner	a citizen of the Creek	Nation.
Name of Mother:	Lou Bruner	a citizen of the Creek	Nation.

Present Postoffice   Star, Ada County, Idaho.

AFFIDAVIT OF MOTHER.

UNITED STATES OF AMERICA, Indian Territory, }
Okmulgee   DISTRICT.

I, Lou Bruner , on oath state that I am Twenty Five years of age and a citizen by Marriage , of the Creek Nation; that I am the lawful wife of Nathan Bruner , who is a citizen, by Birth of the Creek Nation; that a Female child was born to me on First day of January , 1902 , that said child has been named Pearl Bruner , and is now living.

Lou Bruner

Applications for Enrollment of Creek Newborn
Act of 1905   Volume XIV

Witnesses To Mark:
   { Letha Bishop
    S.P. Wilson

    Subscribed and sworn to before me this 11" day of   April , 1905.

                      L. B. Wehr
                         Notary Public.

AFFIDAVIT OF ATTENDING PHYSICIAN OR MID-WIFE.

UNITED STATES OF AMERICA, Indian Territory,
    Okmulgee   **DISTRICT.**

    I, Maggie Bishop , a Mid-wife , on oath state that I attended on Mrs. Lou Bruner , wife of Nathan Bruner on the First day of January , 1902 ; that there was born to her on said date a Female child; that said child is now living and is said to have been named Pearl Bruner

                      Maggie Bishop

Witnesses To Mark:
   { Letha Bishop
    S.P. Wilson

    Subscribed and sworn to before me this 11" day of   April , 1905.

                      L. B. Wehr
                         Notary Public.

BIRTH AFFIDAVIT.
DEPARTMENT OF THE INTERIOR.
COMMISSION TO THE FIVE CIVILIZED TRIBES.

    IN RE APPLICATION FOR ENROLLMENT, as a citizen of the Creek Nation, of Dennis Flinn Proctor , born on the 12 day of September , 1902

Name of Father: Toney E. Proctor   a citizen of the   Creek   Nation.
Weogufke Town
Name of Mother: Susan Proctor   a citizen of the   Creek   Nation.
Coweta Town

                      Postoffice   Okmulgee, I.T.

Applications for Enrollment of Creek Newborn
Act of 1905   Volume XIV

AFFIDAVIT OF MOTHER.

Child present.

UNITED STATES OF AMERICA, Indian Territory,
    Western   DISTRICT.

I, Susan Proctor, on oath state that I am about 29 years of age and a citizen by blood, of the Creek Nation; that I am the lawful wife of Toney E. Proctor, who is a citizen, by blood of the Creek Nation; that a male child was born to me on 12 day of September, 1902, that said child has been named Dennis Flinn Proctor, and was living March 4, 1905.

Susan Proctor

Witnesses To Mark:

Subscribed and sworn to before me this 10 day of April, 1905.

Drennan C Skaggs
Notary Public.

AFFIDAVIT OF ATTENDING PHYSICIAN OR MID-WIFE.

UNITED STATES OF AMERICA, Indian Territory,
    Western   DISTRICT.

I, Amanda Sanger, a Midwife, on oath state that I attended on Mrs. Susan Proctor, wife of Toney E. Proctor on the 12th. day of September, 1902; that there was born to her on said date a Male child; that said child was living March 4, 1905, and is said to have been named Dennis Flinn Proctor

her
Amanda x Sanger
mark

Witnesses To Mark:
  Fannie E. Brightman
  Frank W Rushing

Subscribed and sworn to before me 15th day of April, 1905.

My Commission Expires Jan. 30, 1909.

Frank W. Rushing
Notary Public.

Applications for Enrollment of Creek Newborn
Act of 1905   Volume XIV

NC 1138.

DEPARTMENT OF THE INTERIOR,
COMMISSIONER TO THE FIVE CIVILIZED TRIBES.

In the matter of the application for the enrollment of Sam Sladen, as a citizen by blood of the Creek Nation.

DECISION.

The record in this case shows that an application was filed, in affidavit form on April 20, 1905, for the enrollment of Sam Sladen, as a citizen by blood of the Creek Nation. Supplemental affidavits, filed January 16, and June 29, 1906 are attached to and made a part of the record herein.

The evidence shows that the names of the parents and that of the applicant are erroneously spelled in the birth affidavits, but it appears conclusively from the evidence and the records of this office that the said Sam Sladen is the child of John Sladen, a non citizen and Nora Williams, whose name appears opposite Creek Indian Roll number 2234, approved by the Secretary of the Interior, March 13, 1902.

It further appears that the said Sam Sladen was born October 19, 1904 and was still living June 27, 1906.

The Act of Congress approved March 3, 1905, (33 Stats. 1048), provides in part as follows:

> "That the Commission to the Five Civilized Tribes is authorized for sixty days after the date of the approval of this act to receive and consider applications for enrollment, of children, born subsequent to May twenty-fifth, nineteen hundred and one, and prior to March fourth, nineteen hundred and five, and living on said latter date, to citizens of the Creek tribe of Indians whose enrollment has been approved by the Secretary of the Interior prior to the approval of this act; and to enroll and make allotments to such children."

It is, therefore, ordered and adjudged that said Sam Sladen is entitled to enrollment as a citizen by blood of the Creek Nation, in accordance with the provisions of the Act of Congress above quoted, and the application for his enrollment as such, is accordingly granted.

Tams Bixby COMMISSIONER.

Muskogee, Indian Territory.
JAN 18 1907

Applications for Enrollment of Creek Newborn
Act of 1905   Volume XIV

BIRTH AFFIDAVIT.

DEPARTMENT OF THE INTERIOR.
COMMISSION TO THE FIVE CIVILIZED TRIBES.

IN RE APPLICATION FOR ENROLLMENT, as a citizen of the Creek Nation, of Sam Claybon, born on the 19th day of October , 1904

Name of Father: John Claybon	a citizen of the U.S.	Nation.
Name of Mother: Dora Williams	a citizen of the Creek	Nation.

Postoffice   Depew, Ind Terr.

AFFIDAVIT OF MOTHER.

UNITED STATES OF AMERICA, Indian Territory,
Western   DISTRICT.

I, Dora Rogers , on oath state that I am 20 years of age and a citizen by blood, of the Creek Nation; that I am the lawful wife of Rufus Rogers , who is a citizen, by *(blank)* of the Cherokee Nation; that a male child was born to me on 19th day of October , 1904 , that said child has been named Sam Claybon , and was living March 4, 1905.

              her
            Dora Rogers x
Witnesses To Mark: mark
 { Wm Vann
  WJ Smith

Subscribed and sworn to before me this 9th day of January , 1906.

         T.W. Flynn
            Notary Public.

AFFIDAVIT OF ATTENDING PHYSICIAN OR MID-WIFE.

UNITED STATES OF AMERICA, Indian Territory,
Western   DISTRICT.

I, Hannah Rogers , a Midwife , on oath state that I attended on Mrs. Dora Rogers , wife of Rufus Rogers on the 19th day of October , 1904 ; that there was born to her on said date a male child; that said child was living March 4, 1905, and is said to have been named Sam Claybon.

            Hannah Rogers
Witnesses To Mark:
 { Wm Vann
  WJ Smith

Applications for Enrollment of Creek Newborn
Act of 1905   Volume XIV

Subscribed and sworn to before me this 9th day of   January , 1906.

        T.W. Flynn
          Notary Public.

BIRTH AFFIDAVIT.

DEPARTMENT OF THE INTERIOR,
COMMISSION TO THE FIVE CIVILIZED TRIBES.

In Re Application for Enrollment, as a citizen of the Creek Nation, of Samuel Sladen , born on the   19   day of   October   , 1904

Name of Father: John Sladen   a citizen of the United States Nation.
Name of Mother: Nora Williams   a citizen of the   Creek-   Nation.

      Post-office Depew Ind Tery

AFFIDAVIT OF MOTHER.

UNITED STATES OF AMERICA, }
 INDIAN TERRITORY,
 Western District.

 I, Nora Williams , on oath state that I am 22 years of age and a citizen by Birth , of the Creek Nation; that I am the lawful wife of   Rufus Rogers , who is a citizen, by Birth of the Cherokee   Nation; that a Male child was born to me on 19 day of October , 1904 , that said child has been named Samuel Sladen , and is now living.

           her
        Nora x Williams
WITNESSES TO MARK: mark
 { P.H. Anderson
  H.A. Stanfield

Subscribed and sworn to before me this 27 day of   June , 1906.

        E.W. Sims
         NOTARY PUBLIC.

My Com Ex July 11-06

Applications for Enrollment of Creek Newborn
Act of 1905   Volume XIV

AFFIDAVIT OF ATTENDING PHYSICIAN OR MID-WIFE.

UNITED STATES OF AMERICA,
  INDIAN TERRITORY,
  Western   District.

I, Hannah Rogers , a Midwife , on oath state that I attended on Mrs. Nora Williams , wife of Rufus Rogers on the 19 day of October , 1904 ; that there was born to her on said date a male child; that said child is now living and is said to have been named Samuel Sladen

Hannah Rogers

WITNESSES TO MARK:
{ P.H. Anderson
{ H.A. Stanfield

Subscribed and sworn to before me this 27 day of June , 1906.

E.W. Sims
NOTARY PUBLIC.

My Com Ex July 11-06

BIRTH AFFIDAVIT.

DEPARTMENT OF THE INTERIOR.
COMMISSION TO THE FIVE CIVILIZED TRIBES.

IN RE APPLICATION FOR ENROLLMENT, as a citizen of the Creek Nation, of   Sam Claybon, born on the 19th day of Oct , 1904

Name of Father: John Claybon   a citizen of the United States Nation.
Name of Mother: Dora Claybon   a citizen of the   Creek   Nation.

Postoffice   Bristow Ind Ter

AFFIDAVIT OF MOTHER.

UNITED STATES OF AMERICA, Indian Territory,
  Western   DISTRICT.

I, Dora Claybon , on oath state that I am 19 years of age and a citizen by blood, of the Creek Nation; that I am the lawful wife of John Claybon , who is a citizen, by Marriage of the Creek Nation; that a male child was born to me on 19th day of October , 1904 , that said child has been named Sam Claybon , and was living March 4, 1905.

her
Dora x Claybon
mark

Applications for Enrollment of Creek Newborn
Act of 1905   Volume XIV

Witnesses To Mark:
  { Samuel L Rogers
  { Berry Womack

                                                                April
Subscribed and sworn to before me this 12th day of ~~October~~ , 1905.

                                                  Richard J Hill
                                                  Notary Public.

My commission expires March 25th 1909

AFFIDAVIT OF ATTENDING PHYSICIAN OR MID-WIFE.

UNITED STATES OF AMERICA, Indian Territory, }
    Western   DISTRICT.   }

    I, Hanah[sic] Rodgers , a midwife , on oath state that I attended on Mrs. Dora Claybon , wife of John Claybon on the 19th day of October , 1904 ; that there was born to her on said date a male child; that said child was living March 4, 1905, and is said to have been named Sam Claybon.

                                                Hannah Rogers

Witnesses To Mark:
  {

Subscribed and sworn to before me this 12th day of April , 1905.

                                              Richard J Hill
                                              Notary Public.

My commission expires March 25th 1909

                                                                     HGH

REFER IN REPLY TO THE FOLLOWING:
NC-1138.

DEPARTMENT OF THE INTERIOR,
COMMISSIONER TO THE FIVE CIVILIZED TRIBES.

                            Muskogee, Indian Territory, October 24, 1905.

Nora Claybon,
      c/o John Claybon,
            Bristow, Indian Territory.

Dear Madam:

    In the matter of the application for the enrollment of your minor child, Sam Claybon, born October 19, 1904, as a citizen by blood of the Creek Nation, you sign your name to your affidavit relative to his birth as Nora Williams.

Applications for Enrollment of Creek Newborn
Act of 1905   Volume XIV

If you are the lawful wife of John Claybon, the father of said child, your name must necessarily be Claybon instead of Williams. For the purpose of correcting the discrepancy as to name there is herewith inclosed a form of birth affidavit which has been properly filled out. You are requested to have the same executed before a notary public, taking care to sign your name to your affidavit as the same appears in the body thereof.

Respectfully,
Tams Bixby
Commissioner.

CTD-19.
Env.

#-1138

Bristow, Ind Terr.   Jan 9th, 1906.

Commission to the Five Civilized Tribes,
    Muskogee, I.T.

Sir:-

Enclose find affidavits of Dora Rogers, mother, and Hannah Rogers, mid-wife, relative to the dirth[sic] of Sam Claybon.
Mrs. Rogers, was enrolled as Dora Williams, as I understand it, she was never lawfully married to John Claybon, she is now lawfully married to Rufus Rogers, a Cherokee Citizen, and, of course, at this time bears his name.

Respectfully,

T. W. Flynn

(The letter below typed as given. Difficult to read.)

Depew, I.T. August 15, 1906.

Mr. Indian Sir:

I write you a few lines in regard of filling for my ground *(illegible)* I have allready *(three words illegible)* to the Commissioner and the claim that it *(remainder of letter llegible)*

Applications for Enrollment of Creek Newborn
Act of 1905 Volume XIV

N C 1138

Muskogee, Indian Territory, March 7, 1907.

Dora Rogers,
    Depew, Indian Territory.

Dear Madam:

You are hereby advised that on March 2, 1907 the Secretary of the Interior approved the enrollment of your minor child, Sam Sladen, as a citizen by blood of the Creek Nation and that the name of the said child appears upon the roll of new born citizens by blood of the Creek Nation enrolled under the Act of Congress approved March 3, 1905, as number 1265.

This child is now entitled to allotment and application therefor should be made without delay at the Creek Land Office, Muskogee, Indian Territory.

                      Respectfully,
                                  Commissioner.

DEPARTMENT OF THE INTERIOR,
COMMISSION TO THE FIVE CIVILIZED TRIBES.
Near Morse, I.T. April 28, 1905.

In the matter of the application for new born children concerning whose enrollment no affidavits could be obtained in time.

Chofulop, being duly sworn, testified as follows: Through Official Interpreter, Alex Posey.

Examination by the Commission.

Q What is your name? A Chofulop
Q What is your age? A (No answer)
Q What is your post office address? A Morse I.T.

Statement: I am a member of the House of Kings of Nuyaka Town. Eundel and Millie Robert, both of Neyaka[sic] Town, have a girl named Indy--it is over two years

Applications for Enrollment of Creek Newborn
Act of 1905   Volume XIV

old, and the other child is unnamed and was born in February. It is a boy, both are living- about the first of February the youngest was born. Post office Morse.

The father of the child is unknown, the mother Fucinda of Nuyaka Town, has a child over a year old--a girl unnamed, living, post office, Morse.

Henry G. Hains, being duly sworn, on his oath, states that the above and foregoing is a true and correct transcript of his stenographic notes as taken in said cause on said date.

Henry G. Hains

Subscribed and sworn to before me this 10th day of May 1905.

Drennan C Skaggs
Notary Public

I, Anna Garrigues, state on oath that the above is a copy of the original.

Anna Garrigues

Subscribed and sworn to before me this 19th day of September 190?

J McDermott
Notary Public.

NC
774

File copy
in 774

N.C. 1140 & 1141.

DEPARTMENT OF THE INTERIOR,
COMMISSIONER TO THE FIVE CIVILIZED TRIBES.
Okemah, I. T., October 20, 1905.

In the matter of the application for the enrollment of Indie Roberts as a citizen by blood of the Creek Nation.

KENDALL ROBERTS, being duly sworn, testified as follows

Through Alex Posey Official Interpreter:

BY THE COMMISSIONER:
Q What is your name? A Kendall Roberts.
Q How old are you? A About thirty-three.
Q What is your post office address? A Morse.
Q Are you a citizen of the Creek Nation? A Yrs, sir.
Q To what town do you belong? A Nuyaka.

Applications for Enrollment of Creek Newborn
Act of 1905 Volume XIV

Q Have you a child named Indie Roberts? A Yes, sir. The child is a girl.
Q Have you made application for the child's enrollment as a Creek New-Born? A Yes, sir. I went before Tupper Dunn (notary) and executed affidavits about the child. I made application at the same time for another child named Cainey Roberts.
Q What was the name of the mother of Indie? A Mary Roberts was the mother of both children.
Q What was the name of the mother of India? A Mary Roberts what the mother of both children.
Q What was your wife's name before her marriage to you? A Mary West.
Q When was Indie born? A January 18, 1903.
Q Is the child also known as Indie Johnson? A No, sir. Indie Johnson is a child of my sister, Wiley Roberts. The child's father was Ahullie Johnson, who is now dead.
Q To what town does Wiley Roberts belong? A Nuyaka.
Q To what town did Ahullie Johnson belong? A Greenleaf.
Q Is Indie Johnson living? A No, sir, she is dead.
Q Did they have another child named Mandoche Johnson? A Yes, sir, That child is also dead. My child, Indie Roberts and Indie Johnson are two different children. Wiley's child was named after its father, Ahullie Johnson, and the mother is known as Wiley Roberts instead of Wiley Johnson.
Q Was your wife ever known as Millie? A No, sir.
Q Was Wiley ever known as Millie: A No, sir.
Q Have you any other children? A I have only one other child living.
Q What is its name? A Johnson Roberts.
Q Has your sister, Wiley Roberts, any other children? A No, sir. She only had two children, Indie and Mandoche.
Q Is your wife Mary Roberts enrolled as Mary Roberts? A Yes, sir.
Q Is your sister, Wiley Roberts, enrolled as Wiley Roberts or Wiley Johnson? A She is enrolled as Wiley Roberts. I notice you have my name spelled Cundel. That is not correct--it is Kendall.

I, D. C. Skaggs, on oath state that the above and foregoing is a full and true transcript of my stenographic notes as taken in said cause on said date.

D. C. Skaggs

Subscribed and sworn to before me this 30 day of Dec 1905.

Edw C Griesel
Notary Public.

Applications for Enrollment of Creek Newborn
Act of 1905   Volume XIV

NC-1140

DEPARTMENT OF THE INTERIOR,
COMMISSION TO THE FIVE CIVILIZED TRIBES.

Muskogee, Indian Territory, December 4, 1905

In the matter of the application for the enrollment of Monoche (or Mandoche) and India Johnson as citizens by blood of the Creek Nation.

Kendall Roberts, being duly sworn, testified as follows (through Jesse McDermott, Official Interpreter):

EXAMINATION BY THE COMMISSIONER:
Q What is your name, age and postoffice? A Kendall Roberts; 33; Morse.
Q Do you know Wiley Roberts? A Yes sir.
Q Is that your sister? A Yes sir.
Q Do you know her father's name? A Osuchee Yarhola.
Q Do you know the mother? A Arsofolech Yarhola.

Said Wiley Roberts is identified as Warley Roberts on Creek Indian card, Field No. 1319, No. 4206.

Q Did she have two children named Monoche (or Mandoche) and Indie Johnson?
A Yes sir.
Q Are they dead? A Yes sir.
Q What is the name of the father of these two children? A Ahullie Johnson.
Q Has Ahullie a boy named Culley Johnson? A Yes sir. He is Culley's father.
Q Was he ever known by "Miller Johnson?" A Ahullie is the only name that I have known him by.
Q Is he dead? A Yes sir.
Q How old was he? A He was a tolerably old man. I couldn't say how old he was.
Q Can you name any of his other children besides Culley? A Culley has three sisters but I don't know their names? They live some distance from where I do and I don't know their names.
Q Is Halley one of them and Maggie? A I think the oldest girl if Jennie.
Q Willie and Clenowes--are they his children? A I don't know I have seen them a number of times, but I don't remember their names.
Q What Creek Indian Town did Ahullie belong to? A He lived in the Greenleaf settlement. I always thought he belonged to that Town.

It appears from a notation on the card of Halley Johnson that he is the child of Miller Johnson and belonged to Wewoka Town. Miller Johnson is identified on Creek Indian card, Field No. 1282, opposite No. 4093, in Wewoka Town. It appears on the 1890 Roll as Aharley, an[sic] it is presumed that said Miller Johnson is the Ahullie Johnson referred to herein.

Applications for Enrollment of Creek Newborn
Act of 1905   Volume XIV

STATEMENT BY THE INTERPRETER:
This man was always known by the white people as Miller Johnson. The Indians had no other name for him except as Ahulley. I am positive that that is his name. My aunt was in business and he had an account with her. She sent me out to collect it. I called for Miller Johnson or Ahulley. There weren't any Indians there who knew a man by the name of Miller Johnson but would refer me to Ahulley. The white people, when I asked them where he lived they told me they didn't know anybody by that name. Possibly he may be the same man as Miller Johnson. I was personally acquainted with the old fellow myself

INDIAN TERRITORY, Western District.
I, J. Y. Miller, a stenographer to the Commissioner to the Five Civilized Tribes, do hereby certify that the above and foregoing is a true and complete translation of my notes as same appear in my stenographic report of this case.

JY Miller

Sworn to and subscribed before me
this the 6th day of December,
1905.

J McDermott
Notary Public.

N.C. 1140.   J.L.De
DEPARTMENT OF THE INTERIOR,
COMMISSIONER TO THE FIVE CIVILIZED TRIBES.

In the matter of the application for the enrollment of Monoche (or Mandochee) Johnson, deceased, and Indian Johnson, deceased, as citizens by blood of the Creek Nation.

DECISION.

The record in this case shows that on May 1, 1905, application was made, in affidavit form supplemented by oral testimony on April 28, 1905, and by further testimony on December 4, 1905, for the enrollment of Monoche (or Mandochee) Johnson, deceased, and Indie Johnson, deceased, as citizens by blood of the Creek Nation, under the provisions of the Act of Congress approved March 3, 1905.

It appears from the evidence filed in this matter that the said Monoche (or Mandochee) Johnson, and India Johnson were born September 19, 1900, and July 1, 1902 respectively and died November 12, 1900 and October 1, 1902, respectively and were the children of Ahullie Johnson and Wiley Roberts, whose names appear opposite Nos. 4093 and 4206 respectively on the approved roll of citizens by blood of the Creek Nation.

The Act of Congress approved March 3, 1905, (33 Stats. 1048), provides in part as follows:

Applications for Enrollment of Creek Newborn
Act of 1905 Volume XIV

"That the Commission to the Five Civilized Tribes is authorized for sixty days after the date of the approval of this act to receive and consider applications for enrollment, of children, born subsequent to May twenty-fifth, nineteen hundred and one, and prior to March fourth, nineteen hundred and five, and living on said latter date, to citizens of the Creek tribe of Indians whose enrollment has been approved by the Secretary of the Interior prior to the approval of this act; and to enroll and make allotments to such children."

It is therefore, ordered and adjudged that said Monoche (or Mandochee) Johnson, deceased, and the said India Johnson, deceased, are not entitled to enrollment as citizens by blood of the Creek Nation, in accordance with the provisions of the Act of Congress above quoted, and the application for their enrollment as such is accordingly denied.

Tams Bixby COMMISSIONER.

Muskogee, Indian Territory.
JAN 18 1907

Copy
DEPARTMENT OF THE INTERIOR.
COMMISSION TO THE FIVE CIVILIZED TRIBES.

In the matter of the death of   Mandochee Johnson   a citizen of the Creek   Nation, who formerly resided at or near   Morse   , Ind. Ter., and died on the 12   day of   November   , 1900

AFFIDAVIT OF RELATIVE.

UNITED STATES OF AMERICA, Indian Territory,
Western   DISTRICT.

I,   Wiley Roberts   , on oath state that I am 24   years of age and a citizen by blood   , of the Creek   Nation; that my postoffice address is   Morse   , Ind. Ter.; that I am   mother   of   Manochee[sic] Johnson   who was a citizen, by blood   , of the Creek   Nation and that said   Mandochee Johnson   died on the   12   day of November   , 1900

(Signed) Wiley Roberts

Witnesses To Mark:

(Seal)

Subscribed and sworn to before me this 17 day of   April   , 1905.

My Com Exp Aug. 19 1908   Tupper Dunn
                                  Notary Public.

Applications for Enrollment of Creek Newborn
Act of 1905 Volume XIV

AFFIDAVIT OF ACQUAINTANCE.

UNITED STATES OF AMERICA, Indian Territory,
Western DISTRICT.

I, Kendall Roberts, on oath state that I am 33 years of age, and a citizen by blood of the Creek Nation; that my postoffice address is Morse, Ind. Ter.; that I was personally acquainted with Mandochee Johnson who was a citizen, by blood, of the Creek Nation; and that said Mandochee died on the 12 day of November, 1900

(Signed) Kendall Roberts

Witnesses To Mark:

(Seal)

Subscribed and sworn to before me this 17 day of April, 1905.

My Com Exp Aug 19-1908   Tupper Dunn
Notary Public.

Copy
DEPARTMENT OF THE INTERIOR.
COMMISSION TO THE FIVE CIVILIZED TRIBES.

In the matter of the death of Indie Johnson a citizen of the Creek Nation, who formerly resided at or near Morse, Ind. Ter., and died on the 1st day of October, 1902

AFFIDAVIT OF RELATIVE.

UNITED STATES OF AMERICA, Indian Territory,
Western DISTRICT.

I, Wiley Roberts, on oath state that I am 24 years of age and a citizen by blood, of the Creek Nation; that my postoffice address is Morse, Ind. Ter.; that I am mother of Indie Johnson who was a citizen, by blood, of the Creek Nation and that said Indie Johnson died on the 1st day of October, 1902

(Signed) Wiley Roberts

Witnesses To Mark:

(Seal)

Applications for Enrollment of Creek Newborn
Act of 1905 Volume XIV

Subscribed and sworn to before me this 17 day of   April , 1905.

My Com Exp
Aug. 19-1908

Tupper Dunn
Notary Public.

AFFIDAVIT OF ACQUAINTANCE.

UNITED STATES OF AMERICA, Indian Territory,
      Western   DISTRICT.

I, Kendall Roberts , on oath state that I am 33 years of age, and a citizen by blood of the Creek Nation; that my postoffice address is   Morse , Ind. Ter.; that I was personally acquainted with   Indie Johnson   who was a citizen, by blood , of the Creek Nation; and that said   Indie Johnson   died on the 1st day of October , 1902

(Signed) Kendall Roberts

Witnesses To Mark:

{   (Seal)

Subscribed and sworn to before me this 17 day of   April , 1905.

My Com Exp
Aug. 19-1908

Tupper Dunn
Notary Public.

(Letter below typed as given.)

NC 1140   Copy

Morse I.T. May 16, 1905.

Commission to the Five Civilized Tribes,
      Muskogee, I.T.

Sir:

I rec'd your request the date of the birth of said children that was being death, so I will advise you the date of the birth of said children.

Well, Monochee was borned on Sept 19, 1900 & she died on November 12 1900 & Indie was borned in July 1st 1902 & she died on October 1st 1902 I advised you all when children was born & when the both died. I remain

(signed) Wiley Roberts.

Applications for Enrollment of Creek Newborn
Act of 1905   Volume XIV

N.C. 1170[sic].

Muskogee, Indian Territory, August 4, 1905.

Wiley Roberts,
    Morse, Indian Territory.

Dear Madam:

    May 1, 1905, there were filed with this office affidavits executed by you in which you state that your minor children, Indie Johnson and Mandochee Johnson, died October 1, 1902 and November 12, 1900 respectively.

    There are herewith enclosed blank proofs of birth and you are requested to sign and execute same before a notary public; care being taken that said notary public affixes his signature and official seal.

    You are advised that this office is unable to identify you on its rolls of citizens of the Creek Nation and you are requested to state the names of your parents, the Creek Indian town to which you belong and your roll number as the same appears on your deeds and allotment certificate.

    This matter should receive your prompt attention.

                                 Respectfully,

                                                   Commissioner.

2 B A
1 env.

                                                                       HGH

REFER IN REPLY TO THE FOLLOWING:
NC-1140
NC-1141

DEPARTMENT OF THE INTERIOR,
COMMISSIONER TO THE FIVE CIVILIZED TRIBES.

Muskogee, Indian Territory, September 19, 1905.

Alex Posey,
    Clerk in Charge Creek Enrollment Field Party,
        Eufaula, Indian Territory.

Dear Sir:

    There is herewith enclosed a copy of the record in the cases of Monoche, or Mandoche, Indie Johnson and Indie Robert, and two other children of Cundel Robert, the names of the latter two children being unknown.

Applications for Enrollment of Creek Newborn
Act of 1905   Volume XIV

You are directed to ascertain whether or not Indie Robert is the same person as Indie Johnson, and whether there are any other duplications among the children in this case.

You will also endeavor to ascertain whether or not Mary Robert, or Mary Johnson, is living or dead, and whether Millie Robert, Wiley Johnson and Mary Robert are one and the same person; and if so, under what name she is enrolled.

Respectfully,

W^mO.Beall
Acting Commissioner.

JYM-19

NC 1140.

Muskogee, Indian Territory, January 19, 1907.

The Honorable,
    The Secretary of the Interior.

Sir:

There is herewith transmitted the record of proceedings in the matter of the application for the enrollment of Manoche (or Mandochee) and Indian Johnson, both deceased, as citizens by blood of the Creek Nation, including the decision of the Commissioner to the Five Civilized Tribes, denying said application.

Respectfully,

Commissioner.

LM-15.

Through the Commissioner
    of Indian Affairs.

NC 1140.

Muskogee, Indian Territory, January 19, 1907.

M. L. Mott,
    Attorney for Creek Nation,
        Muskogee, Indian Territory.

Dear Sir:

There is herewith enclosed one copy of the decision of the Commissioner to the Five Civilized Tribes in the matter of the application for the enrollment of Manoche (or Mandochee) and Indie Johnson, both deceased, as citizens by blood of the Creek Nation, denying said application.

Applications for Enrollment of Creek Newborn
Act of 1905   Volume XIV

The decision, with a copy of the proceedings had in the case, is this day transmitted to the Secretary of the Interior for his review and decision. The final decision of the Secretary will be made known to you as soon as the Commissioner is informed of the same.

        Respectfully,

              Commissioner.

LM-14.

HGH

REFER IN REPLY TO THE FOLLOWING:
NC 1140.

DEPARTMENT OF THE INTERIOR,
COMMISSIONER TO THE FIVE CIVILIZED TRIBES.

Muskogee, Indian Territory, January 19, 1907.

Wiley Roberts,
 c/o Ahullie Johnson,
  Morse, Indian Territory

Dear Madam:

There is herewith enclosed one copy of the decision of the Commissioner to the Five Civilized Tribes in the matter of the application for the enrollment of your minor children, Manoche (or Mandochee) and Indie Johnson, both deceased, as citizens by blood of the Creek Nation, denying said application.

The decision, with a copy of the proceedings had in the case, is this day transmitted to the Secretary of the Interior for his review and decision. The final decision of the Secretary will be made known to you as soon as the Commissioner is informed of the same.

        Respectfully,

          Tams Bixby Commissioner.

Register.
LM-12.

COPY

DEPARTMENT OF THE INTERIOR,
LAND   Office of Indian Affairs,
6870-1907.
      Washington. February 21, 1907.

  The Honorable,

    The Secretary of the Interior.

Applications for Enrollment of Creek Newborn
Act of 1905   Volume XIV

Sir:

There is enclosed a report from the Commissioner to the Five Civilized Tribes, dated January 19, 1907, transmitting the record relative to the application made on May 1, 1905, for the enrollment of Monoche (or Mandochee) and Indie Johnson, both deceased, as citizens by blood of the Creek Nation. On January 18, 1907, the Commissioner held that the applicants were not entitled to enrollment.

The record shows that the applicants were the children of citizens by blood of the Creek Nation and were born on September 19, 1900 and July 1, 1902, respectively, and died on November 12, 1900 and October 1, 1902, respectively.

Under the Act of March 3, 1905 (33 Stat. L. 1048) the applicants are not entitled to enrollment.

It is therefore recommended that the decision of the Commissioner to the Five Civilized Tribes adverse to the applicants be approved.

Very Respectfully,
C. F. Larrabee,
Acting Commissioner.

J.P.B.-NL.

J.P.

C O P Y.

DEPARTMENT OF THE INTERIOR.

WASHINGTON.

I.T.D. 4854, 4888, 4892-07.
4906, 4908, 4912, 4914-"
4916, 4918, 4366, 4822-"
LRS. 4842, 4910, 4900,   -"

February 28, 1907.

DIRECT

Commissioner to the Five Civilized Tribes,
  Muskogee, Indian Territory.

Sir:

Your decisions in the following Creek citizenship cases adverse to the applicants are hereby affirmed, viz:

Applications for Enrollment of Creek Newborn
Act of 1905   Volume XIV

Title of case.	Date of your letter of transmittal.
Louisa Hartley, (Freedman)	December 13, 1906.
Effie May Splawn, et al, (Freedman)	January 19, 1907.
Zepherina Ross, (Freedman)	January 19, 1907.
Thomas Thomas, deceased,	January 19, 1907.
Yah-pah-ney, deceased,	January 18, 1907.
Irene Tucker, deceased, (Freedman)	January 17, 1907.
Owens Fleming, (Freedman)	January 19, 1907.
Willie Lindsey, deceased,	January 18, 1907.
Manoche (or Mandochee) and Indie Johnson,	January 19, 1907.
Annie Malone, (Freedman)	October 13, 1906.
Henrietta[sic] Hollands (Freedman)	December 13, 1906.
Wrichel Hadrick,	January 10, 1907.
Reuben Humphreys, et al (Freedman)	January 17, 1907.
Alice Humphreys, (Freedman)	January 19, 1907.

Copies of Indian Office letters submitting your reports and recommending that the decisions be affirmed, are inclosed.

A copy hereof and all the papers in the above-mentioned cases have been sent to the Indian Office.

Respectfully,

A.F.Mc
3-1-07.

Jesse E. Wilson.
Assistant Secretary.

14 inc. and 29 for Ind. Of.

JWH

N C 1140

Muskogee, Indian Territory, March 8, 1907.

Wiley Roberts,
% Ahullie Johnson,
Morse, Indian Territory.

Dear Madam :--

You are hereby advised that under date of February 28, 1907, the Secretary of the Interior affirmed the decision of the Commissioner to the Five Civilized Tribes, denying the application for the enrollment of your deceased minor children, Monoche and Indie Johnson, as citizens by blood of the Creek Nation.

Respectfully,

Commissioner.

Applications for Enrollment of Creek Newborn
Act of 1905   Volume XIV

DEPARTMENT OF THE INTERIOR,
COMMISSION TO THE FIVE CIVILIZED TRIBES.
Near Morse, I.T. April 28, 1905.

In the matter of the application for new born children concerning whose enrollment no affidavits could be obtained in time.

Chofulop, being duly sworn, testified as follows: Through Official Interpreter, Alex Posey.

Examination by the Commission:

Q What is your name? A Chofulop.
Q What is your age? (No answer)
Q What is your post office address? [sic] Morse, I.T

Statement: I am a member of the House of Kings, of Nuyaka Town. Eundel and Millie Robert, both of Neyaka[sic] Town, have a girl named Indy--it is over two years old, and the other child is unnamed and was born in February. It is a boy, both are living--about the first of February the youngest was born. Post Office, Morse.

The father of the child is unknown, the mother Funcinda of Nuyaka Town,-- has a child over a year old--a girl unnamed. living   Post Office, Morse.

Henry G. Hains, being duly sworn, on his oath, states that the above and foregoing is a true and correct transcript of his stenographic notes as taken in said cause on said date.

Henry G. Hains

Subscribed and sworn to before me this 10th day of May, 1905.

Drennan C Skaggs
Notary Public.

N.C. 1140 & 1141.

DEPARTMENT OF THE INTERIOR,
COMMISSIONER TO THE FIVE CIVILIZED TRIBES.
Okemah, I. T., October 20, 1905.

In the matter of the application for the enrollment of Indie Roberts as a citizen by blood of the Creek Nation.

KENDALL ROBERTS, being duly sworn, testified as follows

Through Alex Posey Official Interpreter:

Applications for Enrollment of Creek Newborn
Act of 1905   Volume XIV

BY THE COMMISSIONER:
Q What is your name? A Kendall Roberts.
Q How old are you? A About thirty-three.
Q What is your post office address? A Morse.
Q Are you a citizen of the Creek Nation? A Yrs, sir.
Q To what town do you belong? A Nuyaka.
Q Have you a child named Indie Roberts? A Yes, sir. The child is a girl.
Q Have you made application for the child's enrollment as a Creek New-Born? A Yes, sir. I went before Tupper Dunn (notary) and executed affidavits about the child. I made application at the same time for another child named Cainey Roberts.
Q What was the name of the mother of Indie? A Mary Roberts was the mother of both children.
Q What was the name of the mother of India? A Mary Roberts what the mother of both children.
Q What was your wife's name before her marriage to you? A Mary West.
Q When was Indie born? A January 18, 1903.
Q Is the child also known as Indie Johnson? A No, sir. Indie Johnson is a child of my sister, Wiley Roberts. The child's father was Ahullie Johnson, who is now dead.
Q To what town does Wiley Roberts belong? A Nuyaka.
Q To what town did Ahullie Johnson belong? A Greenleaf.
Q Is Indie Johnson living? A No, sir, she is dead.
Q Did they have another child named Mandoche Johnson? A Yes, sir, That child is also dead. My child, Indie Roberts and Indie Johnson are two different children. Wiley's child was named after its father, Ahullie Johnson, and the mother is known as Wiley Roberts instead of Wiley Johnson.
Q Was your wife ever known as Millie? A No, sir.
Q Was Wiley ever known as Millie: A No, sir.
Q Have you any other children? A I have only one other child living.
Q What is its name? A Johnson Roberts.
Q Has your sister, Wiley Roberts, any other children? A No, sir. She only had two children, Indie and Mandoche.
Q Is your wife Mary Roberts enrolled as Mary Roberts? A Yes, sir.
Q Is your sister, Wiley Roberts, enrolled as Wiley Roberts or Wiley Johnson? A She is enrolled as Wiley Roberts. I notice you have my name spelled Cundel. That is not correct--it is Kendall.

I, D. C. Skaggs, on oath state that the above and foregoing is a full and true transcript of my stenographic notes as taken in said cause on said date.

D. C. Skaggs
Subscribed and sworn to before me this 30 day of Dec 1905.

Edw C Griesel
Notary Public.

Applications for Enrollment of Creek Newborn
Act of 1905   Volume XIV

NC 1142

Mr. Bixby

    Here is a case I told Creek division to investigate but they have not been able to send it

(Illegible) and there is no longer any time

(Illegible) OK on the record.   AWC

                                                                               OCH

NC-1142   JWH

                 DEPARTMENT OF THE INTERIOR,
          COMMISSIONER TO THE FIVE CIVILIZED TRIBES.

    In the matter of the application for the enrollment of Louana Johnson as a citizen by blood of the Creek Nation.

DECISION.

    The record in this case shows that on May 3, 1905, application was made, in affidavit form, for the enrollment of Louana Johnson as a citizen by blood of the Creek Nation.

    The evidence shows that said Louana Johnson is the child of Tolitha Jefferson and Peter Johnson.

    An examination of the records of this office fails to show that the names of Tolitha Jefferson or Peter Johnson, or either of them, appear upon the approved roll of citizens by blood of the Creek Nation; that their names, or either of them, appear upon the 1890 authenticated tribal roll or the 1895 pay roll of the Creek Nation; that they, or either of them, have ever been admitted to citizenship in the Creek Nation by any of the Creek tribal authorities, the Commission to the Five Civilized Tribes or the United States Court in Indian Territory.

    The evidence further shows that said Louana Johnson was born March 4, 1903, and was living April 22, 1905.

    This office has attempted to obtain further evidence in this case, but the parents of said child have failed to furnish any further information.

    It is, therefore, ordered and adjudged that the said Louana Johnson is not entitled to be enrolled as a citizen by blood of the Creek Nation, under the provisions of the Act of Congress approved March 3, 1905, (33 Stat. L., 1048), and the application for her enrollment as such is accordingly denied.

                                               Tams Bixby   COMMISSIONER.

Muskogee, Indian Territory,
   FEB 27 1907

Applications for Enrollment of Creek Newborn
Act of 1905   Volume XIV

N.C. 1142

Muskogee, Indian Territory, June 22, 1906.

Tolitha Johnson,
    Beggs, Indian Territory.

Dear Madam:

    In the matter of the application for the enrollment of your minor child, Louana Johnson, as a citizen by blood of the Creek Nation, you are advised that it is required that you furnish this office with the affidavits of yourself and the midwife in attendance at the birth of said child. For this purpose there is inclosed blank form of affidavit. Said affidavit should show the name of the child, the names of its parents, the date of its birth and whether or not it was living on March 4, 1905.

    This matter should receive your prompt attention.

                            Respectfully,

BA   Commissioner.

NC 1142.

Muskogee, Indian Territory, February 27, 1907.

Tolitha Johnson,
    c/o Peter Johnson,
        Beggs, Indian Territory.

Dear Madam:

    There is herewith enclosed one copy of the decision of the Commissioner to the Five Civilized Tribes in the matter of the application for the enrollment of your minor child, Louanna Johnson, as a citizen by blood of the Creek Nation, denying said application.

    The decision, with a copy of the proceedings had in the case, is this day transmitted to the Secretary of the Interior for his review and decision. The final decision of the Secretary will be made known to you as soon as the Commissioner is informed of the same.

                            Respectfully,

                                                 Commissioner.

Register.
LM- 212.

Applications for Enrollment of Creek Newborn
Act of 1905 Volume XIV

NC 1142.

Muskogee, Indian Territory, February 27, 1907.

M. L. Mott,
    Attorney for Creek Nation,
        Muskogee, Indian Territory.

Dear Sir:

    There is herewith enclosed one copy of the decision of the Commissioner to the Five Civilized Tribes in the matter of the application for the enrollment of Louana Johnson, as a citizen by blood of the Creek Nation, denying said application.

    The decision, with a copy of the proceedings had in the case, is this day transmitted to the Secretary of the Interior for his review and decision. The final decision of the Secretary will be made known to you as soon as the Commissioner is informed of the same.

        Respectfully,

                Commissioner.

LM- 213.

NC 1142.

Muskogee, Indian Territory, February 27, 1907.

The Honorable,
    The Secretary of the Interior.

Sir:

    There is herewith transmitted the record of proceedings in the matter of the application for the enrollment of Louana Johnson, as a citizen by blood of the Creek Nation, including the decision of the Commissioner to the Five Civilized Tribes, denying the application.

        Respectfully,

                Commissioner.

LM-214.

Through the Commissioner
    of Indian Affairs.

Applications for Enrollment of Creek Newborn
Act of 1905 Volume XIV

DEPARTMENT OF THE INTERIOR
WASHINGTON

JF
FHE

I.T.D. 7764-1907.

LRS

March 4, 1907.

Direct.

Commissioner to the Five Civilized Tribes,
　　Muskogee, Indian Territory.

Sir:

　　The Department has considered the following citizenship cases received with your letters of February 25, 26 and 27 1907, and Indian Office letter of March 2, 1907 (Land 21229 et al), copy inclosed, and in accordance with the recommendation made by you and the Indian Office the application in each case is rejected:

Title of case.

　　George and Julia McIntosh, deceased (freedmen[sic])
　　Belle and Delpha May Brown (Freedmen)
　　Peggy McCoy (Freedman)
　　Lena McGirt (Creek)
　　Julia Grayson deceased (Creek)
　　Cosarpe, Ithas Harjo and Mewike (Creeks)
　　Ophila Harjo (Creeks)
　　Louana Johnson (Creek)
　　Sampson Harjo (Creek)
　　Ivy Richardson (Cherokee freedman)
　　Hester and Myrtle Powell (Cherokee freedman)
　　George Sutherland (Cherokee)
　　Lawrence Smith (Creek freedman)
　　John W. Vaughn et al., (Cherokees)
　　Louie A. Lafallier, (Cherokee)

　　A copy hereof has been sent to the Indian Office.

Respectfully,
E. A. Hitchcock,
Secretary.

i[sic] inclosure. WCF 4/4/06.

Applications for Enrollment of Creek Newborn
Act of 1905   Volume XIV

DEPARTMENT OF THE INTERIOR
OFFICE OF INDIAN AFFAIRS   (Copy.
WASHINGTON.

Land
References   March 2, 1907.
at bottom
of letter.

The Honorable,
        The Secretary of the Interior.

Sir:

There are forwarded herewith several reports of Commissioner Bixby and records in the following names citizenship cases, together with the Commissioner's decisions denying the applications for enrollment of the persons involved in each case:

Cherokee citizens by blood	John W. Vaughn, et al.
Cherokee citizens by intermarriage	George Sutherland Louis A Lafallier.
Cherokee freedmen	Hester and Myrtle Powell Ivy Richardson
Creek citizens by blood	Sampson Harjo Louana Johnson Ophila Harjo Cosarpa, Ithas Harjo and Mewike Julia Grayson Lena McGirt Belle Brown and Delpha May Brown, Lawrence Smith, George and Julia McIntosh Peggy McCoy.

The office has examined the record in each of the above cases and recommends for approval the decisions of the Commissioner denying the applications.

There are also forwarded herewith briefs and affidavits tonbe[sic] considered in connection with the following cases, which have heretofore been forwarded to the Department:

Chickasaw citizens by blood	M. D. Carson, Indian Territory et al.
Chickasaw intermarried citizen	Martin M. Yoakum

Applications for Enrollment of Creek Newborn
Act of 1905 Volume XIV

Choctaw citizen by blood	Hazy Ann Vandergriff
Choctaw intermarried citizen	Mattie Doak
Choctaw intermarried citizen	Emma Crawford
Choctaw intermarried citizen	Mary Jane Williams

Very respectfully,
C. F. Larrabee,
Acting Commissioner.

AJW-EM

21229-1907	21271-1907	21265-1907
21226	21270	21221
21230	21269	21222
21236	21277	21224
21237	21268	21248
21273	21267	21223
21272	21266	21225

NC-1142

Muskogee, Indian Territory, March 15, 1907.

Mars & Mars,
    Attorneys at Law,
        Sapulpa, Indian Territory.

Gentlemen:

    You are hereby advised that the Secretary of the Interior under date of March 2, 1907, affirmed the decision of the Commissioner to the Five Civilized Tribes denying the application for the enrollment of Louana Johnson, as a citizen by blood of the Creek Nation.

Respectfully,
Commissioner.

Applications for Enrollment of Creek Newborn
Act of 1905   Volume XIV

NC-1142

Muskogee, Indian Territory, March 15, 1907.

Peter Johnson,
    Beggs, Indian Territory.

Dear Sir:

    Replying to your letter of March 13, 1907, you are hereby advised that the Secretary of the Interior under date of March 2, 1907 affirmed the decision of the Commissioner to the Five Civilized Tribes denying the application for the enrollment of your minor child, Louana Johnson, as a citizen by blood of the Creek Nation.

                  Respectfully,

                              Commissioner.

Nc[sic]-1142

Muskogee, Indian Territory, March 15, 1907.

Tolitha Johnson (or Jefferson)
    Beggs, Indian Territory.

Dear Madam:

    Replying to your letter of March 13, 1907, you are hereby advised that the Secretary of the Interior under date of March 2, 1907 affirmed the decision of the Commissioner to the Five Civilized Tribes denying the application for the enrollment of your minor child, Louana Johnson, as a citizen by blood of the Creek Nation.

                  Respectfully,

                              Commissioner.

Applications for Enrollment of Creek Newborn
Act of 1905 Volume XIV

DEPARTMENT OF THE INTERIOR.
COMMISSION TO THE FIVE CIVILIZED TRIBES.

In the matter of the death of   Bert Dunn   a citizen of the   Creek Nation, who formerly resided at or near   Okemah   , Ind. Ter., and died on the   15   day of   October , 1904

AFFIDAVIT OF RELATIVE.

UNITED STATES OF AMERICA, Indian Territory, }
Western Judicial   DISTRICT.

I,   Susie Dunn , on oath state that I am   31   years of age and a citizen by blood , of the Creek   Nation; that my postoffice address is   Okemah   , Ind. Ter.; that I am   mother   of   Bert Dunn   who was a citizen, by blood   , of the Creek   Nation and that said   Bert Dunn   died on the   15   day of   October , 1904

Susie Dunn

Witnesses To Mark:
{
Subscribed and sworn to before me this 28 day of April, 1905.

HG Malot
Notary Public.
My Com Exp 2 July 1906

AFFIDAVIT OF ACQUAINTANCE.

UNITED STATES OF AMERICA, Indian Territory, }
Western Judicial   DISTRICT.

I,   Tupper Dunn , on oath state that I am   31   years of age, and a citizen by blood   of the Creek   Nation; that my postoffice address is   Okemah   , Ind. Ter.; that I was personally acquainted with   Burt[sic] Dunn   who was a citizen, by blood   , of the   Creek   Nation; and that said   Bert Dunn   died on the   15   day of   October   , 1904

Tupper Dunn

Witnesses To Mark:
{
Subscribed and sworn to before me this 28 day of April, 1905.

HG Malot
Notary Public.
My Com Exp 2 July 1906

Applications for Enrollment of Creek Newborn
Act of 1905   Volume XIV

BIRTH AFFIDAVIT.

DEPARTMENT OF THE INTERIOR.
COMMISSION TO THE FIVE CIVILIZED TRIBES.

IN RE APPLICATION FOR ENROLLMENT, as a citizen of the Creek Nation, of Bert Dunn, born on the 6 day of October, 1903

Name of Father:	Tupper Dunn	a citizen of the Creek	Nation.
Name of Mother:	Susie Dunn	a citizen of the Creek	Nation.

Postoffice   Okemah I.T.

AFFIDAVIT OF MOTHER.

UNITED STATES OF AMERICA, Indian Territory, }
   Western Judicial   DISTRICT.

I, Susie Dunn, on oath state that I am 31 years of age and a citizen by blood, of the Creek Nation; that I am the lawful wife of Tupper Dunn, who is a citizen, by blood of the Creek Nation; that a male child was born to me on 6 day of October, 1903, that said child has been named Bert Dunn, and was ~~living March 4, 1905~~. (living Oct 6th 1904 and there was no one attended

Susie Dunn

Witnesses To Mark:
{

Subscribed and sworn to before me this 8 day of May, 1905.

HG Malot
Notary Public.

DEPARTMENT OF THE INTERIOR.
COMMISSION TO THE FIVE CIVILIZED TRIBES.

IN RE APPLICATION FOR ENROLLMENT, as a citizen of the Creek Nation, of Bert Dunn, born on the 6 day of October, 1903

Name of Father:	Tupper Dunn	a citizen of the Creek	Nation.
Name of Mother:	Susie Dunn	a citizen of the Creek	Nation.

Postoffice   Okemah Ind Terr

Applications for Enrollment of Creek Newborn
Act of 1905   Volume XIV

AFFIDAVIT OF MOTHER.

UNITED STATES OF AMERICA, Indian Territory,
Western   DISTRICT.

I, Susie Dunn , on oath state that I am 33 years of age and a citizen by Blood , of the Creek Nation; that I am the lawful wife of Tupper Dunn , who is a citizen, by Blood of the Creek Nation; that a male child was born to me on 6 day of October, 1903 , that said child has been named Bert Dunn , and ~~was living March 4, 1905~~. Died Oct 15th 1904

Susie Dunn

Witnesses To Mark:
{

Subscribed and sworn to before me this 8 day of August , 1905.

HG Malot
Notary Public.

My Com Exp 2 July 1906

AFFIDAVIT OF ATTENDING PHYSICIAN OR MID-WIFE.

UNITED STATES OF AMERICA, Indian Territory,
Western   DISTRICT.

I, Tupper Dunn , a husband , on oath state that I ~~attended on Mrs~~. am the Husband of Sussie[sic] Dunn my , wife of Creek Nation IT on the 6 day of October , 1903 ; that there was born to her on said date a male child; that said child ~~was living March 4, 1905~~ (Died Oct 15 1904), and is said to have been named Bert Dunn

Tupper Dunn

Witnesses To Mark:
{

Subscribed and sworn to before me this 8 day of August , 1905.

HG Malot
Notary Public.

My Com Exp 2 July 1906

Applications for Enrollment of Creek Newborn
Act of 1905   Volume XIV

NC 1145								ISN
									CM

DEPARTMENT OF THE INTERIOR,
COMMISSIONER TO THE FIVE CIVILIZED TRIBES.

In the matter of the application for the enrollment of Bert Dunn, deceased, as a citizen by blood of the Creek Nation.

STATEMENT AND ORDER

The record in this case shows that on April 29, 1905, application was filed with the Commission to the Five Civilized Tribes, in affidavit form, for the enrollment of Bert Dunn, deceased, as a citizen by blood of the Creek Nation. Supplemental affidavits were filed in this case on May 10 and August 11, 1905.

The evidence shows that said Bert Dunn was born October 6, 1903 and died October 15, 1904.

It is, therefore, adjudged that there is no authority of law for the enrollment of the said Bert Dunn, deceased, as a citizen by blood of the Creek Nation, and the application for his enrollment as such is hereby ordered dismissed.

				Tams Bixby COMMISSIONER.
Muskogee, Indian Territory,
    FEB 19 1907

DEPARTMENT OF THE INTERIOR,
COMMISSION TO THE FIVE CIVILIZED TRIBES.

IN RE APPLICATION FOR ENROLLMENT, as a citizen of the Creek Nation, of Bert Dunn, born on the 6 day of October, 1903.

Name of Father: Tupper Dunn, a citizen of the Creek Nation.
Name of Mother: Susie Dunn, a citizen of the Creek Nation.

				Postoffice Okemah Ind Terr

AFFIDAVIT OF MOTHER.

UNITED STATES OF AMERICA, Indian Territory,   )
)
Western. . . . . .District.   )

I, Susie Dunn, on oath state that I am 33 years of age and a citizen by blood, of the Creek Nation; that I am the lawful wife of Tupper Dunn, who is a citizen, by blood, of the Creek Nation; that a male child was born to me on 6 day of October, 1903; that said child has been named Bert Dunn, and died Oct 15th 1904.

Applications for Enrollment of Creek Newborn
Act of 1905   Volume XIV

Susie Dunn.

Witnesses to Mark:

(Must be Two) (_____
(Witnesses) (_____

Subscribed and sworn to before me this 8 day of August, 1905.

                                   H. G. Malot,
                                          Notary Public.

My Com Exp 2 July 1906

AFFIDAVIT OF ATTENDING PHYSICIAN OR MID-WIFE.

UNITED STATES OF AMERICA, Indian Territory,   )
)
Western. . . . . .District.   )

      I, Tupper Dunn, a husband, on oath state that I am the husband of Sussie Dunn my wife of Creek Nation I.T. on the 6 day of October, 1903; that there was born to her o said date a male child; that said child (died Oct 15 1904) and is said to have been named Bert Dunn.

                                    Tupper Dunn.

Witnesses to Mark:

Must be Two) (_____
(Witnesses) (_____

Subscribed and sworn to before me this 8 day of August, 1905.
(Seal)

                                   H. G. Malot,
                                         Notary Public.

My Com Exp 2 July 1906

(Indorsed)   IN RE
                    Application for Enrollment of
                           INFANT CHILD

                      As a citizen of
                      _____ nation

                Approved _____190__
                    _____Commissioner
                     Rec'd 8-11-05

Applications for Enrollment of Creek Newborn
Act of 1905   Volume XIV

DEPARTMENT OF THE INTERIOR,
COMMISSION TO THE FIVE CIVILIZED TRIBES.

In the matter of the death of Bert Dunn, a citizen of the Creek Nation, who formerly resided as or near Okemah, Ind. Ter., and died on the 15 day of October, 1904.

AFFIDAVIT OF RELATIVE.

UNITED STATES OF AMERICA,   )
)
Western Judicial District.   )

I, Susie Dunn, on oath state that I am 31 years of age and a citizen, by blood, of the Creek Nation; that my post office address is Okemah, Ind. Ter.; that I am mother of Bert Dunn, who was a citizen, by blood, of the Creek Nation; and that said Bert Dunn died on the 15 day of October, 1904.
(Seal)   Susie Dunn.

Subscribed and sworn to before me this 28 day of April, 1905.

My Com Exp 2 July 1906.   H. G. Malot,
                                                                                    Notary Public.

AFFIDAVIT OF ACQUAINTANCE.

UNITED STATES OF AMERICA   )
)
Western Judicial District.   )

I, Tupper Dunn, on oath state that I am 31 years of age, and a citizen, by blood of the Creek Nation; that my post office address is Okemah, Ind. Ter.; that I was personally acquainted with Burt[sic] Dunn who was a citizen, by blood, of the Creek Nation; and that said Bert Dunn died on the 15 day of October, 1904.

    Witness to Mark: Tupper Dunn.

(Must be Two) (_____
(Witnesses) (_____

Subscribed and sworn to before me this 28 day of April, 1905.
                                                        H. G. Malot
(Seal)   Notary Public.
My commission exp 2 July 1906.

Applications for Enrollment of Creek Newborn
Act of 1905   Volume XIV

(Indorsed)
           IN RE
       THE DEATH OF
          Bert Dunn
       a citizen of the
        Creek Nation.
    Approved_____
          _____Commissioner

DEPARTMENT OF THE INTERIOR
COMMISSIONER TO THE FIVE CIVILIZED TRIBES.
FILED 4-29-05
          Tams Bixby Commissioner.
(Rec'd) APR 29 1905.

Birth Affidavit.
    DEPARTMENT OF THE INTERIOR,
COMMISSION TO THE FIVE CIVILIZED TRIBES.

IN RE APPLICATION FOR ENROLLMENT, as a citizen of the Creek Nation, of Bert Dunn, born on the 6 day of October, 1903.

Name of Father: Tupper Dunn, a citizen of the Creek Nation.
Name of Mother: Susie Dunn, a citizen of the Creek Nation.

          Postoffice..........Okemah, I. T.

AFFIDAVIT OF MOTHER.

UNITED STATES OF AMERICA, Indian Territory,)
)
Western Judicial District.   )

    I, Susie Dunn, on oath state that I am 31 years of age and a citizen by blood, of the Creek Nation; that I am the lawful wife of Tupper Dunn, who is a citizen, by blood, of the Creek Nation; that a male child was born to me on 6 day of October, 1903; that said child has been named Bert Dunn and (living Oct. 6th 1904,) and there was no one attended.
                                    Susie Dunn.

    Witnesses to Mark:

(Must be Two) (_____
(Witnesses) (_____

Applications for Enrollment of Creek Newborn
Act of 1905   Volume XIV

Subscribed and sworn to before me this 8 day of May, 1905.

(Seal) H. G. Malot,
Notary Public.

My Com Exp 2 July 1906

(Indorsed)   IN RE
Application for Enrollment of
INFANT CHILD
Bert Dunn
as a citizen of
Creek Nation.

N.C. 1145

Muskogee, Indian Territory, August 4, 1905.

Susie Dunn,
Okemah, Indian Territory.

Dear Madam:

April 29, 1905, there was filed with this office your affidavit in which it is stated that your child, Bert Dunn, died October 15, 1904.

There is herewith enclosed a blank for proof of birth which should be properly executed before a notary public; care should be taken that he affixes his signature and official seal to same.

You are advised that this office is unable to identify said Bert Dunn as a citizen by blood of the Creek Nation and you are requested to state your maiden name, the names of your parents, the Creek Indian town to which you belong, and, if possible, the number which appears on your deeds to land in the Creek Nation.

Respectfully,

Commissioner.

1 1 B A

Applications for Enrollment of Creek Newborn
Act of 1905   Volume XIV

NC 1145.

Muskogee, Indian Territory, February 19, 1907.

Susie Dunn,
    c/o Tupper Dunn,
        Okemah, Indian Territory.

Dear Madam:

    There is herewith enclosed one copy of the statement and order of the Commissioner to the Five Civilized Tribes, dated February 19, 1907, dismissing the application made by you for the enrollment of your minor child, Bert Dunn, deceased, as a citizen by blood of the Creek Nation.

                      Respectfully,

                              Commissioner.

Register.
LM-2-19-07.

N.C. 1146.   I.D.
DEPARTMENT OF THE INTERIOR,
COMMISSIONER TO THE FIVE CIVILIZED TRIBES.

    In the matter of the application for the enrollment of Anna Tiger as a citizen by blood of the Creek Nation.

ORDER

    The record in this case shows that on May 8, 1905, there was filed with the Commission to the Five Civilized Tribes at Muskogee, Indian Territory, the application of Mary Tiger for the enrollment of her minor child, Anna Tiger as a citizen by blood of the Creek Nation.
    The evidence shows that said Anna Tiger was born May 24, 1902, and that she was living March 4, 1905.

Applications for Enrollment of Creek Newborn
Act of 1905   Volume XIV

An examination of the records of this Office shows that no application was made for the enrollment of said Anna Tiger prior to May 8, 1905.
The Act of Congress approved March 3, 1905 (Public No. 212) provides:

"That the Commission to the Five Civilized Tribes is authorized for sixty days after the date of the approval of this act to receive and consider applications for enrollment, of children, born subsequent to May twenty-fifth, nineteen hundred and one, and prior to March fourth, nineteen hundred and five, and living on said latter date, to citizens of the Creek tribe of Indians whose enrollment has been approved by the Secretary of the Interior prior to the approval of this act; and to enroll and make allotments to such children."

It is, therefore, ordered that there is no authority of law for the enrollment of said Anna Tiger as a citizen by blood of the Creek Nation, and that the application for her enrollment as such should be and the same is hereby dismissed.

Commissioner.

Muskogee, Indian Territory.

Department of the Interior.
COMMISSION TO THE FIVE CIVILIZED TRIBES.

In Re Application For Enrollment, as a citizen of the Creek Nation, of Anna Tiger, born on the 24" day of May 1902.

Name of Father: Ben Tiger a citizen of the Creek Nation.
Name of Mother: Mary Tiger a citizen of the Creek Nation.

Postoffice Broken Arrow, Ind. Ter.

AFFIDAVIT OF MOTHER.

United States of America,)
  Indian Territory,   )
Western District.   )

I, Mary Tiger, on oath state that I am 40 years of age and a citizen by blood of the Creek Nation; that I am the lawful wife of Ben Tiger, who is a citizen by blood of the Creek Nation; that a female child was born to me on day of , 190, that said child has been named , and was living March 4, 1905. was born to me on the 24" day of May 1902; that said child has been named Anna Tiger, and is now living.

Applications for Enrollment of Creek Newborn
Act of 1905   Volume XIV

Witness to mark: Frank L. Haynes Lasley Haynes	her Mary x Tiger mark

Subscribed and sworn to before me this 2" day of May 1905.

                                      Z.I.J. Holt
                                      Notary Public.

My commission expires May 9", 1907.

Affidavit Of Attending Midwife.

United States of America,
Indian Territory,
Western District.

I, Sukey Haikey Haynes, a Midwife, on oath state that I attended on Mrs. Mary Tiger, wife of Ben Tiger on the 24" day of May 1902; that there was born to her on said date a female child; that said child is now living, and is said to have been named Anna Tiger.

Witness: T.H. Smith Willie N. Grant	her Sukey Haikey x Haynes mark

Subscribed and sworn to before me this 6" day of May 1905.

                                    Z.I.J. Holt
                                    Notary Public.
My commission expires 5/9/07.

Applications for Enrollment of Creek Newborn
Act of 1905   Volume XIV

DEPARTMENT OF THE INTERIOR,
COMMISSION TO THE FIVE CIVILIZED TRIBES.

Muskogee, Indian Territory, April 15, 1905

In the matter of the application for the enrollment of certain new-born children as citizens of the Creek Nation.

Alex Posey, being duly sworn, testified as follows:

EXAMINATION BY THE COMMISSION:
Q State your name, age and postoffice address. A Alex Posey; 31; Muskogee.
Q Are you a citizen of the Creek Nation? A Yes sir.
Q Got your land, have you? A Yes sir.
Q Have you been engaged recently in the "field work" of the Dawes Commission in securing evidence about Creek citizens or new-borns? A Yes sir.
Q Have you a list of children for whom application could not be made and about whom you have succeeded in obtaining some information? A Yes sir.
Q You may state the conditions and the names of those children that you desire to make application for. A Yes sir.
Q Name then. A Posey Fish, a child of Lewis and Meleya Fish, born June January 30, 1905. The father of this child appeared before the Commission at Dustin in March, 1905, to make application for said child, but learning that the affidavits of the mother and midwife would be required, he returned home, promising to come back the next day with the mother of the child, and midwife and execute proper affidavits. This he failed to do.

INDIAN TERRITORY, Western District.
I, J. Y. Miller, a stenographer to the Commission to the Five Civilized Tribes, do hereby certify that the above and foregoing is a true and complete translation of my notes as same appear in my stenographic report of this case.

JY Miller

Subscribed and sworn to before me
   this the 15th day of April,
1905.

Drennan C Skaggs
Notary Public.

Applications for Enrollment of Creek Newborn
Act of 1905 Volume XIV

BIRTH AFFIDAVIT.

DEPARTMENT OF THE INTERIOR.
COMMISSION TO THE FIVE CIVILIZED TRIBES.

IN RE APPLICATION FOR ENROLLMENT, as a citizen of the Creek Nation, of Posey Fish, born on the 30 day of Jan, 1905

Name of Father: Lewis Fish   a citizen of the Creek Nation.
Name of Mother: Meleya Fish   a citizen of the Creek Nation.

Postoffice   Trenton, I.T.

AFFIDAVIT OF ATTENDING PHYSICIAN OR MID-WIFE.

UNITED STATES OF AMERICA, Indian Territory,
Western DISTRICT.

are personally acquainted with We, the undersigned , ~~a~~, on oath state that ~~I~~ we ~~attended on~~ Mrs. Meleya Fish, wife of Lewis Fish ~~on the day of , 1~~ ; that there was born to her on ~~said date~~ January 30, 1905 a female child; that said child was living March 4, 1905, and is said to have been named Posey Fish

           (Illegible) x Stevens
Witnesses To Mark: mark
  { DC Skaggs   her
    Alex Posey   x Tahakee
           mark

Subscribed and sworn to before me 7 day of October , 1905.

         Drennan C Skaggs
         Notary Public.

BIRTH AFFIDAVIT.

DEPARTMENT OF THE INTERIOR.
COMMISSION TO THE FIVE CIVILIZED TRIBES.

IN RE APPLICATION FOR ENROLLMENT, as a citizen of the Creek Nation, of Posey Fish, born on the 30 day of January , 1905

Name of Father: Lewis Fish   a citizen of the Creek Nation.
Cussehta
Name of Mother: Meleya Fish   a citizen of the Creek Nation.
(Illegible) Tullahasse

Postoffice   Hanna, I.T.

Applications for Enrollment of Creek Newborn
Act of 1905   Volume XIV

AFFIDAVIT OF MOTHER.

UNITED STATES OF AMERICA, Indian Territory, }
Western   DISTRICT.

    I, Meleya Fish , on oath state that I am 35 years of age and a citizen by blood , of the Creek Nation; that I am the lawful wife of Lewis Fish , who is a citizen, by blood of the Creek Nation; that a female child was born to me on 30 day of January, 1905 , that said child has been named Posey Fish , and is now living. and was living March 4, 1905.

                                                      her
                                      Meleya x Fish
                                            mark

Witnesses To Mark:
  { DC Skaggs
    Alex Posey

    Subscribed and sworn to before me this 30 day of   May   , 1905.

                                      Drennan C Skaggs
                                        Notary Public.

AFFIDAVIT OF ATTENDING PHYSICIAN OR MID-WIFE.

UNITED STATES OF AMERICA, Indian Territory, }
Western   DISTRICT.

                                                        my wife
    I, Lewis Fish , ~~a (blank)~~ , on oath state that I attended on ^ Mrs. Meleya Fish , ~~wife of~~ (blank) on the 30 day of January , 1905 ; that there was born to her on said date a female child; that said child is now living and was living March 4, 1905 and is said to have been named Posey Fish
                                       his
                                   Lewis x Fish

Witnesses To Mark: mark
  { DC Skaggs
    Alex Posey

    Subscribed and sworn to before me this 30 day of   May   , 1905.

                                      Drennan C Skaggs
                                        Notary Public.

Applications for Enrollment of Creek Newborn
Act of 1905   Volume XIV

NC 1152.

Muskogee, Indian Territory, January 16, 1907.

Millie Hale,
    c/o David Hale,
        Bearden, Indian Territory.

Dear Madam:

There is herewith enclosed one copy of the Statement and Order of the Commissioner to the Five Civilized Tribes, dated January 15, 1907, dismissing the application made by you for the enrollment of your minor child, Bunnie Hale, deceased, as a citizen by blood of the Creek Nation.

                Respectfully,

                            Commissioner.

LM-69.

BIRTH AFFIDAVIT.

DEPARTMENT OF THE INTERIOR.
COMMISSION TO THE FIVE CIVILIZED TRIBES.

IN RE APPLICATION FOR ENROLLMENT, as a citizen of the Creek Nation, of Bunnie Hale, born on the 13 day of June , 1903

Name of Father: David Hale   a citizen of the   Creek   Nation.
Name of Mother: Millie Hale   a citizen of the   Creek   Nation.

                Postoffice   Bearden I.T.

AFFIDAVIT OF MOTHER.

UNITED STATES OF AMERICA, Indian Territory,
    Western Judicial   **DISTRICT.**

I, Millie Hale , on oath state that I am 29 years of age and a citizen by blood , of the Creek Nation; that I am the lawful wife of David Hale , who is a citizen, by blood of the Creek Nation; that a male child was born to me on 13 day of June , 1903 , that said child has been named *(blank)* , and was living ~~March 4, 1905~~. Oct 28-04

                    Millie Hale

Witnesses To Mark:

Applications for Enrollment of Creek Newborn
Act of 1905 Volume XIV

Subscribed and sworn to before me this 17 day of May , 1905.

My com exp. Aug 19-1908   Tupper Dunn
                                Notary Public.

AFFIDAVIT OF ATTENDING PHYSICIAN OR MID-WIFE.

UNITED STATES OF AMERICA, Indian Territory,
    Western Judicial   DISTRICT.

I, David Hale , a midwife , on oath state that I attended on Mrs. Millie Hale , wife of me on the 13 day of June , 1903 ; that there was born to her on said date a male child; that said child was living ~~March 4, 1905~~ Oct., 28-04, and is said to have been named Bunnie Hale

                                David Hale
Witnesses To Mark:
{

Subscribed and sworn to before me this 17 day of May , 1905.

My com exp. Aug 19-1908   Tupper Dunn
                                Notary Public.

BIRTH AFFIDAVIT.
DEPARTMENT OF THE INTERIOR,
COMMISSIONER TO THE FIVE CIVILIZED TRIBES.

ENROLLMENT OF MINORS. ACT OF CONGRESS, APPROVED APRIL 26, 1906.

IN RE APPLICATION FOR ENROLLMENT, as a citizen of the   Creek   Nation, of Bunnie Hill , born on the 13 day of June , 1902 and died October 29, 1904.

Name of Father: David Hill (Roll No. 6242)   a citizen of the   Creek   Nation.
Name of Mother: Millie Hill (Roll No 6243)   a citizen of the   Creek   Nation.

Tribal enrollment of father Fish pond   Tribal enrollment of mother Arbeka N F

                Postoffice   Bearden Indian Territory

Applications for Enrollment of Creek Newborn
Act of 1905   Volume XIV

AFFIDAVIT OF MOTHER.

UNITED STATES OF AMERICA, Indian Territory,
Western   District.

    I, Millie Hill, on oath state that I am about 29 years of age and a citizen by blood, of the Creek Nation; that I am the lawful wife of David Hill, who is a citizen, by blood of the Creek Nation; that a male child was born to me on 13 day of June, 1902, that said child ~~has been~~ was named Bunnie Hill, and ~~was living March 4, 1906~~. died October 29, 1904

Millie Hill

WITNESSES TO MARK:
{

Subscribed and sworn to before me this 29 day of May, 1906.

Alex Posey
Notary Public.

Department of the Interior,
COMMISSION TO THE FIVE CIVILIZED TRIBES.

    In the matter of the death of Bunnie Hale a citizen of the Creek Nation, who formerly resided at or near Bearden, Ind. Ter., and died on the 29 day of October, 1904

AFFIDAVIT OF RELATIVE.

UNITED STATES OF AMERICA,
   INDIAN TERRITORY,
Western   District.

    I, David Hale, on oath state that I am 29 years of age and a citizen by blood, of the Creek Nation; that my postoffice address is Bearden, Ind. Ter.; that I am Father of Bunnie Hale who was a citizen, by blood, of the Creek Nation and that said Bunnie Hale died on the 29 day of October, 1904

David Hale

Witnesses To Mark:
{

    Subscribed and sworn to before me this 31 *day of* March, 1905.

My Com. Exp. Aug 19-1908   Tupper Dunn
Notary Public.

Applications for Enrollment of Creek Newborn
Act of 1905   Volume XIV

AFFIDAVIT OF ACQUAINTANCE.

UNITED STATES OF AMERICA,
  INDIAN TERRITORY,
Western Judicial   District.

I, Wotko Harjo , on oath state that I am 62 years of age, and a citizen by blood of the Creek Nation; that my postoffice address is Bearden , Ind. Ter.; that I was personally acquainted with Bunnie Hale who was a citizen, by blood , of the Creek Nation; and that said Bunnie Hale died on the 29 day of October , 1904.

Wotko Harjo

Witnesses To Mark:
  Tupper Dunn

Subscribed and sworn to before me this 31 day of March , 1905.

My Com. Exp. Aug 19-1908   Tupper Dunn
                                           Notary Public.

N.C. 1152.   I.D.
DEPARTMENT OF THE INTERIOR,
COMMISSIONER TO THE FIVE CIVILIZED TRIBES.

In the matter of the application for the enrollment of Bunnie Hill, deceased, as a citizen by blood of the Creek Nation.

O R D E R

The record in this case shows that on May 22, 1905, there was filed with the Commission to the Five Civilized Tribes at Muskogee, Indian Territory, the application of David Hill, for the enrollment of his minor child, Bunnie Hill, deceased, as a citizen by blood of the Creek Nation.

The evidence shows that said Bunnie Hill, deceased, was born June 13, 1903, and that he died in the month of October, 1904.

The Act of Congress approved March 3, 1905, (33 Stats. 1071), provides:

"That the Commission to the Five Civilized Tribes is authorized for sixty days after the date of the approval of this act to receive and consider applications for enrollment, of children, born subsequent to May twenty-fifth, nineteen hundred and one, and prior to March fourth, nineteen hundred and five, and living on said latter date, to citizens of the Creek tribe of Indians whose enrollment has been approved by the Secretary of the Interior prior to the approval of this act; and to enroll and make allotments to such children."

Applications for Enrollment of Creek Newborn
Act of 1905 Volume XIV

It is, therefore, ordered that there is no authority of law for the enrollment of said Bunnie Hill, deceased, as a citizen by blood of the Creek Nation, and that the application for his enrollment as such should be, and the same is, hereby dismissed.

Tams Bixby Commissioner.

Muskogee, Indian Territory.
JAN 15 1907

DEPARTMENT OF THE INTERIOR,
COMMISSIONER TO THE FIVE CIVILIZED TRIBES.
Muskogee, Indian Territory, December 8, 1905.

In the matter of the application for the enrollment of Budy Cain, Elmer Sawyer et al as citizens by blood of the Creek Nation.

J.R. Dunzy being duly sworn testified as follows:

Q What is your name? A J.R. Dunzy
Q What is your age? A going on forty.
Q What is your post office address? A Wetumka.
Q Are you a citizen of the Creek Nation? A Yes, sir
Q Are you a notary public? A Yes, sir.
Q When does your commission expire? A In 1906
Q Have you been acting as a notary public for the last two or three years? A Yes, sir.
Q You can talk Creek can't you? A Yes, sir. I have been Notary Public ever since the United States court began.
Q We have here an affidavit of Nicey Cain about her child Budy Cain executed before you, also affidavit of Selina Cain the midwife about that child, executed before you on April 3, 1905. This affidavit was not received by the Dawes Commission until May 4, 1905, can you explain why that affidavit was held from April 3 until May 4? A I couldn't explain how that was because all the applications I had, I made out eight or ten at a time, and the last batch I made out I sent them so they would be here by the fourth of May
Q You made out a lot of affidavits about new born children? A Yes, sir
Q Did you yourself transmit them to the Commission? A Yes, sir mailed them at the post office.
Q Didn't you actually keep some affidavits a week or more? A No, sir
Q Did you know what was the time limit for these applications to be in? A Yes, sir
Q Did you read the notices sent out? A Yes, sir
Q Did you know, when you received these applications? A Yes, sir

Applications for Enrollment of Creek Newborn
Act of 1905 Volume XIV

Q The fact is it was the 2nd and not the 4th of May it expires? A Yes, sir
Q Did you know that at that time? A Yes, sir
Q Didn't you actually transmit some affidavits after that date? A Yes, sir
Q We have a number of affidavits that were executed before you and were received after May 2 and looks to me like you mailed them after that time? A Must have been held over at the post office
Q We have some in which the post mark shows that they were put in the post office after that date? A He must have held that lot there, they do that in some of the post offices I know of because I knew you should have them here at that time and I sent them in time.
Q This affidavit about Budy Cain was made out on April 3 and received by the Commission on May 4th, do you claim you transmitted that on April 3rd? A I don't remember.
Q This about Budy Cain was made out April 3 and we didn't receive it until May 4th? A It must have been held somewhere.
Q You remember this identical affidavit and you put it in yourself? A Yes, sir
Q Is that your writing and your signature? A (showing letter) A Yes, sir that was the last lot over at Bernards.
Q You wrote this letter then? A Yes, sir, that was about five or six of them
Q You wrote this letter then? A Yes, sir, that was about 5 or 6 of them.
Q We have a letter written at Bernard signed by you on May 3, 1905, in which you say "I herewith inclose you affidavits of mostly Snake people whom has made their affidavits I was away a few days when I amed[sic] to send them in by the last of April but I hope this will not cause any delay of those entitle[sic] to enrollment. All these affidavits I have signed is done free gratis to those full bloods excepting 2 negroes[sic] which one Fleming I fear is not correct statement made by the partys[sic] concerned
Q This letter was written on the 3rd of May and was put in the post office as shown by the post mark on May 3 and was received by the Commission on May 4th? A Yes, sir, it was delayed I suppose but I don't remember exactly
Q You held them up and sent them too late? A Yes
Q A while ago you said you didn't send them in too late? A I just didn't remember
Q The law was plain, it didn't say the the[sic] affidavits must be executed or mailed by May 2 but that they must be at the Commission by that time. The Notice read: Such applications may be made at any time up to and inclusive of May 2, 1905, personally at the general office of the Commission at Muskogee, Indian Territory. Applications by mail should be addressed to the Commission to the Five Civilized Tribes, Muskogee, Indian Territory, and mailed in ample time to reach the Muskogee office of the Commission not later than May 2, 1905. I have read you the notice of the Commission I will now read you the law as contained in that notice: That the Commission to the Five Civilized Tribes is authorized for sixty days after the date of the approval of this act to receive and consider applications for enrollment of children born subsequent to May twenty five, nineteen hundred and one, and prior to March fourth, nineteen hundred and five, and living on said latter date, to citizens of the Creek tribe of Indians whose enrollment has been approved by the Secretary of the Interior prior to the date of the approval of this act; and to enroll and make allotments to such children. Notice is hereby given that the Commission to the Five Civilized Tribes will up to and inclusive of midnight May 2, 1905, receive applications for the enrollment of infant children born subsequent to May 25, 1901 and prior to March 4, 1905, and who were living on said

Applications for Enrollment of Creek Newborn
Act of 1905 Volume XIV

latter date to citizens of the Creek tribe of Indians whose enrollment has been approved by the Secretary of the Interior prior to March 3, 1905.
Q I will ask you do you remember having held up any affidavits? A I don't remember any time but that time, there was 25 or 3o[sic] of them in that batch. There was about 10 in that letter
Q And most of them were made out the month before? A No, sir they were the last ones I made
Q One party in this Cain matter testified as follows: A Did you go with your wife Nisey Cain before J.R. Dunzy, notary public, at the time she made affidavit about the birth of Budy Cain? A Yes, sir. Q At the time you went before Mr. Dunzy did you think that he was connected with the Commission to the Five Civilized Tribes in any way? A Yes I was told by several around there that he was employed that way and I went to him to have our papers fixed up. A Did Mr Dunzy charge you anything for fixing up your papers? A No, sir A And when your wife made that affidavit you thought there was nothing more to be done in the making of the application s that correct? A Yes, sir. He told me at the time I made out the affidavit that he was intending to send several others off and that he would send mine off with them. A I didn't intentionally send them too late.

I, Anna Garrigues, state on oath that the above and foregoing is a true and correct transcript of my stenographic notes as taken in said cause on said date.

                                              Anna Garrigues

Subscribed and sworn to before me
this 8 day of December 1905.
                                              J McDermott
                                                  Notary Public.

NC 1153

DEPARTMENT OF THE INTERIOR,
COMMISSIONER TO THE FIVE CIVILIZED TRIBES.
MUSKOGEE, INDIAN TERRITORY.
JANUARY 8, 1907.

In the matter of the application for the enrollment of SAMUEL SAWYER, as a citizen by blood of the Creek Nation.

<u>WESLEY SAWYER,</u> being first duly sworn by Henry G. Hains, a Notary Public, testified as follows, through sworn interpreter, William McCombs.

Questions by Commissioner:

Q: What is your name? A: Wesley Sawyer.
Q: How old are you? A: About 34.

Applications for Enrollment of Creek Newborn
Act of 1905   Volume XIV

Q: What is your post-office address? A: Weleetka now.
Q: What is the name of your father? A: Moses Sawyer.
Q: What is the name of your mother? A: Synda Sawyer.
Q: What Creek Indian Town do you belong to? A: Thlopthlocco.
Q: Did you ever belong to Broken Arrow town? A: I first belong to Broken Arrow town and I was transferred to Thlopthlocco town.
Q: What was the name of your first wife? A: Ellen.

(Witness is identified as Wesley Sawyer opposite Creek Indian Roll number 3846)

Q: Is Ellen living? A: She is dead.
Q: Did you have any children by your first wife, Ellen? A: I only had one child but it died right away.
Q: What was the name of your next wife? A: Eliza.
Q: What was the name of her father? A: Nixey.
Q: Nixey Fife was it? A: Yes sir.
Q: What was the name of her mother? A: Jennie.

She is identified as Eliza Fife opposite Creek Indian Care number 4705.

Q: Is Eliza living? A: She is dead also.
Q: When did she die? A: January 20, 1905.
Q: Did you have any children by her? A: Yes sir.
Q: What are their names? A: Almon and Samuel.
Q: Are both of these children living or dead? A: Both are living.
Q: When was Almon born? A: March 7, 1903.

(Witness presents a memorandum book in which is written March 7, 1903).
Q:[sic]
Q: When was your child Samuel Sawyer born? A: Samuel was born the same day his mother died, January 20, 1905.

(Witness is advised that instead of the affidavit of the mother which is usually required, we desire the affidavit of two disinterested witnesses in regard to the birth of that child, a blank form for that purpose is herewith handed the witness with the instructions that the same should be properly executed and returned to this office within 10 days because the time of enrollment is so near up.

Q: What was the name of the midwife or physician who attended your wife at the birth of this child? A: I was with her alone and she died very suddenly and I didn't have time to get a doctor.
Q: That is when Samuel was born? A: Yes sir.
Q: Who was there when your first child Almon was born? A: There wasn't any one present I was the only one present when Almon was born.
Q: Where are those two children now? A: The oldest one is living with me and the youngest one is living with a close neighbor.

Applications for Enrollment of Creek Newborn
Act of 1905   Volume XIV

This is all the testimony given in said cause on said date.

Julia C. Laval, being first duly sworn states that as Stenographer to the Commissioner to the Five Civilized Tribes, she reported the proceedings has in the above entitled cause on January 8, 1907 and that the above and foregoing is a true and complete transcript of her stenographic notes as taken in said cause on said date.

                                                Julia C Laval

Subscribed and sworn to before
me, a Notary Public on January 8, 1907.

                                            Edward Merrick
                                            Notary Public.

NC 1153

AFFIDAVIT OF DISINTERESTED WITNESS.

UNITED STATES OF AMERICA,
INDIAN TERRITORY,   SS
Western DISTRICT.

We, the undersigned, on oath state that we are personally acquainted with Eliza Sawyer, dead   wife of   Wesley Sawyer   ; that there was born to her a male   child on or about the   7"   day of   March 1903   ; that the said child has been named   Almon Sawyer   and was living March 4, 1906.

                                            his
                                  Chotkey x Foster
                                        mark

Witnesses: his
  HGHains   William x Field
                                        mark

  J.C. Laval

Subscribed and sworn to before me this 8 day of January 1907.

                                            Henry G. Hains
                                            Notary Public.

Applications for Enrollment of Creek Newborn
Act of 1905 Volume XIV

NC 1153

AFFIDAVIT OF DISINTERESTED WITNESS.

UNITED STATES OF AMERICA,
INDIAN TERRITORY,   SS
Western DISTRICT.

    We, the undersigned, on oath state that we are personally acquainted with Eliza Sawyer, dec'd   wife of   Wesley   ; that there was born to her a   male child on or about the   20   day of   January 1905   ; that the said child has been named   Samuel Sawyer   and was living March 4, 1906.

                                                                his
                                        Chotkey x Foster
                                               mark

Witnesses: his
    HGHains   William x Field
                                               mark
    J.C. Laval

Subscribed and sworn to before me this 8 day of January 1907.

                                               Henry G. Hains
                                               Notary Public.

(The letter below is handwritten and typed as given.)

LOUIS DUNZY

_____Dealer in_____

General Merchandise

Barnard, Ind. Ter.   5/3^d *190* 5

Commission to 5 Tribes
    Muskogee, Ind Terr.
                           Dear Sir: I herewith inclose your affidavits of mostly Snake people whoom has made their affidavits. I was away a few days when I amed to send those in by the last of April. But I hope this will not cause any delay of those entitle to enrolment.
                 Yours Truly
                           J.R. Dunzy

Applications for Enrollment of Creek Newborn
Act of 1905   Volume XIV

P.S. All these affidavits I have signed is done free gra*(illegible)* to those full Bloods excepting 2 negroes[sic] which one Fleming I fear is not correct statement made by the Partys concerned.

                         Respectfully
                         JR Dunzy
                         N.P.

POOR ORIGINAL – *(illegible)*

BIRTH AFFIDAVIT.

DEPARTMENT OF THE INTERIOR.
COMMISSION TO THE FIVE CIVILIZED TRIBES.

IN RE APPLICATION FOR ENROLLMENT, as a citizen of the Creek Nation, of Almon Sawyer, born on the 7th day of March, 1903

Name of Father: Wesley Sawyer   a citizen of the Creek Nation.
Name of Mother: Eliza Sawyer   a citizen of the Creek Nation.

                Postoffice   Fentress I.T.

                father
AFFIDAVIT OF ~~MOTHER~~.

UNITED STATES OF AMERICA, Indian Territory,
    Western   DISTRICT.

I, Wesley Sawyer, on oath state that I am 32 years of age and a citizen by blood, of the Creek Nation; that I am the lawful ~~wife~~ husband of Eliza Sawyer, who is a citizen, by blood of the Creek Nation; that a male child was born to ~~me~~ her on 7th day of March, 1903, that said child has been named Almon Sawyer, and was living March 4, 1905.
                         his
                Wesley x Sawyer
Witnesses To Mark: mark
   { William Hill
     Thos H. Dunson

    Subscribed and sworn to before me this 22 day of April, 1905.

                      J.R. Dunzy
                        Notary Public.

Applications for Enrollment of Creek Newborn
Act of 1905 Volume XIV

AFFIDAVIT OF ATTENDING PHYSICIAN OR MID-WIFE.

UNITED STATES OF AMERICA, Indian Territory, } Western DISTRICT.

I, Wesley Sawyer , a ~~husband~~ , on oath state that I attended on Mrs. Eliza Sawyer , wife of my self on the 7th day of March, 1903 ; that there was born to her on said date a male child; that said child was living March 4, 1905, and is said to have been named Almon Sawyer

his
Wesley x Sawyer
mark

Witnesses To Mark:
{ William Hill
Thos H. Dunson

Subscribed and sworn to before me this 22nd day of April , 1905.

J.R. Dunzy
Notary Public.

BIRTH AFFIDAVIT.

DEPARTMENT OF THE INTERIOR.
COMMISSION TO THE FIVE CIVILIZED TRIBES.

IN RE APPLICATION FOR ENROLLMENT, as a citizen of the Creek Nation, of Samuel Sawyer , born on the 20th day of January , 1905

Name of Father: Wesley Sawyer   a citizen of the Creek Nation.
Name of Mother: Eliza Sawyer   a citizen of the Creek Nation.

Postoffice Fentress I.T.

---

father
AFFIDAVIT OF ~~MOTHER~~.

UNITED STATES OF AMERICA, Indian Territory, } Western DISTRICT.

I, Wesley Sawyer , on oath state that I am 32 years of age and a citizen by blood , of the Creek Nation; that I am the lawful ~~wife~~ Husband of Eliza Sawyer , who is a citizen, by blood of the Creek Nation; that a male child was born to ~~me~~ her on 20th day of January , 1905 , that said child has been named Samuel Sawyer , and was living March 4, 1905.

his
Wesley x Sawyer
mark

Witnesses To Mark:
{ William Hill
Thos H. Dunson

Applications for Enrollment of Creek Newborn
Act of 1905 Volume XIV

Subscribed and sworn to before me this 22^d day of   April , 1905.

J.R. Dunzy
Notary Public.

AFFIDAVIT OF ATTENDING PHYSICIAN OR MID-WIFE.

UNITED STATES OF AMERICA, Indian Territory, }
Western   DISTRICT.

I, Wesley Sawyer , a   husband , on oath state that I attended on Mrs. Eliza Sawyer , wife of my self on the 20th day of   January , 1905 ; that there was born to her on said date a   male child; that said child was living March 4, 1905, and is said to have been named   Samuel Sawyer   his

Witnesses To Mark: Wesley x Sawyer
  { William Hill   mark
    Thos H. Dunson

Subscribed and sworn to before me this 22^d day of   April , 1905.

J.R. Dunzy
Notary Public.

| REFER IN REPLY TO THE FOLLOWING:
N.C. 1153. | **DEPARTMENT OF THE INTERIOR,**
COMMISSIONER TO THE FIVE CIVILIZED TRIBES. |

Muskogee, Indian Territory, June 22, 1906.

Wesley Sawyer,
    Fentress, Indian Territory.

Dear Sir:

    In the matter of the application for the enrollment of your minor children, Almon Sawyer and Samuel sawyer, as citizens of the Creek Nation, you are advised that it is required that you furnish this office with the affidavits of yourself and the midwife in attendance at the birth of said children. For this purpose there are inclosed blank forms of birth affidavits. Said affidavits should show the names of the children, the names of their parents, the date of their birth and whether or not they were living on March 4, 1905.
    This matter should receive your prompt attention.

Applications for Enrollment of Creek Newborn
Act of 1905   Volume XIV

Respectfully,
Tams Bixby
Commissioner.

2 BA

REFER IN REPLY TO THE FOLLOWING:

NC 1152.

DEPARTMENT OF THE INTERIOR,
COMMISSIONER TO THE FIVE CIVILIZED TRIBES.

Muskogee, Indian Territory, October 22, 1906.

Wesley Sawyer,
    Wetumka, Indian Territory.

Dear Sir:

    Receipt is acknowledged of your letter of October 16, 1906, in which you ask to be advised if further evidence is necessary in the matter of the application for the enrollment of your minor children, Alma[sic] and Samuel Sawyer, as citizens of the Creek Nation.

    In reply you are advised that before the right to enrollment of said children can be finally determined, it will be necessary that you furnish this office with the affidavit of the mother and of the midwife or physician in attendance at their birth; blank forms for that purpose are herewith enclosed, which you are requested to have properly executed and returned to this office in the enclosed envelope.

    You are further advised that you should furnish this office with the maiden name of the mother of said children, the names of your parents and the parents of said mother, the Creek Indian towns to which each of you belongs, and your roll numbers as same appear on your allotment certificates or deeds to land in the Creek Nation.

    Wesley Sawyer, son of Moses and Cindy Sawyer, appears on the roll of citizens by blood of the Creek Nation as the husband of Ellen Sawyer, and you are requested to state whether she is the mother of said children.

Respectfully,
Tams Bixby   Commissioner.

2 BA
Env.

Applications for Enrollment of Creek Newborn
Act of 1905   Volume XIV

N.C. 1153

Muskogee, Indian Territory, March 1, 1907.

Eliza Sawyer,
    Care Wesley Sawyer,
        Fentress, Indian Territory.

Dear Madam:

    You are hereby advised that on February 15, 1907, the Secretary of the Interior approved the enrollment of your minor children, Almon and Samuel Sawyer, as citizens by blood of the Creek Nation, and that the names of said children appear upon the roll of new born citizens by blood of the Creek Nation, enrolled under the Act of Congress approved March 3, 1905, as numbers 1223 and 1224.

    These children are now entitled to allotments and application therefor should be made without delay at the Creek Land Office, Muskogee, Indian Territory.

                      Respectfully,
                        Commissioner.

NC 1154   OCH
                                                                                                 JCL

DEPARTMENT OF THE INTERIOR,
COMMISSIONER TO THE FIVE CIVILIZED TRIBES.

    In the matter of the application for the enrollment of Lula Deer as a citizen by blood of the Creek Nation.

DECISION.

    The record in this case shows that on May 4, 1905, application was made, in affidavit form, for the enrollment of Lula Deer as a citizen by blood of the Creek Nation, under the provisions of the Act of Congress approved March 3, 1905, (33 Stats. L, 1048).
    The evidence and the records of this office show that said Lula Deer is the child of Miley Deer whose name appears as "Mary Deer" upon a schedule of citizens by blood of the Creek Nation and Joe Deer, whose name appears upon a schedule of citizens by blood of the Creek Nation, approved by the Secretary of the Interior, March 28, 1902, opposite numbers 7359 and 7458, respectively.

Applications for Enrollment of Creek Newborn
Act of 1905   Volume XIV

The evidence shows that said Lula Deer was born November 10, 1903, and was living March 4, 1905.

Although the application herein was not made within the time specified by the provisions of the Act of Congress approved March 3, 1905, (33 Stats. L. 1048) jurisdiction to consider the same, under said Act was given to this office and the Department by the provisions of Section one, of the Act of Congress approved April 26, 1906, (34 Stats. L. 137).

It is therefore, ordered and adjudged that said Lula Deer is entitled to enrollment as a citizen by blood of the Creek Nation, under the provisions of the Act of Congress approved March 3, 1905, (33 Stats. L., 1048) and the application for her enrollment as such is accordingly granted.

Tams Bixby COMMISSIONER.

Muskogee, Indian Territory.
FEB 16 1907

BIRTH AFFIDAVIT.

DEPARTMENT OF THE INTERIOR.
COMMISSION TO THE FIVE CIVILIZED TRIBES.

IN RE APPLICATION FOR ENROLLMENT, as a citizen of the Creek Nation, of Lula Deer, born on the 10 day of November , 1903

Name of Father:	Joe Deer	a citizen of the	Creek	Nation.
Name of Mother:	Miley Deer	a citizen of the	Creek	Nation.

Postoffice   Barnard, I.T.

AFFIDAVIT OF MOTHER.

UNITED STATES OF AMERICA, Indian Territory,
   Western   DISTRICT.

I, Miley Deer , on oath state that I am 32 years of age and a citizen by blood , of the Creek Nation; that I am the lawful wife of Joe Deer , who is a citizen, by blood of the Creek Nation; that a female child was born to me on 10 day of November , 1903 , that said child has been named Lula Deer, and was living March 4, 1905.

her
Miley x Deer
mark

Witnesses To Mark:
 { Jos H. Harjo
   J.R. Dunzy

Subscribed and sworn to before me this 29th day of March , 1905.

Applications for Enrollment of Creek Newborn
Act of 1905   Volume XIV

          J.R. Dunzy
           Notary Public.

AFFIDAVIT OF ATTENDING PHYSICIAN OR MID-WIFE.

UNITED STATES OF AMERICA, Indian Territory, ⎫
 Western   DISTRICT.   ⎬
            ⎭

  I, Kogee King , a mid-wife, on oath state that I attended on Mrs. Miley Deer, wife of Joe Deer on the 10 day of November, 1903 ; that there was born to her on said date a female child; that said child was living March 4, 1905, and is said to have been named Lula Deer   her
            Kogee x King
Witnesses To Mark: mark
 { Jos. H. Harjo
  J.R. Dunzy

  Subscribed and sworn to before me this 29th day of March , 1905.

          J.R. Dunzy
           Notary Public.

(Letter below typed as given.)

        Louis Dunzy
         dealer in
       General Merchandise.

       Barnard, Ind Ter. 5/3d, 1905

Commission to 5 Tribes
  Muskogee Ind Terr

   Dear Sir

     I herewith inclose you affidavits of mostly Snake people whom has made the affidavits I was away a few days when I amed to send those in by the last of April But I hope this will not cause any delay of those entitle to enrolment.

       Yours truly,
       J.R. Dunzy

P S All these affidavits I have signed is done free gratis to those full bloods excepting 2 negroes[sic] which one Fleming I fear is not correct statement made by the partys concerned.

Applications for Enrollment of Creek Newborn
Act of 1905   Volume XIV

Respectfully,
J R Dunzy
N.P.

This letter was received May 4th, 1905 in an envelope postmarked "Mon. & Ft. Worth R.P.O. May 3, 1905 Tr 10."

N.C. 1154.

Muskogee, Indian Territory, June 22, 1906.

Miley Deer,
    Barnard, Indian Territory.

Dear Madam:

In the matter of the application for the enrollment of your minor child, Lula Deer, as a citizen of the Creek Nation, you are advised that it is required that you furnish this office with the affidavits of yourself and the midwife in attendance at her birth. For this purpose there is inclosed blank form of affidavit. Said affidavit should show the name of the child, the names of its parents, the date of its birth and whether or not it was living on March 4, 1906.

You are requested to furnish this office with information which will identify you and Joe Deer, the father of said child, on the roll of citizens of the Creek Nation.

This matter should receive your prompt attention.

Respectfully,
BA   Commissioner.

JWH

N C 1154

Muskogee, Indian Territory, March 9, 1907.

Miley Deer,
    % Joe Deer,
        Barnard, Indian Territory.

Dear Madam :--

You are hereby advised that on March 2, 1907, the Secretary of the Interior approved the enrollment of your minor child, Lula Deer, as a citizen by blood of the Creek Nation, and that the name of said child appears upon the roll of new born citizens by blood of the Creek Nation, enrolled under the Act of Congress approved March 3, 1905, as number 1282.

Applications for Enrollment of Creek Newborn
Act of 1905   Volume XIV

    This child is now entitled to allotment and application therefor should be made without delay at the Creek Land Office, Muskogee, Indian Territory.

                      Respectfully,
                                      Commissioner.

(Letter below typed as given.)

                        Louis Dunzy
                          dealer in
                    General Merchandise.

                  Barnard, Ind Ter. 5/3d, 1905

Commission to 5 Tribes
    Muskogee Ind Terr

        Dear Sir

                I herewith inclose you affidavits of mostly Snake people whom has made the affidavits I was away a few days when I amed to send those in by the last of April But I hope this will not cause any delay of those entitle to enrolment.

                      Yours truly,
                          J.R. Dunzy

P S All these affidavits I have signed is done free gratis to those full bloods excepting 2 negroes[sic] which one Fleming I fear is not correct statement made by the partys concerned.

                    Respectfully,
                        J R Dunzy
                            N.P.

This letter was received May 4th, 1905 in an envelope postmarked "Mon. & Ft. Worth R.P.O. May 3, 1905 Tr 10."

Applications for Enrollment of Creek Newborn
Act of 1905   Volume XIV

N.C. 1155.

Muskogee, Indian Territory, June 22, 1906.

Miley Deer,
    Barnard, Indian Territory.

Dear Madam:

    In the matter of the application for the enrollment of your minor child, Mattie Deer, as a citizen of the Creek Nation, you are advised that it is required that you furnish this office with the affidavits of yourself and the midwife in attendance at her birth. For this purpose there is inclosed blank form of affidavit. Said affidavit should show the name of the child, the names of its parents, the date of its birth and whether or not it was living on March 4, 1906.

    This matter should receive your prompt attention.
                      Respectfully,

BA   Commissioner.

NC 1155.

Muskogee, Indian Territory, February 14, 1907.

Barney Deer,
    Barnard, Indian Territory.

Dear Sir:

    April 29, 1905, an affidavit was executed in the matter of the application for the enrollment of your minor child, Mattie Deer, as a citizen by blood of the Creek Nation. This office desires information as to whether said child is living and if not living, the date of her death.

    There is herewith enclosed blank form of birth affidavit, which please have properly filled out and execute before a Notary Public, or other officer authorized to administer oaths, and forward at once to this office.

    The Act of Congress approved April 2, 1906, (34 Stat., 137) L., 137), provides in part as follows:

> "That the rolls of said tribes affected by this Act shall be fully completed on or before the fourth day of March, nineteen hundred and seven, and the Secretary of the Interior shall have no jurisdiction to approve the enrollment of any person after said date."

    You are urged to give this matter your immediate attention, in order that the rights of this child may be protected.

Applications for Enrollment of Creek Newborn
Act of 1905 Volume XIV

1 B.A.

Respectfully,

Commissioner.

NC 1155.

Muskogee, Indian Territory, February 14, 1907.

J. R. Dunzy,
    Barnard, Indian Territory.

Dear Sir:

    April 29, 1905, an affidavit was executed before you in the matter of the application for the enrollment of Mattie Deer, a child of Miley Deer and Barney Deer, as a citizen by blood of the Creek Nation.

    This office desires information as to whether said child is living and if not living, the date of her death.

    You are earnestly requested to have one or more persons who know whether or not this child is living or dead, to execute an affidavit setting forth the facts and forward the same at once to this office.

    The Act of Congress approved April 26, 1906 (34 Stat. L., 137), provides in part as follows:

> "That the rolls of said tribes affected by this Act shall be fully completed on or before the fourth day of March, nineteen hundred and seven, and the Secretary of the Interior shall have no jurisdiction to approve the enrollment of any person after said date."

    You are requested to furnish this office with this information in order that the rights of this child may be protected.

Respectfully,

Commissioner.

NC 1155.

Muskogee, Indian Territory, February 14, 1907.

Miley Deer,
    Barnard, Indian Territory.

Dear Madam:

    April 29, 1905, an affidavit was executed by you in the matter of the application for the enrollment of your child, Mattie Deer as a citizen by blood of the Creek Nation.

Applications for Enrollment of Creek Newborn
Act of 1905   Volume XIV

This office desires information as to whether said child is living and if not living, the date of her death.

There is herewith enclosed blank form of birth affidavit, which please have properly filled out and execute before a Notary Public, or other officer authorized to administer oaths, and forward at once to this office.

The Act of Congress approved April 26, 1906 (34 Stat. L., 137), provides in part as follows:

"That the rolls of said tribes affected by this Act shall be fully completed on or before the fourth day of March, nineteen hundred and seven, and the Secretary of the Interior shall have no jurisdiction to approve the enrollment of any person after said date."

You are urged to give this matter your immediate attention, in order that the rights of this child may be protected.

Respectfully,

Commissioner.

1 B.A.

NC 1158.

DEPARTMENT OF THE INTERIOR,
COMMISSIONER TO THE FIVE CIVILIZED TRIBES.
December 31/06   Muskogee I.T.

In the matter of the application for the enrollment of Fred Harjo, as a citizen by blood of the Creek Nation.

HAGIE GREEN, being duly sworn, by O.C. Hinkle, a Notary Public, testified as follows, through Official Interpreter, Jesse McDermott.

Examination by Commissioner.

Q What is your name? A Hagie Green.
Q What is your age? A About 30.
Q What is your post office address? A Wetumka.
Q Do you know Steven and Kogee Harjo? A Yes sir.
Q Is Kogee Harjo are[sic] relation of yours? A My sister.

Applications for Enrollment of Creek Newborn
Act of 1905   Volume XIV

Q She is the wife of Steven Harjo? A Yes sir.
Q Did they have a child by the name of Fred Harjo? A Yes sir, but the child is dead now.
Q Was it a little girl; was it a male child? A Male child.
Q When did he die? A I don't know exactly, but I think last August was a year ago.
Q How old was it when it died? A About two years old.
Q Where do you live? A North of Wetumka.
Q Are you a citizen of the Creek Nation? A Yes sir.

----------oOo----------

SALLIE GREEN, being duly sworn, by O.C. Hinkle, a Notary Public, testified as follows, through Official Interpreter, Jesse McDermott.

Examination by Commissioner.
Q What is your name? A Sallie Green.
Q Where do you live? A North of Wetumka.
Q Are you a citizen of the Creek Nation? A Yes sir.
Q Are you the wife of Hagie Green? A Yes sir.
Q Do you know Steven and Kogee Harjo? A Yes sir.
Q Did they have a male child named Fred? A Yes sir.
Q Is he living or dead? A Dead.
Q When did he die? A Last summer was a year ago.
Q He didn't die last summer? A No sir.
Q Died summer before that? A Yes sir.

Lona Merrick, being duly sworn, states that the above and foregoing is a true and correct transcript of her stenographic notes as taken in said cause on said date.

Lona Merrick

Subscribed and sworn
to before me this 31st day of Jan. 1907.

Oliver C. Hinkle
Notary Public.

BIRTH AFFIDAVIT.

DEPARTMENT OF THE INTERIOR.
COMMISSION TO THE FIVE CIVILIZED TRIBES.

IN RE APPLICATION FOR ENROLLMENT, as a citizen of the Creek Nation, of Fred Harjo, born on the 28th day of February, 1903

Name of Father:	Stephen Harjo	a citizen of the	Creek	Nation.
Name of Mother:	Kogee Harjo	a citizen of the	Creek	Nation.

Applications for Enrollment of Creek Newborn
Act of 1905   Volume XIV

Postoffice   Wetumka I.T.

AFFIDAVIT OF MOTHER.

UNITED STATES OF AMERICA, Indian Territory,
Western   DISTRICT.

I, Stephen Harjo , on oath state that I am 25 years of age and a citizen by blood , of the Creek Nation; that I am the lawful ~~wife~~ Husband of Kogee Harjo , who is a citizen, by blood of the Creek Nation; that a male child was born to ~~me~~ her on 28th day of February , 1903, that said child has been named Fred Harjo , and was living March 4, 1905.

his
Stephen x Harjo
mark

Witnesses To Mark:
  Amos King
  J.R. Dunzy

Subscribed and sworn to before me this 22^d day of April , 1905.

J.R. Dunzy
Notary Public.

AFFIDAVIT OF ATTENDING PHYSICIAN OR MID-WIFE.

UNITED STATES OF AMERICA, Indian Territory,
Western   DISTRICT.

I, Lucy R. Gotts , a Mid-wife , on oath state that I attended on Mrs. Kogee Harjo , wife of Stephen Harjo on the 28th day of February , 1903 ; that there was born to her on said date a male child; that said child was living March 4, 1905, and is said to have been named Fred Harjo

her
Lucy R. x Gotts
mark

Witnesses To Mark:
  Amos King
  J.R. Dunzy

Subscribed and sworn to before me this 22^d day of April , 1905.

J.R. Dunzy
Notary Public.

Applications for Enrollment of Creek Newborn
Act of 1905   Volume XIV

NC 1158.

DEPARTMENT OF THE INTERIOR,
COMMISSIONER TO THE FIVE CIVILIZED TRIBES.
January 31, 1907, Muskogee, I.T.

In the matter of the application for the enrollment of Fred Harjo, as a citizen by blood of the Creek Nation.

HAGIE GREEN, being duly sworn, by O.C. Hinkle, a Notary Public, testified as follows, through Official Interpreter, Jesse McDermott.

Examination by Commissioner.

Q What is your name? A Hagie Green.
Q What is your age? A About 30.
Q What is your post office address? A Wetumka.
Q Do you know Steven and Kogee Harjo? A Yes sir.
Q Is Kogee Harjo are[sic] relation of yours? A My sister.
Q She is the wife of Steven Harjo? A Yes sir.
Q Did they have a child by the name of Fred Harjo? A Yes sir, but the child is dead now.
Q Was it a little girl; was it a male child? A Male child.
Q When did he die? A I don't know exactly, but I think last August was a year ago.
Q How old was it when it died? A About two years old.
Q Where do you live? A North of Wetumka.
Q Are you a citizen of the Creek Nation? A Yes sir.

----------oOo----------

SALLIE GREEN, being duly sworn, by O.C. Hinkle, a Notary Public, testified as follows, through Official Interpreter, Jesse McDermott.

Examination by Commissioner.
Q What is your name? A Sallie Green.
Q Where do you live? A North of Wetumka.
Q Are you a citizen of the Creek Nation? A Yes sir.
Q Are you the wife of Hagie Green? A Yes sir.
Q Do you know Steven and Kogee Harjo? A Yes sir.
Q Did they have a male child named Fred? A Yes sir.
Q Is he living or dead? A Dead.
Q When did he die? A Last summer was a year ago.
Q He didn't die last summer? A No sir.
Q Died summer before that? A Yes sir.

Lona Merrick, being duly sworn, states that the above and foregoing is a true and correct transcript of her stenographic notes as taken in said cause on said date.

Applications for Enrollment of Creek Newborn
Act of 1905 Volume XIV

Lona Merrick

Subscribed and sworn
to before me this 31st day of Jan. 1907.

Oliver C. Hinkle
Notary Public.

NC 1158.
OCH
EK

DEPARTMENT OF THE INTERIOR,
COMMISSIONER TO THE FIVE CIVILIZED TRIBES.

In the matter of the application for the enrollment of Fred Harjo, deceased, as a citizen by blood of the Creek Nation.

DECISION.

The record in this case shows that on May 4, 1905, application was made, in affidavit form for the enrollment of Fred Harjo, as a citizen by blood of the Creek Nation, under the provisions of the act of Congress approved March 3, 1905 (33 Stat. L., 1048). Further proceedings were had January 31, 1907.

The evidence and the records in this office show that said Fred Harjo was the son of Stephen Harjo and Kogee Harjo, whose names appear upon a schedule of citizens by blood of the Creek Nation, approved by the Secretary of the Interior March 28, 1902, opposite numbers 8938 and 8939, respectively.

The evidence further shows that said Fred Harjo was born February 28, 1903, and died subsequent to March 4, 1905.

Although the application herein was not made within the time specified by the provisions of the Act of Congress approved March 3, 1905 (33 Stat. L., 1048), jurisdiction to consider same under said Act of Congress was given this office and the Department by the provisions of Section 1 of the act of Congress approved April 26, 1906 (34 Stats. L., 137).

It is therefore, ordered and adjudged that said Fred Harjo, deceased, is entitled to be enrolled as a citizen by blood of the Creek Nation under the provisions of the Act of Congress approved March 3, 1905 (33 Stat. L., 1048), and the application for his enrollment as such is accordingly granted.

Tams Bixby COMMISSIONER.

Muskogee, Indian Territory.
FEB 14 1907

Applications for Enrollment of Creek Newborn
Act of 1905   Volume XIV

(Letter below typed as given.)

Louis Dunzy
dealer in
General Merchandise.

Barnard, Ind Ter. 5/3d, 1905

Commission to 5 Tribes
    Muskogee Ind Terr

    Dear Sir

        I herewith inclose you affidavits of mostly Snake people whom has made the affidavits I was away a few days when I amed to send those in by the last of April But I hope this will not cause any delay of those entitle to enrolment.

Yours truly,
J.R. Dunzy

P S All these affidavits I have signed is done free gratis to those full bloods excepting 2 negroes[sic] which one Fleming I fear is not correct statement made by the partys concerned.

Respectfully,
J R Dunzy
N.P.

This letter was received May 4th, 1905 in an envelope postmarked "Mon. & Ft. Worth R.P.O. May 3, 1905 Tr 10."

N.C. 1158.

Muskogee, Indian Territory, June 22, 1906.

Stephen Harjo,
    Wetumka, Indian Territory.

Dear Sir:

    In the matter of the application for the enrollment of your minor child, Fred Harjo, as a citizen by blood of the Creek Nation, you are advised that it is required that you furnish this office with the affidavits of yourself and the midwife in attendance at the birth of said child. For this purpose there is inclosed blank form of birth affidavit. Said affidavits should show the name of the child, the names of its parents, the date of its birth and whether or not it was living on March 4, 1906.

    You are requested to furnish this office with information which will identify you and Kogee Harjo, the mother of said child, on its roll of citizens of the Creek Nation.

    This matter should receive your prompt attention.

Applications for Enrollment of Creek Newborn
Act of 1905 Volume XIV

Respectfully,

BA   Commissioner.

JWH

N C 1158

Muskogee, Indian Territory, March 9, 1907.

Kogee Harjo,
% Stephen Harjo,
Wetumka, Indian Territory.

Dear Madam :--

You are hereby advised that on March 2, 1907, the Secretary of the Interior approved the enrollment of your minor child, Fred Harjo, as a citizen by blood of the Creek Nation, and that the name of said child appears upon the roll of new born citizens by blood of the Creek Nation, enrolled under the Act of Congress approved March 3, 1905, as number 1283.

This child is now entitled to allotment and application therefor should be made without delay at the Creek Land Office, Muskogee, Indian Territory.

NC 1159.

DEPARTMENT OF THE INTERIOR,
COMMISSIONER TO THE FIVE CIVILIZED TRIBES.
Muskogee, I.T. January 31, 1907.

In the matter of the application for the enrollment of Philliby Harjo, as a citizen by blood of the Creek Nation.

HAGIE GREEN, being duly sworn, by O.C. Hinkle, a Notary Public, testified as follows, through Official Interpreter, Jesse McDermott.

Examination by Commissioner.
Q What is your name? A Hagie Green.
Q What is your post office address? A Wetumka.
Q Are you a citizen of the Creek Nation? A Yes sir.
Q Where do you live? A North of Wetumka.
Q Do you know Sango and Rosey Harjo? A I know the parties but I don't know anything about their children.
Q Is Sango ever called Shanco Harjo, sometimes? A Yes sir.
Q What is the name of his mother? A Mandy.
Q Has he a brother named Sandy? A Yes sir.
Q What is Shanco Harjo's father's name? A Ochee Harjo.

Applications for Enrollment of Creek Newborn
Act of 1905 Volume XIV

Q Do you know whether they had any children? A They have one child about the size of my little girl here.
Q How old is this little girl? A Three years old, this child of Shanco's is little older than this little girl.
Q Do you know its name? A No sir
Q Do you know whether it is called Philliby Harjo? A I don't know the names of their children at all.
Q Do you know whether this child is a boy or girl? A The child I have reference to is a little girl, little older than my child here.
Q Are you sure it is a girl? A Rosey Wollow's child is a little girl, I know that.
Q Is Rosey Harjo the wife of Shanco Harjo? A She was but they have separated.
Q Who has the child, the father or mother? A Mandy had custody of the child.
Q What is her post office address? A I don't know.
Q Does Shanco Harjo live with his mother? A I don't know.
Q What is Shanco's post office address? A I don't know that either.
Q Do you know Rosey Harjo by any other name? A No sir.
Q Has she an Indian name? A She may have an Indian name but I don't know, I am not well acquainted with her.
Q Was she ever called Rosey Wollow? A Yes sir.
Q Do you know her parents? A No sir.

Shanco Harjo, is shown, by the records of this office, to have appeared as Shanco Harjo upon a schedule of citizens by blood of the Creek Nation approved by the Secretary of the Interior March 28, 1902, opposite number 6398. His mother Mandy Harjo and brother, Sandy Harjo appear with him on Creek Indian card number 2069.

Q What Creek Indian town does Sango Harjo and Mandy Harjo belong to? A Wewokache, or Little Wewoka.

-------ooOoo-------

SALLIE GREEN, being duly sworn, by O.C. Hinkle, a Notary Public, testified as follows, through Official Interpreter, Jesse McDermott.

Examination by Commissioner.
Q What is your name? A Sallie Green.
Q Do you know Rosey and Sango Harjo? A I know of them but I am not personally acquainted with them.
Q Do you know them by name? A Yes sir.
Q You know them when you see them? A Yes sir.
Q Do you [sic] who Sango Harjo's mother is? A Mandy.
Q Please state the name? A Mandy.
Q Has he a brother named Sandy Harjo? A Yes sir.
Q Do you know what Creek Indian town they belong to? A I don't know but I think they belong to little Wewoka.
Q Has Sango and Rosey a child? A Yes sir.
Q Have you ever seen the child? A Yes sir.

Applications for Enrollment of Creek Newborn
Act of 1905 Volume XIV

Q Do you know its name? A I don't know. I have never heard the name.
Q Do you know whether it is a girl? A Yes sir it is a girl.
Q Do you [sic] who the father of the child is? A Yes sir.
Q Who is he? A Sango.
Q Rosey Harjo made an affidavit for the enrollment of her child Philliby Harjo and stated in said affidavit that said child was a male child.

Statement by Hagie Green: The child we have reference to it may be that Sango has had another child by a different woman, we don't know anything about that. We know that Sango and Rosey Harjo had a child, a little girl.

Lona Merrick, being duly sworn, states that the above and foregoing is a true and correct transcript of her stenographic notes as taken in said cause on said date.

Lona Merrick

Subscribed and sworn to before me this 31st day of January, 1907.

Oliver C Hinkle
Notary Public.

NC 1159.   OCH
                                                                         EK

DEPARTMENT OF THE INTERIOR,
COMMISSIONER TO THE FIVE CIVILIZED TRIBES.

In the matter of the application for the enrollment of Philliby Harjo, as a citizen by blood of the Creek Nation.

DECISION.

The record in this case shows that on May 4, 1905, application was made, in affidavit form for the enrollment of Philliby Harjo, as a citizen by blood of the Creek Nation, under the provisions of the Act of Congress approved March 3, 1905 (33 Stat. L., 1048). Further proceedings were had January 31, 1907.

The evidence and the records in this office show that said Philliby Harjo is the child of Sango Harjo, whose name appears as "Shanco Harjo" upon a schedule of citizens by blood of the Creek Nation, approved by the Secretary of the Interior March 28, 1902, opposite No. 6398, and Rosey Harjo, whose name has not been identified upon any approved schedule of citizens by blood of the Creek Nation.

The evidence further shows that said Philliby Harjo was born October 3, 1904, and was living March 4, 1905.

The evidence in this case is not as full and complete as has heretofore been required by this office to establish a right to be enrolled as a citizen of the Creek Nation, but in view of the provisions of the Act of Congress approved April 26, 1906 (34 Stats.

Applications for Enrollment of Creek Newborn
Act of 1905 Volume XIV

L., 137), fixing March 4, 1907, as the date after which the Secretary of the Interior shall have no jurisdiction to approve the enrollment of any person as a citizen of said Nation, it is believed that the evidence herein should be considered sufficient to establish the facts necessary to support the applicant's right to enrollment.

Although the application herein was not made within the time specified by the provisions of the Act of Congress approved March 3, 1905 (33 Stat. L., 1048), jurisdiction to consider same under said Act of Congress was given this office and the Department by the provisions of Section 1 of the Act of Congress approved April 26, 1906 (34 Stats. L., 137).

It is therefore, ordered and adjudged that said Philliby Harjo is entitled to be enrolled as a citizen by blood of the Creek Nation, under the provisions of the Act of Congress approved March 3, 1905 (33 Stat. L., 1048), and the application for his enrollment as such is accordingly granted.

Tams Bixby COMMISSIONER.

Muskogee, Indian Territory.
FEB 7- 1907

BIRTH AFFIDAVIT.

DEPARTMENT OF THE INTERIOR.
COMMISSION TO THE FIVE CIVILIZED TRIBES.

IN RE APPLICATION FOR ENROLLMENT, as a citizen of the Creek Nation, of Philliby Harjo , born on the 3^d day of Oct , 1904

Name of Father: Sango Harjo   a citizen of the   Creek   Nation.
Name of Mother: Rosey Harjo   a citizen of the   Creek   Nation.

Postoffice   Wetumka I. Terr

AFFIDAVIT OF MOTHER.

UNITED STATES OF AMERICA, Indian Territory,
Western   DISTRICT.

I, Rosey Harjo , on oath state that I am 25 years of age and a citizen by blood, of the Creek Nation; that I am the lawful wife of ———, who is a citizen, by blood of the Creek Nation; that a male child was born to me on 3^d day of Oct , 1904 , that said child has been named Philliby Harjo , and was living March 4, 1905.

her
Rosey x Harjo
mark

Witnesses To Mark:
 Sam Yargee
 Wash Lony

Applications for Enrollment of Creek Newborn
Act of 1905   Volume XIV

Subscribed and sworn to before me this first day of April, 1905.

       J.R. Dunzy
        Notary Public.

AFFIDAVIT OF ATTENDING PHYSICIAN OR MID-WIFE.

UNITED STATES OF AMERICA, Indian Territory,
(blank)   **DISTRICT.**

 I, non Rosey Harjo, a acted herself, on oath state that I attended on Mrs. Rosey Harjo herself, wife of *(blank)* on the 3^d day of Oct, 1904; that there was born to her on said date a *(blank)* child; that said child was living March 4, 1905, and is said to have been named *(blank)*

         her
       Rosey x Harjo
Witnesses To Mark: mark
 { Sam Yargee
  Wash Lony

Subscribed and sworn to before me this first day of April, 1905.

       J.R. Dunzy
        Notary Public.

(Letter below typed as given.)

      Louis Dunzy
      dealer in
    General Merchandise.

      Barnard, Ind Ter. 5/3d, 1905

Commission to 5 Tribes
 Muskogee Ind Terr

   Dear Sir
    I herewith inclose you affidavits of mostly Snake people whom has made the affidavits I was away a few days when I amed to send those in by the last of April But I hope this will not cause any delay of those entitle to enrolment.

      Yours truly,
      J.R. Dunzy

P S All these affidavits I have signed is done free gratis to those full bloods excepting 2 negroes[sic] which one Fleming I fear is not correct statement made by the partys concerned.

      Respectfully,
      J R Dunzy
       N.P.

Applications for Enrollment of Creek Newborn
Act of 1905   Volume XIV

This letter was received May 4th, 1905 in an envelope postmarked "Mon. & Ft. Worth R.P.O. May 3, 1905 Tr 10."

REFER IN REPLY TO THE FOLLOWING:

N.C. 1159.

DEPARTMENT OF THE INTERIOR,
COMMISSIONER TO THE FIVE CIVILIZED TRIBES.

Muskogee, Indian Territory, June 22, 1906.

Rosey Harjo,
    Wetumka, Indian Territory.

Dear Madam:

    In the matter of the application for the enrollment of your minor child, Philliby Harjo, as a citizen by blood of the Creek Nation, you are advised that it is required that you furnish this office with the affidavits of yourself and the midwife in attendance at the birth of said child. For this purpose there is inclosed a blank form of birth affidavit. Said affidavits should show the name of the child, the names of its parents, the date of its birth and whether or not it was living on March 4, 1906.

    You are requested to furnish this office with this information which will identify you and Sango Harjo, the father of said child, on its roll of citizens of the Creek Nation.

    This matter should receive your prompt attention.

                           Respectfully,
                           Tams Bixby   Commissioner.

BA

NC 1159

                       Muskogee, Indian Territory, January 30, 1907.

J. R. Dunzy, Esq.
    Barnard, Indian Territory.

Dear Sir:

    The records of this office show that on May 4, 1905 the affidavit of Rosa Harjo was received in the matter of the application for the enrollment of Philliby Harjo as a citizen by blood of the Creek Nation. Said affidavit appears to have been executed before you on April 1, 1905, and was transmitted with your letter of May 3, 1905. Owing to the fact that said affidavit was not received on or before May 2, 1905 this child cannot be enrolled under the provisions of the Act of Congress approved March 3, 1905.

Applications for Enrollment of Creek Newborn
Act of 1905   Volume XIV

June 22, 1906, this office addressed a letter to Rosa Harjo, inclosing a birth affidavit for supplemental proof, but the letter was returned unanswered. There is herewith inclosed a birth affidavit which you are requested to have executed by said Rosa Harjo and one other person who has sufficient knowledge of the facts with reference to said Philliby Harjo, and when properly executed please transmit to this office in the inclosed envelope.

There is but a short time remaining in which to enroll this child should it be found entitled to enrollment, as the Act of Congress approved April 26, 1906, provides in part as follows:

"That the rolls of the tribes affected by this act shall be fully completed on or before the fourth day of March, nineteen hundred and seven, and the Secretary of the Interior shall have no jurisdiction to approve the enrollment of any person after said date."

In view of the provision of law above quoted this matter should receive prompt attention.

      Respectfully,

          Commissioner.

B A
Env.

NC 1159.

      Muskogee, Indian Territory, March 7, 1907.

Rosey Harjo,
  Care of Sango Harjo,
    Wetumka, Indian Territory.

Dear Madam:

You are hereby advised that on March 2, 1907 the Secretary of the Interior approved the enrollment of your minor child, Philliby Harjo, as a citizen by blood of the Creek Nation and that the name of said child appears upon the roll is new born citizens by blood of the Creek Nation enrolled under the Act of Congress approved March 3, 1905, as number 1266.

This child is now entitled to allotment and application therefor should be made without delay at the Creek Land Office, Muskogee, Indian Territory.

      Respectfully,

          Commissioner.

Applications for Enrollment of Creek Newborn
Act of 1905   Volume XIV

(Letter below typed as given.)

Louis Dunzy
dealer in
General Merchandise.

Barnard, Ind Ter. 5/3d, 1905

Commission to 5 Tribes
   Muskogee Ind Terr

    Dear Sir
        I herewith inclose you affidavits of mostly Snake people whom has made the affidavits I was away a few days when I amed to send those in by the last of April But I hope this will not cause any delay of those entitle to enrolment.

Yours truly,
J.R. Dunzy

P S All these affidavits I have signed is done free gratis to those full bloods excepting 2 negroes[sic] which one Fleming I fear is not correct statement made by the partys concerned.

Respectfully,
J R Dunzy
N.P.

This letter was received May 4th, 1905 in an envelope postmarked "Mon. & Ft. Worth R.P.O. May 3, 1905 Tr 10."

N.C. 1160.   I.D.

DEPARTMENT OF THE INTERIOR,
COMMISSIONER TO THE FIVE CIVILIZED TRIBES.

In the matter of the application for the enrollment of Lizzie Scott as a citizen by blood of the Creek Nation.

ORDER.

The record in this case shows that on May 4, 1905, there was filed with the Commission to the Five Civilized Tribes at Muskogee, Indian Territory, the application of Wiley Scott for the enrollment of his minor child, Lizzie Scott, as a citizen by blood of the Creek Nation.

The evidence shows that said Lizzie Scott was born January 5, 1902, and the she was living March 4, 1905.

It does not appear from the records of this office that application was made prior to May 4, 1905, for the enrollment of said Lizzie Scott as a citizen by blood of the Creek Nation.

The Act of Congress approved March 3, 1905, (Public No. 212), provides:

Applications for Enrollment of Creek Newborn
Act of 1905   Volume XIV

"That the Commission to the Five Civilized Tribes is authorized for sixty days after the date of the approval of this Act to receive and consider applications for enrollments of children born subsequent to May twenty five, nineteen hundred and one, and prior to March fourth, nineteen hundred and five, and living on said latter date, to citizens of the Creek tribe of Indians whose enrollment has been approved by the Secretary of the Interior prior to the date of the approval of this act; and to enroll and make allotments to such children."

It is, therefore, ordered that there is no authority of law for the enrollment of said Lizzie Scott, as a citizen by blood of the Creek Nation, and that the application for her enrollment as such should be and the same is hereby dismissed.

                                                Commissioner.

Muskogee, Indian Territory,

BIRTH AFFIDAVIT.

DEPARTMENT OF THE INTERIOR.
COMMISSION TO THE FIVE CIVILIZED TRIBES.

IN RE APPLICATION FOR ENROLLMENT, as a citizen of the Creek Nation, of   Lizzie Scott, born on the   5   day of   January   , 1902

Name of Father:	Wiley Scott	a citizen of the	Creek Nation.
Name of Mother:	Rosanna Scott	a citizen of the	Creek Nation.

                       Postoffice   Wetumka Ind Ter.

AFFIDAVIT OF MOTHER.

UNITED STATES OF AMERICA, Indian Territory,
    Western   DISTRICT.

I,   Wiley Scott , on oath state that I am 35 years of age and a citizen by blood , of the Creek Nation; that I am the lawful ~~wife~~ husband of Rosanna Scott , who is a citizen, by blood of the Creek Nation; that a female child was born to ~~me~~ her on 5 day of January , 1902 , that said child has been named Lizzie Scott , and was living March 4, 1905.

                                                his
                                     Wiley x Scott
Witnesses To Mark: mark
   { Henry W Shaber
     John Smith

Applications for Enrollment of Creek Newborn
Act of 1905   Volume XIV

Subscribed and sworn to before me this 8th day of April, 1905.

J.R. Dunzy
Notary Public.

AFFIDAVIT OF ATTENDING PHYSICIAN OR MID-WIFE.

UNITED STATES OF AMERICA, Indian Territory, }
    Western   DISTRICT.

I, Melissa Bird, a mid-wife, on oath state that I attended on Mrs. Rosanna Scott, wife of Wiley Scott on the 5th day of January, 1902; that there was born to her on said date a female child; that said child was living March 4, 1905, and is said to have been named Lizzie Scott

                                            her
                                Melissa x Bird

Witnesses To Mark: mark
  { Henry W Shaber
    John Smith

Subscribed and sworn to before me this 8th day of April, 1905.

J.R. Dunzy
Notary Public.

NC-1162

**DEPARTMENT OF THE INTERIOR,
COMMISSIONER TO THE FIVE CIVILIZED TRIBES.**

Muskogee, Indian Territory, September 27, 1905.

In the matter of the alleged application for the enrollment of Budy King as a citizen of the Creek Nation.

Daniel Cain, being duly sworn, testified as follows (through Jesse McDermott, Official Interpreter):

Applications for Enrollment of Creek Newborn
Act of 1905   Volume XIV

EXAMINATION BY THE COMMISSIONER:
Q What is your name? A Daniel Cain.
Q How old are you? A I am about 32 or 3,
Q What is your postoffice address? A Bearden.
Q What is the name of your wife? A Nicey Cain.

    The witness is identified as Daniel Cain, whose name appears on Creek Indian card, field No. 1805, and his name is contained in the partial list of citizens by blood of the Creek Nation approved by the Secretary of the Interior March 28, 1902, Roll No. 5726. The name of his wife, Nisey Cain, appears on the same card, opposite Roll No. 5727.
Q Are the father of Budy Cain? A Yes sir.
Q When was Budy Cain born? A I am not certain, but I think he will be three years old next Spring.
Nicey Cain, in her affidavit, states he was born the 9th day of May, 1903; is that correct? A Yes, that is correct. The child was born on the 9th day of May.
Q Did you go with your wife, Nisey Cain, before J. R. Dunzy, notary public, at the time she made affidavit about the birth of Budy Cain? A Yes sir.
Q At the time you went before Mr. Dunzy, did you think that he was connected with the Commission to the Five Civilized Tribes, in any way? A Yes. I was told by several around there that he was employed that way, and I went to him to have our papers fixed up.
Q Did Mr. Dunzy charge you anything for fixing up your papers? A No sir.

    On file with this Office are affidavits of Nisey Cain and Selma Cain relative to the birth of said Budy Cain. These affidavits are dated April 3, 1905, and were filed on May 4, 1905, with the Commission to the Five Civilized Tribes, together with several affidavits in other cases sworn to before J. R. Dunzy. The envelopes transmitting these and the other affidavits referred to is postmarked "May 3, 1905."

Q Is your child, Budy Cain, living now? A Yes sir.
Q Was it the general impression in the neighborhood in which you lived that Mr. Dunzy was in the employ of the Commission and was receiving applications for the Commission? A It was stated in the papers that the applications could be made before notaries, and as he being a notary, I thought he was a the proper man to go to.
Q You got the impression from the circular issued by the Commission to the Five Civilized Tribes that when you swore to the affidavit before the notary public, you had made an application for the enrollment of the child, did you? A Yes sir.
Q And when your wife made that affidavit before Dunzy, you thought there was nothing more to be done in the making of the application? is that correct? A Yes sir. He told me at the time I made out the affidavit that he was intending to send several others off and that he would send mine off with them.

INDIAN TERRITORY,)
Western District.   )   I, J. Y. Miller, a stenographer to the
)   Commissioner to the Five Civilized Tribes, do
)   hereby certify that the above and foregoing is a

Applications for Enrollment of Creek Newborn
Act of 1905 Volume XIV

true and complete translation of my notes as same appear in my stenographic report of this case.

            JY Miller

Sworn to and subscribed before me
 this the 28th day of September,
1905.   Edw C Griesel
              Notary Public.

(Letter below typed as given.)

         Louis Dunzy
          dealer in
        General Merchandise.

        Barnard, Ind Ter. 5/3d, 1905

Commission to 5 Tribes
 Muskogee Ind Terr

  Dear Sir
    I herewith inclose you affidavits of mostly Snake people whom has made the affidavits I was away a few days when I amed to send those in by the last of April But I hope this will not cause any delay of those entitle to enrolment.

      Yours truly,
       J.R. Dunzy

P S All these affidavits I have signed is done free gratis to those full bloods excepting 2 negroes[sic] which one Fleming I fear is not correct statement made by the partys concerned.

      Respectfully,
       J R Dunzy
        N.P.

This letter was received May 4th, 1905 in an envelope postmarked "Mon. & Ft. Worth R.P.O. May 3, 1905 Tr 10."

BIRTH AFFIDAVIT.

DEPARTMENT OF THE INTERIOR.
COMMISSION TO THE FIVE CIVILIZED TRIBES.

    IN RE APPLICATION FOR ENROLLMENT, as a citizen of the Creek Nation, of Budy Cain , born on the 9th day of May , 1903

Name of Father:	Daniel Cain	a citizen of the Creek	Nation.
Name of Mother:	Nicy Cain	a citizen of the Creek	Nation.

Applications for Enrollment of Creek Newborn
Act of 1905   Volume XIV

Postoffice   Bearden I.T.

AFFIDAVIT OF MOTHER.

UNITED STATES OF AMERICA, Indian Territory, }
    Western   DISTRICT.

    I, Nicy Cain, on oath state that I am 35 years of age and a citizen by blood, of the Creek Nation; that I am the lawful wife of Daniel Cain, who is a citizen, by blood of the Creek Nation; that a female child was born to me on 9th day of May, 1903, that said child has been named Budy Cain, and was living March 4, 1905.

                                            her
                                       Nicy x Cain
Witnesses To Mark: mark
{ Jimmy McGirt
{ Louis Dunzy

    Subscribed and sworn to before me this 3^d day of April, 1905.

                                       J.R. Dunzy
                                          Notary Public.

AFFIDAVIT OF ATTENDING PHYSICIAN OR MID-WIFE.

UNITED STATES OF AMERICA, Indian Territory, }
    (blank)   DISTRICT.

    I, Selina Cain, a mid-wife, on oath state that I attended on Mrs. Nicy Cain, wife of Daniel Cain on the 9th day of May, 1903; that there was born to her on said date a female child; that said child was living March 4, 1905, and is said to have been named Budy Cain

                                            her
                                       Selina x Cain
Witnesses To Mark: mark
{ Jimmy McGirt
{ Louis Dunzy

    Subscribed and sworn to before me this 3^d day of April, 1905.

                                       J.R. Dunzy
                                        Notary Public.

Applications for Enrollment of Creek Newborn
Act of 1905 Volume XIV

(Letter below typed as given.)

Louis Dunzy
dealer in
General Merchandise.

Barnard, Ind Ter. 5/3d, 1905

Commission to 5 Tribes
Muskogee Ind Terr

Dear Sir
I herewith inclose you affidavits of mostly Snake people whom has made the affidavits I was away a few days when I amed to send those in by the last of April But I hope this will not cause any delay of those entitle to enrolment.

Yours truly,
J.R. Dunzy

P S All these affidavits I have signed is done free gratis to those full bloods excepting 2 negroes[sic] which one Fleming I fear is not correct statement made by the partys concerned.

Respectfully,
J R Dunzy
N.P.

This letter was received May 4th, 1905 in an envelope postmarked "Mon. & Ft. Worth R.P.O. May 3, 1905 Tr 10."

DEPARTMENT OF THE INTERIOR.
COMMISSION TO THE FIVE CIVILIZED TRIBES.

In the matter of the death of Bettie Yargee a citizen of the Creek Nation, who formerly resided at or near Wetumka , Ind. Ter., and died on the 28th day of February , 1904

AFFIDAVIT OF RELATIVE.

UNITED STATES OF AMERICA, Indian Territory, }
Western DISTRICT.

I, Louisa Yaholar , on oath state that I am 32 years of age and a citizen by blood , of the Creek Nation; that my postoffice address is Wetumka , Ind. Ter.; that I am the mother of Bettie Yargee who was a citizen, by blood , of the Creek Nation and that said Bettie Yargee died on the 28 day of Feby , 1904

Applications for Enrollment of Creek Newborn
Act of 1905   Volume XIV

                                                    her
                                       Louisa x Yaholar
Witnesses To Mark: mark
  { Louis Dunzy

Subscribed and sworn to before me this 15th day of April, 1905.

                                          J.R. Dunzy
                                          Notary Public.

AFFIDAVIT OF ACQUAINTANCE.

UNITED STATES OF AMERICA, Indian Territory, ⎫
      Western   DISTRICT. ⎭

    I, Winey Scott, on oath state that I am 50 years of age, and a citizen by blood of the Creek Nation; that my postoffice address is Wetumka, Ind. Ter.; that I was personally acquainted with Bettie Yargee who was a citizen, by blood, of the Creek Nation; and that said Bettie Yargee died on the 28th day of Feb, 1904

                                        her
                                    Winey x Scott
Witnesses To Mark: mark
  { Louis Dunzy

Subscribed and sworn to before me this 15th day of April, 1905.

                                          J.R. Dunzy
                                          Notary Public.

NC 1164   JLD
DEPARTMENT OF THE INTERIOR,
COMMISSIONER TO THE FIVE CIVILIZED TRIBES.

    In the matter of the application for the enrollment of Bettie Yargee, deceased, as a citizen by blood of the Creek Nation.

                . . . .

STATEMENT AND ORDER.

    The record in this case shows that on May 4, 1905, application was made in affidavit form for the enrollment of Bettie Yargee, deceased, as a citizen by blood of the Creek Nation, under the provisions of the Act of Congress approved March 3, 1905.

Applications for Enrollment of Creek Newborn
Act of 1905 Volume XIV

It appears from the affidavit filed in this matter that said Bettie Yargee, deceased, was born February 5, 1904, and died February 28, 1904.

The Act of Congress approved March 3, 1905, (33 Stats., 1048) provides:

"That the Commission to the Five Civilized Tribes is authorized for sixty days after the date of the approval of this act to receive and consider applications for enrollment, of children, <u>born subsequent to May twenty-fifth, nineteen hundred and one, and prior to March fourth, nineteen hundred and five, and living on said latter date</u>, to citizens of the Creek tribe of Indians whose enrollment has been approved by the Secretary of the Interior prior to the approval of this act; and to enroll and make allotments to such children."

It is, therefore, ordered that the application for the enrollment of said Bettie Yargee, deceased, as a citizen by blood of the Creek Nation, be, and the same is hereby dismissed.

Tams Bixby Commissioner.

Muskogee, Indian Territory.
JAN 4- 1907

N.C. 1165

DEPARTMENT OF THE INTERIOR,
COMMISSIONER TO THE FIVE CIVILIZED TRIBES.

In the matter of the application for the enrollment of Nancy Green as a citizen by blood of the Creek Nation.

ORDER.

The record in this case shows that on May 4, 1905, there was filed with the Commission to the Five Civilized Tribes at Muskogee, Indian Territory, the application of Haggie Green for the enrollment of her[sic] minor child, Nancy Green, as a citizen by blood of the Creek Nation.

The evidence shows that said Nancy Green was born June 17, 1903, and that she was living March 4, 1905.

It does not appear from the records of this office that application was made prior to May 4, 1905, for the enrollment of said Nancy Green, as a citizen by blood of the Creek Nation.

The Act of Congress approved March 3, 1905, (Public No. 212), provides:

Applications for Enrollment of Creek Newborn
Act of 1905 Volume XIV

"That the Commission to the Five Civilized Tribes is authorized for sixty days after the date of the approval of this act to receive and consider applications for enrollment, of children, born subsequent to May twenty-fifth, nineteen hundred and one, and prior to March fourth, nineteen hundred and five, and living on said latter date, to citizens of the Creek tribe of Indians whose enrollment has been approved by the Secretary of the Interior prior to the approval of this act; and to enroll and make allotments to such children."

It is, therefore, ordered that there is no authority of law for the enrollment of said Nancy Green, as a citizen by blood of the Creek Nation, and that the application for her enrollment as such should be and the same is hereby dismissed.

Commissioner.

Muskogee, Indian Territory,

BIRTH AFFIDAVIT.

DEPARTMENT OF THE INTERIOR.
COMMISSION TO THE FIVE CIVILIZED TRIBES.

IN RE APPLICATION FOR ENROLLMENT, as a citizen of the Creek Nation, of Nancy Green, born on the 17th day of June, 1903

Name of Father: Haggie Green   a citizen of the   Creek   Nation.
Name of Mother: Sallie Green   a citizen of the   Creek   Nation.

Postoffice   Wetumka I.T.

AFFIDAVIT OF MOTHER.

UNITED STATES OF AMERICA, Indian Territory,
   Western   DISTRICT.

I, Haggie Green, on oath state that I am 30 years of age and a citizen by blood, of the Creek Nation; that I am the lawful ~~wife~~ husband of Sallie Green, who is a citizen, by blood of the Creek Nation; that a female child was born to ~~me~~ her on 17th day of June, 1903, that said child has been named Nancy Green, and was living March 4, 1905.

his
Haggie x Green
mark

Witnesses To Mark:
  { HW Shaber

Applications for Enrollment of Creek Newborn
Act of 1905   Volume XIV

Subscribed and sworn to before me this 5th day of   April   , 1905.

J. R. Dunzy
Notary Public.

AFFIDAVIT OF ATTENDING PHYSICIAN OR MID-WIFE.

UNITED STATES OF AMERICA, Indian Territory, }
Western   DISTRICT.

I, Lucy Stewart , a mid-wife , on oath state that I attended on Mrs. Sallie Green, wife of Haggie Green on the 17th day of June , 1903 ; that there was born to her on said date a female child; that said child was living March 4, 1905, and is said to have been named Nancy Green

her
Lucy x Stewart
mark

Witnesses To Mark:
{ HW Shaber

Subscribed and sworn to before me this 5th day of   April   , 1905.

J. R. Dunzy
Notary Public.

NC 1166.

Muskogee, Indian Territory, *(illegible date)*.

Peter King,
   Bearden, Indian Territory.

Dear Sir:

In the matter of the application for the enrollment of your min or child, George King, as a citizen by blood of the Creek Nation, you are advised that it is required that you furnish this office with the affidavits of the mother of said child, and the midwife in attendance at its birth, *(illegible)* the name of the child, the names of its parents, the date of its birth and whether said child was living March 4, *(illegible)*, and for this purpose

Applications for Enrollment of Creek Newborn
Act of 1905   Volume XIV

there is herewith enclosed a blank affidavit. This matter should receive your immediate attention.

You are further advised that this office is unable to identify you and Lizzie King, the mother of said child, upon the rolls of citizens of the Creek Nation, and it will be necessary that you furnish this office with the maiden name of your wife, the names of your parents and other members of your family, the Creek Indian towns to which [sic] belong, the names and roll numbers as same appear on your deeds or allotment certificates to land in the Creek Nation, and any other information which will enable this office to identify you and said Lizzie King on its records.

Respectfully,

1 BA   Commissioner.

DEPARTMENT OF THE INTERIOR,
COMMISSIONER TO THE FIVE CIVILIZED TRIBES.
Eufaula, I. T., September 11, 1905.

In the matter of the application for the enrollment of Annie Deere as a citizen by blood of the Creek Nation.

LOWINA DEERE, being duly sworn, testified as follows:

Through Alex Posey Official Interpreter:

BY THE COMMISSIONER:
Q What is your name? A Lowina Deere.
Q How old are you? A I do not know.

Witness appears to be about twenty-five years of age.

Q What is your post office address? A Eufaula.
Q Are you a citizen of the Creek Nation? A I am a citizen of the Seminole Nation.
Q Have you a child named Annie Deere? A Yes, sir.
Q What is the name of her father? Esul Deere.

Applications for Enrollment of Creek Newborn
Act of 1905   Volume XIV

Q Is he a citizen of the Creek Nation? A Yes, sir.
Q To what town does he belong? A Okfuske Canadian.
Q Is he your lawful husband? A Yes, sir.
Q When was Annie born? A July 10, 1902.
Q Have you made application for the enrollment of Annie as a citizen of the Seminole Nation? A Yes, sir.
Q Do you with to have the child enrolled in the Seminole Nation? A Yes, sir.
Q Who attended on you at the birth of Annie? A Susie Deere.

---oooOOOooo---

I, D. C. Skaggs, on oath state that the above and foregoing is a full and true transcript of my stenographic notes as taken in said cause on said date.

D. C. Skaggs

Subscribed and sworn to before me this 16 day of October 1905.

Edw C Griesel
Notary Public.

N.C. 116[sic]

DEPARTMENT OF THE INTERIOR,
COMMISSIONER TO THE FIVE CIVILIZED TRIBES.
Eufaula, Indian Territory, December 6, 1905.

In the matter of the application for the enrollment of Annie Deere as a citizen by blood of the Creek Nation.

Lydia Pologee being duly sworn testified as follows through Alex Posey official interpreter.

By Commissioner.

Q What is your name? A Lydia Pologee, I am enrolled as Loda Pologee.
Q What is your age? A I am over twenty. (Witness appears to be about thirty.)
Q What is your post office address? A Eufaula.
Q Are you a citizen of the Creek Nation? A Yes, sir
Q Of what town are you a member? [sic] Okfuske Canadian.
Q Do you know Esul Deere? A Yes, sir, he is my brother.
Q Is he known by any other name? A Yes, sir, his proper name is Israel Pologee but I think he is enrolled as Esul Pologee.
Q Do you know his wife Louina Deere? A Yes, sir.
Q What was her name before she married Esul Pologee? A Louina Beaver
Q Is she a citizen of the Creek Nation? A No, sir, Seminole.
Q Have they a child named Annie Deere? A Yes, sir

Applications for Enrollment of Creek Newborn
Act of 1905 Volume XIV

I, Alex Posey, on oath state that the above and foregoing is a true and correct transcript of my notes as taken in said cause on said date.

Alex Posey

Subscribed and sworn to before
me this 22 day of December 1905.

Edw C Griesel
Notary Public.

C 1167

DEPARTMENT OF THE INTERIOR,
COMMISSION TO THE FIVE CIVILIZED TRIBES.

Muskogee, Indian Territory, April 15, 1905

In the matter of the application for the enrollment of certain new-born children as citizens of the Creek Nation.

Alex Posey, being duly sworn, testified as follows:

EXAMINATION BY THE COMMISSION:
Q State your name, age and postoffice address. A Alex Posey; 31; Muskogee.
Q Are you a citizen of the Creek Nation? A Yes sir.
Q Got your land, have you? A Yes sir.
Q Have you been engaged recently in the "field work" of the Dawes Commission in securing evidence about Creek citizens or new-borns? A Yes sir.
Q Have you a list of children for whom application could not be made and about whom you have succeeded in obtaining some information? A Yes sir.
Q You may state the conditions and the names of those children that you desire to make application for. A Yes sir.
Q Name them. A Annie Deere. Born July 10, 1902, a child of _____ Deere and Louina Deere. The father belongs to Okfuskee Canadian, and the mother is a citizen of the Seminole Nation. *(Handwritten to the side: Eufaula)*

Noda Pologee I understand has some children, but I have not been able to learn their names, or the name of their father. The mother lives near Eufaula. *(Handwritten to the side: Eufaula)*

Maxey Lewis, of Eufaula Canadian Town, I learn has one child, but I have not been able to learn its name or the name of its mother. *(Handwritten to the side: Eufaula)*

Q This information you received from relatives right around there on April 15, 1905?
A Yes sir.

Applications for Enrollment of Creek Newborn
Act of 1905   Volume XIV

Q Were you informed that the parents of these children were unwilling to make application for their enrollment? A Yes sir.
Q This was the only way the rights of these children could be save by? A Yes, sir. I made every effort to obtain direct information from the parents, but in every instance they refused to give testimony.

INDIAN TERRITORY, Western District.

I, J. Y. Miller, a stenographer to the Commission to the Five Civilized Tribes, do hereby certify that the above and foregoing is a true and complete translation of my notes as same appear in my stenographic report of this case.

JY Miller

Subscribed and sworn to before me
this the 15th day of April,
1905.

Drennan C Skaggs
Notary Public.

N.C. 1167.   F.H.W.
                                                     A.G.
DEPARTMENT OF THE INTERIOR,
COMMISSIONER TO THE FIVE CIVILIZED TRIBES.

In the matter of the application for the enrollment of Annie Deere as a citizen by blood of the Creek Nation.

DECISION.

The record in this case shows that on September 11, 1905, an application was filed, in affidavit form for the enrollment of Annie Deere as a citizen by blood of the Creek Nation, under the provisions of the Act of Congress approved March 3, 1905. Further proceedings were had before a creek enrollment field party at Eufaula, Indian Territory, September 11, 1905 and December 6, 1905. A copy of the transcript of testimony taken April 15, 1905, "in the matter of the application for the enrollment of certain new-born children as citizens of the Creek Nation" and a supplemental affidavit filed May 22, 1906, are attached to and made a part of the record herein.

The evidence in this case shows that the applicant is the minor child of Lou Annie Deere, an alleged citizen of the Seminole Nation, and Esal Deere, whose name is identified on a roll of citizens by blood of the Creek Nation approved by the Secretary of the Interior March 28, 1902, opposite No. 8748. The surname of the applicant is shown in the original affidavit filed in this matter as Deere and in the supplemental affidavit as Deer. The surname of the father of the said applicant as shown on the approved roll being Deere, the application filed herein is considered as being made for the enrollment of Annie Deere.

Applications for Enrollment of Creek Newborn
Act of 1905   Volume XIV

The evidence further shows that there is a discrepancy in the dates given for the birth of the said applicant but it is clearly shown by a preponderance of evidence that the said Annie Deere was born July 10, 1902, and was living March 4, 1905.

After a careful examination of the records in the possession of this office, neither the mother, under any of the various names by which she is referred to in the evidence, nor the name of the said applicant is identified on the approved roll of citizens by blood of the Seminole Nation, nor does it appear that application has been made for their enrollment as such.

The records of this office fail to show that the mother is a citizen of or an applicant for citizenship in the Creek Nation.

Although the application herein was not made within the time prescribed by the Act of Congress approved March 3, 1905, jurisdiction to consider the same was given to this office and the Department by the provisions of Section 1 of the Act of Congress approved April 26, 1906.

It is, therefore, ordered and adjudged that the said Annie Deere is entitled to be enrolled as a citizen by blood of the Creek Nation, under the provisions of the Act of Congress approved March 3, 1905 (33 Stats., 1048) and the application for her enrollment as such is accordingly granted.

Tams Bixby COMMISSIONER.

Muskogee, Indian Territory.
FEB 2 – 1907

BIRTH AFFIDAVIT.

COPY.
DEPARTMENT OF THE INTERIOR.
COMMISSION TO THE FIVE CIVILIZED TRIBES.

IN RE APPLICATION FOR ENROLLMENT, as a citizen of the Creek Nation, of Annie Deere, born on the   10th day of   July , 1902

Name of Father: Esul Deere   a citizen of the   Creek   Nation.
Okfuskee Canadian
Name of Mother: Louina Deere   a citizen of the Seminole Nation.

Postoffice   Eufaula, Ind. Terr.

AFFIDAVIT OF MOTHER.

UNITED STATES OF AMERICA, Indian Territory,
    Western   DISTRICT.

I, Louina Deere , on oath state that I am about 35 years of age and a citizen by blood , of the Seminole Nation; that I am the lawful wife of Esul (Isreal) Deere , who is a citizen, by blood of the Creek Nation; that a female child was born to me

Applications for Enrollment of Creek Newborn
Act of 1905 Volume XIV

on the 10th day of July , 1902 , that said child has been named Annie Deere , and was living March 4, 1905.

(Signed) Louina x Deere
her mark

Witnesses To Mark:
{ DC Skaggs
  Alex Posey

Subscribed and sworn to before me this 11 day of September , 1905.

(Signed) Drennan C Skaggs
Notary Public.

AFFIDAVIT OF ATTENDING PHYSICIAN OR MID-WIFE.

UNITED STATES OF AMERICA, Indian Territory, }
   Western   DISTRICT.

I, Susie Deere , a midwife , on oath state that I attended on Mrs. Louina Deere , wife of Esul Deere on the 10 day of July , 1902 ; that there was born to her on said date a female child; that said child was living March 4, 1905, and is said to have been named Annie Deere Susie Deere after giving above data, refused to sign affidavit

Witnesses To Mark:
{ ....
  ....

Subscribed and sworn to before me this .... day of ...., 190....

Notary Public.

BIRTH AFFIDAVIT.

DEPARTMENT OF THE INTERIOR.
COMMISSION TO THE FIVE CIVILIZED TRIBES.

IN RE APPLICATION FOR ENROLLMENT, as a citizen of the Creek Nation, of Annie Deere, born on the 10th day of July , 1902

Name of Father: Esul Deere   a citizen of the Creek   Nation.
Okfuskee Canadian
Name of Mother: Lowina Deere   a citizen of the Seminole Nation.

Postoffice   Eufaula, Ind. Terr.

Applications for Enrollment of Creek Newborn
Act of 1905   Volume XIV

AFFIDAVIT OF MOTHER.

UNITED STATES OF AMERICA, Indian Territory,
Western   DISTRICT.

    I, Lowina Deere , on oath state that I am about 35 years of age and a citizen by blood , of the Seminole Nation; that I am the lawful wife of Esul (Isreal) Deere , who is a citizen, by blood of the Creek   Nation; that a female   child was born to me on the 10th day of   July , 1902 , that said child has been named   Annie Deere , and was living March 4, 1905.

                                          her
                                  Lowina x Deere
Witnesses To Mark: mark
{ DC Skaggs
  Alex Posey

    Subscribed and sworn to before me this 11 day of   September   , 1905.

                               Drennan C Skaggs
                               Notary Public.

AFFIDAVIT OF ATTENDING PHYSICIAN OR MID-WIFE.

UNITED STATES OF AMERICA, Indian Territory,
Western   DISTRICT.

    I, Susie Deere , a   mid-wife , on oath state that I attended on Mrs. Lowina Deere , wife of Esul Deere on the 10 day of July , 1902 ; that there was born to her on said date a female   child; that said child was living March 4, 1905, and is said to have been named Annie Deere   Susie Deere after giving above data, refused to sign affidavit

Witnesses To Mark:
{

    Subscribed and sworn to before me this .... day of ...., 190... .

                               Notary Public.

Applications for Enrollment of Creek Newborn
Act of 1905   Volume XIV

BIRTH AFFIDAVIT.

DEPARTMENT OF THE INTERIOR,
COMMISSIONER TO THE FIVE CIVILIZED TRIBES.

ENROLLMENT OF MINORS. ACT OF CONGRESS, APPROVED APRIL 26, 1906.

IN RE APPLICATION FOR ENROLLMENT, as a citizen of the   Creek   Nation, of Annie Deer , born on the *(blank)*   day of   July , 1903

Name of Father: Israel Deer   a citizen of the   Creek   Nation.
                                     Annie Beaver
Name of Mother: Lou Annie Deer nee Lou   a citizen of the   Seminole   Nation.

Tribal enrollment of father   Creek Roll   Tribal enrollment of mother   Seminole

Postoffice   Okmulgee Ind. Ter

AFFIDAVIT OF MOTHER.

UNITED STATES OF AMERICA, Indian Territory,
Western   District.

I, Lou Annie Deer , on oath state that I am about 30 years of age and a citizen by blood , of the Seminole   Nation; that I am the lawful wife of Israel Deer , who is a citizen, by blood of the Creek   Nation; that a female   child was born to me on *(blank)* day of   July , 1903 , that said child has been named Annie Deer , and was living March 4, 1906.

                                                                        her
                                                    Lou Annie x Deer

WITNESSES TO MARK: mark
    J H Winston
    BH Nicholas

Subscribed and sworn to before me this   5ᵗʰ   day of   May , 1906.

My Comm ex Jan 17-07   BH Nicholas
                                                            Notary Public.

AFFIDAVIT OF ATTENDING PHYSICIAN OR MID-WIFE.

UNITED STATES OF AMERICA, Indian Territory,
Western   District.

I, Susie Deer , a midwife , on oath state that I attended on Lou Annie Deer , wife of   Israel Deer   on the   *(blank)*   day of   July , 1903 ; that there was born to her on said date a   female   child; that said child was living March 4, 1906, and is said to have been named Annie Deer

Applications for Enrollment of Creek Newborn
Act of 1905   Volume XIV

                                    her
                             Susie x Deer
WITNESSES TO MARK: mark
 { Martin Kanard
   H L Marshall

Subscribed and sworn to before me this   15th   day of   May , 1906.

                                   Charles Whitaker
My Commission expires Aug 29 1909   Notary Public.

N.C. 1167

                         Muskogee, Indian Territory, October 24, 1905.

Chief Clerk,
    Seminole Enrollment Division.

Dear Sir:

    There is herewith enclosed one copy of the testimony of September 11, 1905, in the matter of the application for the enrollment of Annie Deere, as a citizen by blood of the Creek Nation.

    The mother of said child states in her testimony of that date that she is a citizen of the Seminole Nation, that said child was born July 10, 1902, that the name of the father of said Annie Deere is Esul or Israel Deere, a citizen of the Creek Nation and that she elects for said child to be enrolled and allotted as a citizen of the Seminole Nation.

    The Creek Enrollment Division of this office is unable to identify said Esul or Israel Deere, as a citizen by blood of the Creek Nation, nor has it been able to secure his election for said child.

    You are requested to advise the Creek Enrollment Division whether or not an application has been made for the enrollment of said Annie Deere, as a citizen by blood of the Seminole Nation and if so what disposition has been made of same.

                         Respectfully,

                                                               Commissioner.

Applications for Enrollment of Creek Newborn
Act of 1905   Volume XIV

HGH

REFER IN REPLY TO THE FOLLOWING:
NC-1167

DEPARTMENT OF THE INTERIOR,
COMMISSIONER TO THE FIVE CIVILIZED TRIBES.

Muskogee, Indian Territory, October 27, 1905.

Alex Posey,
    Clerk in Charge, Creek Enrollment Field Party,
    Okemah, Indian Territory.

Dear Sir:

    There are enclosed herewith copy of new-born Creek Indian card, No. 1167 and a copy of the testimony in the matter of the application for the enrollment of Annie Deere as a citizen by blood of the Creek Nation.

    It appears from the testimony in said case that the name of the father of said child is Esul Deere, a citizen of the Creek Nation, and that the name of the mother of said child is Louina Deere, a citizen of the Seminole Nation. This Office is unable to identify the father of said child as a citizen of the Creek Nation; or its mother as a citizen of the Seminole Nation. You are accordingly directed to take additional testimony in said case for the purpose of identifying the father and mother of said Annie Deere. It is suggested that the correct name of the father may be Esal Polokee.

                    Respectfully,
                      Tams Bixby   Commissioner.
JYM-27-1

GWW

REFER IN REPLY TO THE FOLLOWING:

DEPARTMENT OF THE INTERIOR,
COMMISSIONER TO THE FIVE CIVILIZED TRIBES.

Muskogee, Indian Territory, October 28, 1905.

Chief Clerk,
    Creek Enrollment Division,

Dear Sir:

    Receipt is hereby acknowledged of your letter of the 24th instant, inclosing a copy of the testimony of Lowina Deere under date of September 11, 1905, in the matter of the application for the enrollment of her daughter Annie Deere as a citizen of the Creek Nation, and in which you request to be informed if an application has been made for the

Applications for Enrollment of Creek Newborn
Act of 1905   Volume XIV

enrollment of Annie Deere as a citizen of the Seminole Nation, and what disposition has been made of same.

In reply you are advised that the Seminole Enrollment Division of this office is unable to identify Lowina Deere as a citizen of the Seminole Nation, nor has it been able to find any record of the application for the enrollment of Annie Deere as a New Born Seminole citizen.

      Respectfully,
      Tams Bixby   Commissioner.

ISM

REFER IN REPLY TO THE FOLLOWING:
N.C. 1167.

DEPARTMENT OF THE INTERIOR,
COMMISSIONER TO THE FIVE CIVILIZED TRIBES.

Muskogee, Indian Territory, January 18, 1907.

Clerk in Charge,
 Seminole Enrollment Division.

Dear Sir:

It appears from the records of this office that on September 11, 1905, an application was made, in affidavit form, for the enrollment of Annie Deere as a citizen by blood of the Creek Nation.

It further appears that on the same date the mother of the applicant, Lowina Deere, also referred to in the records of this office as Louina Deere, Lou Annie Deere, nee Lou Annie Beaver, testified that she was a citizen of the Seminole Nation and that she had made application for her minor child, Annie Deere, and still desired to have her enrolled as a citizen of the Seminole Nation.

It appears in evidence that the said Lou Annie Deer or Beaver was lawfully married to the father of the applicant Esul Poloke, who is identified as a citizen of the Creek Nation, opposite roll No. 8748.

You are requested to notify the Creek Enrollment Division whether or not the name of the mother of the applicant appears as a duly enrolled citizen of the Seminole Nation, under any of the various names above mentioned.

It is further desired that the Creek Enrollment Division be notified whether or not application has been made for the said applicant who is variously named as follows: Annie Deer (or Deere), Annie Poloke and Annie Beaver.

      Respectfully,
      Tams Bixby   Commissioner.

Applications for Enrollment of Creek Newborn
Act of 1905   Volume XIV

N C 1167.

Muskogee, Indian Territory, March 7, 1907.

Esal Deere,
    Eufaula, Indian Territory.

Dear Sir:

    You are hereby advised that on March 2, 1907 the Secretary of the Interior approved the enrollment of your minor child, Annie Deere, as a citizen by blood of the Creek Nation and that the name of said child appears upon the roll of new born citizens by blood of the Creek Nation enrolled under the Act of Congress approved March 3, 1905, as number 1267.

    This child is now entitled to allotment and application therefor should be made without delay at the Creek Land Office, Muskogee, Indian Territory.

                        Respectfully,

                                  Commissioner.

DEPARTMENT OF THE INTERIOR,
COMMISSION TO THE FIVE CIVILIZED TRIBES.

Muskogee, Indian Territory, April 15, 1905

    In the matter of the application for the enrollment of certain new-born children as citizens of the Creek Nation.

    Alex Posey, being duly sworn, testified as follows:

EXAMINATION BY THE COMMISSION:
Q State your name, age and postoffice address. A Alex Posey; 31; Muskogee.
Q Are you a citizen of the Creek Nation? A Yes sir.
Q Got your land, have you? A Yes sir.

Applications for Enrollment of Creek Newborn
Act of 1905   Volume XIV

Q Have you been engaged recently in the "field work" of the Dawes Commission in securing evidence about Creek citizens or new-borns? A Yes sir.

Q Have you a list of children for whom application could not be made and about whom you have succeeded in obtaining some information? A Yes sir.

Q You may state the conditions and the names of those children that you desire to make application for. A Yes sir.

Q Name them. A Annie Deere. Born July 10, 1902, a child of _____ Deere and Louina Deere. The father belongs to Okfuskee Canadian, and the mother is a citizen of the Seminole Nation.

    Noda Pologee I understand has some children, but I have not been able to learn their names, or the name of their father. The mother lives near Eufaula.

    Maxey Lewis, of Eufaula Canadian Town, I learn has one child, but I have not been able to learn its name or the name of its mother.

Q This information you received from relatives right around there on April 15, 1905? A Yes sir.

Q Were you informed that the parents of these children were unwilling to make application for their enrollment? A Yes sir.

Q This was the only way the rights of these children could be save by? A Yes, sir. I made every effort to obtain direct information from the parents, but in every instance they refused to give testimony.

INDIAN TERRITORY, Western District.

    I, J. Y. Miller, a stenographer to the Commission to the Five Civilized Tribes, do hereby certify that the above and foregoing is a true and complete translation of my notes as same appear in my stenographic report of this case.

                                                             JY Miller

Subscribed and sworn to before me
   this the 15th day of April,
1905.

                                               Drennan C Skaggs
                                                   Notary Public.

DEPARTMENT OF THE INTERIOR,
COMMISSIONER TO THE FIVE CIVILIZED TRIBES.
Eufaula, I. T., September 11, 1905.

    In the matter of the application for the enrollment of certain new born children as citizens of the Creek Nation.

                JANIE LAWSON, being duly sworn, testified as follows:

BY THE COMMISSIONER:

Applications for Enrollment of Creek Newborn
Act of 1905 Volume XIV

Q What is your name? A Janie Lawson.
Q How old are you? A Twenty-six.
Q What is your post office? A Eufaula, I. T.
Q Are you a citizen of the Creek Nation? A No, sir. United States citizen.
Q Do you know Maxey Lewis? A Yes, sir.
Q Do you know the name of his wife? A No, sir, I don't believe I do. I have seen them and been acquainted with them long enough to know her name.
Q Are they both close neighbors of yours? A Yes, sir.
Q Have they any new born children? A Yes, sir, they have two.
Q About how old is the oldest one? A About three years old. The baby I think, was born in January. It is older than my baby and my baby was born in February.
Q Are they both boys? A Yes, sir, I think they are.
Q You don't know the names of these children do you? A No, sir.

JENNIE LEWIS, being duly sworn, testified as follows:

Through Alex Posey Official Interpreter:

BY THE COMMISSIONER:
Q What is your name? A Jennie Lewis.
Q How old are you? A About thirty.
Q What is your post office address? A Eufaula.
Q Are you a citizen of the Creek Nation? A Yes, sir.
Q To what town do you belong? A Tulsa Canadian.
Q Have you any children for whom you have made no application? A I have two.
Q What are their names? A <u>Billy and Natecha Lewis</u>.
Q When was Billy born? A In September 4, 1902.
Q When was Natecha born? A January 16, 1905.
Q What is the name of the father of these two children? A Maxey Lewis.
Q To what town does he belong? A Eufaula Canadian.

---oooOOOooo---

I, D. C. Skaggs, on oath state that the above and foregoing is a full and true transcript of my stenographic notes as taken in said cause on said date.

D. C. Skaggs

Subscribed and sworn to before me this 16 day of October 1905.

Edw C Griesel
Notary Public.

Applications for Enrollment of Creek Newborn
Act of 1905 Volume XIV

BIRTH AFFIDAVIT.

DEPARTMENT OF THE INTERIOR.
COMMISSION TO THE FIVE CIVILIZED TRIBES.

IN RE APPLICATION FOR ENROLLMENT, as a citizen of the *(blank)* Nation, of Billy Lewis, born on the 4 day of September, 1902

Name of Father: Maxey Lewis   a citizen of the   Creek   Nation.
Eufaula Canadian
Name of Mother: Jennie Lewis (nee Canard)   a citizen of the   Creek   Nation.
Tulsa Canadian

                       Postoffice   Eufaula, I.T.

AFFIDAVIT OF MOTHER.

UNITED STATES OF AMERICA, Indian Territory,
     Western   DISTRICT.

     I, Jennie Lewis, on oath state that I am about 30 years of age and a citizen by blood, of the Creek Nation; that I am the lawful wife of Maxey Lewis, who is a citizen, by blood of the Creek Nation; that a male child was born to me on the 4 day of September, 1902, that said child has been named Billy Lewis, and was living March 4, 1905.

                                    her
                        Jennie x Lewis
Witnesses To Mark: mark
   { Alex Posey
     DC Skaggs

     Subscribed and sworn to before me this 11 day of September, 1905.

                       Drennan C Skaggs
                       Notary Public.

AFFIDAVIT OF ATTENDING PHYSICIAN OR MID-WIFE.

UNITED STATES OF AMERICA, Indian Territory,
     (blank)   DISTRICT.

                                  are personally acquainted with
     We, the undersigned, ~~a~~, on oath state that ~~I~~ we ~~attended on~~ Mrs. Jennie Lewis, wife of Maxey Lewis ~~on the day of , 1~~; that there was born to her on Sept 4, 1902 ~~said date~~ a male child; that said child was living March 4, 1905, and is said to have been named Billy Lewis

                       T.I. Washington
Witnesses To Mark: Ella B. Scott
   {

Applications for Enrollment of Creek Newborn
Act of 1905   Volume XIV

Subscribed and sworn to before me this 11 day of   September , 1905.

Drennan C Skaggs
Notary Public.

DEPARTMENT OF THE INTERIOR,
COMMISSIONER TO THE FIVE CIVILIZED TRIBES.
MUSKOGEE, INDIAN TERRITORY.
JULY 3, 1906.

In the matter of the application for the enrollment as citizens of the Creek Nation, of minor children born to duly enrolled citizens, members of the so called Snake faction.

Alex Posey, being duly sworn, testified as follows:

Q: What is your name? A: Alex Posey.
Q: What is your age? A: 33.
Q: What is your post office address? A: Muskogee.

Statement by Mr. Posey: The following information concerning new born children was received by me at various points in the field subsequent to May 2, 1905.

SALLIE HILL, daughter of John Hill of Okchiye town and Malindy Hill of Okfuskee Canadian town; age of child unknown, post office address of parents, Eufaula, I. T.; information received May 12, 1905.

_____ MITCHELL, child of Waitie Mitchell, a Seminole citizen and Mandy Mitchell, of Tulledega Town (see I-2824); child about two years old, sex unknown, post office address of the parents Hanna, I.T. Information received May 24, 1905.

_____ Sevier, child of Louis Sevier, of Tulsa Canadian town (see I-1783), and Amanda Thompson, of Tookpafka town (see I-2207); child about four years old, female; post office address of parents, Burney, I. T. Information received May 20, 1905.

SONNIE FIELDS, child of Walter Field, of Quassarte No. 2 (C.I. 2615) and Eliza Field, nee Harjo, of Artussee town (C.I. 1558) child born June 2, 1904; male; post office address of parents, Dustin, I. T. Information received June 15 1905.

Applications for Enrollment of Creek Newborn
Act of 1905 Volume XIV

(Note to side of entry: N.C. #1170)

BILLIE BIRD, child of Thomas and Sallie Bird of Weogufke town: over a year old; post office address of parents, Hanna, I. T. Information received June 15, 1905.

HETTIE MITCHELL, child of Lewis Mitchell, of Eufaula Canadian town (C.I. 3248), and Bittie Mitchell, also of Eufaula Canadian town, (C.I. 3248), child born February 19, 1896, and living; post office address of parents, Eufaula, I.T. Information received Mary 18, 1905.

FIRSEY MITCHELL, child of Lewis Mitchell, of Eufaula Canadian town (C.I. 3248), and Bittie Mitchell, also of Eufaula Canadian town, (C.I. 3248); child born March 3, 1898, and living sex unknown; post office address of parents, Eufaula, I.T. Information received Mary 18, 1905.

_____ SEVIER, child of Louis Sevier, of Tulsa Canadian town (see C.I. 1783), and Amanda Thompson, of Tookpafka town (see C.I. 2207); child about a year old, male; post office address of parents, Burney, I. T. Information received May 20, 1905.

SELANIE MITCHELL, child of Lewis Mitchell, of Eufaula Canadian town (C.I. 3248), and Bittie Mitchell, also of Eufaula Canadian town, (C.I. 3248); child born May 3, 1901, and living; female; post office address of parents, Eufaula, I.T. Information received Mary 18, 1905.

_____ JACOB, child of Sampson Jacob of Tulledega town and Selanie Jones, of Arbeka North Fork town, child about four years old; female; post office address of parents Burney, I. T. Information received May 20, 1905.

_____ JACOB, child of Sampson Jacob of Tulledega town and Selanie Jones, of Arbeka North Fork town, child about four years old; female; post office address of parents Burney, I. T. Information received May 20, 1905.

HETTIE TUFFER, child of Tuffer and Sene, both of Pokuntalahassee[sic] town (C.I. 6961); child about six years old; post office of the parents, Trenton I. T. Information received June 14, 1905

SAM POLOKE, child of Esal Poloke of Eufaula Canadian town, (C.I. 3602), and Louisa Polke, nee Beaver, a Seminole; child born October 18, 1905; post office of parents, Eufaula, I.T. Information received May 8, 1906.

RHODA WILDCAT, child of Sandy Wildcat of Arbeka North Fork town (C.I. 1576), and Losanna Wildcat, also of Arbeka North Fork town (C.I. 1576), child over five years old; post office address of parents, Weleetka, I. T. Information received May 5, 1905.

Applications for Enrollment of Creek Newborn
Act of 1905   Volume XIV

JOHN WHITLOW, child of William Whitlow and Semhoye Whitlow; age of child unknown; post office address of parents, Dustin, I.T. Information received May 5, 1905. The Creek towns to which the parents belong are unknown.

NELLIE WEST, child of Lumsey West, of Kialigee town (C.I. 1541) and Emma West, of Thlewarthle town; child over five years old; post office address of parents, Henryetta I. T. Information received May 5, 1905.

HANNAH MOSES (or BEAR), child of Moses Bear, a Seminole, and Nancy Bear, of Thlewarthle town, child born March 2, 1894, and living; post office address of parents, Keokuk Falls, O.T. Information May 1905.

MAUD MOSES (or BEAR), child of Moses Bear, a Seminole and Nancy Bear, of Thlewarthle town, child born February 1, 1898, and living; post office address of parents, Keokuk Falls, O.T. Information May 1905.

TURNER MITCHELL, child of Mitchell Sarwanoka of Okfuskee Canadian town, (C.I. 3583), and Nancy Sarwanoka, of Eufaula Canadian town, (C.I. 3583); child born March 15, 1899, and living; post office address of parents, Eufaula, I. T. Information received April, 1905.

BESSIE MITCHELL, Child of Mitchell Sarwanoka of Okfuskee Canadian town, (C.I. 3583), and Nancy Sarwanoka, of Eufaula Canadian town, (C.I. 3583); child born February 22, 1901, and living; post office address of parents, Eufaula, I. T. Information received April, 1905.

BESSIE SMITH, child of Belcher Smith of Greenleaf town (C.I. 2218) and Hinty Smith (town unknown) child about four years old; post office address of Parents, Okemah, I. T. Information received May 13, 1905.

EDMUND BARNETT, child of Austin Barnett, of Okchiye town (C.I. 3076) and Liza Barnett, (town unknown) child over four years old, post office address of parents, Mellette, I. T. Information received May, 1906.

JOHN _____, child of Sanie, of Alabama town, age unknown; post office address of parents, Weleetka, I. T. Information received March 29, 1906.

Lona Merrick, being duly sworn, states that the above and foregoing is a true and correct transcript of her stenographic notes as taken in said cause on said date.

Lona Merrick

Subscribed and sworn to before me this 11th day of August, 1906.

(SEAL)   Signed)   Edward Merrick.
                                    Notary Public.

Applications for Enrollment of Creek Newborn
Act of 1905 Volume XIV

I, Julia C. Laval on my oath state that the above and foregoing is a true and correct copy of the original.

Julia C. Laval

Subscribed and sworn to before me this 15 day of December, 1906.

Edward Merrick.
Notary Public.

N.C. _____

DEPARTMENT OF THE INTERIOR,
COMMISSIONER TO THE FIVE CIVILIZED TRIBES.
WELEETKA, I. T., November 14, 1906.

In the matter of the application for the enrollment of Sonie Fields as a citizen by blood of the Creek Nation.

ELIZA HARJO, being first duly sworn by, and examined through Alex Posey, a Notary Public, and Official Interpreter, testified as follows:

BY THE COMMISSIONER:

Q What is your name? A Eliza Harjo.
Q How old are you? A 30 or over.
Q What is your postoffice address? A Weleetka.
Q Are you a citizen of the Creek Nation? A Yes sir.
Q To what Creek town do you belong? A Artussee.
Q Have you a minor child named Sonie Fields? A Yes sir, but the child is now dead.
Q When was Sonie born? A June 2, 1904.
Q When did he die? A Died June 30, 1905.
Q Who is the child's father? A Walter Fields, of Quassartie town No. 2.
Q Is Walter Fields our lawful husband? A No sir, we were never lawfully married and are not now living together.
Q Were you ever married? A Yes sir, I was married to Muppeyah, who was also known as Fushutche Harjo, who is now dead.
Q Have you any children enrolled? A Yes sir, Sandy, Sampson, Dudley, Jonah and Joe Harjo, all children of Muppeyah or Fushutche Harjo.
Q Have all of these children been enrolled and given allotments of land? A Yes sir.
Q You did not make application for the enrollment of your deceased child, Sonie, while the Commissioner was receiving applications for the enrollment of new born children in 1905, did you? A No sir, I wanted to go before the Commission at Dustin and make application for the child's enrollment but was prevented by the child's illness form doing so, but I appeared before you afterwards and gave information about the child.
Q Who attended on you at the birth of your child? A There was no one present.

Applications for Enrollment of Creek Newborn
Act of 1905   Volume XIV

    James B. Myers, being first duly sworn, states, that as stenographer to the Commissioner to the Five Civilized Tribes, he recorded the testimony in the foregoing proceedings, and that the above is a true, and correct transcript of his stenographic notes thereof.

                              James B Myers

Subscribed and sworn to before me,
this   10 day of Dec, 1906.   Alex Posey
                                        Notary Public.

JBM

Western District
Indian Territory   SS

    We, the undersigned, on oath state that we are personally acquainted with Eliza Harjo   not wife of   Walter Field   ; and that on or about the   2   day of June , 1904 , a   male   child was born to them and has been named   Sonnie Field ; and that said child was living March 4, 1905. and died on or about June 30, 1905

    We further state that we have no interest in the above case.

                                 her
                           Sally x Lowe
                                mark
                                 her
                         Maggie x Harjo
                                mark

Witness to mark.
  Alex Posey
  JB Myers
  Alex Posey
  JB Myers

Subscribed and sworn to before
me this 27 day of Dec 1906.
                                        Alex Posey
                                          Notary Public.

AFFIDAVIT OF TWO DISINTERESTED WITNESSES.

United States of America, (
Western District,   (ss.
Indian Territory.   (

    We, the undersigned, on oath state that we are personally acquainted with   Eliza Harjo   the   unlawful   wife of   Walter Fields   ; that there was born to her a

Applications for Enrollment of Creek Newborn
Act of 1905 Volume XIV

male child on or about the 2^d day of June, 1904; that the said child has been named Sonnie Fields, and was living March 4, 1905.
We further state that we have no interest in the above case.

Witnesses to mark.
J McDermott

Mary Harjo

Mary Harjo
his
Joe x Mahola
mark

Subscribed and sworn to before me, this 15 day of January, 1907.

J McDermott
My Commission   Notary Public.
Expires July 25" 1907

BIRTH AFFIDAVIT.

DEPARTMENT OF THE INTERIOR,
COMMISSIONER TO THE FIVE CIVILIZED TRIBES.

ENROLLMENT OF MINORS. ACT OF CONGRESS, APPROVED APRIL 26, 1906.

IN RE APPLICATION FOR ENROLLMENT, as a citizen of the Creek Nation, of Sonnie Fields, deceased, born on the 2 day of June, 1904

Name of Father: Walter Fields (C.I. 2615)   a citizen of the Creek Nation.
Name of Mother: Eliza Harjo (C.I. 1558)   a citizen of the Creek Nation.

Tribal enrollment of father Quassarte No. 2   Tribal enrollment of mother Artussee

Postoffice   Weleetka, Indian Territory

AFFIDAVIT OF MOTHER.

UNITED STATES OF AMERICA, Indian Territory,
Western   District.

I, Eliza Harjo, on oath state that I am about 35 years of age and a citizen by blood, of the Creek Nation; that I am not the lawful wife of Walter Fields, who is a citizen, by blood of the Creek Nation; that a male child was born to me on 2nd day of June, 1904, that said child has been named Sonnie Fields, and was living March 4, 1905. and died June 1905

WITNESSES TO MARK:
{ Alex Posey
  JB Myers

her
Eliza x Harjo
mark

Subscribed and sworn to before me this 14 day of November , 1906.

Alex Posey
Notary Public.

REFER IN REPLY TO THE FOLLOWING:

NC 1170.

DEPARTMENT OF THE INTERIOR,
COMMISSIONER TO THE FIVE CIVILIZED TRIBES.

Muskogee, Indian Territory, December 21, 1905.

Alex Posey,
Clerk in Charge Creek Enrollment Field Party,
Dustin, Indian Territory.

Dear Sir:

In the matter of the application for the enrollment of Sonnie Field born June 2, 1904 to Walter Field and Eliza Harjo both citizens by blood of the Creek Nation, you are directed to secure the affidavits of two disinterested witnesses relative to the birth of said child.

Respectfully,

Wm O.Beall
Acting Commissioner.

N.C. 1170.

Muskogee, Indian Territory, March 1, 1907.

Eliza Harjo,
Care Walter Field,
Weleetka, Indian Territory.

Dear Madam:

You are hereby advised that on January 25, 1907, the Secretary of the Interior approved the enrollment of your minor child, Sonnie Field, as a citizen by blood of the Creek Nation, and that the name of said child appears upon the roll of new born citizens by blood of the Creek Nation, enrolled under the Act of Congress approved March 3, 1905, as No. 1225.

Respectfully,

Commissioner.

Applications for Enrollment of Creek Newborn
Act of 1905   Volume XIV

N.B.C. 494

DEPARTMENT OF THE INTERIOR,
COMMISSIONER TO THE FIVE CIVILIZED TRIBES.
Wetuma[sic], Indian Territory, November 2, 1906.

In the matter of the application for the enrollment of Minnie Yahola as a citizen by blood of the Creek Nation.

ADDIE YAHOLA, Being duly sworn, testified as follows: (through Jesse McDermott official interpreter)

By Commissioner:

Q What is your name? A Addie Yahola.
Q What is your age? A About twenty one.
Q What is your postoffice address? A Wetumka, c/o Joe Brooks.
Q Are you a creek[sic] citizen? A Yes.
Q Have you a child named Minnie Yahola? A Yes.
Q When was that child born? A It was in April but I do not know the date or year.
Q Is Minnie living? A No.
Q When did she die? A I do not know that. Amos Harjo my half-brother has a record of her birth and death both.
Q Where does he live? A Over west of here about two miles.
Q Who is the father of Minnie? A Wiley Yahola who is now dead.

AMOS HARJO, being duly sworn, testified as follows: (through Jesse McDermott official interpreter)

By Commissioner:

Q What is your name? A Amos Harjo.
Q What is your age? A About twenty nine.
Q What is your postoffice address? A Barnard.
Q Do you know Addie Yahola? A Yes, she is my halfsister.
Q Do you know a child of hers named Minnie? A Yes.
Q When was that child born? A In April 1904, the 14th I think.
Q Is Minnie Living[sic]? A No.
Q When did she die? A Here is the record of her death.

The witness presents a memorandum book and on nearly the last page of said book appears the following entry: (In Creek writing) The date of Minnie's birth is April 14, 1904. She finished her days January 12, 1906, Friday, Age 1 year and 9 months.

Q When was this record made? A I made that record just about three days after Minnie died. I was not at home when she died or I would have made the record on the day she died.

---oooOOOooo---

Applications for Enrollment of Creek Newborn
Act of 1905   Volume XIV

I, Jesse McDermott, on oath state that the above and foregoing is a full and true transcript of my notes as taken in said cause on said date.

Jesse McDermott

Subscribed and sworn to before me this 3rd day of November, 1906.

(Name Illegible)

My Commission Expires Aug. 17, 1908.   Notary Public.

N.C. 1149.   I.D.

DEPARTMENT OF THE INTERIOR,
COMMISSIONER TO THE FIVE CIVILIZED TRIBES.

In the matter of the application for the enrollment of Minnie Yahola as a citizen by blood of the Creek Nation.

ORDER.

The record in this case shows that on June 14, 1905, there was filed with the Commission to the Five Civilized Tribes at Muskogee, Indian Territory, the application of Addie Yahola for the enrollment of her minor child, Minnie Yahola, as a citizen by blood of the Creek Nation.

The evidence shows that said Minnie Yahola was born April 14, 1904, and that she was living March 4, 1905.

It does not appear from the records of this office that any application was made prior to June 14, 1905, for the enrollment of said Minnie Yahola as a citizen by blood of the Creek Nation.

The Act of Congress approved March 3, 1905, (Public No. 212), provides:

> "That the Commission to the Five Civilized Tribes is authorized for sixty days after the date of the approval of this act to receive and consider applications for enrollment, of children, born subsequent to May twenty-fifth, nineteen hundred and one, and prior to March fourth, nineteen hundred and five, and living on said latter date, to citizens of the Creek tribe of Indians whose enrollment has been approved by the Secretary of the Interior prior to the approval of this act; and to enroll and make allotments to such children."

It is, therefore, ordered that there is no authority of law for the enrollment of said Minnie Yahola as a citizen by blood of the Creek Nation, and that the application for her enrollment as such should be and the same is hereby dismissed.

_____
Commissioner.

Muskogee, Indian Territory,
October 24, 1905

Applications for Enrollment of Creek Newborn
Act of 1905   Volume XIV

DEPARTMENT OF THE INTERIOR.
COMMISSION TO THE FIVE CIVILIZED TRIBES.

In the matter of the death of   Minnie Yahola   a citizen of the   Creek Nation, who formerly resided at or near   Wetumka , Ind. Ter., and died on the 12" day of   January , 1906

AFFIDAVIT OF RELATIVE.

UNITED STATES OF AMERICA, Indian Territory, }
    Western   DISTRICT.

I, Addie Barnett (nee Yahola) , on oath state that I am   about 21   years of age and a citizen by blood , of the   Creek   Nation; that my postoffice address is   Wetumka , Ind. Ter.; that I am the mother   of   Minnie Yahola   who was a citizen, by blood , of the Creek   Nation and that said   Minnie Yahola died on the 12   day of January   , 1906   her

                                        Addie x Barnett nee Yahola

Witnesses To Mark: mark
{ J McDermott
  Joe Brooks

Subscribed and sworn to before me this 2" day of November, 1906

My Commission   J McDermott
Expires July 25" 1907   Notary Public.

AFFIDAVIT OF ACQUAINTANCE.

UNITED STATES OF AMERICA, Indian Territory, }
    Western   DISTRICT.

I, Joe Brooks , on oath state that I am   about 34 years of age, and a citizen by blood   of the Creek   Nation; that my postoffice address is   Wetumka   , Ind. Ter.; that I was personally acquainted with   Minnie Yahola   who was a citizen, by blood , of the   Creek Nation; and that said   Minnie Yahola   died on the   12   day of   January , 1906

                                Joe Brooks

Witnesses To Mark:
{

Subscribed and sworn to before me this 2 day of Nov. , 1906.

Applications for Enrollment of Creek Newborn
Act of 1905 Volume XIV

J McDermott
Notary Public.

BIRTH AFFIDAVIT.

DEPARTMENT OF THE INTERIOR.
COMMISSION TO THE FIVE CIVILIZED TRIBES.

IN RE APPLICATION FOR ENROLLMENT, as a citizen of the Creek Nation, of Minnie Yahola, born on the 14 day of April, 1904

Name of Father: Wiley Yahola   a citizen of the Creek Nation.
Name of Mother: Addie Yahola   a citizen of the Creek Nation.

Postoffice   Wetumka I.T.

AFFIDAVIT OF MOTHER.

UNITED STATES OF AMERICA, Indian Territory, } Western DISTRICT.

I, Addie Yahola, on oath state that I am 25 years of age and a citizen by blood, of the Creek Nation; that I am the lawful wife of Wiley Yahola, who is a citizen, by blood of the Creek Nation; that a female child was born to me on 14th day of April, 1904, that said child has been named Minnie Yahola, and was living March 4, 1905.

                               her
                      Addie x Yahola
Witnesses To Mark: mark
 { J. A. Ostrom
   Louis Dunzy

Subscribed and sworn to before me this 3^{d} day of June, 1905.

J.R. Dunzy
Notary Public.

AFFIDAVIT OF ATTENDING PHYSICIAN OR MID-WIFE.

UNITED STATES OF AMERICA, Indian Territory, } Western DISTRICT.

I, Mary Lowe, a mid-wife, on oath state that I attended on Mrs. Addie Yahola, wife of Wiley Yahola on the 14th day of April, 1904 ; that there was born to her on said date a female child; that said child was living March 4, 1905, and is said to have been named Minnie Yahola

Applications for Enrollment of Creek Newborn
Act of 1905 Volume XIV

                                                  her
Witnesses To Mark: Mary x Lowe
  { J. A. Ostrom   mark
    Louis Dunzy

Subscribed and sworn to before me this 3^d day of June , 1905.

                                              J.R. Dunzy
                                                  Notary Public.

                                                                                                  ISM

REFER IN REPLY TO THE FOLLOWING:
N.C. 1149.

DEPARTMENT OF THE INTERIOR,
COMMISSIONER TO THE FIVE CIVILIZED TRIBES.

                                  Muskogee, Indian Territory, June 20, 1906.

Addie Yahola,
    Wetumka, Indian Territory.

Dear Madam:

      In the matter of the application for the enrollment of your minor child, Minnie Yahola, as a citizen of the Creek Nation, you are hereby advised that it is required that you furnish this office with the affidavits of yourself and the midwife in attendance at the birth of said child. For this purpose there is inclosed herewith blank form of birth affidavit. Said affidavits should show the name of the child, the names of its parents, the date of its birth and whether or not it was living on March 4, 1906.

      You are further advised that in order that you and Wiley Yahola, the father of said child, may be identified upon the rolls of citizens of the Creek Nation, it will be necessary that you furnish this office with your maiden name, the names of your parents and other members of your family, the Creek Indian town to which you belong and the roll number as same appears upon your and your said husband's deeds or allotment certificates to land in the Creek Nation.

      This matter should receive your prompt attention.

                                  Respectfully,
                                  Tams Bixby
BA   Commissioner.

Applications for Enrollment of Creek Newborn
Act of 1905   Volume XIV

NBC 494.

Muskogee, Indian Territory, October 25, 1906.

Jesse McDermott,
    Wetumka, Indian Territory.

Dear Sir:

    In the matter of the application for the enrollment of Minnie Yahola, born April 14, 1904, to Addie and Wiley Yahola, as a citizen of the Creek Nation, you are advised to procure proof as to whether said child was living March 4, 1906.

    Application was made in affidavit form for the enrollment of said child June 14, 1905, too late to be enrolled under the act of March 3, 1905, and letters to the parents of said child requesting the above proof have been returned unclaimed.

    Blank form of birth affidavit, is herewith enclosed which you are requested to have properly executed and returned to this office at an early date.

                      Respectfully,

                                      Commissioner.

1 BA

NC 1171

Muskogee, Indian Territory, March 7, 1907.

Wiley Yahola,
    Care of Joe Brooks,
        Wetumka, Indian Territory.

Dear Sir:

    You are hereby advised that on March 2, 1907 the Secretary of the Interior approved the enrollment of your minor child, Minnie Yahola, as a citizen by blood of the Creek Nation and that the name of said child appears upon the roll of new born citizens by blood of the Creek Nation enrolled under the Act of Congress approved March 3, 1905, as number 1268.

    This child is now entitled to allotment and application therefor should be made without delay at the Creek Land Office, Muskogee, Indian Territory.

                      Respectfully,

                                      Commissioner.

Index

ADAMS
   D Mollie 239
   Mollie 243
AHARLEY 263
AHULLEY................................. 264
ALEXANDER
   L 129
   L, MD 129
   Rasp... 187
ALLEN
   R C 85,222
ANDERSON
   Lucy...................141,142,143,145
   P H.................................. 256,257
   Ruth 142
   Susan 141
ANNIE
   Millie.. 54
ARBUCKLE
   Selina...................................... 223
ARTUSSEE
   Annie 192,193,194,195
   John 192,193,194,195
   Mose...................192,193,194,195
ASBURY
   Jimsy 22
   Wicey 22

BARNETT
   Addie 365
   Alice 36,37
   Austin 358
   Charley 35
   Charlie 35,36
   Dave 38,39
   Edmund 358
   John 34,35
   Liza.. 358
   Mary 34,37,38,39,153,154,155
   Nancy 38,39
   Sukey.........................34,35,36,37
   Thomas 153,154
   Tom 34,35,36,37,38

A W 177,179,180
BASHAW
   Laura 87
BEALL
   Wm O 269,362
BEAMS
   Annie ... 152,153,154,155,156,157
   Charles 153,154,155,156,157,158
   Charles W................................157
   Charlie 152
   Fishie M 156,157
   Rhoda 152,153,154,155,156,
   157,158
   Tishie M 152,154,155,157,158
   Tissie M....................................157
BEAR
   Hannah 358
   Lena.........8,20,23,24,25,26,28,29
   Lydia 20,21,22,23,24,25,28,29
   Maud 358
   Moses 358
   Nancy 358
   Thomas..20,21,22,23,24,25,28,29
   Thos..24,27
BEARDEN
   Sarah E 10
BEAVER
   Annie 351
   Heliswa..................................8,26
   Kaska......................................8,26
   Lou Annie 348,351
   Louina 342
   Louisa.......................................357
   Peter 96,97
   Phebe 95,96
   Phebie.................97,102,103,104
BEIDLEMAN
   Geo C 208
BEIDLEMAN & WINSTON 213
BEIDLEMAN & WINSTOR......212
BETHEL
   David F................................93,94
   Dora......................................93,94

Index

Julia Lavinia 93,94
BIGHEAD
   Celina 40
   Salina 123,124,125,126,127
   Sam 123,124,125,126,127
   Sampson 125,126
BIRD
   Billie 357
   Geo Y, Jr 248,249
   Melissa 332
   Sallie 357
   Thomas 357
BISHOP
   Letha 252
   Maggie 252
BIXBY
   Commissioner 279
   Mr 275
   Tams .... 5,43,47,50,63,64,66,76, 82,100,106,125,126,133,157,160, 163,173,174,190,211,212,231,244, 254,259,265,270,275,285,288,300 ,309,311,321,326,328,338,345, 350,351,367
BLAND 130
   Billie 131,132,133
   Jennie 131,132,133,134,135
   Lewis 131,132,133,134,135
   Lucy 132,135
   Winford 133,134,135
BLEND
   Roley 130
BOLING
   Dixie Self 246,247,248
   Martha F 246,247,248,250
   W F 246,247,248,250
   Walter Gilmore 250
BONNET
   H R 17
BOONE
   Thomas L 81
BRADY
   Clayton 248,249

BRASHAR
   Andrew 80,181
BRIGHTMAN
   Fannie E 253
BROOK
   Jeanetta 3
BROOKS
   Joe 363,365,368
BROWN
   Belle 278,279
   Delpha May 278,279
   John I 31
BRUNER
   Adaline 188
   Lou 250,251,252
   Nathan 250,251,252
   Pearl 250,251,252
BUFORD
   Charles 237
BURGES
   Lyddia C 244
BURGESS
   Ben 238,240,246
   Benjamin E 239,241,242,243, 244,245
   Benjiman 238
   Lyddia 239
   Lyddia C 242,243,244,245
   Lyddia E 239,243
   Lydia 240
   Lydia C 238,242,245
   May 238,245
   Raymond 243
   Raymond B 238,239,240,242, 243,244,245,246

CAIN
   Budy 300,301,302,333,334,335
   Daniel 332,333,334,335
   Nicey 300,333
   Nicy 334,335
   Nisey 302,333
   Selina 300,335

Selma 333
CAKOCHEE 146
CANARD
   Jennie 355
   Susan 115,118
CARRUTH
   Dicey 158
   Lewis 158
   Thomas 158,160
CARSON
   M D 279
CASTILE
   Hosey 161
   Lizzie 161
CASTILLO
   Etta 233
CASTLEBERRY
   J E 140
CHARTE
   Cristie 22
   Loney 21,22,23
   Rhoda 22
CHECOTAH
   Sam 54
CHECOTE
   Martin L 40
   Samuel J 57,58
CHILDERS
   Chisso 184,185
   Chissoe 184
   Effie 184,185,186
   Millie 184,185,186
CHOFULOP 260,273
CHRISTIAN
   Nathanial D 186
CHUPCO
   Jenely 146
   John 146
   Johnson 146
   Leetka 146
   Letka 146
CLAWSON
   W R 98,101

CLAYBON
   Dora 257,258
   John 255,257,258,259
   Sam 255,257,258,259
CLENOWES 263
CLOUD
   Cinda 164
   Laslie 164
   Lizzie 164,165,166
   Stephen 167
COLBERT
   Daniel 121,122,123
   Jemima 121,122,123
   William 121,122,123
COLLINS
   Jacob M 31,32,33
   Lewis 81
   Nancy D 31,32,33
   Roy 31,32,33
CORSER
   Ben 23
COSARPA 279
COSARPE 278
CRAWFORD
   Emma 280
CROSBY
   G W 203,204,205
CROWSON
   Robert 92
CUNDEL 262,274
CUPKO
   Heneha 147
CUSSAMACHA 28

DAN
   Lizzie 214
   Mary 214
   Somecher 214
DAVIDSON
   C A 90
   Charles A 26,91,241
   Chas A 26,27,91,241,242
DAVIS

Index

Bert 103,104
Josiah G 250
Sam C 166
Saml C 167
Sam'l C 167
Wisey 229
DAY
  E B 69,70
DEER 344
  Annie 348,351
  Barney 315,316
  Israel 348
  Joe 311,312,313
  Lawyer 96
  Lou Annie 348,351
  Lula 310,311,312,313
  Mary 310
  Mattie 315,316
  Miley ... 310,311,312,313,315,316
  Susie 348,349
DEERE
  Annie 19,341,342,343,344,
  345,346,347,349,350,351,352,353
  Charlie 75,76,77,78,79
  Esal 344,352
  Esul 341,345,346,347,349,350
  Israel 349
  Isreal 345,347
  Lou Annie 344,351
  Louina 19,342,343,345,346,
  350,351,353
  Lowina 341,346,347,350,351
  Lumdey 76
  Lumsey 77,78,79
  Maley 75,76,77,79
  Mary 76
  Noah 75,76,77,79
  Susie 25,342,346,347
DEERISAW
  Barney 80
  Toche 80
  Tuxey 80
DEN

Lizzie 216,217
Mary 215,216,217
Somihchar 216,217
Somihehar 215
DERRISAW
  Barney 82,83,84
  Toche 82,83,84
  Tuxey 82,83,84
DERRSAW
  Barey 81
  Barney 80,81
  Togie 80,81
  Tuxey 80,81
DEW
  Legus 221
  Liela 221
  Madella E 221
DILL
  W H 215
DOAK
  Mattie 280
DODGE
  Elizabeth 185
DONOVAN & GRIESEL 110
DOYLE
  Arthur 86,87
  Author 88,89
  Clarrance William 86,88,89
  Lara 89
  Laura 88
  Lava 86
  Mose 89,90,92,93
  Roseter E 89,92,93
  Sarah A 89,93
  Thomas E 89,90,92,93
DREW
  Bettie 85
  Legus C 222
  Leila 222
  Lela S 221
  Madella E 222
DUBOSE
  A 236

Index

A, MD 236
DUNN
  Bert............282,283,284,285,286, 287,288,289,290
  Burt................................ 282,287
  Susie 282,283,284,285,286, 287,288,289,290
  Sussie............................. 284,286
  Tupper 215,216,262,265,266, 267,274,282,283,284,285,286,287, 288,290,297,298,299
DUNSON
  Thos H......................306,307,308
DUNZY
  J R..............300,302,305,306,307, 308,311,312,313,314,316,319,327, 328,330,332,333,334,335,336,337 ,340,366,367
  Louis...305,312,314,322,330,334, 335,336,337,366,367
DYSON
  Wesley M 117,119,120

EDWARDS
  J O... 113
EPSEY 223
ESKRIDGE
  C C 199,200,202

FAIN
  J N 17
  J N, MD................................... 17
FARROW
  Anna 18
FIELD
  Eliza..................................... 356
  Sonnie....................356,360,362
  Walter 356,360,362
  William................................ 304,305
FIELDS
  Sonie..................................... 359
  Sonnie................................... 361
  Walter 359,360,361

FIFE
  Eliza 303
  Jennie 303
  Nixey....................................303
FINCH
  Luther 144
FISH
  Lewis...................293,294,295
  Lwqia 295
  Meleya.................293,294,295
  Poawy 295
  Posey 293,294,295
FISHER
  Rosie........34,35,37,38,39,154,155
  Seaborn........34,35,37,38,154,155
  Seaorn......................................39
FIXICO
  Janily 149
FLEMING 306,314,322
  Owens..................................272
FLESHER
  M B 238
FLYNN
  T W 255,256,259
FORD
  P M..90
FORTER-POKOSKA
  Jennie 135
FOSTER
  Chotkey 304,305
  Jennie 131
  Minnie 115
  Noah 110,111
  Sallie..........115,116,117,118,119, 120,121
  Sam...............................131,136
FOWLER
  J W 122
FOX
  Ada.............172,174,177,178,183
  Addie.........173,174,176,177,179, 180,181,182
  Ettie 171,173

James..........174,176,177,179,182
Jeannetta........................170,171
Jennetty....................172,173,183
Jim.............170,172,173,175,176,
177,178,183
Jimmie........173,174,175,180,181
Sandy.........171,173,174,175,176,
177,178,179,180,181,182,183
FUCINDA............................261,273

GANO
   Katy...8,26
   Nicey..8,26
GARRIGUES
   Anna.......71,131,147,165,261,302
GIERKES
   Wm F A.................................126
GILLIS
   E L..29
   Elizabeth.........................185,186
   Ellen..185
   Elmer....................................29,30
GOLING
   Martha F.................................249
   W F..249
   Walter Gilmore......................249
GOTTS
   Lucy R....................................319
GRAHAM
   M F...................................120,121
GRANT
   Willie N..................................292
GRAY
   Lewis......................................110
   Millie......................................110
GRAYSON
   Annie......................................235
   Julia..................................278,279
GREEN
   Haggie......................338,339,340
   Hagie.................317,320,323,325
   Nancy.......................338,339,340
   Sallie...........318,320,324,339,340

GREENE
   M A...................................234,235
GREENHAW
   Bessie.....................................247
   Mary A............................247,248
   Mattie.....................................247
GRIESEL
   C...71
   E C.........42,52,59,61,99,110,112,
   116,118,123,128,129,132,134,135,
   139,143,150,152,159,193,198,206
   ,214,220,228,229
   Edw C....2,3,4,15,21,23,45,52,68,
   69,116,118,119,127,152,164,187,
   188,189,190,200,201,203,207,210,
   224,242,262,274,334,342,343,354
   Edward C................................207
GUIRE
   John..156

HADRICK
   Wrichel..................................272
HAGAN
   Charley....................................92
HAINS
   G H...305
   H G.....56,96,97,102,103,162,304
   Henry G.1,14,44,45,147,251,261,
   273,304,305
HALE
   Bunnie...............296,297,298,299
   David.......................296,297,298
   Millie.................................296,297
HALLEY......................................263
HAMILTON
   Dr..12
HARDIN
   Mary.......................................237
HARJO
   Ahalok....................................162
   Ahpahle..................................224
   Ahpale.............................223,225
   Amos......................................363

Index

Arbuckle 223,224,225
Bennie 219,220
Chanco 324
Christy 148,197
David 96,98,99,105
Dudley 359
Edwad 43
Edward 42
Eliza 40,359,360,361,362
Ella Ruth 217,218
Ethel 40,41
Fred 317,318,319,320,321, 322,323
Fushutche 359
H M 207,217,218
Hannah 94,95,96,100,101,102, 103,104,105
Hepsey . 175,177,179,180,181,182
Ithas 278,279
Joe 359
Jonah 359
Jos H 311,312
Kate M 217,218
Kogee 317,318,319,320, 321,322,323
Lewis 146,148,196,219,220
Liza 41,42,121,122
Lizzie 40
Maggie 360
Mandy 324
Mary 361
Ochee 323
Ophila 278,279
Peter 95,96,97,98,99,100,101, 103,104,126
Philliby 323,324,325,326, 328,329
Robert 94,96,97,98,104,105
Rosa 328,329
Rosey ... 323,324,325,326,327,328
Sampson 278,279,359
Sandy 323,324,359
Sango ... 323,324,325,326,328,329

Shanco 323,324,325
Sophia 95
Stephen 318,319,321,322,323
Steven 317,318,320
Sukie 146
Sulphur 40,41,42
Sundulla 95
Sunduller 97,102
Susie 95,97,98,99,100,101,102, 103,104,105
Thomas 192,194
Willie 146
Wisey 219,220,226
Wotko 299
Yardeka 225
HAR-KA-WA-THLANY 70
HARLAN
  J 88
HARRIS
  A W 137
  A W, MD 137
HARRISON
  R P 87,88
  Robert P 87
HARRY
  Edmond 167
  Martha 235
HARTLEY
  Louisa 272
HARVISON
  Geo S 192,194
HARY
  Cornelius 167
HATFIELD 13
  Charles W 11,16
  Mr 12
HAWKINS
  George 199,201
HAYNES
  Frank L 292
  Lasley 292
  Sukey Haikey 292
HAYNEY

Sam 53
HE-KA-WA-THLA-NY 69
HENEHA
　Eannah 200
HENNEHA
　Eannah 202
HICKMAN
　M C 153,154,156
HILL
　Bunnie 297,298,299,300
　David 297,298
　John 356
　Malindy 356
　Millie 297,298
　Richard J 234,235,236,258
　Sallie 356
　William 306,307,308
HINHA
　Lelah 199,202
HINKLE
　O C 317,318,320,323,324
　Oliver C 318,321,325
HITCHCOCK
　E A 278
HODGE
　Peter 95
HOLLANDS
　Henrietta 272
HOLMAN
　Dora 93,94
HOLT
　Z I J 30,233,292
HOMAHTA
　Chepe 8,26
　Folle 8,26
HUDDLESTON
　C A 216
HUGHES
　G C 70
HUMPHREYS
　Alice 272
　Reuben 272

INGRAM
　R J 179,180
　T J 177
ISHULKER 99

JACK
　Betsey 166
JACOB
　Jeanetta 224,227
　Jeannetta 231,232
　John 224,226,227
　Nicey 229,231,232
　Sam 225,226,227,228
　Sampson 357
　Shawnee 228,231,232
JACOBS 226
　Jeanetta 225,230
　Jeannetta 228,229
　John 225,226,228,230
　Nicey 226,229
　Sam 225
　Sampson 225
　Shawnee 223,225,228,229,230
JANAWAY
　Preston 177,179,180
JANNAWAY
　Preston 178
JANWAY
　Preston 81,89,92,93,172,173
JEFFERSON
　Tolitha 275,281
JENNIE 263
JIMHOKER 165
JOHNSON
　Ahullie 262,263,264,270,
　　272,274
　Culley 263
　Gabriel 110
　Harpley 110,111,112,113,114
　India 263,264,265
　Indian 264,269
　Indie 262,263,264,266,267,
　　268,269,270,271,272,274

376

Jeanetta 112,114
Jennetta 112,113,114
Jennette 110,111
Keeper 110,111,112,113,114
Louana 275,276,277,278,279, 280,281
Lydia 24,27
Mandoche 262,263,268,274
Mandochee 264,265,266,268, 269,270,271,272
Manoche 269,270,272
Mary 269
Miller 263,264
Monoche 263,264,265,268, 271,272
Monochee 267
Onate 8,26
Peter 275,276,281
Susanna 8,26
Susie 1,2,3,4,5,6,7,8
Susue 2
Tolitha 276,281
Wiley 262,269,274
JONES
 Louisa 11,16
 Selanie 357

KANARD
 Martin 349
KELL
 Katie 140
KELLEY
 Marshall 140,141,142,143, 144,145
 Newman 140,141,142,143, 144,145
 Susan 141,142,143,144,145
KELLY
 Amy 1,2,3,4,5,6,7,8,26
 James 5,6,8
 Jim 1,2,3,4,5,7
KENDALL 262,274
KENNEDA

Chloe 199,202
KEYES
 C M 234,235
KIDDO
 Ben 23
KIMBLE
 C C 126
KING
 Amos 319
 Budy 332
 George 340
 Kogee 312
 Lizzie 341
 Peter 340
KNIGHT
 Ramsey 199,202

LAFALLIER
 Louie A 278
 Louis A 279
LARRABEE
 C F 280
 Cv F 271
LAVAL
 J C 304,305
 Julia C 304,359
LAWSON
 Janie 353,354
LETTS
 Frank B 9,10
 Oscar Lovick 9,10
 Susan L 9,10
LEWIS
 Billy 354,355
 Daniel 6
 Jennie 354,355
 Johnson 1,4,6
 Maxey 19,343,353,354,355
 Natecha 354
LIBROWSKI
 Senora 122
LINDSEY
 Willie 272

Index

LITTLE
  Liddie C 241
  Lydia 238
LOGAN
  S J 44,47
  Sam 45,109
  Sam J 50
LONEY
  Racael 174
  Rachael 174,181
  Rachel 177,179,180,182
LONG
  Sam 171
LONY
  Wash 326,327
LOSKEY 226
LOUDERMILK
  S E 32
LOWE
  Losanna 146
  Louie 146
  Mary 366,367
  Sally 360
  Sukey 36
LUCUS
  J B 237
LYBRAND
  R H 241
LYNCH
  Robert E 167,168,169,185,186

McADOO
  W C 145
McCOMBS
  Arthur E 85
  Bill 23
  Jannetta 85
  Tookah 84,85
  William 21,302
McCOY
  Peggy 278,279
McDERMOTT
  J 41,42,55,58,59,60,61,80,
  88,92,99,112,123,124,127,128,129,
  130,131,132,135,137,138,139,143
  ,150,152,159,165,167,174,175,
  180,181,187,188,189,190,193,198,
  210,214,218,220,228,230,240,261
  ,264,302,365,366
  Jesse 8,42,53,54,59,60,61,69,
  78,79,83,99,112,116,118,123,127,
  128,129,132,134,135,139,143,147,
  150,159,174,176,187,188,189,190
  ,193,198,210,214,220,228,229,
  238,263,317,318,320,323,324,332,
  363,364,368
McDERMOTT, ... 175
McDRMOTT
  J 361
McELWAIN
  B F 87
McGEE
  R C 91
McGILL
  Rosetta 90
McGIRT
  Jimmy 335
  Lena 278,279
McINTOSH 162
  Ben 70
  Bertha 71,74
  Bertha A 71,72,73,74
  Charles Curtis 71,72,73,74
  Charles E 72,73,74
  Charley 161
  Charlie 70,71,72
  Charlie E 71,72,74
  David 161
  George 278,279
  Julia 278,279
  Katie 161
  L G 170
  Lee 161
  Polly 234
  Rosa 226
McLAGAN

Geo 40
McNAE
   Bettie 236,237
   Emma 236,237
   Robison 236,237
MAGGIE 263
MAHOLA
   Joe 361
MALONE
   Annie 272
MALOT
   H G 282,283,284,286,287,289
MANSKER
   D J 31
MARS & MARS 280
MARSHALL
   Charley 67
   Charlie 68,69,70
   H L 349
   Henry 67,68,69,70
   Martha 67,68,69,70
MARTIN
   Wm T, Jr................................. 171
   Wm, Jr 14
MATHIS
   W B 69,70
MEADOWS
   James D 186
MERRICK
   Edward 111,304,358,359
   Lona 95,96,97,102,103,110,
   111,162,165,166,318,320,321,325,
   358
MEWIKE 278,279
MIDDLETON
   Sintha.............................. 138,139
MIKEY
   Lizzie 214
MILLER
   Bettie 113
   J Y 19,55,88,91,124,242,
   264,293,333,334,344,353
MILLIE 262,274

MITCHELL
   Bessie 358
   Bittie......................................357
   Firsey....................................357
   Hepsey..................................126
   Hettie 357
   Lewis.....................................357
   Mahlahsee 8,26
   Mandy 356
   Selanie 357
   Turner...................................358
   Waitie 356
MITCHENER
   W C 218
   W C, MD 218
MONDAY
   Annie 52,53,54,56,57,58,59,
   61,62,63,64,65,66,67
   Edna 52,53,54,55,56,60,61,62,
   63,64,66,67
   Elizabeth................53,54,62,63,65
   Jennette..54
   Lizzie....52,53,54,55,56,57,58,59,
   60,61,62,63,64,65,66
   March 52,54,55,56,57,58,59,
   60,61,62,63,64,66
   Martin...54
MORRISON
   S A................................117,120
MORROW
   J B 237
MORTON
   Joseph C 138,140
   P K...121
MOSE
   Hannah 358
MOSES
   Maud 358
MOSS
   F L 175,176
MOTT
   M L......................10,183,269,277
   Mr.......................................12,13

MOWBRAY
   Geo W 239,240,241,243
   Geo W, Rev 241
MULLINS
   Ed 16
MUPPEYAH 359
MYERS
   Betsey 127,128,129
   J B 229,360,361
   James B 24,360
   Laura M 127,128
   Oscar D 129
   Wm F 127,128,129

NAGEE 124
NEWMAN
   Wm C 145
NICHOLAS
   B H 348

ORCUTT
   Alice 72,73
OSTROM
   J A 366,367

PAKOSKA
   Billie 130,133
   Jennie 131
   Joe 130
   Lewis 130
   Lucy 130
   Winford 130,131
PANTHER
   J F 187,188
PARKER
   R E 140
PARRISH
   Zera E 32,33,52,207
   Zera Ellen 15
PATTON
   Dora 137
   Emma 137,138,139,140
   J P 137,138,139,140

   Leo Ora 139,140
   Lora 138,139
PERRYMAN
   Anna 29,30
PHILLIPS
   Johnson J 27
PINKEY
   Jimmie 163,164
   Lilia 164
   Lillia 163,164
   Willie 163,164
PINKY
   Eliza 161
   Jimmie 161,163
   Jimmy 162
   Lilia 161
   Lizzie 161,162
   Willie 162
PITTS
   Barbee 15
   Emma 10,11,12,13,14,15,
   16,17,18
   Frank 11
   Frank F 11,13,15
   Frank Field 15,16
   Frank Fields 17
   Major Barbee 10,11,12,13,14,
   15,16,17,18
   William 13
   William Robinson 13
PLUMLEE
   R S 222
   R S, MD 222
POKOSKA
   Jennie 135,136
   Lewis 135,136
   Lucy 136
   Winford 135,136
POLK
   Dan 28,29
POLKE
   Louisa 357
POLLARD

A J 30
A J, MD 30
POLOGEE
   Esul 342
   Loda 342
   Lydia 21,22,23,342
   Neda 21,22
   Noda 19,343,353
POLOKE
   Annie 351
   Esal 357
   Esul 351
   Lydia 28
   Sam 357
   Susie 29
POLOKEE
   Esal 350
POSELL
   Hester 278,279
   Myrtle 278,279
POSEY
   Ale 354
   Alex 1,3,7,8,18,19,21,22,24,
   25,26,28,29,46,49,75,77,96,146,
   148,149,164,166,195,196,197,207,
   209,219,220,223,224,225,226,227
   ,229,231,260,261,268,273,293,
   294,295,298,343,346,347,350,352,
   355,356,359,360,361,362
   Wm 172,178
POSTKA 147
POSTOAK
   Charley 234,235,236
   Jennie 235,236
   Julia 234
   Rachel 234,235,236
PROCTOR
   Dennis Flinn 252,253
   Susan 252,253
   Toney E 252,253
PULSUMA 123
PYLE
   Theodore T 180

RAIFORD
   Arthur E 84
   Jannetta 84
   Tookah 84
RANDALL
   Lizzie 53
   Mina 53,54
   Minor 57
RANDEL
   Minah 59,61
RAY
   Laura 204
REGMER
   C E 57
RICHARD
   Eastman 44,45,46,47,48,49,
   50,51
   Jennetta 45
   Mane 46
   Minnie 44,45,46,47,48,49,
   50,51
   Sam 45
   Samuel 45
   Yana 46,48,49
   Yanah 48,51
   Yarna 45,47
   Yarner 44
RICHARDSON
   Ivy 278,279
ROBERT
   Cundel 268
   Eundel 260,273
   Indie 268,269
   Indy 260,273
   Mary 269
   Millie 260,269,273
ROBERTS
   Cainey 262,274
   Indie 261,262,273,274
   Johnson 262,274
   Kendall 261,263,266,267,273,274
   Mary 262,274
   Warley 263

Index

Wiley..........262,263,264,265,266, 267,268,270,272,274
RODGERS
  Hanah 258
ROGERS
  Dora.........................255,259,260
  Hannah 255,257,258,259
  Mary Ellen............................ 221
  Rufus 255,257,259
  Samuel L 258
ROSS
  Zepherina.............................. 272
RUBLE
  George W 94
RUSHING
  Frank W................................ 253
RUSSELL
  W H 57

SAMPSEY.................................. 124
SAMPSON
  Dan.. 229
SANGER
  Amanda 253
SANIE.. 358
SARTY 8,26
SARWANOKA
  Mitchell 358
  Nancy 358
SAUNDERS
  Walter A 40
SAWYER
  Alma...................................... 309
  Almon........303,304,306,307,308, 310
  Cindy 309
  Eliza...........303,304,305,306,307, 308,310
  Ellen 303,309
  Elmer 300
  Moses 303,309
  Samuel.......302,303,305,308,309, 310

  Synda.................................... 303
  Wesley........302,304,305,306,307, 308,309,310
SCHOCK
  E E 35,36,37,38,39,154, 155,156
  E E, NP................................. 153
SCOTT
  Ella B....................................355
  James 98,101,103,104
  Jennie 219
  Kizzie 121,122
  Lizzie........................330,331,332
  Rosanna...........................331,332
  Setepake 8,26
  Wiley........................330,331,332
  Winey...................................337
SEBER..................................... 165
  Jimmie.............. 164,165,166,167, 168,169,170
  Lizzie............... 164,165,166,167, 168,169,170
  Mrs 165
  Sampson 164,165,166,167, 168,169,170
SELUMBER
  Robert................................... 171
SEMIHOYE.................223,224,225
SENE 357
SESSIONS
  Litsey L 142,144
SEVERS
  F B..207
SEVIER
  Louis...............................356,357
SHABER
  H W 339,340
  Henry W 331,332
  Smith 332
SHALBY
  David 69
SHARP
  Dug................................192,194

SHELBY
  David 68
SHERWOOD
  L E 136
  Mrs Roena 136
SHOCK
  E E 34
SILWA 217
SILWAR 215
SIMPSON
  Estelle 94
SIMS
  E W 256,257
SKAGGS
  D C 1,2,3,4,7,20,21,23,25,46,
  49,75,77,148,149,171,196,197,219,
  223,224,226,227,262,274,294,295
  ,342,346,347,354,355
  Drennan C 6,7,19,25,48,49,
  72,75,77,85,107,147,253,261,273,
  293,294,295,344,346,347,353,355,
  356
SLADEN
  John 254,256
  Sam 254,260
  Samuel 256,257
SLOZN
  Lillie 146
  Lodie 146
  Peter 146
SMITH
  A A 237
  Belcher 358
  Bessie 358
  Hinty 358
  Joe 171
  John 331
  Lawrence 278,279
  T H 292
  W J 255
SNAKE 44,109,146,225,301,
305,312,314,322,327,330,334,336,
356

SNOW
  Martha 68
SOON
  Sallie 159
SPENCER
  W J 72,73
SPLAWN
  Effie May 272
STANFIELD
  H A 256,257
STEWART
  Lucy 340
SULPHUR
  James 20
SUTHERLAND
  George 278,279

TAHAKEE 294
TAYLOR 162
  Abram 161
  Jemima 122
  Lilia 162
  Lizzie 192
  M D 250
  M D, MD 250
  Maleah 198
  Roley 195,196
  Sammy 161
  Sissie 162
  Wiley 196
  Wisey 220
THATCHER
  Charley Dee L 232,233
  Nancy 232,233
  S B 232,233
THLOCCO
  Neha 95
THOMAS
  Thomas 272
THOMPSON
  Amanda 356,357
TIGER
  Albert 159

Index

Anna 290,291,292
Ben 291,292
Dicey 158,159
Janily 149
Jinalee 147,148,149,151
Jnalee 150
Kitka 149
Lietka 147,148,149,150
Litka 149,151
Martha 68
Mary 290,291,292
Nancy 147,148,149,151
Thomas 159
William 8,26
TILLEY
 Annie 203,204,205
 Eannah 199,200,201,202, 203,205
 Frank 199,200,201,204,205
 James 199,200,201,202,203, 204,205
 Laura 204,205
 Laura May 201,202,203
 May Laura 205
TIMOTHY
 Eliza 105,106,107,108,109
 Ella 105,106,107,109
 John 48,105,106,107,108,109
TONEY
 Foley 146
 Lijah 146,196
 Lodger 196,197
 Maleah 196
 Meleah 196
 Miles 197
 Rogers 196
 Wiley 195,196,197
TOONEY
 Lodger 198
 Maleah 198
 Wiley 198
TUCKER
 Irene 272

TUFFER
 Hettie 357
TYLER
 Nancy 219

VANDERGRIFF
 Hazy Ann 280
VANN
 Wm 255
VAUGHN
 John W 278,279
VIERSEN
 A A 144

WALKER
 Annie 225,226
 Cheparnoche.........................226
 E H 172,178
 Sleche 225,226
 Willie 224,225
WARD
 Della 128
WASHINGTON
 T I 355
WEAVER
 Emma 236,237
 Mary 237
WEHR
 L B 252
WEST
 Emma 358
 J 113
 Lumsey 358
 Mary 262,274
 Nellie 358
WHITAKER
 Harles 349
WHITE
 Adeline 2,7
WHITLOW
 John 358
 Semhoye 358
 William 358

WILCOX
C E 87
WILDCAT
Losanna 357
Rhoda 357
Sandy 357
WILLIAMS
Dora 255,259
Eli 206,207,208,209,210, 211,212,213
Haddie 212
John 206,207,208,209,210, 211,212,213
Mary 207,208,209,210,211,212
Mary Jane 280
Nora 254,256,257,258
WILLIE 263
WILSON
Annie 186,187,188,190,191
Enus 188,189,190,191
Grace ... 186,187,188,189,190,191
Jesse E 272
S P 252
Thomas 186,187,188,189, 190,191
WINSTON
H 208
J H 208,348
WISENER
B J 116,117,119
Ben J 115,116,118,120,121
Bessie 115,116,117
Minnie 115,118,119,120,121
Susan 115,116,117,118, 119,120,121
WOLF
Robert 209
WOLLOW
Rosey 324
WOMACK
Berry 258
WOODFIN
Mollie 204

WRIGHT
E A 221
Lela S 221
Mary Ellen 221
S T 111
YAHDIHKA
Cinda 146
Joe 146
YAHOLA
Addie 363,364,365,366, 367,368
Minnie 363,364,365,366, 367,368
Wiley 363,366,367,368
YAHOLAR
Louisa 336,337
YAH-PAH-NEY 272
YARGEE
Bettie 336,337,338
Sam 326,327
YARHOLA
Arsofolech 263
Osuchee 263
YEARGAIN
Green 239,243
YETTEKAHAJO
Wisey 219
YOAKUM
Martin M 279

www.ingramcontent.com/pod-product-compliance
Lightning Source LLC
Chambersburg PA
CBHW020304030426
42336CB00010B/897